D0054104

Soundings

HENRY HOLT AND COMPANY
NEW YORK

Soundings

THE STORY OF THE REMARKABLE WOMAN WHO MAPPED THE OCEAN FLOOR

Hali Felt

Henry Holt and Company, LLC
Publishers since 1866
175 Fifth Avenue
New York, New York 10010
www.henryholt.com

Henry Holt® and ® are registered trademarks of Henry Holt and Company, LLC.

Library of Congress Cataloging-in-Publication Data

Felt, Hali.
   Soundings : the story of the remarkable woman who mapped the ocean floor /
Hali Felt.—1st ed.
      p. cm.
   Includes index.
   ISBN 978-0-8050-9215-8 (hardback)
   1. Tharp, Marie.   2. Cartographers—United States—Biography.
3. Geomorphologists—United States—Biography.   4. Women cartographers—United
States—Biography.   5. Submarine topography.   I. Title.
   GA407.T43F45 2012
   526.092—dc23
   [B]   2011044178

Henry Holt books are available for special promotions and premiums.
For details contact: Director, Special Markets.

First Edition 2012

Designed by Meryl Sussman Levavi

Printed in the United States of America

10 9 8 7 6 5 4 3 2 1

This book is for my grandmother
Hilda Hubsher Rifkin (1928–2009),
who taught me to tell stories.

Soundings

$\mathcal{M}$Y MOTHER USED TO DRAW MAPS. NOT IN THE CARTO-graphic sense—she had no training in that field—but rather in the sense that she rendered them, drew and painted and inked up sheets of paper depicting areas of land that she had studied. She spent hours at the library poring over atlases in the reference section, photocopying in segments the huge pages of the books, then taping them together so she'd have something to work from at home.

She liked to complain about all the research she had to do to create even the smallest map. This made sense; as a freelance magazine illustrator, the time she spent on research went largely uncompensated. But she had to do it if her maps were going to meet her editors' approval, and I think it was actually her favorite part. I remember waking up in the middle of the night when I was little and stumbling in my bare feet to the other side of our apartment. I could hear the soft laugh track of whatever she had on the television to keep her company as she worked, and as I got closer to her studio I could see the electric light spilling out of it, as if daylight had arrived a few hours early in just this room. And there she'd be, all splayed out on her studio floor, the copied maps spread out like a carpet and a pencil between her teeth. When I found her on these nights, she'd almost never be looking down at the maps or at the television.

Instead, she'd be staring off into what would have been the distance if her futon, her flat files, and her dresser hadn't been in the way. I thought she must be thinking about mountains or maybe even plains, and the borders between countries that could shift if she allowed even a tiny tremor in her hand to travel down the wood of her pencil, through the lead, onto the paper. Her illustrations were always meticulous, though; looking at them, I found it obvious that she reveled in all the necessary detail.

While she also drew other things, such as plants, or a Pennsylvania-German type of folk art called fraktur, or hands demonstrating how to, say, lace a shoe, I latched onto the maps without any urging. As a kid I sent away for an orienteering manual that taught me how to navigate through the wilderness with only a map and compass; as a teenager I bought journals and calendars with maps printed on them; and when I moved away from home, I decorated the walls of my bedrooms with maps. I, too, loved how beautiful they were, the grids of streets, the curves of rivers, the green amoebas of parks or forests—maps were true, but they were also art, a starting point for me to imagine what they represented, what they meant, what was actually on the ground.

I suppose, then, that it isn't surprising that the story of the cartographer Marie Tharp piqued my interest. It was very early on New Year's Day 2007, and I discovered her in the *New York Times Magazine*, part of the 2006 roundup of all the notable people who had died throughout the past year. Some were famous; some were not. The photograph on the cover showed names constructed out of neon tubes and the letters spelling out the words "Marie Tharp" came just after the ones that spelled out "Betty Friedan." Inside the magazine were articles about all these people, short biographical pieces whose intent was unclear. In reading we were not necessarily to mourn, but rather to appreciate the posthumous congregation the *Times* had organized—or at the very least to acknowledge that the people we were reading about should be remembered, even if they wouldn't be.

Marie Tharp, the header of the article about her said, was a "contrary map maker." In the article's first line the author wrote that Marie had red hair and cut a fine figure. In its second line I learned that she had studied English and music before going to graduate school for geology. In the second paragraph I learned that she and her scientific partner, an Iowan named Bruce Heezen, "rewrote 20th century geophysics." It was not until the next paragraph that I learned what exactly she had done: from the 1950s to the 1970s she mapped the entire ocean floor and discovered a rift valley that circled the globe.

Science, I have to say, had never been my thing. I avoided it in high school and then college, taking only what was required to graduate. I placed my faith in the subjective. I believed that the act of creation was worth more than a quest for explanations. And so when I first read that article about Marie Tharp in the *Times* I was attracted to certain elements of the story, to the use of words such as "imagine," "intuit," and "creativity." I loved the idea of a map having been produced as a "supreme act of rigorous creativity," tried to imagine her thirty-year-long "Hamlet-like" relationship with the "hulking" Heezen.

By the time I reached the end of the article I'd learned that they were "a couple" in a way that lay "outside of the bell-shaped curve," fought like "cats and dogs," and had just finished a map of the entire ocean floor when tragedy struck. "Bruce Heezen had printer's proofs of the map with him in 1977," the article said, "when he suffered a fatal heart attack on a research vessel off the coast of Iceland. A widow in all but name, Marie Tharp continued to live in [her] house in South Nyack until her death." The article also said that Marie's discovery of a rift valley running down the center of the Atlantic essentially proved the theory of continental drift (which said that the Earth's surface was made up of moving plates), but when I first read the article what stood out to me was that no one believed her—when she initially discovered what came to be called the Mid-Oceanic Rift, her claims were dismissed as "girl talk." I thought I was reading a classic—the story of an outcast eccentric, a female scientist whose reputation had been the victim of mid-century American gender bias. I was wrong, but also right: the whole story, the true story, was much more complicated.

AFTER I FIRST read about Marie and had looked at images of her maps from the 1950s, '60s, and '70s, I turned to Google Earth for a modern glimpse of the ocean floor. I was disappointed; the oceans fill almost three-quarters of the Earth's surface, but the images illustrating them just showed vast swaths of woolly cobalt. When I clicked my cursor to zoom in on any of these spots, I was confronted with pixilated blue nothingness, the virtual equivalent of sailing to the edge of a flat Earth. I told myself that it made sense that nothing was there. Your average person, after all, probably does not need a street view of his new neighborhood on a faraway undersea mountain, does not need step-by-step driving directions to the Mid-Atlantic Ridge. On the other hand, most of the people I knew who liked Google Earth used it to explore and meander more than anything else. They'd go to places they knew they'd probably never be able to visit in their lives—islands and volcanoes and rain forests and deserts that they could just drop down into and learn something about without the expense of actually traveling.

The emptiness of the oceans was infuriating—average people like me couldn't explore the ocean floor. Marie's maps had been around for decades, and I knew that other scientists must have been collecting information since then—where had all that data gone? I had learned that the ocean floor was not blank and I could not go back to thinking it was; just as there is not a miniature band huddled inside the radio and schoolteachers do not spend the evenings of their lives camped out in their classrooms, the world does not end where the oceans begin. So as I learned more about Marie and her maps, I'd occasionally visit the oceans of Google Earth, let myself plummet down into their cold virtual blue, and imagine the topography she discovered stretched out before me, her illustrations like grand-scale slipcovers for the deep.

And then, on February 2, 2009, the oceans got their due. In the version of Google Earth released that day, you could engage in what Google's publicity called "a plunge into the oceans of the world" to explore shipwrecks, watch clips of old Jacques Cousteau footage, and learn about marine protected areas; most important to me, though, was a new feature that allowed users to see Marie's World Ocean Floor Panorama wrapped around the globe. It's now possible to look at the Earth as she envisioned it: the features of the ocean floor painted in all different shades of blue (sky, suede, corn, and midnight); the continents' rich ripe yellows and peaches and oranges; bruised brick reds where mountains burst through the skin of the plains—the whole map much more beautiful than the muddy shades of Google Earth's terrestrial satellite images.

That's the big picture view. All its parts—the continents and the oceans, the highs and the lows—are necessary to tell the story of Marie's life, but if I had to choose the most significant locations of her life there would be five. Bellefontaine, Ohio, where her father bought a farm so that his family (Marie and her mother) could finally settle after almost two decades of nomadic living; the second would be Lamont Hall, the hub, in the 1950s, of the Lamont Geological Observatory, formed and headed by a scientific innovator named Maurice Ewing, who gave Marie her first research position and introduced her to both Bruce Heezen and the ocean floor; the third would be the Mid-Atlantic Ridge, a deep-sea feature surveyed by Ewing and Bruce and then studied by Marie, whose discovery forever changed human understanding of the Earth; the fourth location would be the Reykjanes Ridge, on the ocean floor off the coast of Iceland, an area that Bruce was studying when he died in 1977, in a U.S. Navy submarine called the *NR-1*; the fifth and final location would be Marie's house in South Nyack, New York: home, workplace, data storage center, archive, and safe haven—the place where Marie, during the thirty years she lived after Bruce was gone, expressed herself most freely, nesting into her idiosyncratically curated collections of art, repurposed clothes, invented recipes, stories, vast correspondence files, and local oddballs.

Thanks to Google Earth, I can collapse space—summon a satellite image of Bellefontaine or Lamont Hall or the Mid-Atlantic Ridge, locations that the now-gone Marie once held dear. Time and matter, however, are much more difficult: although I've spent hours staring at photo album sheets filled with pictures of Marie, I can't break through walls—not the ones out of which the buildings at those locations are constructed and not the ones Marie erected around the events and emotions in her life that she wanted to forget. I can't see Bruce exactly as she saw him and I can't explain the true nature of their relationship—they were the only two people in the world who could have outlined the boundaries of their thirty-year-long partnership, who could have defined just how deep the "more" in "more than colleagues and friends" went.

During the time I've spent learning about Marie I've come to terms with these limitations. Because there's one other curious thing about her work: its importance, much like the oceans in general, gets little attention. Without Marie's first map of the ocean floor, the scientists who developed the first theoretical models of plate tectonics would have had nothing to look at—and, therefore, no theories to develop. Yet there are no books devoted to Marie, only a handful of articles. Histories of that period in geology usually refer to her only in a single sentence or in a caption for one of her maps. By the time I discovered her in the *Times* on

New Year's Day 2007, she'd been allowed to settle into obscurity. Even in that article, the sensational aspects of her life drowned out the scientific value of her work. For all my own limitations, I told myself as I ran into all sorts of walls during the years I spent working on this project, if I could restore the detail to Marie's life, I could restore the import of her work, so that there'd be more to her than the sensational or eccentric, more than just the highs and lows.

I KNOW NOW that in order to understand Marie Tharp the scientist you also have to understand Marie Tharp the woman. The *Times* got that much right. But the task does not end with her clothes and whether or not she was dominated by a bunch of postwar male egos. Those things are very relevant, but they don't explain the extent to which the science she practiced became personal and instinctive. It's easy to focus on the fanfare and drama in a life like hers, but it's the places where the tremor escapes notice—the in and out of alarm clocks, wash rags, and frying eggs; light tables, ink pens, and smooth sheets of white paper; erasers, fathoms, and final drafts; lunch and more work and breathing and cooking dinner and waiting until the last moment before darkness to turn on the electric lights; pulling the drafting lamp over an unfinished map, the light shining down on the spot where nothing's been drawn; the night stretching out, a sweater pulled taut against the winter cold, a sip of water, the hash marks of a mountain, the long lines of a continent, the stained pads of fingers, the slit of a rift valley reaching up toward a pole, the quiet of a house, the crumbs and eraser shavings on the floor, staring up at the wall; a hand on the railing, feet pressed into stairs, bare feet on cold tile, running a bath, sweater off, shirt off, pants off, etc., and the steam fogging all the surfaces; a head under water, a spine pressed into enamel, breasts rising up like islands, tub walls steep-sided as submarine canyons, floating content between it all; and falling asleep, and dreaming—where she is the most stubbornly herself. All of it, in other words, smashed together to make something united and whole.

One of the most basic principles of geology is that of uniformitarianism. This doctrine states that the present is the key to the past, that what we see taking place here on Earth today is part of a uniform and continuously repeating set of processes. No one can explain precisely, moment by moment, how the surface of the Earth was formed, but if we look closely at what's here now (two of Africa's continental plates being pulled apart to form the Great Rift Valley), we can form theories about what happened in the past (the supercontinent Pangaea separating, fragmenting, and being pulled apart to form the continents we live on today).

Along with uniformitarianism there's also something called catastrophism, which says that the Earth's surface has been formed as the result of a series of sudden, discrete, violent events. Glacial Lake Missoula bursting through its ice dam, dumping billions of gallons of water per second into eastern Washington, creating the Scablands. A ten-kilometer-wide meteor slamming into the ground at Chicxulub and wiping out about 70 percent of the Earth's species. A man you've worked with on a map for thirty years of your life up and dying on you while he's down in some submarine: there are certain events in life that stand out in raised relief.

It used to be that most scientists believed exclusively in uniformitarianism, that they had created for the world a neatly bound historical package. This required the creation of long vast time lines, everything connected by one narrative line leading straight like an arrow to the present. In the past few decades, however, scientists have embraced catastrophism, too. With its potent periodic outbursts, catastrophism allows for a photo album conception of the Earth's history: stretches of black and a then quick glossy scene. Combine it with uniformitarianism and you get a more realistic sort of story, one in which moments have value not because they conform to one another or constantly rebel against their surroundings—one or the other—but because both happen, illuminating and providing context for each other.

I like using scientific ideas when I write, looking at the articles and maps and photos relating to Marie and her work that I have and putting them together in an attempt to figure out the story of her past. But even though I've got those documents, I'm still missing the most important part of all: her. Marie can't narrate for me a play-by-play of her entire life, but I can take the things in front of me and weave them together to make something whole.

And I can take myself, act as a mediator, use my own experiences with discovery and eccentricity and sadness to fill in some of the emotional blanks that are left between the hours of interviews, the ephemera. I can take the dusty things I discover crushed at the bottoms of folders and I can use my imagination and I can say this is all that I know and here is how it might have made Marie feel. So you'll run into me occasionally in this story, a kind of understudy: Marie got sick, you see, and then she died, and in order to keep her from becoming too big or too small, a PowerPoint of generic caricatures (scientist, woman, artist, spinster) on infinite loop, I want to give her story a little palpable emotion, even if it isn't hers, to try to keep her whole, a little Pangaea.

Part One

A hill is a transitional accommodation to stress, and ego may be a similar accommodation. A waterfall is a self-correcting maladjustment of stream to structure, and so, for all I know, is technique.

—JOAN DIDION, *Democracy*

CHAPTER 1

*A*T ITS MOST BASIC LEVEL, MY JOB AS A WRITER IS NOT very alluring. It has its moments, of course, as with most occupations. The exciting days when I spoke for hours on the phone with one or another of Marie's colleagues. Or when I ended up at her house the night before its new owner took possession of it, helping a few of her old friends box up the last of her things—that was exciting. Or once, when I went to the cemetery in Iowa where Bruce was buried, next to his father, in a grave that would probably have been his mother's if he hadn't beat her to it (she's buried in Pittsburgh, next to her last husband). Small scraps of gauzy fabric were scattered all around on the grass like giant snowflakes and when I squatted down to pick one up off Bruce's headstone I realized that they were weathered old pieces of silk flowers and flags, decomposing until one day they would disappear. I stood there on top of his grave for a while, which I knew was probably bad luck, but I couldn't resist; it was the closest I could get to either one of them.

It was creepy, and a little bit thrilling. What if I laid down, I thought, stretched out on the grass in the sun, and took a nap until the shadow of the Heezen family monument touched my face? These are the kinds of things a writer thinks. Or they're the kinds of things I think. I didn't do it, of course. I could hear a lawn mower close by and worried what the high school kid who found me would think. After that, though, I went to the house Bruce grew up in—a huge mansion the color of butter on a bluff overlooking the Mississippi. It didn't look like anyone was home, but I knocked on all the doors anyway, one by one, hoping to be invited in, imagining what I'd say if I were. I'm writing a book, I would say, perkily, and the housewife who answered the door would take one look at my cardigan and sensible clogs and invite me in for a tour. I had no idea a famous scientist grew up here, she'd exclaim over the tea she served me after we'd figured out which bedroom had been Bruce's. But no one answered the door, so I walked around the side of the house and stared up at the third-floor gables, and took pictures of the view and the trees and the Beware of Dog sign, and doing this, too, was a little bit creepy and thrilling; I didn't stay very long.

While researching Marie, I often found myself forced to say the words "I'm not a scientist" whenever anyone asked me what I was writing about. They'd pause; I'd shake my head. "At *all*?" they'd ask, as if their rephrasing might reveal that I was actually about one-sixteenth scientist, the way some people are part Irish or Swiss. "No," I'd say, "but there are things that make up for that and anyway"—here I'd usually wiggle my eyebrows—"don't you believe the present holds the key to the past?" If they said yes, I'd tell them that I agreed and that that belief had its beginnings in geology. "It's called uni-formi-tari-anism. What do you think of *that*?"

On a bookshelf in my living room there's an old olive green book with the title *Geomorphology* stamped on its spine in gold. It belonged to Bruce and was given to me on the day I spent at Marie's house. The spine is fraying and broken and the book can't stand up on its own, so I made a protective portfolio for it, fashioned from thick cardboard covered in golden silk, to hold it up straight and keep out dust. Also in my living room: a whole filing cabinet filled with documents photocopied from the Heezen-Tharp Collection at the Library of Congress—interviews in which Marie talks about her childhood, photographs of her throughout her life, transcripts of tapes Bruce made near the end of his life. There's also a stack of hatboxes containing all sorts of random things—one of Marie's address books, a falling-apart cigar box holding letters between Marie's brother and her father, a falling-apart shoe box marked "Family Letters, 1920s," stacks of holiday greeting cards people sent to Marie when she was in grad school, tiny flattened boxes that once held Bruce's heart medication.

On my fridge there's a copy of Marie's Atlantic Ocean Floor map that appeared in *National Geographic* magazine in the 1960s. On my bulletin board there's a photocopy of a black-and-white photo of Marie and Bruce posed awkwardly in topcoats. There are diagrams of the ocean floor rolled around old wrapping paper tubes in my linen closet, and in my bedroom is a huge dainty-legged table that looks about ready to buckle under the weight of what it's holding up. Stacks of books about the ocean two and a half feet tall. File folders stuffed with transcripts of interviews. Papers and books embellished with fluorescent orange sticky notes that poke from between the pages like the stubby limbs of an animal smashed inside. To the right of my computer I've built my own miniature natural history museum: a milky white geode that looks like a cauliflower floret on the outside, a smooth rock with perfect round craters bored into it, a small wooden model of a stegosaurus skeleton, some dried thistle heads that look like skewered sea urchins, a postcard of Marie's World Ocean Floor Panorama, a playing-card-size portrait of her, a Polaroid photo of the pond next to my grandfather's cabin, and a thick-stalked jade plant ris ing up over it all.

Taped to the wall next to my desk are some pages I photocopied from Marie's scrapbooks. On one page, Maries from almost every decade of her life crowd against each other: small square photos of her as an adolescent in the 1930s, with a smile too big for her face and untamed hair brushing her bomber jacket's shearling collar; a strip of four pictures from a photo-booth, whose flashbulb has illuminated her in various stages of laughter, picking up her radiant skin, her high cheekbones, the metallic thread of her intricately patterned shift and the gleam of her pinned hair; a color snapshot of late-period Marie in her living room, commanding from her leopard-print couch, one arm behind her head and the other hovering near a stack of papers. The Bruce page looks like one of those kinder-garten classroom posters that has faces exhibiting a wide range of emotions—in small passport photos arranged into a perfect grid, a dapperly dressed thirty-something Bruce shows that he's not only capa-ble of happy, sad, and angry, but that his round face can also do assertive, inquisitive, suspicious, and reprimanding.

The sheet I love most, though, is the one that includes both Marie and Bruce—black-and-white portraits of them in their fifties. There isn't a single shot that captures them both within one frame, but it's clear that they were in close proximity when the pictures were taken: it's evening, the quality of the lamplight hitting their faces identically is both bright and soft, their summer clothes are loose and rumpled, and both project something best described as a deep and comfortable intimacy. There is no composure here, just relaxed faces sometimes smiling, sometimes simply looking. Marie has (uncharacteristically) undone her hair so that it falls down past her shoulders, Bruce's head is tilted, eyes and chin (uncharacteristically) gentle. They're caught tender in these photos, faces angled toward each other; I can almost hear them exchanging soft murmurs across the scrapbook's page, even though they're dead and gone, even though the pictures are almost fifty years old.

My life has become what you might call saturated—with Marie, with her work, with things relating to the ocean floor and oceanography and geology—and so has my mind. The transformation of facts into a scene, then, has become effortless. It is what I imagine simple algebra must be like for a mathematician. I read some facts, Marie's reply to an interview question: "Well, anyhow, the first thing I remember—this is unbelievable— lying in a bed with wheels on it outdoors, and I was looking up at this house with a 'peaky' roof, and I couldn't understand why I was looking up and it was peaky, because when I was inside it was flat, you know, a flat ceiling." "Oh, how wonderful," the interviewer replied, and they keep talking for another few hundred pages, but my imagination goes off running. Shapes, or rather the outlines of shapes—a house, a bed, a baby— drawn with thick crude lines. The outlines are facts. Or the facts are outlines? I'm not sure, but either way, I'm the one who comes in decades later—an adult with a steady hand, coloring everything bright but staying inside those lines.

MARIE'S FIRST MEMORY is this: she's very small and the sky is very big and she's lying outside on a bed that has wheels on it. She ignores the things down at her level in order to cast her eyes up. No blanket, no teddy bear, no bottle or mother or father are mentioned in this memory; for her, it's all about a house.

She's looking up at her house, at a peaky tall roof, and something about it is bothering her. She lies there on her back in that way babies do, rocking gently from side to side like a turtle trying to right itself. Even though Marie is too preoccupied with the roof to notice, her mother is probably nearby, keeping an eye on her as she stews their laundry in a huge iron pot. Marie tilts her face. When she does this she can make the sun disappear and her eyes stop feeling so squinty. She moves her face again and the sun comes back, does this a few more times before she remembers what was originally bothering her. The roof thing doesn't make sense because she knows that when she's inside the house the part of the roof that she can see is flat. She doesn't know the word for roof yet, or the word for ceiling. But she knows that her house has a lid; until now she's noticed it only from the inside, where it's flat and smooth above her. Now, though, it's angled toward the sky, as if while her mother was rolling her crib through the yard some giant plucked an invisible string, jerking the lid skyward along a single central line, transforming a plain into a peak.

"Believe it or not," Marie said by way of introduction to this story, "it's amazing." One of those things whose significance she doesn't explain but we can take an easy guess at.

By the time Marie neared the end of her life people started wanting to hear her story and so she started telling it. Interviewers came to call, a few articles were written, she pops up scattered in a few chapters. Marie was good at keeping secrets and telling stories and she had lived a long and cluttered life. But she was also getting old, and things were probably getting murky: the things that she had tried to forget, or at least make less painful, had been filed away in the backs of cabinets or had disappeared entirely. There are lots of holes in her story because by the time she died in 2006 she had no family and her only friends were the Tharpophiles: devotees who had worked for (or with) her on her maps in her South Nyack, New York, home, most of whom were significantly younger. There was no one left, in other words, to correct and fill in memories.

Certain details are fact, though.

Marie was born in 1920 in Ypsilanti, Michigan, to William Edgar Tharp and Bertha Louise Newton. William, who Marie referred to as "Papa" until she died, began working for the U.S. Department of Agriculture's Bureau of Soils in 1904. He was thirty-four years old, had never been to college, and had been to only one year of high school in Stuart,

Iowa, before the school declared him learned enough to graduate and then immediately reclaimed him as a teacher. He hated it; he quit the job after one year but had nightmares about it for years.

William worked in a plant nursery after that, saving up enough money to buy his parents a house before he took the civil service test that got him into the Bureau of Soils. He came late to everything he did, or maybe just waited until he was good and ready: he didn't marry his first wife, Ethel Griffin, who came from a family of butchers and patent medicine hawkers in Stuart, until after he started working for the government. They had one child, named Orlo but called Jim, before Ethel died of an asthma attack in Piney Woods, Mississippi. Because of all the traveling William had to do, he left Jim to be raised by Ethel's parents in Stuart. Even after William got married again, to Marie's mother, Bertha, Jim stayed with his grandparents; Grandma Griffin had no respect for second wives and Bertha had no respect for uppity old ladies. Bertha refused to set foot in Stuart, which is why Marie didn't meet Jim until he showed up when she was in high school. Until then he was mostly a story, someone she heard about from time to time, someone who grew up with creeks and lots of boy cousins who eventually blotted out his mother's death, someone who as a teenager was disfigured and blinded in one eye by a ricocheting projectile from a toy cannon his father sent him for Christmas. He and her father corresponded weekly, and "somewhere along the way," Marie said, "the decision was made to send him to the School of Forestry at Ames, Iowa. Jim's only complaint was the ROTC had parades on Saturday afternoons when he would have rather been hunting."

Bertha had been a high school German teacher before, as Marie says her father always used to remark, she "traded one job for another." Bertha died when Marie was fifteen and, in most of Marie's recollections, is ghostly and off to the side—watching her, waiting for her. She was forty and William was fifty when Marie was born, and according to Marie they were married in 1912 or 1917. Either way, they met in a boardinghouse in Frankfurt, Indiana, seven years after William's first wife died. I picture William sneaking a glance at Bertha over the top of a book in a parlor.

As parents, William and Bertha seem to have been past an age when coddling their only child was an option. They were devoted, but they trusted her to find her own way, let her explore the unknown so she'd gain confidence from her own forward motion. Like one of the years when they lived in Washington, D.C. (they went every four years, so William could go to the Soil Bureau's main office to oversee the printing of the maps he had worked on since his last visit), Marie and her mother were at the U.S. Capitol and Marie ran away from her and up the steps to the top of the dome. She stayed there awhile and her mother didn't even worry, just sat down on a bench and let her daughter survey the city from above. Eventually Marie trotted back, followed by a guard who'd caught her where he thought she wasn't supposed to be.

Because they spent so much time moving around, the Tharp family (William, Bertha, and Marie) knew the value of packing light. They knew, whether by choice or circumstance, that there was an economics to nearly everything, and they tended to be prudent. Trade-offs were a part of life. Consistency was swapped for financial security. Friendships did not exist, not really, but the three Tharps were so "tightly-knit," such a "happy bubbly family," that they once induced envious tears in a neighboring widower who stopped to pay his regards one Christmas Eve. The moving they had to do for William's job made them "perennial gypsies"; they had one another, but that's about it.

Marie attended more than a dozen schools before she graduated from high school. The recorded number changes—sometimes it's as high as eighteen and other times as low as fifteen—but the number I reach when I count them all up is seventeen, clearly nothing to scoff at. There was kindergarten in Tippecanoe, Indiana, where her father called her "tippe two" because he didn't like the name Marie; half of first grade in Peru, Indiana, and the other half in Marion, Alabama; back to Ypsilanti for second grade; then to Hartford City, Indiana; then to Washington, D.C., for a whole year. After that they took a train to Albia, Iowa; went to Selma, Alabama; Rockwell City, Iowa; Orrville, Alabama; spent a whole year in Florence, Alabama; then went to Adams County, Ohio; back to D.C.; to Cooperstown, New York; to Oneonta; and then to Bellefontaine, Ohio, where her father bought a farm to fix up and where her mother died less than a year later. Marie barely ever talked about losing her mother, just a few vague things here and there about how she'd been reaching an age when her mother could have taught her a lot (about what, she doesn't say); about watching her as she lay dying as summer passed into fall, next to a window overlooking a maple losing its leaves; about how she took over the "fun" parts of keeping house when her mother was gone.

In her memories, Marie was often alone. "Usually I was the new kid on the block, the stranger that no one had anything to do with. By the time I'd develop friends, we'd move on," she said. One season they lived in a four-room furnished flat in Washington, D.C., where Marie claimed as her kingdom the space behind a couch placed diagonally across a corner. Another season they lived in a colossal old mansion in Albia. Her father had rented it for twenty-five dollars a month and she had two whole rooms to lord over—one to sleep in, another for her toys—and lots of other empty rooms to wander through in the afternoons when the air hung like wet clothes on a line. She loved this emptiness, the way her little wooden animals skittered on the bare floors; she separated the cows from the sheep and put them out on the parquet floor to graze; she took all the furniture out of her dollhouse to make it into an airplane hangar.

Her sparsely populated childhood often took on a surreal and sometimes whimsical quality, filled as it was with extremes—in temperature, in size, in out-of-placeness. When she was six, in Peru, her father drove her out to the Ringling Brothers headquarters on Sunday afternoons to see the animals on vacation from touring. There were lions and tigers and elephants lolling in the Indiana oat fields like tourists at the beach. Her father, an amateur poet, wrote a poem titled "When the Circus Comes Back to Peru," which got published in the local paper. The next year, when he was down in South Carolina by himself and Marie and her mother were in Ypsilanti taking care of Marie's dying grandmother, he wrote poems about the 1928 presidential candidate Alfred Smith and also to the calendar on his hotel wall, which had a picture of a girl on it. The Alfred Smith poem got published; the calendar girl poem did not. ("We never could get over that," Marie said, "them thinking it was too, I don't know, suggestive. It was just a nice calendar.") In Washington, D.C., in 1929 they watched Herbert Hoover get inaugurated: "we sat out in the rain in the bleachers and got to see the whole parade," Marie said. "It was gorgeous for a kid." The pouring rain, the top hats and horses, and the men slowly waving from open-roofed cars were still lodged in her memory decades later.

Winters down south and summers up north meant that Marie didn't experience much in the way of winter until she was a teenager in Cooperstown, New York. That was the year her father surveyed Suwannee County in Florida and wasn't allowed to take his family along because there weren't any schools. The meteorological conditions of her childhood were generally warm, to say the least. In Marion it was so hot in the after-noons that they didn't have to go back to school after lunch, so she sat by herself on the stone wall by the Methodist church and watched people's faces as they walked by. In the Albia mansion it was so hot that you couldn't touch the carved wooden banister. One summer, in Washing-ton, D.C., it was so hot that Marie and her mother hid out all afternoon at the Unitarian church trying to cool off by watching a movie about Admiral Byrd's adventures at the South Pole.

Even as a child, Marie was what my own grandfather would have referred to as a "real pistol," a "firecracker," or a "piece of work," depending on the situation. (When I got so excited three days before we were sup-posed to go to the beach that I couldn't sit still or sleep or eat and kind of just jangled around making everyone nervous, I was a firecracker.) Marie, in fifth grade, standing off to the side and watching her schoolmates leap around on the playground during mandatory recess, thinking, "Why do we have to put up with this nonsense," was a piece of work. And when Marie's parents tried to send her to Sunday school and she "flatly refused"—citing in her defense the fact that because they moved so much, she basi-cally had to put up with strangers all week long and she wasn't about to start doing the same on weekends—she would have been a real pistol. When I read this story, I pictured a miniature version of Marie's older self standing before two amused adults and gesturing wildly, with shoes untied and some wooden jungle creatures at her feet.

This kind of scene is easy to imagine—but it's necessary, too. Because while Marie's later life was well documented in both picture and word, I have only a handful of photographs of Marie as a child—one I'm certain is of her and another I'm pretty sure is of her. The huge cache of photos she left behind is almost entirely of the years after she got to New York. Any that aren't are of Bruce and his affluent family, who vacationed frequently—Bruce next to a man in a primitive diving suit; Bruce struggling to hold a giant just-caught fish high in the air; Bruce looking uncomfortable in a white linen suit with some palms in the background—are of him in later life, as a scientist (sitting at a table of other scientists, Marie at his side and looking at him instead of the camera; squeezing his bulk down through the hatch of a bobbing submersible).

One of the pictures of child Marie is black and white and fading. The contrast needs to be amped up and the border thinned, but the composition is nice and the subject fitting. In it, Marie stands near the edge of a dirt road next to her father's surveying tripod. The road cuts through a dried-out old field, something that had been plowed some time ago and has only a few papery stalks sticking up. The trees are knobby-kneed preadolescents grouped at her back and the tripod is an arrow pointing only to her. The mechanic's jumpsuit she's wearing ends about six inches above her ankles and her bangs are cut straight across her brow. She's got a thigh resting on one of the posts of the tripod; if she were any older her hip would probably be cocked, but as it is she's just straight up and down. My favorite part about this picture (and the next one, the one I'm not sure is of her) is that she's totally ignoring the camera. There's no indication that she has any idea the picture is being taken. She's completely engrossed with whatever it is she's drawing or writing with that pencil clutched in her hand.

The second photograph complements the first one nicely. It is charming where the other is gritty, dainty where the other is tomboyish. Marie has the same severe haircut, but her face looks a little pudgier, which makes me think she might be slightly younger in it. This picture is sepia-toned, and behind Marie the shadows of leaves spread out batik-like on a barn door. She wears a dress, and oxfords, and sits at a child-size farm table. I might even be able to see a bracelet pushed halfway up her forearm. Again, she's totally engrossed in what she's drawing or writing.

When I first discovered these pictures I could feel the possibilities in them stretching out, as if Marie were still alive, still young and with her whole life about to happen: drawing and drawing, alone and immersed in her work. As if there'd been a shift in the air, the way the sky turns green and still before a summer thunderstorm and all the people and animals hurry home. These moments never shock, they are not the actual storm but the time before it, when you remember all the storms you've been through before and are able to say, of course, I know what is coming: we will meet, we will each say or do something that seems right, a sentence or a gesture that softly falls into place but in retrospect is heavy as a brick.

THE FIRST TIME Marie ever saw the ocean was in Pascagoula in 1925 or 1926—she could never be sure which year of her childhood was spent where. But her family lived there one winter while her father finished up a survey of Mobile County.

In Pascagoula the land is the same height as the sea. But the trees stop and the grasses stop and the sand lies there and lets the water cover and uncover it each day. Marie and her mother go down the steps of the boardinghouse, take the steps one at a time, a little hand inside a big one like seashells tucked together. There's the crossing of streets with names such as Beach and Canal and Lakeview, and Marie's mother reading the street signs out loud to her. There's the feeling of stepping onto the sand for the first time, and it distracts her for a while, the way her feet sink into it after they step off the road that sets off the beach and the way her behind sinks into it, too, as she sits down to take off her shoes and socks.

But the water! Oh, she says at first, just a little noise beneath the sound of the waves, and then she looks back at her mother's face. Her mother takes her hand again and they start to cross the wide, empty beach. It's low tide and Marie is a little apprehensive, so the approach is slow; the water advances and retreats like a shy animal. But then Marie steps onto wet sand, and the water comes back to lick her feet. It's like nothing she's ever seen before, like the ice of a pond after the snow's been swept off for skating, like static on a television, or wind moving through wheat fields. The closest thing she can think of is a blue woolen blanket, the waves like her toes squirming underneath. A little while later, when she sees her first movie, *Ben Hur*, she can't understand why the ocean on the screen doesn't get her wet, too.

On the beach there's a giant wreck of a boat, just a skeleton, and then the next day when they go back it's almost all covered up with water. So her mother tells her about something called a tide, about the moon pulling the water up close to its face and then pushing it back again. Every day, her mother says, the way Papa goes to work and comes home, or the way we move north and then come south again.

That's the story of Marie seeing the ocean for the first time, and how she thought it was the most amazing thing she ever saw, and how she didn't see it again until she moved to New York more than twenty years later. But somehow the memory stayed intact, the ocean a drop beaded up on a blouse, water that didn't soak in until she needed it.

$\mathcal{J}$N THE AUTUMN OF 1926, THE YEAR MARIE ENTERED FIRST grade, a German named Alfred Lothar Wegener traveled to New York City to attend the American Association of Petroleum Geologists' annual meeting. Wegener was an astronomer, geologist, meteorologist, and record-holding balloonist. In 1911 he had published his first book, *Thermodynamik der Atmosphäre* (*Thermodynamics of the Atmosphere*). In 1912 he had traveled to Greenland and, when he and his three companions narrowly escaped death after a glacier they were climbing calved, became part of the first expedition ever to overwinter there; the following spring the group made the longest on-foot crossing of the ice cap. In 1914 he was bedridden after sustaining injuries in World War I and, during his recuperation, developed an idea that had been nagging at him for years.

It had started, the story goes, after Christmas of 1910, when his roommate received the *Allgemeiner Handatlas*, a general atlas filled with 139 main maps and 161 side maps. The two men pored over the color maps until Wegener had a sort of scientific epiphany—a lick of lightning to the head or just a soft, gentle brain click. "Presently," he wrote to his wife, Else, "an idea came to me. Look at the world map again, please: doesn't the east coast of South America fit precisely with the west coast of Africa, as if they had been connected formerly?" This idea is not itself revolutionary. Schoolchildren regularly notice this congruity long before they're introduced to geology of any kind. In 1596 a Flemish geographer named Abraham Orte-lius noticed that the "projecting parts of Europe and Africa" fit "along with the recesses of America" and looked as if they had been "torn away" from each other. And in 1838 a Scottish philosopher named Thomas Dick wrote, in his book *Celestial Scenery; or, the Wonders of the Planetary System Dis-played: Illustrating the Perfections of Deity and a Plurality of Worlds*, that if western Africa snuggled up to the horn of Brazil, "one compact continent" could be formed, and may once have existed as such until they were "rent asunder by some tremendous power."

When Wegener wrote to his wife about the congruity of South Amer-ica and Africa in 1910 it was nothing new. But Wegener didn't know that. The rest of the world didn't know that in 1910 and they didn't know it in 1915, either, when Wegener published *Die Entstehung der Kontinente und Ozeane (The Origin of Continents and Oceans)*, in which he made an interdisciplinary argument that the Earth's surface was constructed from continental plates that moved laterally. At one point, he said, they had all been part of a single land mass called Pangaea, a supercontinent that had been breaking apart and wandering across the surface of the Earth for billions of years. As proof for this theory, Wegener offered the following: the aforementioned observation that the continents fit together like a jigsaw puzzle; that the order and age of the strata (layering of rocks) matched on opposite sides of the Atlantic; that the fossil record within those layers contained evidence of similar species clustered along the coasts; and that the structures on the surfaces of the continents also matched, as if, he wrote, "we were to refit the torn pieces of a newspaper by matching their edges and then check whether the lines of print ran smoothly across. If they do, there is nothing left but to conclude that the pieces were in fact joined in this way."

Wegener called his theory "continental drift." This meant that the continents were moving; with this theory, he had "released the continents from the Earth's core and transformed them into icebergs of gneiss [a type of granite, pronounced "nice"] on a sea of basalt," wrote fellow country-man Hans Cloos in his 1947 book, *Gespräch mit der Erde (Conversation with the Earth)*. "It let them float and drift, break apart and converge. Where they broke away, cracks, rifts, trenches remain; where they collided, ranges of folded mountains appear."

Because World War I was in full swing in 1915, the first edition of Wegener's book didn't make it past Germany. But Wegener, who hadn't let spending a winter on an ice cap beat him, persevered. In 1922, the third edition of his book was published and translated into English, French, Russian, Spanish, and Swedish, giving geologists across the globe something to agree on: this Wegener, they asked one another, he sounds more like a nut job than not, right?

What gave the idea of spooning continents revolutionary momentum was the openness of Wegener's mind. What arrested that momentum was the narrowness of the larger scientific community with which Wegener interacted. In her history of plate tectonics, science historian Naomi Oreskes points out that the "vitriolic" response to Wegener's theory had much to do with the philosophy of science in America at the time. "Americans," she says, "were widely committed to the method of multiple working hypotheses—the idea that scientific evidence should be weighed in light of competing (multiple) theoretical explanations, which one held provisionally until the weight of evidence was sufficient to compel assent. This provisional stage was thought to require a long time—certainly years, perhaps even decades."

In 1922, when translations of *The Origin of Continents and Oceans* first appeared, one of the main ideas in circulation that addressed the formation of the Earth's surface included the principles of isostasy, or equal standing. Think of cubes of different frozen liquids floating in a bowl of water. Their various densities will cause them to float higher or lower in the water, just as the varying densities of the continents and ocean basins will cause them to "float" higher or lower on the Earth's mantle. One of the other main ideas was uniformitarianism (the present is the key to the past), but in the early part of the twentieth century uniformitarianism was an independent concept, not yet tempered by catastrophism (sporadic violent events), which meant that there were no exceptions: if South America was tropical now it was tropical millions of years ago, and therefore could not have, as Wegener suggested, migrated across the globe from a nontropical zone.

Such was the climate into which Wegener entered when he attended the 1926 meeting of the American Association of Petroleum Geologists. It was supposed to be a symposium, but the spoken arguments stacked up against Wegener, with only the convenor speaking in his favor, and one other geologist arguing for reservation of judgment. As different speakers took the podium and verbally protected the sanctity of American geology, displaying levels of passion that ranged from generalized human zeal to that of a grizzly protecting her cubs, Wegener smoked his pipe. His opponents' arguments against him included these: he argued too hard, he advocated a cause, his presentation was unconvincing, the rocks on either side of the Atlantic did not actually match up, he could not come up with a mechanism to describe how this "drift" had taken place, he was audacious to propose that continents could battle their way through the ocean floor, leaving mountains in their wake (particularly in light of his inability to produce a mechanistic explanation for how this could happen).

The wording of many of the attacks seemed directed more at Wegener's person than his theory. A "drunken" upper crust, said one geologist of continental drift, "hopelessly floundering" on the Earth's "sober" mantle. "A beautiful dream," said another, "the dream of a great poet. One tries to embrace it, and finds that he has in his arms a little vapor of smoke." The words "blind," "auto-intoxication," "fairy tale," and "dangerous" were used. But it is a statement from an unnamed geologist and quoted by one of continental drift's most ardent opponents that gets at what I think the real problem was: "If we are to believe Wegener's hypothesis we must forget everything which has been learned in the last seventy years and start all over again."

Despite the obvious bias, a bound copy of the proceedings titled *Theory of Continental Drift* appeared in March 1928. The abundantly named W. A. J. M. van Waterschoot van der Gracht, who had spoken in favor of Wegener's theory of continental drift, solicited three additional pro-drift papers to round things out a bit. None were from Americans and in order to see an interesting case study in the economics of dissent, you have only to travel to the current website of the American Association of Petroleum Geologists, where you can read about the publication in a special commemorative issue of *Explorer*, their society magazine. "Despite the unpopularity of the theory," they write, "AAPG was well-advised in having arranged the special symposium on continental drift. Proceeds from the meeting not only covered costs, but also paid for publication of the symposium papers. Income from the volume ($3.50 postpaid) was set aside in a new Revolving Publication Fund, 'to become the nucleus for printing books and papers in addition to the regular Bulletin.' Thus began," they end, gleefully, "AAPG's Special Publications program."

Wegener did not live to see his ideas vindicated. He died in 1930 while on another expedition to Greenland, this time to conduct the first year-long observation of the weather there. He had some supporters while he was alive—among them, a South African geologist named Alexander du Toit, who was struck by the geologic and biological similarities of Africa and South America that he'd seen firsthand. But for the most part, Alfred Wegener's theory of continental drift would have to wait for an American girl born in Ypsilanti to grow up, assembling the perfect combination of talents and knowledge along the way.

CHAPTER 3

O N ONE LEVEL, FOR MOST OF THE FIRST TWENTY YEARS OF her life, Marie did not publicly display much interest in science. But on another level, it seems that she was, throughout her childhood and adolescence, quietly gathering bits of scientific knowledge like gossip, trying to deduce whether her private crush might be worthy of pursuit. This is why the passion that consumed her later life strikes me as all the more genuine: it stands out in such strong relief to what came before.

She loved going into the field with her father; as a small child she would sit in the back of her father's green government truck "making mudpies and generally being a nuisance." Or not; it seems Marie's father liked taking her out into nature just as much as she liked to go. They'd search for arrowheads to add to his vast collection: "he could always find them," Marie said, "because he knew where they lived." Marie eventually inherited this collection, just as she inherited her father's acuity for what he called "reading nature." Some of the arrowheads she had framed, mounted, and arranged like stone butterflies. Others she had made into a necklace that she habitually wore with a chiffon dress; when not in use, the necklace came to be displayed on a bronze bust she sculpted of her father, placed there by one of the Tharpophiles, lending Papa Tharp's effigy a rakish air.

Marie loved to tell one particular story about trekking out into the midwestern countryside with her father. There are soft rolling hills and stands of trees with bark like tiny mud flats that have dried and cracked in the sun. Marie walks behind her father, watching her own boots squish into the mud and fallen leaves. When she looks up it's either at her father's back—his brown work shirt tucked into his pants, his pants tucked into boots—or to look up ahead, for tufts of moss or seedlings or some interesting rocks that might make good camping spots for her dolls. It is nearing the end of the day and the sunlight is a rich brothy yellow flashing down through the trees. Occasionally they stop and squat down to look at an interesting plant, bracketing it with two pairs of cloth-covered knees. Once, they share an apple split with William's pocket knife. On this particular outing, Marie's father has his camera. They stop, and he takes a picture.

"He wanted me for a yardstick more than anything," Marie's recollection of this story begins. "Oh," she says in the middle, "I remember Papa taking a picture of me once, I was pointing to a big tumor on a tree." "But at least—" Marie's story on this picture ends, and it was the "at least" that used to make me think this was a story about disappointment. She was being used, I thought indignantly. Now I see it differently: they shared this lovely moment, a father measuring one thing he loved with another. Marie as metric.

When she got to be eleven, her father taught her to drive his truck. She could be seen careening down red dirt roads, past the cotton fields of the South. And then, out of the blue, in the seventh grade in Florence, Alabama, she became the "third president" of the science club. "I never understood why," she said, and then followed it up with an anecdote that she apparently wanted to serve as proof. She had missed the whole point, she said, when her mother tried to explain where babies come from and Marie replied, "Do the men have the little boys?"

There are more stories like this, of young Marie trying to learn things that she couldn't seem to grasp. On astronomy: "I couldn't see those figures in the stars." On trying to learn perspective in art class: "I did all right except I couldn't do the backgrounds, so my teacher would have to fill them in for me." Yet there are also others in which it is possible to see a systematic mind growing, even before she hit the double digits. Looking down from where they sat in a balcony in church, Marie would go through and count the different types of heads: "black hats, brown hats, white heads, brown heads, bald heads." And in first grade: "We went to school in a great big old mansion with columns. There were seven or eight of us, and we sat around in a circle with the teacher in the middle, and she had all these kids around her sitting still, and she'd go to this one 'How much is one plus two?' And the kid would say 'Three.' 'How much is one plus four?' The kid would say, 'Five.' And she kept going around. I figured out what she was going to say when she got to me, and so then I knew right away that nine plus five was fourteen, so that's the way I got through those early years."

And then there was Florence, Alabama, where Marie got to spend one whole school year in the same place, where she took school field trips on weekends to study trees and rocks, where she collected a big bag of snake skeletons and skins and took them home, terrifying her mother. It was where she had a class called Current Science, in which she and her classmates learned all about what contemporary scientists were working on, which she loved, but whose optimistic tone discouraged her from thinking that there was anything left to discover. And Florence was where she had her first crush—in fact the only one she ever talked about in any of the interviews she granted—on a boy named Xenophon Nicolopoulos, who was "the smartest boy in the class in every subject." He was the "second president" of the science club. She sat beside him. He was, she says, "just one of those things."

I don't think so, though. Marie told a story about how once, while she was living in Florence, she went roller-skating with her friend Quava Hart out by the dam. They skated, she said, down wide cement roads for a city that was laid out but never built, evidence of a businessman's fantasy. I imagine the streets straight and smooth as the cool blue lines of graph paper; there's no one else for miles around. Their metal skates are clacking hard on the ground. Where houses should be there are just weeds, scrub, and brambles. The squares of the grid are empty. All those choices, all that zigzagging. If they turn right or left they can slow down a little, devote more energy to imagining what the people and houses would look like if they were there, if someone filled in these grids. But if they keep going straight they can go faster and faster, legs pushing into the ground, fists pushing into the air, lungs about to burst with all the effort, their hair whipped back from their faces by the wind as they propel themselves forward.

I think Florence was where it all started coming together for Marie, where she began forming a sense of herself, where she began to see how experiences and desires could shape her. There are some who say that your first love affects you more than any other love. Others say that your first love can reflect who you want to be. Still others say this: that you'll always be looking for what first let you down, a lifelong chase to find what failed you.

MARIE TALKED ABOUT the Appalachians as if they were the first mountains she ever saw as a kid, even though she probably saw others before. "Mountains to me meant mountains like the Alps, rock towered and snow covered," she said.

The three Tharps are driving to D.C. from Hartford, Indiana, in the family's Model T coupe. Marie is about seven years old, and tiny enough to sprawl out on the back window ledge, staring up at the clouds whizzing by. The car is packed with their belongings. There's even a box up front between her parents. Her legs are bent and they sway from side to side as the car begins its drive through the lazy curves of the Appalachians.

In the Midwest, the landscape she's most used to at this point in her life, you can see most changes in topography coming, or feel them because your body has gotten used to the straight flat roads. But about halfway through Ohio the predictability stops, and slow changes in grade become random, so she's surprised when her father swivels his head to tell her that they're going over the mountains; she thought it would be something sudden and jarring, like slipping off a mossy rock into a creek—only backward. Where, she asks, craning her neck to look out one of the side windows. Right here, he says, and turns back to the road.

Marie's been waiting for this announcement for what seems like forever. She learned about the Alps in geography class and, ever since, has tumbled the whole concept of mountains around in her head until they've been reduced to just one range: the Alps—glaciers, peaks, and all. That's what she's expecting. She looks out the other window: nothing. Where, she asks again. We're in them, her father says. She climbs down into a small space between some boxes on the backseat so she can look out the windshield: the road with trees on either side. No mountains. Where, she asks, her voice getting whiny. She makes a ruckus climbing back up onto the window ledge: still nothing. How can you be in the middle of something and not be able to see it? She gives the window a little kick and promptly falls asleep.

Later, when she wakes up, the sun has set and the light in the car is violet and jade. Her mouth is dry as cotton and she lets her face fall toward the window. And there they are, behind her: not mountains, not really, just some fog-shrouded cardboard cutouts retreating in the distance. "One of the most colossal disappointments in my whole life," she called them, more than fifty years later. "Not a goddamn mountain in sight."

MARIE AS AN adolescent was not so different from Marie as a child. Physically slight and bristling with intelligence, she still regarded herself as an outsider and valued her mother and father above all else, traits that would combine to affect her unevenly, leaving her both calloused and raw.

Her freshman year of high school, in Cooperstown, New York, was only the second time in her life she got to stay at a single school for a whole year. In the winter and spring of 1933/34, her father was assigned to a few of the more remote counties in Florida, where there weren't any schools; while he traveled south, Marie and her mother stayed on in Cooperstown.

Marie's experiences there were mixed—but vivid. Even in her seventies, when she gave the only interview in which she spoke at length about her childhood and adolescence, she still gave Cooperstown a lot of mental real estate: she missed her father a lot, but she mostly loved her school. "I was telling someone the other day I thought the New York school system that I went to was the best in the country I ever saw." It was the biggest she'd attended, with a different teacher for each subject—algebra, Latin I, ancient history, English, and then gym. And for the first time in her life, Marie had a group of friends to hang out with. They started high school together and then "sort of flocked together," going to each other's houses, lying around talking and gossiping. It was, she said, "quite nice."

Cooperstown was tough, too. That winter it was fifty below—"the coldest winter on record before or since. So my Ma sent me to school in ski pants, and I got drug into the principal's office and bawled out: 'You do not come to school in long pants. You'll stay an hour after school for a week because you showed up in long pants.' What could you do? You stayed after school for a week." So Marie's mother bought two blankets, plaid on one side and brown on the other, and made a long coat out of them. If her daughter was going to be forced to wear skirts, Bertha was going to make sure her nearly bare legs were as warm as possible.

Marie's memory of her mother's experiences in Cooperstown were overwhelmingly negative: thinking her husband had left her, the towns-people were "very unfriendly" to Bertha. She was unaccepted, lonely. "It was," Marie said, "terrible for her." But Bertha learned to cope; she and Marie had always been very close. They were, by necessity, each other's closest friend—and they stayed that way, often spending their evenings reading out loud together, trying not to miss William too much. When he came home from Florida, their little family unit was reunited; Marie and her mother were so proud and happy and relieved to have him back that Bertha sent Marie down to the landlady to announce his return, "but they wouldn't deign to come out and greet him. Typical of Cooper-stown. We considered retiring and living in that area but it was too unfriendly, horribly unfriendly."

So they moved to Oneonta, where Marie started studying the violin. "That year," she recalled, "was rather notable." She caught the whooping cough, and was ill enough that she missed six weeks of school. Her mother wore herself out taking care of her, because she "whooped it up all night." And then it was time for William to retire after thirty-one years working for the Bureau of Soils. They spent the spring in Washington, where Marie's mother hired someone to tutor Marie in Latin and algebra because she'd missed so much school and because Bertha wanted her to be able to start her sophomore year of high school wherever they decided to settle. When the retirement finally came through, they all got back in their Model T and drove west to Bellefontaine, Ohio, where Marie had spent part of her eighth-grade year, and where they'd left a bunch of furniture in storage; they thought Bellefontaine could be their headquarters that fall while they looked around for a place to settle.

William had written a paper describing the ideal farm he'd like to buy when he retired: surrounding a large brick house set way back from the road in a grove of trees would be flat land, rolling land, pastureland, cropland, and an orchard—and after a couple days spent driving around in the car looking for such a place, he found it. Everything was run-down. Fences toppled, barn falling over, house in disarray. But when he took Marie and her mother to look at it, in the pouring rain no less, they all loved it. They still loved it the next day when they returned to look at it in the sun, so William paid cash for it the day after that and pretty soon they moved into the farmhouse, four miles outside the corporation line in Bellefontaine, Ohio (town motto: ". . . home is where your story begins"). The first night on the farm, Marie slept on an army cot in the kitchen, listening to the house: the wind and the doors that banged and all the other country sounds.

By that time, Marie had missed so much school and was still so run-down from her bout of whooping cough that she "decided to stay out all the rest of that year," to pause midway before she left home for college. "It was just assumed that I would go to college and I was supposed to—what else was there to do but be a teacher?" Her mother had been happy teaching, so she figured she could be, too.

"They didn't specify that I had to do that, but it was assumed I couldn't be a soil surveyor like Papa because I was a girl, as much as I loved his work, maps, outdoors, in the field with him." Her options were the same as those of all the other young women at the time: secretary, bookkeeper, nurse, schoolteacher, librarian; high school girls couldn't take shop or metalworking, couldn't learn what Marie called the "modest beginnings" of how to handle tools, even if they wanted to. "That was only open to guys . . . I didn't resent it because I accepted the fact that they would never be available to me. I got more resentful in college."

By spring, the Tharps had eased nicely into their farm. They bought several pieces of furniture from the people who'd sold them the house, including a big double desk that Marie still owned sixty years later. Other than that, they didn't have much furniture: a living room suite and beds and kitchen and dining room tables. Minimal. "We had the whole house to rattle around in and dream and stuff. And I had that whole year at home, helping out, because I wasn't going to school—the local high school principal knew I was there, we discussed it with him, but he looked the other way, I guess because I was already a year ahead. I was excited about settling down into one place."

And then Bertha died—her daughter just a teenager, only months after her family settled down, having spent her entire short married life on the move.

Marie's October 27, 1994, interview with Helen Shepherd, from the Society of Woman Geographers—the same interview in which she felt adequately comfortable talking about the early years of her life—is the only time Marie addresses her mother's death in any detail. At the very end of side A of tape 5, Marie digresses and starts talking about the "whole new world" she had access to on the farm, particularly the creek that ran through the property—"when it rained it would cut gullies and deepen." This leads to her talking about the sudden appearance of her brother Jim—"so he built fourteen dams and it slowed down the erosion and created little pockets of things where the plants would grow and the birds would come"—which leads to her thoughts about her mother's death.

Jim, Marie said, came home after her mother died. "He came back and stayed there permanently. She had died and Papa was—it was very sad. Jim came home in December. He tried to get home by Christmas, drove from Washington state when he quit the Forest Service, and drove the southern route in the winter. He drove, but he took time to visit scenes and people and relatives, didn't make it until the day after Christmas. I'll never forget. He just showed up at the back door with his car full of stuff and there he was. That was something."

How did you feel, the interviewer asked Marie. What was that like?

"We were so glad to see him, because Papa was still shook up at losing Mom and it was a very sad time when she died."

Tell me, had she been ill, Marie?

"She was only ill for three months, for one summer, but she laid in bed and watched this little maple tree which was growing outside in the yard. We put her in the library and she laid there looking out the window, and I thought, as I watched the little maple tree lose its leaves, that she was losing her life, too. But I didn't think it would come so soon. Then they came and took her away in an ambulance, because we couldn't take care of her at home. Then I went to school, Papa was out in the hay field taking in the hay, and then she up and died. They hadn't told us it was going to be that soon. So it was pretty sad."

Do you remember taking care of her?

"I didn't do much taking care of her. No."

Did you have somebody come in to take care of her?

"Actually, my father had gone up to Ypsilanti and fetched my mother's sister down from there, who had never married, my aunt Lulu. She was an old maid, very religious, and he got her down there and gave her a room, and we tried to make her part of the family, but we couldn't quite, because she was sort of resentful that her sister had had a chance to get married and travel and have a family, but she helped out a lot. She did household work, which was why I could get through high school with good grades. I didn't have to do the meals or the dishes. She did the chores."

So she had come down before your mother died and then stayed after?

"I don't know whether she came before Mom died or not. I think she was there a few weeks before Mom died . . . Yeah, just a short time, because I remember Mommy said, 'Oh, now you'll have somebody to make cookies for you.'"

On the tape, Marie says her mother's death took place in 1935, but Bertha Louise Tharp's death certificate says that she died on September 8, 1936, from kidney failure as the result of an unspecified carcinoma. Bertha hadn't been seen by a doctor since the beginning of July, but "if she suffered," Marie said, "she kept it all to herself." Marie witnessed her mother bear pain privately, and it must have made an impression, for Marie would do the same in her own life: if her mother could do it, she figured she could, too.

*T*HESE DAYS I THINK ABOUT MARIE'S LIFE AS COMPOSED OF equal parts circumstance and desire, so that by the time she reached the age when her choices began to matter, she was perfectly suited to take advantage of the opportunities that presented themselves. This is not to say that something magical occurred; Marie fit her times and was able to recognize a destination when she saw it.

She entered Ohio University in the fall of 1939 as a nineteen-year-old, having taken a year off to stay at the farm after graduating from high school. She was, therefore, older than many of her peers. Her mother was dead, her father was nearly seventy, and she had chosen Ohio University in Athens because it was small and had a less religious slant than many of the other schools in the state. When speaking about her late teens, Marie mentioned saving up things in her head to tell her mother—as if she had not died, just gone on vacation—and of being an academic snob, of holding the women in the home economics department in "complete contempt." When compounded with the year at the farm before college, I can't help but see these moves as protective. This notion of dealing with loss by hibernation by retreating and stockpiling for the future is not, I think, uncommon. Nor do I think that in her case it was altogether negative: most people seemed to baffle her, and she hadn't acquired the experience that would later let her confidently decide how to interact with them.

Marie began her college career as an art major. She started with a sketching class and then moved on to design theory, where a Miss York lectured the students and then sent them off to do projects that would be critiqued by the class. It was Miss York who once sent a girl up in front of the class and analyzed her outfit, explained why the girl's choice of a black sweater, a yellow and black tweed skirt, and black socks worked well as a design. It was Miss York who wouldn't let students use color until their second semester, Miss York whose blue eyes could devastate the students in her Intro to Design class during a critique, Miss York who was horrified when one of Marie's classmates tipped her off about the chewing gum Marie had used to hold her modern sculpture together. Marie said that Miss York was a prude for objecting to the gum but also acknowledged the need to understand the basics of realism (form) before adding in modernist "frivolities" (chewing gum). She did not, however, take Miss York's second-semester class, and as a result, she said, "to this day, color doesn't exist for me. I'm really color blind, theoretically."

In Marie's second semester of college, she decided that she would become a music major. She had played the violin since high school, but although she stayed in the symphony, she apparently could not make the devotional leap required for a major in music. In her third semester, she took up German and zoology. "I was interested in those, but I never got good grades in them, I think because I had a hard time adjusting to the schedule of college—you know, I wasn't used to Monday, Wednesday, Friday." She tried paleobotany because the students went outside and dug fossils out of the creek; she tried philosophy and loved it ("I would have stuck with it if it hadn't been for this overhanging threat of finding a job"); she tried English but got Bs ("what a blast that was"); took education and hated it.

During the several interviews conducted with her before she died, Marie never mentioned any college friends or boyfriends. It seems she kept her baggage light during college, sharing a room with a Russian named Nina Plotnikoff in a boardinghouse (it was Nina who had been breaking the house rule by surreptitiously listening to a radio in their room the Sunday Pearl Harbor was bombed, Nina who interrupted Marie's studies to tell her), submerged in the anonymity of campus, looking from the outside like all her war-era sisters. This is what I tend to fixate on when I think about this period in Marie's life. Marie referred to these young women as sheep, and complained about the fashion rules she had to abide by for her four years at OU. "They made us wear heels and hose once or twice a week for dinner. You had to get dressed up," she said, remembering. "And you had to practice being hostess. Oh god, it was terrible." Skirts were full or straight, fifteen and a half inches from the floor; the women wore saddle shoes and anklets, high-necked sweaters with pearls, and short haircuts with neat, curled bangs. If you were wild you had a double strand of pearls.

Marie called it regimentation, and certainly it was, but I also think it protected her. If she looked like everyone else she could keep stockpiling information without interruption, collecting bits of knowledge from a wide range of disciplines, knitting them into something that would serve her later. If she were in college today there would be choices to make, a personal style to project so that like-minded souls could home in on her, wanting to become friends, urging her to externalize her most private emotions and stripping her of the privacy she clearly prized.

In college, Marie found geology instead of friends. It wasn't a lightning bolt; she just took historical geology and liked it. A semester later she tried physical geology and met the "nearest to a mentor I ever saw." His name was Dr. Clarence Dow and he was a fat, jovial man whose office door was always open and who must have recognized a blossoming talent when he saw it. He was the one who suggested she take drafting, a skill not usually necessary to become a geologist, but one that he knew would improve her chances of getting a job in a discipline dominated by men and old traditions. There was a good chance that no one would let her do fieldwork, but if she could draft, she could work in an office. Marie got a C in the class (of seventy-three students, three were women), but said that she learned a lot. "It was very important to learn the tools, and it was a beginning of learning to see things in three dimensions."

When she was a senior, Marie saw a flyer hanging on the bulletin board outside Dow's office. The University of Michigan, it said, was offering an accelerated geology degree with the guarantee of a job in the petroleum industry upon graduation. As this was 1942, and most of the men were off fighting in World War II, it was understood that most of the students would be female. When Marie consulted Dow, he told her to try it. "It only takes two years," she remembered him telling her. "You don't like it, you can do something else."

That December she marched over to talk to the dean, who had been one of her philosophy professors, and informed him that she was ready to graduate, and why. He was shocked. The process usually moved in the opposite direction—his office informing a student that she could graduate—but when they added up all her credits, Marie had ten more than she needed. Majors in English and music, and several loose groupings of classes that the secretary didn't attempt to form into minors. "Within three weeks I got the hell out of there." Just a week later, she had explained her plans to her father and taken out a $400 loan to pay her tuition at the University of Michigan; in January 1943 she stepped off a train into an Ann Arbor blizzard, the snow so thick she couldn't see in front of her.

DURING THE WAR, the women in the geology department at the University of Michigan were called the "PG girls." PG was short for *petroleum geology*. The program would teach them what they needed to know, and girls who had always been referred to as "smart cookies" (as in "C'mon, just take her out! I'm telling you, she's one smart cookie") would jump at such an opportunity.

Marie liked the PG girls but says she never really got close to any of them—"we just sort of tolerated each other and went off and did our homework" were her exact words—meaning that in Ann Arbor, as in Athens, Ohio, she "lived alone, walked alone, ate alone." That was her nature, but her experience at Michigan also reflected the ways in which she was different: the program required only two years of college, and although Marie was pursuing her master's degree, most of the girls were still undergraduates. She was older. Her level of thinking would have to be higher and she would have to produce a thesis; it was expected that she come prepared for total geological immersion. And while that's what she wanted, her immersion just a few weeks prior had been in the humanities: poetry, painting, and philosophy. She was quickly overwhelmed by all the work.

Her first summer there, the girls went to Camp Davis in Wyoming, where they got to study rocks firsthand. They stopped at what Marie called "all the interesting geological places"—the Black Hills, Devils Tower, the Great Plains—mapping outcrops and looking at mountain thrusts. They lived in tin huts, wore blue jeans tucked into tall hiking boots, and warmed themselves by a fire in the morning. Marie would wander off on hikes by herself, observing nature the way she used to do with her father. But most of the time grad school was textbooks and papers, classes and sleeping and the winter cold of Ann Arbor.

It's impossible to say what exactly Marie was taught because she said almost nothing about it. A petroleum geologist named Kenneth Landes was chairman of the department. Armand Eardley, who according to Marie "authored the first tectonic summary of a continent" (it happened to be North America, and was called *Structural Geology of North America*), taught structural geology. An unnamed cast taught sedimentation, invertebrates, and mineralogy. In the almost twenty years that had passed since the American Association of Petroleum Geologists publicly flayed Alfred Wegener's theory of continental drift, not too much had changed. Wegener himself was dead, which was convenient for the men who'd disagreed with him, but there was still no definitive theory that explained how the Earth's crust formed. Mountains, oceans, continents, islands, valleys—even the Earth's simplest features were still a source of contention.

One textbook from the time "admitted" that "the cause of crustal deformation is one of the great mysteries of science and can be discussed only in a speculative way. The lack of definite knowledge on the subject is emphasized by the great diversity and contradictory character of attempted explanations." The two examples the textbook gave were contraction theory, which "represents the interior of the Earth as a slowly contracting mass, on which the outer shell collapses like the skin of a shriveling apple," and continental drift, which had "whole continents shift[ing] horizontally through long distances." Both were dismissed—contraction theory because it explained the formation of only some mountains, and continental drift because of a lack of "motive power." As for other explanations for the cause of crustal deformation, there were simply too many, the authors said, and not enough space to catalogue them all.

Marie recalled being taught what continental drift was, but not in a way that suggested it was a realistic possibility. As late as 1952, Kenneth Landes, the chairman of the geology department at Michigan, wrote a paper entitled "Our Shrinking Globe," so it's safe to say that contraction theory was part of the curriculum there in 1945. Professors at other schools were not as hesitant to tap into the "diversity and contradictory character of attempted explanations" as the textbooks in use at Marie's university. At Harvard, the graduate students of then-prominent structural geologist Marlin Billings were subjected to a lecture in which nineteen possibilities were given to explain how mountains had been formed. Nineteen! Other than contraction theory and continental drift, the list included geosynclinal theory and isostasy. Geosynclinal theory posited that sediments accumulated in troughs called geosynclines. These troughs sank as the weight of the sediments they held accumulated; eventually, the heat in them also accumulated, changing the sediments to rock. The result was a "mountain-making crisis" wherein the whole pile was lifted up into a mountain chain.

Isostasy was essentially a state of equilibrium. It proposed that the rock of Earth's crust "floated" on top of the layer of rock beneath it. And depending who you asked, that could be because the Earth's crust varied in either density or thickness. In the density model, mountains were light and valleys were heavy; mountains rose higher into the air because they were more buoyant than valleys. In the thickness model, mountains were areas of thick crust and valleys were areas of thin crust; just as mountains rose higher into the air than valleys, so did their roots extend deeper down into the earth.

Vague? Yes! Why would geosynclines that had been sinking under the weight of accumulated sediment suddenly pop up into mountains? How long did the process take? How can it be that mountains are light? Why was all this piecemeal vertical movement acceptable but Wegener's laterally drifting continents were not? These questions were not answered definitively by textbooks or professors, but isostatic movement of the Earth's crust was taught as reality anyway. Textbooks put on brave faces for their audiences, declaring that further study would shortly bring the answers to such questions if pupils could be faithful just a little longer.

What stands out most about the period is an uncertainty—which, by the time Marie was in grad school, had escalated into a medium-grade professional hysteria, geologists pressing to find a unifying theory that would open into a vast new world of geoscience. It was as if Wegener had yelled "Fire!" when he first published *The Origin of Continents and Oceans*. Few geologists believed him, but extensive smoke, hot walls, and smoldering floorboards had been observed; while they could allow that the building seemed unstable, they couldn't agree on a way out. And anyway, what space could they occupy if they evacuated?

Textbooks were vague. Lectures raised more questions than they answered. In one of the few stories she related about her time at Michigan, Marie recalled a talk and visit from the state geologist. At a post-presentation tea, the PG girls were given the chance to ask him questions. What was it like to be in this field? What would a job in the real world be like? Just what, the girls' questions implied, were they getting themselves into? "And lo and behold what did this geologist say," Marie recalled. "He said the geologist is the best one on the spot to make an educated guess." The geologist's best tool, in other words, was the ability to look at an incomplete picture and make a hypothesis about what that picture meant. The field, then, was both exhilarating and frustrating—frustrating to those who wanted to be told that there was a solid foundation they could believe in, exhilarating to those who liked guessing. The field was leveling; authorities did not have many more answers than the newcomers.

By 1945 Marie had completed the four semesters required for her geology degree and was tackling a fifth semester of physics, math, and chemistry because she "felt guilty not knowing anything." Plus, geology alone had not given her or anyone else the answer to how the Earth's surface had been formed, so maybe physics, math, and chemistry would help. By immersing herself in these classes, she was following a guess. She recognized the gaps in her knowledge and was taking courses she knew would fill them in. The result would be tangled—a hole in a fabric darned through complex maneuvering of interlocking strings, not just covered up by slapping on an iron-on patch.

Her professors worried. They thought, she said, that she "didn't seem to have any direction." She was not behaving the way she was supposed to; in the same way that English/music majors rarely made sudden decisions to enter graduate programs in geology, graduate geology students did not often stay in school longer than required to gain a deeper understanding of the basic sciences. Her interdisciplinary wandering made them nervous that she would drop geology altogether, so when an assistant geologist job came down the line from an oil company in Tulsa, they offered it to her.

In the summer of 1945, Marie Tharp graduated from the University

of Michigan with a master's in geology and a job in the petroleum industry. Her thesis was titled "Subsurface Studies of the Detroit River Series."
Its purpose was to "investigate the extent and thickness of the salt in the
Detroit River series and its relationship to the formation as a whole," its
conclusion that the "sediments of the Detroit River series were deposited
in an inland sea which may have been isolated at several times." Nothing
big, she said in retrospect; it probably became a chapter of Kenneth
Landes's textbook. Her move to Oklahoma would temporarily focus her
attention on land and the oil that could be found in it, but her toes were
wet; she'd return to moving seas before too long.

*M*EN HAVE BEEN ATTEMPTING TO MEASURE THE DEPTHS of the oceans for hundreds of years; the process of doing so, no matter the technology involved, is called sounding. In 1521 Ferdinand Magellan is said to have conducted the first recorded single-spot sounding: he lowered a weighted line into the Pacific and, when it reached a depth of 750 meters, declared the ocean "immeasurable." Mid-eighteenth-century naturalists guessed that the oceans must be between 20 and 35 kilometers deep. In 1854 navy man John Mercer Brooke improved upon the process for conducting single-spot soundings, known as "heaving the lead": tying a cannonball to the end of a length of strong twine on which each fathom had been marked off, then "heaving the lead" over the side of the boat and waiting until it was believed to have hit the bottom. Brooke's improvement rigged the cannonball so that when it hit the bottom a hollow, tallow-coated brass rod shot into the sediment, capturing it so that it could be raised back up to the surface and examined under a microscope.

The Brooke Deep-Sea Sounding Apparatus was a big deal; two years later, in 1856, Matthew Fontaine Maury used it while making a contour map of the Atlantic Ocean floor with lines drawn in at one, two, three, and four thousand fathoms. This map was the first to hint at a ridge running down the length of the Atlantic, the ridge that Marie, nearly a century later, discovered was rifted and ran worldwide. " 'What is to be the use of these deep sea soundings?' is a question that often occurs," Maury wrote in his book *The Physical Geography of the Sea*. "And it is as difficult to be answered in categorical terms as [Benjamin] Franklin's 'What is the use of a new-born babe?' Every physical fact, every expression of nature, every feature of the earth, the work of any and all of those agents which make the face of the earth what it is, and as we see it, is interesting and instructive. Until we get hold of a group of physical facts, we do not know what practical bearings they might have." Maury, whose prose was prone to fantastical digressions, would become known as the Father of Oceanography and a favorite of modern marine geologists.

In 1856 Benjamin Franklin's grandson Alexander Dallas Bache calculated the average depth of the Pacific by using tidal gauge records to determine the velocities of the first tsunami waves of a recent Japanese earthquake. From 1872 to 1876 the HMS *Challenger* traveled 125,000 kilometers with the goal of systematically surveying the world's oceans. It was a true tour de force on the part of the scientific crew—the ship stopped every 200 miles to take soundings, with temperature and currents measured at various levels in the water column, and the bottom dredged for sediment, flora, and fauna. From their discovery that the ocean floor was covered with a thick layer of "ooze" composed of the skeletons of surface plankton and that, under the microscope, those skeletons showed no evidence of abrasion, scientists concluded that the ocean floor was a place of absolute stillness. One scientist called it a place of "perfect repose." This understanding of the world's oceans remained practically unchanged for another fifty years. That the most exciting things discovered on the *Challenger* expedition were living—faceted foraminifera and strange pale invertebrates—did little to encourage interest in the geological or topographical aspects of the deep sea. The expedition, which had resulted in fifty volumes' worth of research and was the most comprehensive study of the topography of the ocean floor in history, included only 492 soundings from 713 days at sea.

The 1901 formation of the International Hydrographic Bureau, improbably headquartered in Monaco and led by Prince Albert I, injected a little glamour into oceanography. Pre–World War I newspaper references to "oceanography" pit the prince against polar explorers; together they dominated the coverage of oceanography. Breathless headlines about "quests"

and expeditions and "the unknown" in the North and South poles counter stories about the prince's discoveries in the deep sea. "THIS CRAB
CANNOT SWIM; Prince of Monaco, deep-sea student, tells of a new
species," declared the *New York Times* on April 19, 1921. To this day the
International Hydrographic Bureau compiles soundings from member
nations to produce the General Bathymetric Chart of the Oceans (aka
GEBCO—a bathymetric chart being the ocean-floor equivalent of your
average topographical map).

It took a big technological leap for oceanographic cartography to
take off. The need for locating underwater masses was prompted by the
Titanic's collision with her famous iceberg in 1912. By the time World
War I broke out in 1914, several rudimentary echo sounders had been
developed. Thus began the reign of sonar.

By sending out an underwater sound wave known as a "ping" and
then measuring the amount of time the ping took to reach a receiver
after bouncing off the ocean floor, one sailor operating an echo sounder
was able to do in seconds what used to take several men hours—without
even having to stop the ship. In order for the whole process to work,
though, the sailor had to 1) press a button sending out the ping, 2) simultaneously set a stopwatch, 3) listen for the echo of the ping (usually not
more than six seconds), and 4) mark down the echo time and the ship's
position. "Ping ping ping ping ping," went the countless echo sounders
whose night-watch sailors had fallen asleep with fingers on the triggers.
You had to listen. And you had to care; by 1923, a *New York Times* article
headed "New Device Measures Ocean Depths by Sound" said that the
United States Navy had abandoned this stopwatch method, as it "involved
the human equation and was not dependable."

From 1925 to 1927, the German research vessel *Meteor* undertook an
expedition that supplanted that of the *Challenger*. The cruise was sponsored by the University of Berlin, which outfitted the ship with the most
up-to-date equipment and thinkers available. There were four different
types of echo sounders, four physical oceanographers, and scientists from
four other disciplines: biology, geology, chemistry, and meterology. Including the crew and officers, there were 133 people on board. Their goal was
systematically to fill in "the details of the physical, chemical and tidal conditions of the whole depth of the ocean," a 1926 article in *The Geographical Journal* said. The *Meteor* traversed the Southern Atlantic thirteen

times. Along these thirteen lines, stretching horizontally from Africa to South America, the echo sounder recorded 67,388 deep-sea soundings, about three to four kilometers apart. Had they been limited to "heaving the lead," such a survey would have taken seven years of sounding, twenty-four hours a day, seven days a week.

In 1927, perhaps impressed by and envious of the *Meteor* expedition, the U.S. National Academy of Sciences appointed a committee on ocean-ography. Its goal was to examine the role of the United States within the worldwide community of oceanographic research. The NAS had appointed a similar committee just eight years prior, in 1919, headed by Harvard zoologist and oceanographer Henry Bryant Bigelow. The committee was charged with the task of developing, along with the Division of Biology and Agriculture, a "cooperative study of ocean life," but the NAS hadn't followed through with enough funding, and by 1923 the committee dis-solved. In 1927 Bigelow was again involved, but this time he was asked to look at the economic and scientific importance of oceanography. Another man, Thomas Wayland Vaughan, the director of Scripps, the only oceano-graphic institute in the United States at the time, was asked to look at the international aspects of oceanography.

The Scripps Institution for Biological Research had been founded in San Deigo in 1908. It was the first marine science center not only in the United States, but in the entire Western Hemisphere. It became part of the University of California in 1912, and when Vaughan was appointed director in 1920, he vowed to broaden Scripps's mission, expanding it into a world-class institution; to reflect this mission better, Scripps became the Scripps Institution of Oceanography in 1925. By 1927, when Vaughan was asked by the NAS to think about the role of the United States in oceanography, he was understandably the expert. And, also unsurpris-ingly, the committee on which he and Bigelow served found that the United States' oceanographic endeavors had been significantly surpassed by those of the nations of northwestern Europe. The committee recom-mended the establishment of an institution on the East Coast that would be comparable to Scripps, and encouraged the future cooperation of all practitioners of oceanography—Scripps, the new East Coast center, and federal agencies such as the Naval Hydrographic Office.

The Woods Hole Oceanographic Institution (WHOI—rhymes with "chewy") became that new East Coast hub. Founded in 1930 with money from the Rockefeller Foundation, it had to start from scratch, just as Scripps had done more than two decades before. WHOI had new buildings, new staff, Bigelow as director, and, most important, something that Scripps did not have: a research vessel. It seems ridiculous to imagine an oceanographic institution without a ship, but that's how it was until August 1931, when construction on the built-to-order *Atlantis* was finished and the boat was delivered to the Woods Hole campus in Massachusetts. (Scripps would get a ship in 1937.) The 142-foot steel-hulled ketch was, as Bigelow requested, "capable of extended voyages and equipped to carry on investigations at all depths in the various fields of sea science." It had staterooms for six scientists, dorm space for students, a hoisting winch (essential to any work that required the submersion of machinery), and a diesel engine that could travel at what was, for the time, the impressive speed of nine knots (or just over ten miles) per hour. American oceanography finally had the right tools (sonar) and a means of locomotion (the *Atlantis*); now all it needed were people who could use these means to visualize new possibilities.

I HAVE, IN AN ARCHIVAL BOX MADE FROM ACID-FREE MATE-rials, a fat envelope addressed to Miss Marie Tharp in Tulsa, Okla-homa. It's one of the things I rescued from Marie's house, and in it are seven letters from seven different PG girls, dated between August and October 1946, a year after Marie graduated from the University of Mich-igan. The papers are all different shades—some whites that have faded to yellow, light blue, gray, one with a pink herringbone pattern. The letters are part of what was known then as a round robin: one girl would write a letter and send it to another girl, who would write a response and mail it and the previous letter on to another girl.

Marie is the last one on the list of addresses. Because she said she never really got close to the PG girls, I've always wondered what it was like for her to read their letters, full of descriptions of sightseeing trips and weddings and lives in which other PG friends played a role. A couple of pairs of the girls were living together, having relocated to such exotic locales as Texas for their new jobs, and several of them either had just gotten married or were about to get married. When I read these letters the first time, the events they described morphed into a rather nightmar-ish Busby Berkeley–esque chorus line—giant wedding rings and smiling

mouths the size of automobiles gliding across a glossy black stage, taunt-
ing Marie's status as a single and mostly solitary woman.

   She, on the other hand, had relocated to Tulsa, where she worked in
the head office of the Stanolind Oil Company—six days a week until the
end of World War II in August 1945. After a VJ Day parade in which so
much confetti filled the air that it looked like a blizzard, the office cut
back to five days a week. In Tulsa, Marie's yearning to be allowed to do the
work that men did intensified. "Not too challenging, nothing to do, hot,"
is how she characterized her time there. As assistant to the senior geologist, she helped decide where to drill and when to stop drilling. She filed.
She pulled maps of the areas in which drilling decisions were being made.
She was "bored as hell," but at least not engaging in a science that she found
even more boring: micropaleontology. That's what most women in petroleum geology had to do, and it pretty much meant "sitting around" staring
into the lens of a microscope "counting bugs." The "bugs" were actually
phytoplankton, index fossils whose presence helps scientists determine if
rocks are likely to contain petroleum. That women with graduate degrees
were doing this task bothered Marie; it was, she said, "simple identification"
that the company could have used "high school students for."

   "I thought it was limited," Marie said of her time at Stanolind. But with
the "astronomical" salary of $200 a month (about twice what a high school
teacher made at the time), she could simultaneously pay off her grad school
loans and continue her education. She picked up where she had left off at
Michigan, taking night classes in math at the University of Oklahoma,
once again heeding the advice of a man she respected. This time it was a
graduate teaching assistant she'd had for physics at Michigan—essentially
her equal, but also her teacher—with whom she had been "chewing the fat"
on the last day of class. He picked up a piece of chalk, started listing the
sciences "in order" on the board. Exact sciences: chemistry on the bottom, physics in the middle, mathematics at the top. Natural sciences were
in another column, but it was the math they were both interested in. Marie
was about to graduate, she told him, had a job in Oklahoma with an oil
company. That's math, too, he said, and Marie never forgot it.

   Her math classes challenged her. Staying busy kept her happy. Answers
did not come easily, but she derived comfort from the effort she put into
the problems, mistakes and solutions both suspending her in a graphite
flutter. Even though she could have afforded one, she never bought a slide

rule—did all her calculations by hand and mind until she found a slide rule lying in the street one night when she was almost finished with her new degree.

During this time, she said, her social life was "largely nonexistent." She had one friend, though, named Freida Jones, whom she'd met in one of her math classes. They'd take bike trips on Saturdays, cycle out of town to a pond and spend the rest of the day floating around trying to keep cool. They'd ride the five miles out to the airport and sit in the cafeteria eating lunch, watching the planes come in. They'd visit the churches of different denominations for Freida's religion class and go to the zoo, too—all on their bikes. Unlike other girls, Marie said, who bought cars first thing after they got jobs. Like Marie, Freida was "real scientific." Later, Freida disappeared, just like the few friends Marie made as a child. "I had her," Marie said, "but I lost track of her."

When asked by an interviewer where her life took her after she left Tulsa in 1948, Marie answered "home," meaning her father's farm in Bellefontaine, Ohio. The transcript indicates a long pause after that single word, a space into which I'd originally inserted Papa Tharp and Marie's brother, Jim, and the farm they called "the Home Place." She said she spent a year there, but at some point it occurred to me that her math had to be wrong. By November 1948, she had to be living in New York—all accounts said so—and she worked at Stanolind in Tulsa for three years, beginning in August 1945. Either she spent less time at home or less time in Tulsa.

Eventually I discovered that Marie had not so much lost track of time as let it run wild in her memory, allowing some days (and the experiences they contained) to swell, pushing others almost totally out of the way. Good days counted double; the periods she wanted to forget were part of the whole, but not counted, not spoken of individually. So while Papa Tharp and Jim and the Home Place may very well have been a part of that long pause between home and New York, something else was, too.

Marie had been married.

Her husband's name was David Flanagan, and for at least a few years Marie Tharp became Marie Flanagan. David served in the Fifth Bombardment Wing of the U.S. Air Force during World War II. He played violin in the Columbus Philharmonic for the 1947/48 season. He was born in Plumwood, Ohio, on March 18, 1920. I have, in the same acid-free box as the PG girls' round robin letters, a few photographs that I assume are of him, since he's playing the violin and wearing an air force uniform. In them, the features of his face all point down—his eyes, his thick eyebrows, the corners of his mouth, and the lobes of his ears. A few other snapshots show him and Marie together. Her body looks slight, but her eyes and lips are dark and aimed at the space behind the photographer instead of at her husband.

While Marie lived in Tulsa, David lived in Columbus. Sometimes they met halfway, in bus stations in Pittsburgh or D.C. From what her friends have been able to tell me, the marriage was not a passionate one. It was also mostly a secret. The friends I spoke to knew only because they'd mistakenly found out, when Marie was nearing the end of her life and her tongue slipped or when one of them was going through a box looking for some obscure document and happened to come across her marriage certificate. They never pushed her to talk about her marriage since she obviously wanted to forget it. "At her memorial service," one of them told me, "people were pulling me aside and whispering, 'Did you know Marie was *married*?' It was one of those secrets that we all knew but didn't talk about."

I wouldn't mention it either, would leave it to die like she wanted if it wasn't for one thing. In all her interviews, when Marie was asked about New York, why she decided to quit her well-paid job with Stanolind and move to Manhattan in 1948 with no prospects, her answer was this: that she was bored, that she wanted a research position, that she wanted something new and exciting to stimulate her mind. But then I found out about the marriage, and after that I found a piece of paper folded up in a box at the Library of Congress. It was a letter from Juilliard to David Flanagan, accepting him as a student for the summer 1948 session, his enrollment in the fall contingent on his performance during that time— which means that when Marie arrived in New York in 1948, she followed more than an intellectual desire.

Based upon this evidence it would be easy to strip Marie of her agency; a move across the country with a husband is a very different adventure from doing it alone. But it's important to note that Marie had had the opportunity to take the easy path before. She could have lived in Columbus with David from the moment they married—but she hadn't. Her life would surely have been less lonely, and she would not have had to deal with the looks Oklahomans cast at her because she was almost thirty and single and working in a man's profession. Despite those difficulties, love or companionship (or whatever descriptor best suits Marie and David's strange relationship) were not enough to move her. She valued geology and her freedom more, and it was only when her marriage presented her with the chance to practice better geology by moving to New York that she chose to compromise some of that freedom. It was a transaction—she gave up a share of independence in order to receive a larger portion of knowledge—a trade-off that she would consciously make throughout her life.

David and Marie were divorced by 1952, and the only words I've found where she directly alludes to this period in her life were scrawled across a cracking piece of yellow lined paper: "My marriage did not survive. Our interests were too disparate. In addition, our friends were scarcely compatible and we both felt out of place in the other's group. My father was concerned and came to visit me. Neither he nor I knew what to do about my erstwhile husband who had recurrent illnesses. We would visit him in the [state] hospital. There were many details which I no longer remember. Eventually he left. I never knew whether he left with a degree or not from Juilliard. He did some teaching and played in some symphonies." I'm told that the impetus for divorce came from Marie. And that was that.

One more thing about this period: she does remember one detail about leaving Tulsa. She needed to sign up for a final course before receiving her math degree. Her advisor suggested accounting—it would help her, he said, to do her own taxes. Marie wanted to take spherical trigonometry (which looks at the relationships of shapes on a sphere). "And guess what he says," she asked that same interviewer who asked her where life took her after Tulsa. "Most of us never have any occasion to do any navigation at sea."

Marie followed her instinct and took spherical trig. The class, she said, was "sort of a comedown" after the higher-level math she'd been taking, but as it turned out she would find the knowledge she picked up there highly valuable. What's interesting to consider, then, is whether her background was the cause of her future interests—revealing in her world an ever-present grid of theorems she had no choice but to follow—or if it just enabled her, gently guiding her toward subjects to which she was already inclined.

* * *

THE *NEW YORK TIMES* said it was going to be rainy and in the mid-sixties, unseasonably warm for the first day of November: "Showers and continued mild today and tomorrow." Marie glances up from the paper and tries not to look like a yokel. She folds the newspaper into a rectangle and tucks it under the arm that's holding her handbag. She squares her shoulders a bit; she's here at Columbia University because she wants a job. It is 1948.

Beneath her heels the bricks are uneven. As she walks, some of them jiggle like loose teeth—they're too far apart to hold one another in place—but it's reassuring because everything else looks perfect, as if she'd wandered onto some soundstage by mistake. She stops on Amsterdam Avenue. Carved into the stone above the entrance to Schermerhorn Hall are the words FOR THE ADVANCEMENT OF NATURAL SCIENCE. SPEAK TO THE EARTH AND IT SHALL TEACH THEE. There's a magnified fog in the air, a mist really, and it's made her hair start to frizz out, escape from the fat curls around her face. She tries to push some of it back.

From the outside she looks sensible. Her clothes are not fancy, but her eyes and her cheekbones could make you look twice. She might be a secretary sent on an errand who's worried she's gotten the wrong building. Like the other day, when she went to the Geological Society because she heard they were doing a book on the geography of oil and she had a degree in geology and had spent the last three years as an assistant geologist for the Stanolind Oil Company of Tulsa, Oklahoma, and—

We ain't got no room for file clerks, the secretary told her. As if she had come all the way to New York to sit around filing things. If she wanted to do that she could have stayed in Tulsa watching the ceiling fan kicking up dust all day.

So Columbia was the next stop. She pushes through the heavy wooden doors of Schermerhorn Hall. Columbia, where the brick-façaded buildings rise up perpendicular from the brick walkways and money and smartness are just another part of the air. Where many of the professors who wrote the textbooks she studied when she was in grad school teach. She clicks across the marble floor to the building directory.

There's some waiting after she ascends the stairs and goes into the geology department office. Maybe there's a student trying to get the secretary to sign something, or perhaps that secretary is on the phone arguing with someone about a check that she assures the caller was sent out weeks ago. So Marie sits, content to wait, and closes her eyes for a moment: acres of low green hills, the shadows of clouds tumbling across them toward her.

The secretary clears her throat. Can I help you, she asks. Marie stands and tells her what she wants. The secretary looks her up and down. Ah, she says, well. I suppose since you've got a degree in math, Dr. Ewing might be able to use you. The phone on her desk rings. But he's at sea right now, the secretary says. Come back in a couple weeks, his geophysical lab is in the basement.

Marie goes back to her rented room. For two weeks she watches David come and go from his classes, doesn't really go anywhere herself until she knows whether she'll get what she came for.

CHAPTER 7

*D*R. MAURICE "DOC" EWING WAS A TEXAN WHO PUB-
lished his first paper, about "Dewbows by Moonlight," in *Science*
when he was eighteen years old. By 1930, when he was twenty-four, he
had a doctorate in physics from Rice University and was teaching at
Lehigh University, recruiting students barely younger than he to drive
out into the countryside, in an old Ford named Floozey Belle, to study
the movement of seismic waves through the earth by setting off TNT
charges at timed intervals. This, of course, was illegal, but several papers
came out of it: "Locating a Buried Power Shovel by Magnetic Measurements," "Seismic Study of Lehigh Valley Limestone," and "Magnetic Survey of the Lehigh Valley." Most of this work was done on the weekends,
paid for out of his $1,800-a-year salary.

In 1934 Doc met two men whose ideas would forever change his
work. It was snowing slightly that November day. The men wore derbies
and thick overcoats with fur collars and during the introductions Doc
focused on the snowflakes resting on the fur: at first just fuzzy white
flecks, the flakes resolved into individual crystals as the men removed
their hats and unbuttoned their coats. The visitors were Richard Field, of
Princeton, and William Bowie, of the U.S. Coast and Geodetic Survey,
and they knew of Doc because for the past few years he'd been showing

up at the annual meeting of the American Geophysical Union, presenting papers that were basic in their findings but that also had implications for solving some key problems in science. No big deal, unless your imagination could transform promise into discovery.

"They wanted to interest me in the study of the continental shelf," Doc recalled in his biography. On a map of the northern Atlantic Ocean, the continental shelf looks like a margin along the East Coast of North America, a buffer zone of relatively shallow seas. "They thought it was a very important geological problem to see if the steep place where the shelf ends was a geologic fault or the result of outbuilding of sediment from the land." The continental shelf ends at what is called a shelf break, after which the slope of the undersea land increases dramatically. "They wondered if seismic refraction measurements, such as I had been working with, could be used. I said yes, it could be done, if one had the equipment and ships." Doc did not have any of this; in fact, he'd never done any work at sea. But "if they had asked me to put seismographs on the moon instead of the bottom of the ocean I'd have agreed, I was so desperate for a chance to do research."

Doc applied for a grant from the Geological Society of America and got it. The question was simple—how deep are the sediments off the coast?—but the answer, and the path to it, were complex. Obviously you could not just stand on the continental shelf and take measurements. There was underwater pressure to contend with, and sunlight can't penetrate more than a few dozen meters below the surface. An indirect method was needed, and Doc's land-based explosion seismology approach had shown that he was gifted in coaxing answers out of the Earth using even the most rudimentary techniques and basic observations.

In 1935 Doc became the first scientist to use explosion seismology at sea, recording the topography from Virginia's Fort Monroe to the edge of the continental shelf, analyzing its composition and distribution. He found that the continental shelf is basically sediment on top of continental crust. If you were to slice down through the Earth, making a cut perpendicular to the Virginia coast, the sediment would look like a wedge—thick at the beach end, thinning as you head out to sea—resting on top of the basement rock of the Earth's crust. This is precisely the type of place where oil forms, but back then, when Doc asked the chairman of New Jersey Standard Oil for some funding to extend his study of the ocean floor's topography, the chairman told him he wouldn't spend five cents of his shareholders' money on such a venture.

When Doc began his work at sea, it was not much appreciated; he was stuck in an interdisciplinary area that just looked gray and staticky to most other scientists. Before Doc, geologists generally turned to physics and chemistry from their office chairs, equations and elements gathered thick round their heads, forces summoned only to make paper-bound conclusions cohere. To Doc, a physicist by training, most geologists were "annoying fellows who spend most of their time poking around trying to explain this or that little detail." The work he'd done on the structure of the continental shelf, though, was different—it was inclusive and massive and uncomfortable. It required explosives. It required movement in oceans, not just thinking on land. It used physics to study geology: geophysics.

Doc was hooked. He realized that trying to understand the planet Earth while studying only the 30 percent of it that was dry was "like trying to describe a football after being given a look at a piece of lacing," a belief that had never crossed the minds of most geologists. The ocean floor needed to be examined, but the difficulties were many. First was the issue of funding, which meant that some entity with deep pockets had to show interest. Oil companies didn't want in. Lehigh University paid Doc's salary, but it wasn't an oceanographic institution. The GSA ended up giving him three small grants—in 1938, '39, and '40—grants that had to cover the costs of tools and salaries for the grad students, who were just as convinced that answers to important problems could be solved by studying the oceans. One of those students, John L. Worzel, met Doc in a freshman physics class; they would work together until Doc's death, Worzel following Doc from institution to institution. Another was Allyn Vine, who would go on to develop the world's first research submersible in the 1960s—named *Alvin*, capable of diving fifteen thousand feet and possessed of portholes through which countless underwater discoveries have been made. In the summer of 1938, Doc paid Vine and Worzel each fifteen dollars a week to work eighteen hours a day, seven days a week, in preparation for a cruise. "We found our wages hard to live on," Worzel said, so they lived out of Worzel's Ford, driving into the countryside at night, sleeping in a makeshift tent constructed from a scavenged tarpaulin, with blankets they stowed in the back of the car during the day.

They all lived for ship time. Because Doc wasn't officially affiliated

with either Woods Hole or Scripps, the only two oceanographic insti-
tutes in the United States back then, he didn't have regular access to a
ship. What he had in those prewar years were two summer weeks as a
guest on Woods Hole's *Atlantis*; during those two-week periods, he and
his team had to wait their turn to do their on-ship work, which left them
just three or four days a year in which to conduct their research. The only
silver lining in this arrangement was that they had lots of time in which
to analyze what had gone wrong with their tools—and something almost
always did.

"Commercially available geophysical instruments didn't exist at
the time. Geophysics as a science didn't really exist," Worzel said. "Most
physicists and geologists thought our nascent exploratory efforts were
bastardizations of their sciences." Add to that the fact that most oceanographers were interested only in the water and the life it contained; few
thought exploring the land beneath the sea was worth the effort. And so,
when they weren't at sea, Doc and his grad students worked feverishly to
build the tools that would allow them to study the ocean floor. They
guzzled oversize cans of fruit salad so they could use the nickel-plated
tins for rust-proof instrument covers, used glasses pilfered from diners
to create vacuum seals, turned a discarded artillery shell into a pressure
chamber, filled an inexpensive heavy rubber weather balloon with pow-
dered TNT, and successfully, against the advice of experts who said it
wouldn't work, sank and detonated it so that they could record how long
the explosion's sound waves took to reach the ocean floor and travel back
to their boat.

During World War II, the "nascent" discoveries of Doc and his team
piled up. The ocean floor was not a place of "perfect repose," as the scientists of the *Challenger* expedition had concluded in the 1870s; the tracks
left behind by both animals and water currents were clearly visible in a
photograph taken in 1940 with the first underwater camera, built by Ewing
and his team. This discovery alone was huge, akin to finding water or life
on another planet, but accompanied by none of the expected fanfare—
perhaps because the rest of the world was at war and the entry of the
United States was imminent.

Also in 1940, Doc took a leave of absence from Lehigh and went to
Woods Hole to work with the newly formed National Research Defense
Committee. Since that first cruise in 1934, Doc had been stockpiling data

about the ways sounds travel in water: underwater acoustics. This information was extremely interesting to the navy, which had gotten only a taste of the power of submarines at the end of the first world war. They knew, however, that submarines and underwater mines were going to be a large part of the new war, and also that they needed to build defenses against these new technologies. But facing them was a massive barrier: water, the adversary whose patterns Doc had been studying for years.

Like all formidable opponents, the oceans had the ability to hide and reveal and distort. Sonar had been around for more than thirty years by that point, but its use wasn't standard; only some ships had it, and often the crews that had it didn't quite know how to use it. Few scientists, save Doc and the other men at Woods Hole with whom he worked closely, really understood that the physical properties of ocean water could have a huge effect on the transmission of sound. The implications for detecting submarines were there, but sonar gave inconsistent results when employed with the assumption that water was simply a substance through which sounds traveled, unaffected. "Sometimes during practice sessions [sonar] tracked subs with uncanny accuracy, and sometimes the [ships] attacked imaginary submarines and steamed without pause over entirely real ones," reads a chapter (titled "The Chief Scientist Dreamed of Cervantes") in Doc's biography.

In 1941, by combining their knowledge about the ocean floor and underwater acoustics with the navy's records of failed attempts to use sonar as a detection device, Doc and Worzel were able to write up a report called "Sound Transmission in Seawater." "Ten thousand calculations had to be done to figure out and plot sound velocities versus distances, depths, pressures, salinity, and temperatures," Worzel said. Based upon those calculations, they declared that seawater contains layers similar to the stratification of land, some of which have remarkably different effects on sound waves. In one layer, which they deemed a "shadow zone," sound waves did not travel at all. Another layer, called the thermocline because it marked a sharp drop in temperature, bounced sound waves off of it as if solid. Submarines could hide, undetected, in either of those two layers.

By 1943 Doc had proved just how useful his research could be. In 1942 he'd used his underwater camera to identify, in one hour, the wreckage of a German U-boat sunk by a U.S. Coast Guard ship off the coast of

North Carolina, something a small fleet of ships and divers had spent a week attempting to do. That same year, he'd brought an armed pursuit in the Nantucket Shoals to a halt; what the Coast Guard thought was a submarine was exposed as a starfish-covered wreck of an old boat by Doc's underwater photographs. And later, Doc discovered the "sound fixing and ranging" (or SOFAR) channel, in which sound waves can travel for thousands of miles; in 1943, to aid in rescue missions, he recommended that pilots and submarines carry four-pound bombs specifically designed to detonate within this channel, but the military was nervous about having that much TNT in the confined quarters of a plane or submarine.

On Fridays, Doc traveled from Woods Hole to Washington, where he was given small assignments that sometimes required the invention of new gadgets. "During the war we used to talk about what fun we were going to have afterwards when we took all these instruments that were being developed and started doing science with them," Doc said. And his prediction came true: when the war was over, newly available funding and technology opened up major possibilities for the field of geophysics. By the end of 1945, he had been asked to form a geophysical lab, in the Manhattan Project's former suite at Columbia University—with the assignment, he said, of establishing a "program of instruction in the geophysical study of the earth."

Not everyone was as prepared for Doc's innovations as Columbia. In fact, probably because much of his work had been classified, it occupied its own kind of shadow zone that remained impenetrable to other scientists. As proclaimed by "the bible of oceanography," a textbook authored in part by Scripps head Harald Sverdup, "from the oceanographic point of view the chief interest of the topography of the seafloor is that it forms the lower and lateral boundaries of the water." Doc's view was the opposite. "The ocean," he said, "is just a murky mist that keeps me from seeing the bottom. To be honest, I wish the whole thing'd just dry up."

Doc's recruits were mostly young men who were uninitiated in the ways that physics, geology, and oceanography were practiced within the academy. They didn't have to abandon reputations or decades of work to practice Doc's new science; they just had to believe in what Doc called "the brutal facts." They had brains whose pathways were still being formed, where those facts could commune freely. They were also workhorses.

Doc held them to the same rigid standards to which he held himself because he wanted to make sure they took nothing for granted. He threatened them. "If you ruin that record," he once told a seasick student developing a seismogram below deck, "I'll break your jaw." (He overcame his own seasickness largely "by fury." It's "like a toothache," he said; "you don't notice it if your house is burning.") He underpaid them. "He always felt that if he could pay half the salary everyone else did, he could do twice the science," a former student said. But when times were tough in the early days, he worked without pay alongside Worzel and Vine in order to continue practicing science. He did not cede anything to formal learning. "He was the only teacher I ever had who fell asleep in his own class," another former student said. "There were times when he came to class tired, badly prepared, obviously having worked all night," said Jack Oliver, a geophysicist who began his career with Doc. But at other times he thrilled his students "by being a man who communicated by his demeanor, and by doing it in your presence, that basic problems [in physics] were to be solved by people who worked hard enough." That was the opinion of Frank Press, a former student who became the president of the National Academy of Sciences. Not *could* be solved, but "were to be solved." Doc *expected* his followers to solve the basic problems of physics, a profound confidence to instill in young men.

When I think of Doc I picture the first photo I ever saw of him, taken before he started showing up for awards in suits and shiny shoes. It shows him on the deck of a ship, shirtless and squatting above the bowels of some piece of machinery. What I most remember is a section of hair that casts a shadow on his forehead, the way it is both bristly and long, and how it sticks straight out of his head like one of those cantilevered houses you see built into Californian cliffsides, the delicate balance of the house relying on the delicate stability of the cliff. And of course there are his muscles; manliness oozes from those early pictures of Doc surrounded by his men at sea—all of them handsome, struggling with winches, lats straining, smiling comfortably at the photographer, their pants rolled up to their knees, toes gripping the deck, believing their work would someday pay off. For most of them it would.

IN 1947, WHEN Dr. Maurice Ewing arrived in Iowa City on a lecture tour, he was big on ideas and adventure but low on bodies; he needed to recruit young men from families that could afford to let their sons engage in high-minded pursuits at low-level (often nonexistent) pay. If his method of studying the Earth was going to take hold in academia and make its way onto the radar of the general public, Doc needed more disciples. And so he spoke of swashbuckling adventures at sea, of TNT and new technologies, of structures on the ocean floor that were only just beginning to be glimpsed.

Attending the Iowa City lecture was a young man named Bruce Charles Heezen, a young man who had, after spending the summer in the field studying the geology of the American West, declared himself a geology major. Bruce was impressed by Doc's lecture, and Doc must have sensed some potential in Bruce: afterward, when they were all standing over a tray of fossils, Doc popped a question, actually spoke directly to him, saying, "Young man, would you like to accompany me on an expedition to the Mid-Atlantic Ridge?"

Bruce was struck dumb. He'd spent his childhood completely sheltered, almost always within sight of his mother—an experience nearly opposite from Marie's. While she was making mud pies, bringing home bags filled with snake skeletons, doing cartwheels, and skating down empty concrete roads, a slightly younger Bruce was engaged in an entirely different type of childhood. He was one of those solemn children you see every so often. His mother sent him to school in suits, and while the other children played games that involved running or kicking and breaking a sweat, he stood off to the side by himself. His father owned a turkey farm. When Bruce's grandfather took him outside to study nature, to look at Indian mounds and trees and flowers, he nodded appreciatively and simply observed; when his father took him on hunting trips he did the same—refused to carry a gun, went along just to be "on the bird's side." "I took offense," Bruce said when recalling his childhood, "to the philosophy of hunters."

Bruce was born in 1924 in Vinton, Iowa. He and his family moved to Muscatine, Iowa, when he was six years old and lived there until he left for college. He went to elementary, junior high, and high school with the same group of kids; he went with some of them to the University of Iowa, too (called the State University of Iowa back then). He had a geographical stability that the young Marie did not, but the social comfort that you'd expect as a result seems to have been drowned out by the clashing personalities of his parents, Esther and Charles. Esther had been a sorority girl at Northwestern, a schoolteacher until she married Charles; according to Bruce, she was beautiful, a marvelous dresser, and very dramatic. She loved to socialize, but didn't find many opportunities in Muscatine outside of her bridge club. Charles was an avid sportsman. He worked as an agricultural agent until the Depression, when he began taking over farms that had been foreclosed on. He was, Bruce said, respected for his competence, but "never extremely well liked. The fact that there was fairly continuous friction between my mother and my father didn't help my position very much because I sort of got into the middle at times. I was a weakling physically. And when we went to town on Saturdays to socialize, I can recall sitting rather impatiently, waiting for the thing to get over so we could go on to some place else."

In the 1920s, Bruce's and Marie's fathers were both on the road, which means that their mothers raised them during their most formative years. While Bruce was dictating page after page of a story about his adventures with a character called Little Bear, his mother copying down his words so he could illustrate them, Marie's mother had enrolled her in private art lessons, an indignant reaction to a paint-by-number coloring book someone had given to Marie as a good-natured gift. By 1939, when Marie began classes at Ohio University, Bruce was in high school, already a volunteer assistant to a science teacher, staying after school, sometimes long into the evening, working away in the lab doing extra projects, helping the instructors get set up for the next day, or talking to like-minded students. "We would get interested in anatomy and we would dissect cats. We would get interested in freshwater biology and look endlessly at the small animals that live in the creek water. Nothing very sophisticated, just sort of playing with science, a fun thing to do. I suspect that when a young kid wants to be a policeman or a fireman he doesn't know what they really do but he likes the look of the uniform. It was that way with us. We liked the looks, we liked the names, it was a fun thing. That went on all through high school."

By January 1943, while World War II was giving Marie the opportunity to study geology at the University of Michigan, the war forced Bruce to put his college career on hold. He had begun classes at the State University of Iowa in the summer, a few days after graduating from high school, but by January his parents had decided to bring him back home.

Farmworkers were scarce, and if he was working on the farm when his draft number came up, he could get an occupational exemption. So he went home, where he worked full time on the farm in a community he "didn't feel very easy in," unaccepted by the children of his parents' friends, alone in much the same way that Marie was during graduate school. He dabbled in photography, he raised tropical fish. He made a pact with himself that he wouldn't be a farmer, that he would have nothing to do with turkeys, that he would find a job where he could travel, one where he would not succumb to occupational monotony. His draft number did come up in early 1945, but he was classified 4-F when doctors discovered he had high blood pressure.

Bruce left the farm to return to school in 1945, his outlook different. He even looked different. In the photo on his identification card from his first stint in college he looks a little angry. There's no space between his eyes, and his brow and mouth are solidly set. He's wearing a sports shirt, probably to rebel against his mother, and he looks like he knows he's smart. In the second ID photo he's wearing a shirt and a tie. His pompadour is bigger, his face is fuller, and there's space above his eyes. He's smiling. And instead of looking cocky, he looks like he knows he's lucky. Throughout the war he received letters from buddies who were fighting overseas. The letters referred obliquely to fear and depression and homesickness, but spoke directly and repeatedly about one thing: how fortunate Bruce was to be at home, with his family.

When Bruce returned to college after the war, he joined a fraternity, started delving into the natural sciences, and began to date girls. He took zoology and physics and English, but what really "caught his fancy" was a course in geology with A. K. Miller, a fossil man. Miller's graduate assistant was named Walter Youngquist, and by the end of the spring semester, Miller and Youngquist were so taken with Bruce that Youngquist invited him on a summer trip to Nevada. "I got a free course in geology, which ran 12 hours a day, not only when we were collecting, but even when we were riding along in the car. We'd talk geology and he would tell me stories and even the jokes were geological." Together they collected 2,100 cephalopods (a class of mollusks) for Youngquist's thesis. After, Bruce continued on to a summer field course, in the Black Hills of South Dakota, with another Iowa professor. By the time he started his junior year in the fall he had spent an entire summer doing geologic fieldwork, produced a report "about as thick as a master's thesis," and had "pretty much decided to become a geologist."

Maybe what Doc saw in Bruce that day in 1947 as they stood above a bunch of fossils was the same thing that Miller and Youngquist had seen. Imagine: opportunity in the form of a question ("Young man," Doc said, "would you like to accompany me on an expedition to the Mid-Atlantic Ridge?") and a young man in a circle of men. Bruce was paralyzed. Luckily, someone nearby, maybe Youngquist, gave him a little nudge and said, "Of course he will." Bruce stammered out a few questions, such as where and when—and so it was that a twenty-three-year-old college junior who'd seen the ocean only a handful of times, who'd had a class or two in physics and a summer studying fossils in the desert, was invited to join an oceanographic expedition.

ON NOVEMBER 17, 1948, Marie comes back to Schermerhorn Hall, having waited the two weeks the secretary said it would take for Dr. Ewing to return from sea. Back across the wobbling bricks, down into the basement, through a door that reads GEOPHYSICAL LAB on it in small letters, and then: immediate chaos. A newsroom in a black-and-white movie or a television version of an emergency room. Marie stands there for a moment, watching. Noise is everywhere; people are everywhere; papers, books, and pencils are everywhere. There is a grinding sound coming from behind one of the closed doors, metal on metal. Cigarette smoke forms a banner in the air. A secretary sits at the head of it all like a coxswain, her typing urging everyone on, and I like to imagine that when she finally looks up, stops typing, and notices Marie, all the movement and sound come to a halt. Marie stares at them, they stare at her. I'm looking for a job, she says, and the glorious mess animates itself again. The only person still paying attention to her is the secretary. A job, she repeats. Yes, says Marie. I asked at the geology department upstairs and someone told me a Dr.—she looks at a slip of paper tucked into her hand—Maurice Ewing might be looking for people. I have a master's in geology and a bachelor's in math and for the past— She stops when the secretary's face softens a little; they both know that Marie is no secretary.

There really isn't anywhere to sit without moving piles of coats and files and coiled lengths of wire, so Marie stands just inside the doorway while the secretary goes to check if Doc is available. At this point, the geophysical lab uses a few rooms formerly occupied by the Manhattan Project: two rooms for the machine shop, one outer office for the grad students and secretary, and one small room for Doc. Even if they hired her, where would they put her? And everyone looks so young—they look like boys, all of them; at twenty-eight she feels she's got to be almost a decade older than they are. She's trying to figure out what exactly goes on in this suite—adding up the grinding noise, the boys hunched over blurry photographs of dirt, the coastal maps on the wall—when the secretary touches her elbow. He says he'll see you, she tells Marie, pointing to a door across the room. Right through there.

If the outer office was crowded, Doc's office is more so. It's dim and hardly more than a large closet and he sort of blends into it, the physical evidence of his work camouflaging his body. His glasses resolve first, reflecting the light from the room behind Marie like a pair of moons. He's looking at her, but his pencil is still moving. And you are . . . he asks.

The fact of the matter is that they don't get too many visitors down in their basement rooms, so as Marie is introducing herself Doc is still trying to figure out what to do with her. He clears off a chair and she sits down. He clears his throat. What brings you here today, he asks, and it's like a floodgate has been opened. She has, after all, spent two weeks figuring out how to answer that question and therefore takes it quite literally, telling Ewing about her soil surveyor father, the number of schools she attended, her love of nature, the English, music, and philosophy majors, the master's in geology, the job in Tulsa, and the second bachelor's in math. And because of what Marie will later refer to as Doc's courteous Texan demeanor, he does not interrupt, despite his growing incredulity at her diverse background.

For Doc, being incredulous did not equal being impressed—all these biographical details interested him, and certainly they were steps along the way to becoming qualified in his eyes, but in her recollections Marie remembered that it was her short answer to a short question that convinced Doc to give her a job. "Can you draft?" Doc asked, and Marie silently thanked good old Dr. Dow before she said yes. "Yes," she said, "I can." And so she was hired, to work as an assistant to the male graduate students, act as a human calculator, and draft copies of simple maps and diagrams. Bruce, meanwhile, was at sea, acting as chief scientist on an expedition, even though he'd only just gotten his undergraduate degree and hadn't yet taken a single graduate course.

Part Two

I did not paint it to be understood, but I wished to show
what such a scene was like.

—J. M. W. TURNER

*T*HERE WAS NOTHING PARTICULARLY NOTEWORTHY ABOUT the beginning of the second phase of Marie's life. As an employee in Doc's geophysical lab, she was closer to the research end of geology than she'd been at the oil company office in Tulsa. And she was at Columbia University—no small feat—where Doc encouraged his students to innovate. But Marie was not involved in that. She was an assistant. It was nothing special; she was replaceable to the job, and the job was replaceable to her.

When Marie started working at the geophysical lab, there were seven women and sixteen men packed into its basement suite. The first woman was Midge "Mrs. Ewing" Ewing, who did the bookkeeping for a time but was then replaced by Betty Clark. There was Jean "The Admiral" Parker, who had been in the WAVES (Women Accepted for Volunteer Emergency Service), was a math and physics major at Hunter College, and then became secretary, coffee maker, typist, and general factotum at the geophysical lab. There were Faye and Emily (last names: escaped), also math majors from Hunter, who served as computers for Joe Worzel, who had himself followed Doc from Woods Hole to Columbia to do gravity measurements and invent instruments. Marie said Joe needed two girls because "gravity has about 20 pages of stupid arithmetical operations that you had to filter out to get the correct gravity reading." Faye married; Emily moved to Alaska. There was the wonderfully named Renee Brilliant, a female theoretical seismologist who was actually a student in the program. Marie was the seventh woman, originally hired as a human calculator for a young seismologist named Frank Press. Her work was "strictly arithmetic. You set up equations in one column," Marie said. "Column one plus column two equals column three, then column three times five equals column four, and so on." She did what calculators do now. Once, in those early days, she did a drawing of a coring rig for Joe Worzel. The drawing was, in Marie's words, "just barely passable, according to them," so she went back to her numbers.

In addition to Doc, the roster of men included: Joe Worzel and Frank Press; Sam Katz, who did seismic refraction work and eventually married Jean Parker; William Donn, a meteorologist from Brooklyn who married Renee Brilliant; Ivan Tolstoy, who at first studied submarine topography but gave that up for theoretical seismology; Paul Wuenschel, gravity; Nelson Steenland, who studied magnetic anomalies; Milton Dobrin, seismic refraction; Gordon Ross Hamilton, underwater acoustics; Dave Ericson, a paleontologist who was studying cores; Jack Northrop, underwater photography; Dick Edwards, geophysics; and Angelo Ludas and Pat-Pat in the machine shop to build all the tools these men needed. The sixteenth man was Bruce, who spent most of his time at sea and, if pressed to name a specialty or two back then, would probably have said sedimentation and submarine topography.

Not all of them were there all the time. Like Bruce, many of the men spent a lot of time at sea, but still—twenty-three people worked in the three rooms they called, simply, Schermerhorn. Indeed, at one point Doc threatened to use Columbia's chapel for storage. At another point, Joe Worzel took Faye, Emily, and Marie down the street to IBM's Watson Lab to look at a circuit diagram for a computer he hoped would be able to do gravity calculations for him. It was disappointing that it wasn't smart enough to do such high-level calculations, but who knows where they would have put it if it had been, what with analog computers being room-size and all. But it's interesting to imagine what would have happened if the diagram had worked, if Doc had found the money to buy and house a computer. What would have been the fates of the three female human computers? Would they have been fired—Faye married and Emily in

Alaska sooner? Or, most important, might access to a computer have opened a door for Marie? With her job obsolete, would she have been free to prove her hand at tasks more intellectually challenging?

Bruce called the atmosphere in Schermerhorn "stimulating if not hectic." The geophysical lab—while able to offer abundant opportunities (senior staff positions, and even directorships of minor programs) to graduate students like him with little or no experience—"was a poor place to pursue academic studies, for the commotion and the noise and the interest in the scientific work led to hopeless distractions from studies, particularly those aimed at subjects of no immediate application." It might, though, have been precisely those distractions that nurtured the minds of those sixteen men.

For example, each noontime the students gathered together for lunch in front of a blackboard to discuss scientific problems and programs. "It was," Bruce remembered, "quite possible for a submarine geologist like me to follow the advanced work in earthquakes, seismology, gravity, magnetics or atmospheric physics." What was considered advanced back then had only recently been developed, and it was entirely possible that significant discoveries had been made by the guy sitting next to you at lunch. Textbooks gave Bruce and his peers a foundation, but that kind of formal learning was fortified by informal learning—what they learned from Doc, their own research, and one another was just as important. At these lunches they debated not just solutions but methods of attack, their sixteen minds studying sixteen different facets of geophysics. It's possible that, like Bruce, the other fifteen viewed their peers as distractions, but it's also possible that they realized the benefits of Schermerhorn's atmosphere: that Doc had taken them in, that the unavoidable compression of the basement was good, that it allowed them to debate and listen intensely. The product was an expansion of ideas, disparate subjects pressing on each other, the young men allowing themselves to be moved by one another, proximity influencing ideology, so that when they were released from their tiny space they would sail into the world with force, as if shot from an intellectual combustion engine.

BETWEEN THE DIRT blowing in from the street and the dust drifting out of the machine shop, the small offices of the geophysical lab are filthy.

Twice a day Marie wipes down her desk. Once a day she eats lunch. Other than that, it's all numbers. Or it's not exactly all numbers but, rather, a never-ending stream of calculations (her job) accompanied by an equally infinite internal narrative (her life). They move forward together, which means that when Marie looks up at the clock and sees that it's just past noon, the grip of the numbers eases and her life gets a little bit bigger. There in front of her is Joe, coming back from the deli with lunch for the boys, who cheer and make a beeline for the machine shop. Many of them, she's told, have the same thing as Doc, every day: salami and cheese sandwiches and beer. Last guy in slams the door, which is the signal for the girls to open their desk drawers to take out their home-packed lunches and hurry over to whichever desk they all somehow know is the one they'll eat at that day. But Marie, the newcomer, takes only her purse out of its drawer and puts on her jacket. The other girls are welcoming—come sit with us, they say cheerfully, tell us about your husband—but Marie can't see being stuck inside all day when there's so much to see outside the office on this mild December day. So she smiles and declines, wipes her desk clean of grit.

What was a glorious mess when she first came here to work has now resolved; she can draw connections between what she concretely senses and what she knows. She knows that the stacks of photographs that look like someone accidentally released the shutter with the lens pointing at the ground are actually shots of the ocean floor; some reveal tiny sediment swirls, movements capable of revising centuries-old beliefs. Each time her feet register the soft shudder of a passing subway car, she knows that the seismograph is registering it, too, forced to interrupt its collection of the Earth's natural tremors because it's in the only place they have for it: under a trapdoor, in a pit that's been hollowed out of Manhattan bedrock, rock that was sediment on the ocean floor before heat and pressure turned it to schist. She hears the grinding coming out of the machine shop halt and knows that Angelo has stopped for lunch, paused his work on some tool that will likely allow a new glimpse or measurement of something in the ocean. The grinding is replaced by the rise and fall of men's voices and the hiss of beer cans being opened. She sees the closed door, but she also sees what separates her from it; surrounding her here, on the outside, are all the forms of data the men behind that door are arguing about. She is quiet, they are talking.

The words SPEAK TO THE EARTH AND IT SHALL TEACH THEE are carved above the entrance to Schermerhorn Hall; as she leaves the building for lunch Marie is aware of their presence on the wall above her, doesn't have to turn in her path to look at them. That inscription provides a neat summary of how the geophysical lab operates. The men go out to sea and speak to the Earth, then they come back to the basement and speak to one another about what they had said to the Earth and how it had replied. Marie, on the other hand, does not speak directly to the Earth. She had not been hired to conduct research and, as a woman, she was not allowed on board a research vessel. Her job was to look at the Earth's replies, to crunch numbers, and generally spend her days immersed in the raw data the men collected. She liked her work. The men were constantly interrupted by expeditions, conferences, classes, and talking to each other; Marie's role left her largely uninterrupted, calculations forming a kind of numerical mantra running constant in her head. Two different kinds of freedom, two different kinds of absorption in one's work.

On the street, Marie buys a hot dog and eats it in three bites as she walks the few blocks to the Cathedral of St. John the Divine. She likes feeling lost in its huge nave, the interior buffed and pale; occasionally she takes a long lunch and walks all the way up to the Cloisters just so she can see the miniatures with their delicate faces carved from stone. Her coat is unbuttoned and as she walks it flaps around her slender torso. She wears an unstructured skirt, gathered at the waist. Scuffed black chunky shoes. Hair a loose mess of frizz around her face. She does not look like the other women, whose hair is pulled into taut rolls on various parts of their heads. Those women walk with their noses pointed forward, as if to keep their tiny hats balanced, and they wear clothes that nip in at the waist and out at the hips and fit tight around their arms. The women carry magazines, wear shoes that are light and heeled, and skip lunch to shop. Marie is not like them but she is not like the men in the office, either. Or, actually, she is like the men of the geophysical lab in one important way: they're working for their futures, and Marie is working for their futures, too.

IN THE SUMMER of 1948, Doc invited Bruce to work on another oceanographic expedition (his second), again on a ship borrowed from Woods Hole. It's easy to picture a shirtless Bruce on the *Atlantis*, saltwater beaded on a bronzed shoulder, sweat salt and sea salt mingling as he pitches a silvery flying fish back from where it came. It had landed on deck and flopped around for a little while, slapping the deck before Bruce figured out what the noise was. The ship is in the Atlantic, studying the Mid-Atlantic Ridge. Or, as Doc will later say in a voice heavily modulated by the editors of a *National Geographic* magazine article he wrote about the expedition, hoping to "pierce the veil of hundreds of fathoms of water with our deep-sea camera, probe this dark undersea world with new instruments, map its hidden geography, and bring up new rocks and sediments eloquent of its structure and age."

Bruce is seasick and trying to hide it, as usual. He's standing in a group of men and it's Sunday, which he knows only because the smell of roasting turkey is somehow wafting up into his nose the way it does every Sunday when the cook serves turkey, making him ill and peeved that he's still confronting turkeys even out here. But he goes back to what he was fussing with, looks out at the ocean and uses it to push Iowa out of his mind, looks at the trigger wire on the deep-sea camera.

The first deep-sea camera was developed by Doc and his student Joe Worzel back in 1938. They called it the Pyrex Penis because the camera was housed in an eight-inch-wide, four-foot-long test tube made of half-inch-thick glass. It had a watertight seal made out of a stretched inner tube, flashbulb reflectors made of coffee cans, and a spring mechanism. When the contraption hit the ocean bottom it took a picture, bounced up like a pogo stick, hit the bottom again to take a second picture, and then released a ballast in order to float back to the surface. The camera that Bruce and the boys are fooling around with on the *Atlantis* is a little less "science fair," but only just. Due to Angelo Ludas's efficient use of the government surplus lists, the test tube is gone; instead, individual elements (camera, flashbulbs, batteries) are enclosed in pressure cases along a steel pipe. What they're trying to do now is synchronize the flash of light with the opening of the shutter, so that mistiming doesn't result in dark or blurry photographs.

This version of the camera is a little less phallic-looking than earlier versions. To make up for that, it still contains the corer—parting the seas to penetrate the ocean bottom—which takes samples ("cores") by plunging a long, hollow tube into the earth. When removed, the result is one tall drink of rock; each layer of sediment represents thousands of years of history and can be studied to determine date and geological composition. That information, in turn, can be used to attempt to construct a story about the origin and history of the ocean basins. By 1948 only about a hundred ocean basin core samples had been taken the world over, not nearly enough to yield a realistic history of the ocean floor. Dredging, a primitive process described by Doc as "groping for rocks in deep water with a metal bag on the end of two or three miles of wire," can bring up rocks that are scattered along the bottom, but the process is like being blindfolded and running your finger across the surface of an antique sideboard: you'll come away with little more than dust with which to determine the piece's provenance.

Bruce and the rest of the men on the *Atlantis* are pretty typical specimens of 1940s American masculinity, but signs of domesticity still appear. All is not machinery and technology and quick slaps on the back; their superstition (women on ships are bad luck) changes them. The ship's flags are socks and boxers, laundry drying in the sun. Turkeys are roasted on Sundays. Shirts must be worn at the mess table. When night falls, some of the men sleep out on the open deck instead of down below, a considerate move that allows them all more space on a boat cramped with men and equipment. When someone jumps overboard for a swim, the others hover about on deck. They try to be nonchalant, but they're more like mother hawks, scanning the waters for sharks or jellyfish. The cook threw a fit once when he tried to bake bread in bad weather and the waves pounding against the ship made it impossible for his dough to rise; now the captain knows to heave to on stormy baking days.

By far the most interesting collision of life and science on this boat involves the fathometer. The fathometer is an echo sounder—a shipboard device that sends out a ping and then records how long it takes to return to the ship, thus determining the distance between the surface and the seafloor—whose stylus automatically traces the outlines of the ocean floor's features on paper, producing what are called fathograms. You have only to turn it on to be able to experience, in real time, the thrill of watching (again, Doc's edited words, cloaking the scene with a voice-over) "the moving strip of recording paper as the level floor of the three-mile-deep ocean basin [gives] way to saw-toothed peaks—like climbing into the Rockies from the Great Plains of Kansas . . . majestic topography [showing] itself as clearly as if we had been flying over it on a day of good visibility."

It is quite an innovation, a great improvement over the "eye and ear" method of earlier sounding devices. The problem is that the fathometer runs off the same generator as everything else on the ship; any time another appliance or instrument is turned on, causing a shift in electrical currents, the power drain causes the fathometer to stop recording. Only no one notices at first. The fuzzy black lines of the record look continuous, even though the occasional loss of power means that the depths and locations no longer match up—while the power is out, the ship continues forward.

My point is this: what if someone gets hungry during a night watch, goes into the galley for a snack? Gets a plate out of a cabinet. Sets it on a counter. Opens the icebox door and grabs a beer. Leaves the door open as he uncaps the bottle. Lets his body swing down into the icebox, hanging from a hand resting on top. Peruses the selection: salami, cheese, some canned peas left over from dinner in a lidded glass container fogged with condensation. He grabs a few slices of salami, tosses them on the plate. Considers the cheese. Decides against it. Ducks in farther to see if he's missing something and then back out when he sees he hasn't. Finally closes the icebox. It's been, let's say, two minutes. That's miles of accuracy, thwarted by hunger.

"USUALLY, IN MY experience at least," Bruce said into his Dictaphone a few years before he died, "chance meetings, at the right moments in time, particularly when one is young, are more important than anything else. Of course, one has to have a certain number of attitudes towards the world and those guide you in what directions you go."

"We just happened to be in the right place at the right time," Marie wrote and I found, written in fading pencil, on an unmarked crumbling sheet of yellow lined paper at the bottom of a box.

Bruce was talking about meeting Doc; Marie, about her discovery of the Mid-Atlantic Rift. Serendipity is emphasized. Modesty rules. But the question of whether Marie and Bruce were afflicted with insecurity or simply had self-deprecating tendencies is hard to answer from this distance. So even though I can spread out in front me all the documents addressing Marie and Bruce's first meeting, read them repeatedly and practically memorize them, I'm still unable to conclusively distill them. Instead, they repeat themselves in my head, a subtly shifting scene of jump cuts.

Document #1: "And when did you first meet Bruce Heezen," an interviewer asked Marie after they hit the bases of childhood, adolescence, and college. "When we were at Columbia," Marie said. "I met him about a month after I started work, and he had just gotten back from the third National Geographic cruise."

Document #2: "Heezen and I arrived at the same place at the same time, down in the basement of Schermerhorn Hall of Columbia University just one block away from busy Broadway near 116th Street in New York City."

Document #3: "I met Bruce Heezen one morning at 0800 in Schermerhorn when we both came to work at what we thought was the regular time. Here in New York no office starts before 0900 because of the commuting problem."

Document #4: "Oh, down in the basement of Schermerhorn. Came to work at eight o'clock, as I had to do in Tulsa, and he also came to work at eight, because that's the way he had been brought up, and there he was sitting there. He had just gotten back from this National Geographic cruise in 1948."

Document #5 (the one time Bruce answered the question): "I came back [from an expedition] and just before Christmas of 1948, I had this [data] and this was the very same time Marie showed up at Schermerhorn Hall and the fact was I met Marie just before Christmas of 1948."

And then, a fuzzy video recording of Marie in the 1990s that captures her breathy high voice: "The first time I saw him I met him in the hall," Marie said and smiled, looked down and then up, directly into the camera for the first time in the interview.

I don't know what either one of them was thinking at this most auspicious moment. I don't know exactly what they said or did, if Marie reached up to touch her hair or Bruce played with his cuff, if the hallway was painted seafoam green, if Marie wore navy blue or gray or if Bruce had a deep tan from his recent expedition. I don't know if Bruce was at the door of the geophysical lab fumbling with his newly cut keys and looked up to see who was clomping down the hallway. If he stays frozen, hunched around the lock, and she squares her shoulders as he watches. If he stands up and she smiles. If the checkered floor is shiny, if his shoes are shiny, if the city street noise hums somewhere above them, if she holds her pocketbook like a shield, how fast she walks and who speaks first.

Hello.

Mouths taste like coffee in the morning so I guess theirs do too.

Hello.

Marie presents her right hand to Bruce so that he can shake it, but he just sort of stares at it for a second.

Marie Tharp. Pleased to meet you.

Bruce Heezen. The same.

A pause. The door has to open in order for them to move forward. Marie looks at the keys in Bruce's hand, at the lock and then at Bruce, who is looking at his shoes.

Were you having trouble with your keys? Or with the lock? I mean, I have my keys right— She sticks a hand into her bag.

Yes, Bruce says. Right, yes, my key wouldn't—

—right here. Marie holds up a key ring.

Bruce looks at her. Who are you exactly? I mean, what exactly is it that you do here?

Marie straightens, runs a hand down the front of her coat. What exactly is it—she looks down and begins taking off her gloves, finger by finger. You. Do. Here?

I'm Bruce Heezen. I just got back from the *Atlantis* cruise. Both hands hanging down by his sides; other men would have pocketed them by now. National Geographic? I was a chief scientist?

I'm Marie Tharp. She unlocks the door, puts her hand on the door-knob. I punch the Monroe calculator for Frank Press. Bruce is four years her junior. She bids him good morning, opens the door to the geophysical lab, goes in.

*T*HE SCIENTIFIC INSTITUTIONS THAT HAD LITTLE FINANCIAL support to speak of in the first half of the 1940s would get pay-offs in the second. David became Goliath. The graduate students tirelessly working for Doc didn't see the spoils manifest themselves in the form of new suits or fancy cars but, rather, in new professional digs. More money meant more space, more space meant bigger projects, bigger projects attracted more attention and money.

Even before Marie started working for Doc, the geophysical lab had been feeling the strain of such small quarters. Nearly two dozen people packed into three rooms made intellectual contemplation all but impossible. Doc's requests for more space to Columbia's administration—even going so far as to include a design for a new building between Schermerhorn Hall and Columbia's powerplant—were denied. And so when, in 1948, MIT approached Doc with an offer to establish a geophysics research group and bring his graduate students along, he considered it. MIT was giving him quite a vote of confidence: an entire estate near New Bedford to house the day-to-day operations. Having their own campus would put Doc's group on at least the same page as the other great oceanographic institutions in the United States—WHOI in Massachusetts and Scripps in San Diego—and perhaps their own boat would follow.

Doc took his boys to tour the New Bedford estate. When they returned he went straight to Dwight Eisenhower, Columbia's president at the time, and Paul Kerr, the head of the geology department. Columbia countered MIT's offer with one of its own: a 125-acre estate across the Hudson, in Palisades, New York, that was about to be donated to Columbia by Florence Lamont, the widow of a prominent New York financier. Columbia promised to raise money to get the new institute off the ground, too. This was a further vote of confidence. And it turned out to be a smart move: after Doc and his boys toured the estate in Palisades, they voted unanimously to stay at Columbia, turning the geophysical lab into the Lamont Geological Observatory. "Lamont" to honor their benefactor, "Geological Observatory" because observing geology described what they were doing more precisely than "geophysical lab." While they might arrive at answers by applying the principles of physics, none of it would be possible without geological observation. The name also staked a bigger claim than either "Woods Hole Oceanographic Institute" or "Scripps Institution of Oceanography."

In one binder of Marie's papers, there are five maps of Lamont Hall, a family mansion transformed into a hotbed of scientific revolution. Marie drew each one, and each one shows an aerial view of a floor of the building. The rooms are labeled according to use, doors and stairs penciled in like the playing board for a game of Clue. These maps are just copies of simple pencil drawings, but they have in them the potential for conjecture. The dozen or so rooms, bedrooms and sitting rooms and bathrooms, a double kitchen, a butler's pantry, a dining room with a terrace, a drawing room and a library, present just enough to trigger the imagination: with their boundaries clearly delineated, the empty rooms beg to be furnished and populated.

There are also documents in which Marie speaks about the early days of Lamont. Her words make the thin lines of the maps grow up into brick façades and wallpapered walls. She speaks about Doc's group using the big new space, and it's easy to imagine them rattling around in those rooms like game pieces in a box. Add Marie's stories about the early days spent in the rooms of Lamont Hall to her maps depicting them and the view becomes three-dimensional, each room a diorama showing how the budding science of geophysics was practiced by this particular group of people.

"I remember when I first came here," Marie said about the new campus. "I took the bus from the station at 165th Street and, following directions, got off at an obscure dirt road in the woods. Joe Worzel met me and we walked the mile or so down a winding road that came out amid some barnlike buildings and onto a circular drive, past an orchard in an uncut meadow." In the barns were cows whose mooing could be heard throughout the day, and every spring the meadow blazed with golden daffodils. Thick-trunked trees framed a view of the Hudson. Paths trailed through the lawns and woods and down to the river. Everyone worked too hard to take more than a basic constitutional on the grounds, and the outdoor facilities were transformed from places of leisure and luxury into laboratories and work spaces. Angelo Ludas, mechanical engineer extraordinaire, built a machine shop in the former greenhouse. The root cellar that the Lamonts had built as a bulwark against possible starving invaders during the Great Depression provided a base for the seismograph that was much more secluded and stable than the pit below Schermerhorn Hall. The seismometer itself went into the drained swimming pool.

"In the beginning—for maybe a year or two," Marie said, "we all commuted from the city, and then gradually people moved out permanently." "Moved out" meant different things for different people. Outbuildings and places where the servants used to live became homes for Doc and his inner circle, but only the inner circle: Doc and his family moved into what became known as the Director's House; Joe Worzel and Frank Press moved their families into the gardener's house and the apartment above the garage. Those three houses became a miniature neighborhood, the campus a playground for the offspring of Doc's workforce. Most of Doc's employees, Marie included, lived off campus, relocating from Manhattan to apartments in nearby Nyack or Palisades or Piermont (all within a few miles of the estate) so that they could be closer to work.

The main house was the focal point of the estate. It was the size of a mansion, only built to resemble a cottage, as if a common exterior could hide such imposing proportions. "Once inside," Marie noted, "all similarities to a cottage disappear." The rooms, she said, were "spacious" and "ample" and done "in the grand style." If there was a theme to the interior's design, it was a preference for an outsize scale: a spiral staircase touched down in the foyer and stretched up to the third floor, giant windows looked out over the lawn, custom oriental carpets pooled across the floors of even larger rooms, and the library was paneled with big wooden planks from a Scottish castle. The place was stately, and the "Lamonters," as Doc's group came to be known, were not.

Within a year or two the stuff of their work overlaid the house, making for an interesting mix of lavish and utilitarian. Drawing boards were set up over bathtubs and filing cabinets over toilets. An atoll formed from desks rose up from the foyer floor. Five of them, in tight formation, constituted the departments of Lamont's "main office": telephone, purchasing, personnel, business manager, port captain. To the right of the main office was the Seminar Room (formerly the living room), site of Friday afternoon seminars and legendary parties—back when, Marie said, the group was still small enough to fit in the room. The seminars' genesis had a lot to do with the professional status of the Lamonters. "Initially the students gave talks of recent papers in their field published by others," Marie said. "Later, the purpose was to give the kids experience speaking in front of a group so when they presented their own papers at scientific meetings they could do it with a certain amount of aplomb. Gradually the talks became reports of the current work of Lamont scientists, and eventually the various disciplines began to have their own seminars." Additions to the room included an expansive chalkboard, an iron easel, and weekly post-seminar parties fueled by the constantly replenished stash of rum the men always brought back from their expeditions.

Many of Lamont's core samples, along with Dave Ericson, who specialized in studying them (or, as Marie said, "always hanging around them," "totally immersed"), were stored in the former dining room; overflow was put in the estate's seven-car garage. Under crystal chandeliers and the watchful eyes of the birds painted on the walls' murals, Ericson tried to develop a climatic record of the Pleistocene epoch (from approximately 2.6 million to 12,000 years before the present); if he could find correlations in cores taken from spots on the ocean floor hundreds of miles apart, he could begin to describe what the climate of that era was like. Dropcloths replaced tablecloths so Ericson could crack cores open to study their length, layering, and color. Samples were scooped out and placed on slides and under microscopes, so Ericson could study the types of sediments and the distribution of microfossils. That's how the dining room became the Core lab. It was off the main office, as was a tiny flight of stairs that led down to the basement.

Hidden in the basement were Laurence Kulp and a few other geo-chemists. They were studying rock samples using radiocarbon dating, which meant measuring the decay of the carbon-14 isotope to determine age. "They wanted," Marie said, "to use dating to establish that the Earth was created in 4004 B.C." This was a creationist approach to the history of the Earth, and it was an anomaly in the field of geology. Ever since the nineteenth century, even the most conservative estimates had been placing the Earth's age at twenty million years. "We called them theochemists," Marie said. They stuck out in more ways than one. "They were really straitlaced, they didn't drink—you'd give them a drink and they'd throw it in a potted plant." In contrast, other Lamonters, by the close of the rowdy Friday afternoon parties, were much more likely to be found face-down in the potted plants.

Kulp's faith was shaken by his carbon-14 research—it had proven his theory of geological creationism atrociously wrong. He stayed at Lamont but moved on to strontium 90, an isotope left behind after nuclear explosions, getting a contract from the Atomic Energy Commission to study radiation's spread and its effect on humans. In 1957 *Time* magazine introduced the study this way: "[C]ollecting 500 samples of fresh human bone from widely separated parts of the world, the Columbia men analyzed them delicately." In a 1995 interview, Marie put it less delicately: the AEC eventually "built him his own building," behind which there was a pond, in which she claimed "they either threw the cadavers when they were through or kept them until they wanted to use them."

It's hard to tell if Marie was put off by Kulp's being a creationist or a teetotaler or the dumped cadavers—or any of those things. They were just one part of her experience at Lamont, vivid facts she remembered forty years after the fact. When she thought of the basement of Lamont Hall she thought of Kulp, and when she thought of Kulp she thought of whiskey splashing the green leaves of a houseplant, of bodies allowed to rest in the bottom of a pond. Each room came with stories about the person who inhabited it—some about work, and some not. The third floor, for instance, was the domain of Mrs. Alma Smith, the housekeeper, even though the official borders of that domain stopped at the boundaries of the tiny kitchen tucked up under the eaves.

Alma and her husband, Harold, had come with the estate. Alma had been the flower arranger for the Lamonts, and Harold had been an electrician. When Columbia acquired the property, Marie said, the Smiths adjusted accordingly. Harold was "broken in as paper changer on the seismographs, then as record changer for meteorological observations." Alma had no flowers to arrange except for special occasions, so she took over cleaning and what we would today refer to as community building. Groups met in her kitchen for tea and buns and to gather what Marie called "moral fortitude," particularly the women whose spouses were at sea. Alma appreciated the Lamonters' work in ways that they appreciated in turn: once, for someone's birthday, she baked a chocolate cake with white icing squiggles reminiscent of a seismogram.

Joe Worzel's office was in the attic, across from where Faye and Emily did their computing. When everyone first moved out to the estate in the Palisades, most of the attic was taken up by a "trunk" room, a photo room, a small room marked "MT" (Marie's initials), and a room for map storage, along with the two offices. Within a few years, though, Faye and Emily had been replaced by data storage, and the trunk room had been turned into Johnny Ewing's office—and Bruce Heezen's bedroom. According to Marie, the reason Bruce was living out of Doc's brother's office was due to several factors, the largest of which was probably Doc's idiosyncratic pay scale. "If a student was married and had a batch of kids," Marie said, "they got a living wage to support the family." Bruce, a bachelor grad student, was paid $90 a month, which is why, Marie explained, "he had to sleep in Johnny's office and live off the beer, fish, hot dog diet." In those early years, Bruce also spent more time at sea than on land; he didn't have the money to lease an apartment, but even if he had, he wouldn't have been around to appreciate it. This fact has become something of legend— some say he slept under Johnny's desk, some said he just slept anywhere in the office, and one person mentioned, in a eulogy for Bruce, that he first encountered Bruce tromping up to the third floor, disheveled and exhausted and lugging a mattress that he dropped on Johnny's floor and promptly went to sleep on.

Bruce's own office on the second floor had formerly been a bathroom. There were holes in the walls where, Marie said, he'd ripped out the pale green fixtures "when Joe Worzel threatened to make it into the ladies' head," and all horizontal surfaces were blanketed with papers. When he wasn't at sea or attending classes, Bruce pored over the different types of data he'd collected on his trips. Unlike Ericson or Kulp, he was not yet a specialist trying to answer a formally articulated question. He knew only that he was vaguely attracted to what was presently happening on the ocean floor. Photographs of the ocean floor gave a close-up picture of what was happening to the most superficial layer of sediment. Cores showed how deep that superficial layer went and what it was composed of. Soundings revealed large-scale features such as canyons and plains. Bruce knew that he wanted to be a geologist above all else, that he wanted to use the increasingly detailed data that Lamont was gathering at sea to create models of what the Earth looked like beneath the water.

Frank Press also had an office on the second floor. He specialized in earthquakes. In the early 1950s these were still largely mysterious, but if anyone could have been called an earthquake expert back then, it was Press. In 1950 and 1952 every issue of the *Bulletin of the Seismological Society of America* carried a paper by him. Some were coauthored with Doc ("Crustal Structure and Surface Wave Dispersion" and "Two Slow Surface Waves Across North America"). All described new discoveries about how various types of seismic waves traveled across land and through water. With this information, Press and others could measure the size of earthquakes, more precisely pinpoint their origins, predict how their shocks were going to affect different areas, and also where and when tsunamis (which are triggered when an earthquake occurs in the seafloor and displaces a huge amount of water) would hit the coasts.

Marie helped with this work, getting paid two hundred dollars a month (more than twice what Bruce was paid) and working in the "daughter's bedroom," which looked out onto the Hudson River, with one or two of the men. She did wave velocity calculations for Press. She drafted a map with New York at dead center, starting with a blank sheet of white paper, drawing a perfect circle to represent the Earth, doing the calculations to make sure longitude lines were properly located and continents were drawn to scale. She drew diagrams and made slides, not just for Press but for some others, too. She hung maps and did other "sundry carpenter jobs." And one day, she pasted a complete set of GEBCO maps (General Bathymetric Chart of the Oceans, the international organization started by Prince Albert of Monaco that collected soundings from all over the world) to the wall of the second-floor landing. There were sixteen sheets in total, each representing a region of the ocean. The maps included spot depths (nonconsecutive numbers randomly scattered, the visual effect like some impossible connect-the-dots activity sheet) and contours (lines connecting points at the same depth, forming closed loops with amoebic curves, filled in by a few shades of blue, the deeper the water the darker the blue). Marie would have had to spend hours staring at these oceans, brushing paste on the backs of the maps, making sure they were centered inside the lines she'd penciled on the walls, smoothing the edges with a damp sponge, then pressing air bubbles to the edges with the side of her hand. When she was done, "the great expanses of single color[s]," as she put it later, felt smooth to the touch, and pleasing to the eye.

The second-floor landing also happened to be the location, for a while, of the only telephone in the building. So unless the Lamonters closed their eyes or stared at their feet or doodled constantly while talking on the phone, they probably also spent hours looking at these very basic maps of the ocean floor that indicated, as Marie put it, "how little was known about the world's ocean[s]." As a result they could, for a short time in the early 1950s, stand and talk on the phone with nearly all the known depths of the ocean floor within view. They could look at tiny black numbers or wide blue expanses; they could let their eyes glide across an unbroken ocean floor. At Lamont in those early days they could focus on some of it, or none of it, or all of it—and know that no matter what they chose, there was plenty of room for everyone to have his own big discovery.

"IT WAS A happy family," Marie said of those first years spent in Lamont Hall. "One group in one place. One direction." That their workplace still looked like a home beneath the scientific equipment and specimens, that Doc was the clear patriarch of that group, serving as advisor to all the grad students, and that by the spring of 1952, Marie had worked with this group for four years—the most continuity she'd ever had with any group of people outside of her immediate family—only enhanced that feeling. But it was 1952, which meant that there was inequality under that veneer of a common scientific goal. The women of Lamont were very much in service to the men, which made the idea of that "happy family" more complex than Marie's "one group . . . one direction" statement.

Marie did not talk much about this inequality and the resulting frustrations. What's important, though, is that she took action: in the spring of 1952 she ran away from Lamont and drove back home to her father's farm in Ohio. She'd become the new factotum at Lamont, trusted, the woman all the men felt comfortable going to when they needed something. She worked the same long hours as they did, in the same house where they did—one group, one direction, a happy family. Except she worked for all of them, not for herself. And while they always said please, always flashed wide smiles, they also always procrastinated. Because many of them were faced with the same deadlines and were presenting at the same conferences, they were all asking Marie to perform the impossible at the same time. One person might need her to process just one more slide before he had to get on the train—but so did six of the others. Through the happy family lens, it was like asking selfless Mom for a favor: that's what moms are for, right? In reality, it was like asking Mom to iron a shirt without noticing that she's also trying to cook for a dinner party— multiplied by the number of requests and the import of the work. A badly drawn diagram is not the same as a wrinkled shirt; if an illustration is not clearly executed, a talk or presentation with immense geological potential might be misunderstood, disregarded.

Added to the pile was Marie's realization that to stay at Lamont in 1952 would have been to accept her fate as a frazzled factotum; Doc was not suddenly going to let her go out on an expedition, let her run her own lab. I don't know that these were her precise thoughts when she left, but I do know that something of her situation at Lamont must have clarified: one day she just quit, while Doc and the men were off in Brussels at one of their conferences.

Or, rather, she leaves; there's no one to make a formal declaration to. She drives back to her apartment in Nyack, stuffs fistfuls of clothing into a suitcase, lugs it downstairs, and hurls it into her trunk. Gets into the car and starts driving west. When she crosses into Pennsylvania from New Jersey, she's still fuming. When she pulls into a small town to fill her gas tank, she stops only long enough to drink a cup of black coffee at a diner counter. She fights the urge to pace while drinking, instead only taps the toes of her oxfords against the base of the stool she's sitting on. She glares at the racks of candy bars and the blackboards with specials written on them; she glares at the patrons looking her up and down. She's still wearing her work clothes, but her blazer is unbuttoned and her hair is coming unpinned.

For the second time in her life she enters the Appalachian Mountains without really noticing them. Her body sways a few degrees to each side as she rounds the curves in the road, the inclination of her body toward the floor increasing as the road winds farther up into the mountains. She's still angry, still glaring—at the blacktop in front of her, the green trees whizzing by, her own eyes in the rearview mirror. As a child she was given independence that most other children weren't—she knows that. And when she went to college her father didn't insist that she suppress her intelligence—she knows that, too. Grad school, in fact, is where everything changed. Instead of gaining respect, it's where she was most treated like a child—subjected to precise schedules, shuttled into that job in Tulsa when she appeared to be disobeying. And at Lamont she's overqualified, allowed to do only the jobs that require minimal brainpower. Plus, she knows she's smarter than some of the younger men who saddle her with their tasks.

So Marie huffs her way through Pennsylvania and the Appalachians. By the time she hits the Ohio border she's a little calmer, and later, when she pulls up beside her father's barn, the dogs barking at her and the stars shining bright, she's calmer still. Slightly sheepish.

Not because it's okay, she tells her father over a sandwich a few minutes later, because it isn't. She's talking about her treatment at Lamont.

Not because it's okay, she tells her brother, Jim, over the eggs he's fried for her breakfast the next morning, because it isn't. Jim nods in reply as he sips coffee from a mug and starts outside to begin the day's work. Marie is still talking as he unlatches the door to the chicken coop and ducks down into it. He doesn't let strangers into his coops and he doesn't let Marie do any farm work, so she talks to him from outside the door, telling him about all the drawings she's had to draft for the grad students' papers. He nods to show her he's listening as he addresses each chicken by name, feeding them, and he nods when the chickens fly into his arms for a scratch on the back. Marie tilts her head up to tell him about the long process of making glass slides for other people's presentations, sending her voice up through the square hole in the floor of the barn's loft as Jim forks nests of hay down through it. He's still nodding as Marie tells him about all the calculations she has to do—constantly, she says—while he milks their old Jersey cow. This cow, he finally says, just won't quit. Marie stops talking. Jim hands her a bucket of milk; let's take this inside, huh? He puts his hand on her back.

She spends the next day with her father. Calmer, but still on a kind of verbal autopilot. Papa Tharp is eighty-two by now, so he leaves most of the farm work to Jim and concentrates on his reading and writing. There are spring vegetables to be canned, though, big straw baskets of asparagus and peas covering the kitchen table. They shell the peas and trim the stalks of asparagus, paring knives slicing off the pale woody ends. Through it all, Marie talks about making her first map for Lamont—drawing longitude lines, eyeballing in continental borders. It showed, she tells her father, the whole world. He raises his eyebrows. With New York in the middle, of course, she adds, rolling her eyes.

Her father keeps the stove going, sterilizes the jars and hands them to Marie, who fills them and sticks them in another pot. Toward the end of the day, she looks down at a jar and sees the peas packed into it—little green globes pressing at one another—and thinks of the Easter when everything Alma cooked was round, the way monochromatic pyramids of beets and eggs and meatballs and scoops of mashed potatoes and other mismatched foods covered the vast seminar table.

The following day she starts telling her father about the good parts of working at Lamont. Good parts, her father asks, his eyes twinkling. They're walking the farm; it is breezy and sunny and everything seems to be cooperating. The fields plowed parallel to the contours of the hills; the leaves of young plants—oat, alfalfa, and corn—reaching for their neighbors; the tips of the poplars in the windbreak curving away from the wind. Black Jacket Creek ambling through it, multiflora rose hedges holding it all together. In her head, Marie alters the sketch of the farm she's carried in her head since her last visit—the poplars a little taller, the hedges more tangled and dense, the crops sown more perfect in their rows.

By the end of the week she's gained a little perspective. When she wakes up she lies in her bed awhile, thinking about Doc and Bruce, Joe and Frank and all the other men back at Lamont. What they're doing, she knows, is essentially good—all the discoveries and papers and new technologies. And she is a part of that. A means to an end—but still. When she emerges from her room and goes down to the kitchen, there's a telegram propped up against the salt and pepper shakers on the kitchen table.

CONSIDER THIS AN EXTENDED VACATION. DOC.

CHAPTER 10

WHEN MARIE RETURNED TO LAMONT AFTER HER "vacation," she found that Doc had given Bruce the responsibility of delegating her time. This was both a gesture of respect and an insult: Bruce was widely considered to be Doc's golden child, and he had more time than Doc to make sure that she was not being overwhelmed. But by setting up Bruce as Marie's protector, Doc was implying that she was not capable of protecting herself, implying that he did not trust her to prioritize her work. He also did not give her permission to turn down tasks she did not reasonably have time for. That was for Bruce to decide.

It's unclear how much contact Marie and Bruce had had up to this point. Their offices on the second floor were connected. Bruce was, presumably, one of the men who had contributed to her blowup. And after a short period of trying to divide Marie's time among everyone who wanted it, he decided to keep her all to himself. They became a team, which marked the beginning of a period in which Marie (in both her own stories and those of others) never appears without either Bruce or her work; the beginning of a period in which her work has the potential to advance the study of the Earth and her own career; the beginning of a period in which she and Bruce start to work on a map of the ocean floor. It is, in other words, the beginning of an intense commitment.

In September 1952, Marie is in her office (the "daughter's room") doing some math when Bruce walks in hugging a stack of cardboard boxes that block his face. He grunts as he bends to put them down and then flops into the chair beside them. The men who share the daughter's room stay bent over their own work. The room is dense with Marie, the data she's working with spread out everywhere, constellations of newspaper clippings and photographs tacked up on the walls; the air is thick with interrupted thoughts. She's been back from Ohio for maybe a month. Bruce has just returned from his latest cruise on the *Atlantis*.

Marie and Bruce sit at opposite sides of the room for a second, staring at the cardboard boxes. Aloft in her drafting chair near the window, Marie sees only the flaps of the one on top, open and askew like petals, rolls of paper sticking out from the middle. Bruce sees the boxes' edges, meeting in dented and crumpled corners. They consider the boxes from their various perspectives for a moment or two before Marie jumps up and makes her approach, stops with her knees touching the stack and looks down into the rolls' empty centers.

Fathometer records, she says, even though she knows that's what they are—he told her that morning he would bring them by later. Fathograms, he says, his word for them different but with the same meaning. "Fathometer records" or "fathograms" or "echo soundings" are all different terms for the same thing: measurements of ocean depths made using fathometers or echo sounders. Whatever the instrument is called, it produces a long scroll, on which are inscribed soundings of the ocean floor. The result is a fuzzy undulating line, each rise and fall representing a vertical change in underwater terrain. Doc has overseen the collection of these records since just after World War II, when the research ships he and his students used began to be outfitted with continuously recording echo sounders. Bruce has been collecting them since his first cruise in 1947. Technology has progressed since then, from those echo sounders that were supposed to record continuously (but got waylaid by, among other things, extended late-night fridge raiding) to ones that operated smoothly by minimizing the possibilities of human interference; the records of what Doc called, in his *National Geographic* article, "the ocean floor's majestic topography," have been accumulating for several years. Before Bruce left on his most recent cruise, he and Marie decided they wanted to use the sounding records to think in general terms about the structure of the ocean. With the addition of the sounding records from the cruise Bruce has just returned from, they felt they could proceed.

Marie lifts a record out of the top box on the stack. Just these, she asks. Bruce laughs and walks around the drafting table to peer down at what Marie had been working on at her desk. Oh no, he says, there's lots more where that came from. His hand grips the shoulder of the blazer she's got hanging on her desk chair, his body angling down closer to the tabletop. Just waiting to be looked at, he says as she shoos him from her work space.

In her hands the roll of paper is smooth and cool and when she sets it on the table she gives it a nudge so it unrolls partway. She's seen sounding records before, but this one makes her exhale a soft *oh* anyway; these will be hers. Bruce watches as she runs a hand down the length of the paper, pressing out its curl, following the 2-D depiction of the ocean floor's swells, foamy-edged and deflated like waves creeping up a beach, watches her grope for the masking tape dispenser with her other hand, then tear off two short strips and tape down the free end of the record so that part of it stretches out panoramic. Her eyes don't leave the record.

What do you think, Bruce asks. This is not a small question and she does not answer immediately, keeps her face pointed at the record. He's not just bringing her data and telling her what to do with it. He's asking her what she thinks and, by doing so, acknowledging that what she thinks might be valuable.

When he comes to stand beside her she tells him what she thinks: I don't know, she says. Which is maybe partly why they'll work so well together. He's used to these records, the depths noted along the vertical axis, distance along the horizontal axis, the seafloor's topography stretching out gently on the page, rises and falls not so much filled as occupied by grainy gradations. When he looks at them, unfurling in real time from the sounder on a ship at sea, he gets completely frustrated, all that information piling up in his brain. He can't stop thinking about it, can't help but want to decipher it all immediately, and when he can't do that he has to walk away, leaving it tangled, a mess to which he promises himself he'll return. Marie is completely different. The words *I don't know* enchant her, the problem presented by all the data is something new and exciting she's never had access to before. The differences between Marie and Bruce are present this early in their relationship, already hinting at compatibility:

he will collect and she will process, she will be more inclined toward patience and uncertainty, she'll sink deep into the project and he'll leave to study other things.

On the other side of the room is a big metal armoire with rolls of blank paper stacked in a pyramid on top. Marie heads for it, then reaches an arm up to grab a roll. Her back is to him and Bruce watches her shirt come untucked, white silk separating from gray flannel to reveal a pale strip of waist. He watches as she comes back and sets the roll down, he watches as she gives it a little shove so that it unrolls like a red carpet, parallel to the sounding record. Together they stare at the two sheets of paper, one blank and white, one hazy and halfway filled. She asks him if he's looking for anything in particular.

Patterns, Bruce says. Things that line up, connections, shapes. He doesn't really know, but he tries to describe what he wants anyway: a topographical profile that will emphasize the vertical changes in the ocean floor. Marie grabs a pencil and sits down in her chair, rolls backward from her table to her desk with her arms crossed over her chest. He mentions outlines of the abyssal plains, says he'd be happy just finding the limit of the continental rise. A continental rise, they both know, is the continent's final dip down to the deep ocean floor; it slopes gradually, and where it ends the abyssal plain begins. Doc explored both these features in isolated locations just a few years before, but no one knows their boundaries or if they're universally present—because no one has taken the time to do a deep analysis of all the soundings that Bruce has just brought into Marie's office. It's a lot of work, work with much potential for discovery—if you happen to be the type of person who's not intimidated by meticulous numbers crunching. Marie is not intimidated.

In fact, she's kind of disappointed that all these exciting data have only inspired Bruce to think of what's already been hinted at. Slow declines and great big saucers of mud? A vast area of land with all the topographical character of the Midwest? That's it, she asks. She wrinkles her brow and taps her pencil fast against the tabletop. They're about equals, educationally speaking—Bruce has just received his master's degree in geology, she earned hers four years ago. Don't you think it's probably a little more exciting than that down there? Bruce scowls. Well, he asks, what do you think is there? This is the first and, quite possibly, tamest of what will become a very long line of disagreements.

Marie has her glasses pushed up in her hair and is twisting her necklace around her finger. No idea, she says. She grins at him, giddy at all the possibilities. Atlantis, she says, who knows, and spins in her chair to face the dark window overlooking the Lamont grounds. We'll see, he replies, and gets up to leave—satisfied or relieved. But Marie doesn't notice. She's imagining the sounding records sunk in the Atlantic, unrolled and soggy, like ribbons of light illuminating the ocean floor.

IN SEPTEMBER 1952 Marie had a stack of boxes in her office, inside of which were rolled-up sounding records that had been collected between the summer of 1947 and September 1952 by Doc and his students on the *Atlantis*. She also had a detailed record of where the ship went during those five years. It made trips of varying lengths between the western coasts of the Americas and the eastern coasts of Europe and Africa. The paths followed during each trip were marked on nautical charts; the paths are called tracks, as if the ship were an animal that left its footprints behind. Latitude and longitude were periodically marked on the record itself, so that depths could be matched to location.

Because ships rarely traveled all the way across the Atlantic in one go, most of the tracks were compilations. A ship would start at, say, Martha's Vineyard and go a quarter of the way across the ocean (where it tooled around awhile doing all kinds of experiments—taking cores, dredging, measuring temperature and salinity, and maybe doing some seismic refractions), then return to the United States; another trip might have only kept records from a quarter of the way across the ocean to the middle of the ocean; yet another trip might have gone straight to Gibraltar before anyone started collecting soundings. In order to get a track that extended all the way from Martha's Vineyard to Gibraltar, Marie spliced those three tracks together like strips of 35-millimeter film, the connected ship tracks like a sequence of scenes in a movie.

When she was done splicing, Marie had six tracks in front of her, the northernmost one going from Martha's Vineyard to Gibraltar, the southernmost one going from Recife, Brazil, to Freetown, Sierra Leone. On paper, the tracks looked like clotheslines strung haphazardly across the Atlantic Ocean, none perfectly horizontal, most sagging toward the middle. All told, the six tracks represented about a hundred thousand miles of

travel by the *Atlantis,* travel during which it produced about three thousand feet of sounding record: the scrolls in cardboard boxes that were
stacked in the corner of her office.

She and Bruce wanted, Marie would later recall, to see "the entire pattern" of the North Atlantic laid out before them, so the next step was to
translate those three thousand feet of sounding records into one drawing—
something that had never been done before. To do that, Marie glued
together several strips of linen paper, then drew six wide "graphs" on the
sheet, the graph for the northernmost track at the top of the sheet, the
graph for the southernmost track at the bottom of the sheet, the others in
between. The graphs had depths marked along the vertical axes—one, two,
three, and four thousand fathoms—and distance marked in five-hundred-
mile increments along the horizontal axes. Each graph looked a lot like a
musical staff: five horizontal lines, a space between each line, perpendicular lines marking off miles instead of measures.

Her next step was to plot the depth of each peak, trough, or change
of slope with a 40:1 vertical exaggeration, a number that represents the
ratio between the vertical scale and the horizontal scale. Each inch on
the vertical axis equaled one nautical mile, and each inch on the horizontal axis equaled forty miles. Marie and Bruce made the conscious
choice to exaggerate—it meant that they'd be able to see subtle changes
on the ocean floor that otherwise might not have been visible. Ridges
would be taller, as if they were made of taffy and had been pulled toward
the water's surface, and valleys would appear to be carved deeper into
the earth. The choice of a 40:1 exaggeration meant that the longest
ship track needed a graph 87.5 inches—or nearly 7.5 feet—wide. "We were
a little naïve in the methods of drafting in those days," Marie said, "and
so we made the original a rather enormous drawing which took [up]
several drafting tables." It was naïve because they were working at a size
difficult to reproduce in a magazine or journal, but it was also smart: by
working so big, they could see those subtle changes that might have disappeared had they done what Marie called the "normal, scrunched-down
drawings" that were "practical to publish."

After she had made the dots marking depths, each one like a note on
a staff, she connected them. This required interpretation. She had a depth
marked approximately every inch, but what happened in between? It was
like looking at a sheet of music on which some of the notes were missing.

A musician could use her knowledge of chord progressions, harmonies, or melodies to improvise her way through such a song, building a new one in the process, and Marie responded similarly, interpolating instead of improvising, drawing lines connecting known depths, hypothesizing where she had no data. Hers was not a mindless act; it was based on her training as a geologist. Not everyone could have interpreted the connections between those depths in the same skilled way as she, just as most people who sit down at a piano and try to improvise produce noise, not music.

When Marie inked in the space below the jagged lines she had drawn, the six transatlantic topographical profiles were complete: six silhouettes of the ocean floor's terrain, inked onto the stafflike graphs. Continental shelves dropped down into continental slopes, continental rises sloped down into those abyssal plains Bruce wanted to find. The island of Bermuda was there, rising up above the water's surface. The wide medial ridge that had been surmised by oceanographers since the late nineteenth century was there, and wherever there weren't plains, tiny stalagmite-shaped mountains gave the floor texture. It was an accomplishment: Marie's profiles were the most detailed representations of the ocean floor ever produced. But she wasn't satisfied; she didn't think she'd discovered anything.

After all, profiles of part of this area had been made before, most comprehensively by some of the oceanographers on the 1925–27 German *Meteor* expedition of the South Atlantic. Those had been published back in the 1930s. Scientists from all over the world had seen them. Indeed, when Bruce himself turned the soundings over to her and mentioned the abyssal plains and continental rises, it was because he'd already had glimpses of those features; Marie had rebelled against his lack of imagination. "I thought that all of these things were so obvious that they did not need such an amount of folderol," she wrote. "[I] was looking further for more sophisticated or more subtle differences." In Bruce's defense, she continued, the features he wanted to outline "had not been previously described in [the] literature." They were "worthwhile things to point out," but to her "they seemed to present no intellectual challenge." She hoped to find something more.

The initial work had taken her about six weeks, and as summer turned to fall, Marie kept studying her profiles. Day after day in "the daughter's room" on the second floor. Sometimes she and her officemates would light fires in the fireplace. She spent a lot of time staring at the Hudson through the big windows. She spent a lot of time looking closely at the ridge whose presence she'd confirmed, a wide bump where the ocean floor gained elevation. It was apparent on all six of the profiles, which meant that it was a range, not just one isolated mountain. And then something happened. "As I looked further at the detail, and tried to unravel it," she said, "I noticed that in each profile there was a deep notch near the crest of the ridge." A deep notch, a rift. This was something new. She kept studying it, checking the sounding records over and over again to make sure she hadn't mis-plotted a depth. When she was certain she was right, she called for Bruce.

Their first big fight followed, a back-and-forth of gestures and stubborn declarations: Bruce laughing dismissively, then shouting about women's intuition; Marie's face screwed up tight like a fist. Bruce's finger jabbing one of the rifts on the huge sheet of white linen spread out between them. The jagged ocean floor profiles looking, in this context, like the teeth of a bear trap. Marie shouting about Bruce's boring old mind; at least, she says, she uses hers for something, and anyway, what is he afraid of?

She knows exactly what he's afraid of. They both know that the existence of such a rift means continental drift. Wegener's theory is so reviled in the United States that it is very well known. Marie, for instance, learned about it from her professors at Michigan. As she wrote many years later in a *Natural History* article, "If there was such a thing as continental drift, it seemed logical that something like a mid-ocean rift valley might be involved. The valley would form where new material came up from deep inside the Earth, splitting the Mid-ocean ridge in two and pushing the sides apart. That, in turn, would move the continents on their various tectonic plates." She starts to say something to this effect, but Bruce doesn't want to hear about it, and he certainly doesn't want to see proof of it. He paces around the room, puts his hands on his hips, accuses her of daydreaming. Marie's just about had it; she's exercising extreme willpower to stop herself from hurling a stapler at his head. She threatens to quit again. Her officemates have evacuated. Girl talk, Bruce finally bellows, referring to the rift. It cannot be. It looks too much like—

Continental drift, Marie says.

Continental drift, Bruce says.

They look at each other. How do you explain something like that?

IN 1952 THE words "continental drift" were fighting words. "At the time," Marie wrote in her *Natural History* article, Bruce and "almost everyone else at Lamont, and in the United States, thought continental drift was impossible." Depending on your intellectual confidence, the mention of continental drift provoked anything from mild anxiety to flat-out horror. Not only did American scientists think continental drift impossible, they also "considered it to be almost a form of scientific heresy," wrote Marie. "To suggest that someone believed in it was comparable to saying there must be something wrong with him or her." Bruce exhibited something close to horror; the only evidence that Marie felt any discomfort with the hypothesis was the extent to which she checked and rechecked her work before telling him.

To understand Marie's assertion of a rift on the ocean floor as the suggestion of a belief in continental drift requires a quick review of her training. In studying to become a geologist, Marie had been taught to look at an individual rock or a specific piece of land and to use details about its structure, composition, and location to deduce its history—this was a rock's "geomorphology," or an explanation of why and how it had formed. Marie said she had "devoured" geomorphology textbooks in school, reading cover to cover both the one assigned and another book she found on her own. She also mentioned an exercise it would have been hard for geology students to escape: "one was frequently given a topographical quadrangle from almost anywhere in the world, and then, from [the features,] asked to deduce the geologic history of the quadrangle." She'd been taught to do this on dry land, and applied the same process to her study of underwater land: when she saw a rift on the ocean floor, she asked herself why it was there and why it looked the way it did. A rift is a crack, and this one was huge, continuous, and could be correlated with seismic activity; the simplest answer she could think of was continental drift.

Simple, but revolutionary: the *Meteor* soundings had been around for almost two decades when Marie made her discovery, but no one had noticed the rift. No one else had seen the big picture of the Mid-Atlantic

Ridge system, tamped down its noise to make the low points of the rift emerge more clearly, connected those points to the area's seismic activity, and then boldly used the word *rift* to describe what they'd found. The closest anyone had come was a man named Günter Dietrich, writing in a 1938 issue of the *International Hydrographic Review*. Although he discerned patterns in small areas, Dietrich wrote, once the area being observed was expanded, a "definite correlation [could] no longer be spoken of": the Mid-Atlantic Ridge was beset by a "confused and tangled mass of crests and valleys." Where he had seen only chaos, Marie deduced a pattern. As Bruce noted in a response to someone who asked why the *Meteor* soundings hadn't made a bigger impression on the scientific community when they were published, "No one hit it right until Marie."

Bruce's praise, of course, was in retrospect. In 1952 he was more concerned with what the rift meant for his future. He was thinking of heresy, not revolution. When Marie showed him the rift valley, he told her to do the whole job over. And she did.

CHAPTER 11

WHILE MARIE REPEATED THE PROCESS OF DRAWING the profiles, Bruce continued to work on an entirely different project. A paper he'd written with Doc, called "Turbidity Currents and Submarine Slumps, and the 1929 Grand Banks Earthquake," was about to be published in the *American Journal of Science*. By studying the timing of the breaks in transatlantic telegraph cables during the earthquake in question, they'd discovered that an underwater avalanche—which they termed a turbidity current—was the cause. Sediment shaken free by an earthquake on the continental rise south of Newfoundland had gathered speed, sliding down the rise, creating a high-speed current that churned through four hundred miles of sea in twelve hours. A dozen cables had been broken, first the ones closest to where the earthquake originated, finally the ones four hundred miles away. These conclusions also formed the bulk of Bruce's master's thesis.

Bell Laboratories was interested in Bruce and Doc's research. Owned in equal parts by Western Electric and AT&T, Bell Labs was where engineers researched and developed the technologies that were built by Western Electric and used by AT&T. It was understandable that Bell would be interested in an explanation for why its cables were breaking, especially since it hadn't been able to figure out a cause itself and was in the process of developing a transatlantic telephone cable system. Bell sent a letter to Columbia. That letter, said Bruce, made it into the hands of Doc, who happened to be looking for new sources of money for Lamont—particularly money to pay Bruce's salary. After some meetings, it was decided that a Lamont–Bell Labs alliance would be mutually beneficial, and an agreement was reached in which Bell would give Columbia $50,000 a year in exchange for Bruce's services.

According to Bruce, the money covered part of his salary, "the salary of some of [his] people, and some small amount of ship time to do specific things for Bell Labs." Bruce was available for consultation and to "work on problems related to their interest[s]." "They wanted to know," he wrote, "exactly what the temperature was at the bottom of the ocean—how it would vary, because they knew that would change the transmission of their cables. They wanted to know exactly the depth of the water. They wanted to know all the kinds of accidents that could happen to them. They wanted to know accurately the shape of the bottom so that they could cut down the amount of slack they had to lay, and therefore save a little money." Bell wanted to know, in other words, where to put its new telephone cables.

Three things happened at about the same time: Marie finished redoing the profiles, Bruce decided he wanted to try to conduct a systematic study of how earthquake epicenters (the exact place where an earthquake originates) related to cables, and he had some "odd help," in the form of a man named Howard Foster, "thrust" at him. The exact sequence of these events is unclear; what's important is that they happened in close proximity to one another.

Marie's profiles, on her second try, had not changed—the rift was still there. Bruce's response to the rift had also not changed. He was unwilling to accept it, so the original goal of working up the soundings stayed the same: creating a general picture of the structures of the oceans. To do that, Marie had to begin converting the profiles, which were two-dimensional, into a more realistic format. Instead of each track being confined to a separate graph, she and Bruce decided, Marie would begin to copy all six tracks onto one map. She actually did this twice: once on the U.S. Navy's classified map of the North Atlantic, and once on GEBCO's map of the same (another copy of which she had glued to wall of the hallway a few years before). These base maps served as templates—she could trace the outlines of the continents bordering the Atlantic and also inte-grate the soundings that the maps included. And by using both maps, she'd get two views of the same area: the navy map was at a scale of 1:5,000,000 (meaning that 1 inch on the map equaled 5 million inches of ocean floor, about 79 miles) and the GEBCO map was at a scale of 1:10,000,000 (meaning that 1 inch on the map equaled 10 million inches of ocean floor, about 158 miles).

The format they "quite suddenly" decided on was a physiographic diagram. These diagrams were sketches of the topographical features of an area, not just simple strokes showing outlines of mountains and hills, but intricate nests of black lines that made the crags and ridges on the ocean floor look three-dimensional. Sketches that showed, Marie said, the terrain as it would look if viewed "from a low flying plane." The method had been created by a Columbia professor of geomorphology named Armin Kohl Lobeck, who had been sent to Versailles after World War I to help world leaders redraw Europe's boundaries. When he got there and observed those powerful men staring blankly at topographical maps, Bruce said, "unable to tell a mountain from a mole hill or a river from a valley or anything from a shoreline," Lobeck developed the physiographic diagram.

Lobeck's geomorphology textbook was one of the ones Marie had "devoured" in school and since she'd started plotting the ocean floor depths, she'd set to devouring another of his titles, *Block Diagrams*, which laid out the process of diagramming land using the physiographic method. "You couldn't have gotten through any kind of geology course in the United States without knowing about the technique," Bruce said. And although neither Bruce nor Marie "ever took any formal courses from him," she said, "Lobeck had tremendous influence on our work." Important to note are the differences between a physiographic diagram of, say, a state and one of the Northern Atlantic's floor. A state can be surveyed firsthand, all of it visible. "Deep sea soundings obtained along a ship's track," Marie said, "were as a ribbon of light where all was darkness on either side."

While Marie was beginning her first physiographic diagram, Bruce was trying to find a connection between earthquake epicenters and cable breaks; he was also trying to figure out how to use Howard Foster. Foster was the son of the chauffeur and housekeeper of a wealthy Woods Hole oceanographer. According to Bruce, the Woods Hole oceanographer had "put up the money for six months' salary" for Foster, who was deaf and had apparently encountered a lot of problems trying to get work elsewhere, despite having earned a degree in fine arts. Not one to turn down free help and with loads of data to wade through for the new Bell contract, Bruce had Foster help him copy data from cable companies in New York. They took trips to the offices of Western Union and the Commercial Cable Company and sat side by side, copying pages of data (cable break times and locations) into notebooks. Periodically, Bruce flew to London for two- or three-week-long trips to visit the headquarters of British cable companies, photographing the pages of data he thought were the most important. While he was away, he had Foster start plotting earthquake epicenters on maps that were at the same scale (1:5,000,000 and 1:10,000,000) as the ones onto which Marie was simultaneously transferring her six transatlantic profiles.

Foster's work was vastly different from Marie's. Unlike her, he did not have to interpolate to connect soundings. Bruce gave Foster the map and a list of latitudes and longitudes and told him to plot them (i.e., place a dot on the map at the correct place). His hiring marked the end of Marie's role as a "computer." Her work could no longer be considered robotic—in fact, beginning with Foster's hiring, Bruce took great care to contrast Marie's work with the work of assistants such as Foster (he was the first, but there would be many others), noting that even her early projects required scientific knowledge in order to decide "what was to be plotted . . . and determining what or which way it should be plotted and what kind of mountain it should be."

So while Marie was translating profiles into sketches on maps, Foster was marking earthquake epicenters on maps—and Bruce had decided that these two data sets should be plotted on maps of the same scale. The choice was simple but innovative; no one, said Bruce, had ever done this before. Before Marie and Bruce, "the seismologist" (someone who studies earthquakes; at Lamont this was Frank Press) "would use one map, and bathymetry" (the technical term for the study of ocean depths) "would be on something else, and cores" (which were the specialty of Lamont's Dave Ericson) "would be on something else." That approach meant three maps, likely at three different scales, in the hands of three people with different specialties who might never show one another their work—not unlike the *Meteor* oceanographers who didn't notice a rift in their profiles. Dead end.

With Marie and Foster plotting data on maps of the same scale, and both of them working closely with Bruce, however, something spectacular happened. When the two maps were placed on a light table—Marie's map showing the topography of the ocean floor beneath Foster's map with dots marking earthquake epicenters—it was clear that the earthquake epicenters did not just cling to the slopes of the Mid-Atlantic Ridge. They fell within Marie's rift, so many dots clustered within the valley that they appeared to fill it, forming a nearly unbroken line up and down its length, an illustration of a correlation that almost persuaded Bruce to believe in the rift valley.

Eureka.

Who placed the maps on the light table? Who noticed the correlation first? Who was even present at such an auspicious moment? Unfortunately there are conflicting answers to those questions.

What follows is from a transcription of a voice recording Bruce made in late 1975.

> Q. After Marie pointed out to you the close coincidence of the location of the epicenters and the location of the rift, was it you or Ewing who decided on this for the method of location of the rift in the South Atlantic?
>
> A. Well, there is a misconception here. Marie did not point out to me the close coincidence between the epicenters and the location of the rift. I had pointed it out to her. She had found the rift valley in the profiles and had convinced herself of the correlation/formation. I was not convinced of the correlation in the profiles. I couldn't announce—[Here the transcription indicates that the tape made a "bad sound." It picks up again with] . . . from then on she used the data of the epicenters very closely for the rift valley correlation. But it wasn't—as I recall—that—Marie did not point out to me about the rift valley correlation.

This next excerpt is also from late 1975, but it's from Marie's perspective. She talks about how Bruce's "rather insulting view" of the rift valley changed when Foster was hired and began plotting out the earthquake epicenters.

> And [when Foster] did this on the same scale of map that I was working on so as to be useful in helping me define the structure of the Mid-Atlantic Ridge, it became obvious that the earthquake epicenter belt and the point [where] I had found the depressions at the rest of the ridge were not [a] coincidence. So, I returned and told Bruce about this and he was this time somewhat apologetic for treating me so badly.

Later, in her unpublished and undated "Opus" (the story of her life mapping the ocean floor and working with Bruce, the "Opus" is the closest Marie ever came to writing an autobiography), Marie told the story somewhat differently.

> The first six transatlantic profiles which I had plotted and pieced together from the echo sounding records of *Atlantis* and some other early vessels did show the prominent valley at the crest of the ridge. This central valley also coincided with the earthquake epicenters. The epicenters were within the limits of error of half a degree or so, which was as accurate as they could be located. I showed Bruce my plot of the central valley and earthquakes and Bruce said, "Can't be, it looks too much like continental drift."

During the last decades of her life the narrative shifted again. In these versions of the story, Marie gave Bruce all of the credit for being the first to recognize the correlation between the earthquake epicenters and the rift valley.

I can't determine which story is true, but I do know that if Howard Foster's desk sat next to Marie's, so that she could see his work, it would have been unlikely for her to have missed the belt of earthquakes developing on his map. I know that the versions of the story in which Marie gave Bruce total credit were published (one in a magazine and the other in a Columbia-produced collection of essays about the early days of

Lamont) and edited by other people. And I know that the only version in which Marie gives herself credit is the version she wrote when Bruce was still alive.

MARIE AND BRUCE'S decision to make physiographic diagrams was motivated by three major factors. The first was that precise depictions of depth were classified. Contours had been used throughout history to show what little was known about the ocean floor—most recently on the GEBCO maps—but as new technologies made it possible to reveal the specific depths of large portions of the ocean floor, the U.S. government decided to classify them due to cold war worries about submarine warfare. A physiographic diagram was "very adaptable for portraying the seafloor," Marie said. "The displacement of peaks and other topographic features due to the vertical exaggeration blurred their actual positions as demanded by a classification regulation." And anyway, she said, "contours cannot differentiate the smooth from the rough areas, which is so important in a visual presentation of topography."

Accessibility was the second reason Marie and Bruce chose this method of diagramming. The sketches were vivid. The viewer didn't need any specialized knowledge to understand them in a basic way. Lobeck's physiographic diagrams were so accessible, in fact, that he became "cartographic supervisor" for a series of books for school-age children and sold his maps to elementary schools. By using this method to map the ocean floor, Marie said, "even a third grader could understand the concept of abyssal plains." The approach also had a distinctive scientific motivation: to illustrate the systematic development of features, rather than formation by chance. A physiographic diagram is at heart a description of "how"; by looking at such a diagram, someone with specialized knowledge would be able to discern a visual argument for the ways the depicted features had been formed.

Although Lamont exponentially increased the quantity of ocean floor data in the 1940s and '50s, there were still swaths of ocean floor hundreds of miles wide for which there were no sounding records. The sketching technique of the physiographic diagram allowed Marie to interpolate between profiles—again using her knowledge to fill in the blanks. After all, she couldn't have a mountain range stop dead just because she didn't have any data; she did what the state geologist who lectured the PG girls at Michigan had suggested was the geologist's greatest power: she made an educated guess.

Marie began her physiographic diagram with a huge sheet of blank white paper. "It was always," Marie said, "Heezen's philosophy to go from the known to the unknown." So the white paper filled first with well-known information. She meticulously measured out a latitude and longitude grid. She traced in the borders of continents. She penciled in the ship tracks. She sketched out the terrain of the ocean floor around the coasts because depth measurements were abundant near land. Because coastal areas are shallow, it had been possible to sound them long before the development of sonar. In fact, it had been necessary; without accurate navigation charts, ports would have been extremely dangerous for the ships entering them.

So Marie started with the coasts, sketched her way down the continental shelf, slope, and rise, across the abyssal plain, and worked her way out to where the Mid-Atlantic Ridge rose up into a crest. She did this using a type of sketching called hachuring, which relies on the accumulation of lines to show the direction and length of a slope. With hachuring, the steep drop of the continental slope would be drawn using short, thick pen strokes; the gentle, barely perceptible changes of the abyssal plains would be drawn with long, thin pen strokes. When she was done, her sketching of the known facts filled in the coastal areas of the Americas, Europe, and northern Africa, and extended in long bridges across the Atlantic. Between the bridges there wasn't anything at all.

Had Marie stopped here, she would have created a nice compilation of depths of the Northern Atlantic ocean that had been plumbed thus far, no doubt a useful tool. But it was her next step that made her work revolutionary: she kept on going. She and Bruce had, after all, found a "definite association" of topography with seismicity—meaning that earthquake epicenters (particularly shallow ones that originated close to the surface of the Earth's crust) clustered in the rift valley. Why not, Marie thought, use this information to make some educated guesses? If the earthquake epicenters clustered in the rift valley, it was logical to assume that, in places where there weren't any soundings, she could consult their locations to hypothesize the location of the rift valley. This made the most sense for those blank white spaces between the bridges. It made less sense when Marie tried to convince Bruce that they could extrapolate—or hypothesize to extend the rift way past areas that had been sounded—in addition to interpolating.

He was still skeptical that the rift valley even existed, but when Marie sketched out the hypothetical extension of the rift, and the ridge system that it cleaved lengthwise, they noticed something else: the earthquake belt led them south through the Atlantic, around the African cape, north into the Indian Ocean, west into the Gulf of Aden, and then made landfall in the form of the East African Rift. A few decades before, Beno Gutenberg and Charles F. Richter had been the first to note that the earthquake epicenters followed the same path as the oceanic ridge. But Marie's rift traveling across the world and winding up as a valley on continental Africa was an entirely different story, one in which earthquake epicenters fell within the boundaries of the rift valleys, were not just scattered haphazard on the ridges' flanks.

When she made profiles of the African rift, at the request of the still-unconvinced Bruce, the topographical similarities were there, too. Not only did the epicenters cluster within the walls of the East African and Mid-Atlantic rifts, but those two rifts were also structurally analogous. That clinched it for Bruce. The discovery was huge: shallow-focus earthquakes seemed to originate in rift valleys, which weren't confined to the Atlantic and Indian oceans. Eight months after Marie began work on those first six profiles, she could sketch one nearly continuous rift valley all across the world, a forty-thousand-mile-long underwater structure, quite possibly the largest geologic feature on Earth.

Eureka.

THERE ARE PRECIOUS few known details of Marie and Bruce's personal relationship. There isn't a single discrete moment in the story where the plot clarifies, where Marie and Bruce do a quick change, swapping out their roles as colleagues and friends to become lovers. The shift, if it happened, is unacknowledged, as if their movement toward each other took place so slowly that neither of them registered the change until long after it had happened.

Their relationship confounded everyone who knew them. For a long time I, too, was haunted by a particular scene of Marie and Bruce that began after I read two quotes from interviews done with them. The quotes careened around, demolishing everything in their paths until my head was just a big stage, dark except for the glow of twin spotlights, empty but for the two of them sitting side by side. Bruce said: "She didn't do anything except what I gave her." Marie said: "My life was all absorbed with Bruce and working for him and I had no feelings." They'd go back and forth like this in my imagination—"except what I gave her," "I had no feelings," "I gave her," "feelings."

In a diary passage from 1954, his thirtieth year, Bruce described himself using language similar to that which he might have used to describe a geologic process. "I guess one changes very little during life and even then only over great periods of time," he wrote. "I am lonely a lot of the time [I] need a wife I guess, but don't know any good prospects now . . . life seems just a little futile at present. But I guess it always does when you reflect too much." Here's Marie, talking to an interviewer in the mid 1990s: "He probably had other girls that he spent the weekends with, but he and I worked together all during the week, and sometimes we'd work on the weekends, but he had other girlfriends." You know that or you suspect that, the interviewer asked. "No, I know that. But I guess they always found more productive people. He wasn't very romantically inclined, because he'd had an unhappy home life. His ma and pa always fought. It wasn't a happy home life. She was so socially minded, and his father was a hard worker, strictly business. She kept busy hunting Bruce up girlfriends. But I was always in the way, because I worked for him."

By 1960, after they'd known each other for about twelve years, the postcards and letters they wrote to each other included words such as *miss you* and *love*. By 1975 you can hear him calling her "honey" on recordings he made for the man who wanted to write a biography of Marie but gave up because she refused to consider a portrait of herself that didn't give Bruce equal treatment. Bruce left half of his estate, including his house, to Marie when he died. Condolence letters regarding his death and addressed to Marie were written as if to a widow and fill several binders at the Library of Congress. In an article about their work in the German magazine *Mare* that I read a dubious Google translation of online, another interviewer drops the question: whether they were a *Liebespaar*, a pair of lovers. "I worked for Heezen," Marie said, tight-lipped as a Mafia secretary. On the question of why she never married, the article said that only after several hours of discussion did she admit the following: "Bruce was against it."

Another German, named Lia Hörmann, weighing in for the magazine *Tirolerin* (*Best Month in Society*!), translates her own text in a letter to Marie: ". . . small waist, swinging long skirt, graceful line. She looked very charming. As he came over to her, she felt his warm manhood, the scent of his skin, and his voice was deep when he said: 'Marie, we will be cartographers of the whole globe, its topography underneath the seas. Science will have to accept that!' In this night they became a loving couple that stuck together for the coming lifetime." "I had to prepare the story for public interest, so it needed some 'warming up' for pleasure," Hörmann wrote to Marie, "and I hope I have succeeded in that in your opinion!" I don't have Marie's reply.

Liebespaar or not *Liebespaar*? These days I don't wonder much about the details of this question. Marie and Bruce are bound at one of the most basic levels of human existence: their stuff, what's left of it, commingles in boxes at the Library of Congress the same way it commingled at Marie's house before she died, the same way Marie and Bruce's lives became completely intertwined while they were still alive. Most people who knew them used the word *couple* at least once when describing them. One of Marie's friends answered immediately when I asked her what they had been to each other: "very much a couple," she said. *Liebespaar*.

Except that the question pops up everywhere, an entanglement that's constantly alluded to. I don't think it's a coincidence that Lia Hörmann "warmed up" her narrative in a way that turned a months-long process of scientific discovery into a single evening of scientific and sexual epiphany. I also don't believe reality unfolded that neatly. What I think is that Marie and Bruce's relationship is hard to understand within the context of American norms. They didn't marry, and they had separate houses the whole time they knew each other. They were a team—and here I think Hörmann was right in a very general sense—bonded by their epic discovery.

They'd stay that way until Bruce's death in 1977, with one exception: any spotlight trained on Marie also shone on Bruce and the rift; any spotlight trained on the rift also shone on Bruce and Marie. But a spotlight trained on Bruce often excluded the rift, and even more frequently excluded Marie; the mapping of the ocean floor was only one part of his career, but it was everything to Marie.

CHAPTER 12

MARIE'S DISCOVERY OF A WORLD-GIRDLING RIFT VALLEY cutting lengthwise through a world-girdling ridge happened in 1952, but news about this momentous discovery did not leave Lamont's campus until 1956, in the form of a paper authored by Doc and Bruce titled "Some Problems of Antarctic Submarine Geology." Marie's name was absent; Doc was the first author listed. In "Some Problems of Antarctic Submarine Geology," the ridge is "believed to be continuous," the median rift zone is "apparently" present throughout, and the ridges "may be traced throughout poorly sounded areas by the aid of an epicenter map." With such tentative and passive language, "Some Problems" sounded the way a good scientific paper should, and projected a modesty Marie's physiographic diagram never could have: on her map, the rift and the ridge were defiantly present.

The "Some Problems" paper, however hesitant, was the biggest assertion Lamont had made about the rift. They'd already let hints of the discovery trickle out. In 1953 Bruce was an author on a paper that included one of Marie's original six transatlantic profiles, though neither the paper nor the profile pointed out the rift valley that was so plainly visible. In 1955 Bruce gave a talk in which he said that the ridge was a continuous feature throughout the world's oceans. He never directly stated that the ocean floor was rifted, but said that the "ridge is remarkably similar in topography and seismicity to African plateaus and rift valleys, suggesting a common origin and similar age." And before the "Some Problems" paper was published in 1956, Doc and Bruce (again, without Marie), at a meeting of the American Geophysical Union, asserted that the rift valley itself extended into Africa.

This controlled release of information, indirect and separated by several years, made it so that other scientists would have to have been studying Lamont's output very closely in order to add up all the pieces—a near impossibility considering that most other scientists were occupied by their own work. The "Some Problems" paper ended the vagueness and obfuscation. It was published just in time for the 1957 International Geophysical Year (IGY), a huge multinational effort to make "coordinated observations of various geophysical phenomena." Not only would other scientists have to take note, but they'd have to take action, too. "Some Problems" might have sounded passive, but it also sounded an alarm: with the possibility of a vaguely outlined forty-thousand-mile rift valley on the ocean floor, there was the possibility for much more discovery, and no self-respecting geologist, geophysicist, or oceanographer wanted to be left out of the game.

A very clever maneuver, you might say, for Doc and Bruce and maybe even Marie to direct the world's attention to those "poorly sounded areas," so that the IGY's extolled virtues of coordination, cooperation, and collaboration might work in their favor. Or maybe just Marie's favor—of the three of them, she was the only one who had devoted her life to the map. She was the only reason that, by the end of 1956, a physiographic diagram of the North Atlantic was complete: as Charles Officer, a grad student at Lamont in the 1950s, said, "Bruce would not have been able to do what he did without Marie, period." Doc's brother (who also worked at Lamont) and sister-in-law concurred. Bruce, they said in a joint interview, would never have been able to map the ocean floor without her; that Doc couldn't have done it without her either seems to be a foregone conclusion. But of the three players—Doc, Bruce, and Marie—only Marie's name was left off the publication.

*   *   *

IN FEBRUARY AND March 1957, Bruce received letters from several American ladies who were concerned for the safety of humanity—the result of an article and illustration in the *New York Times*, which publicly announced the discovery of the rift valley. The *Times* article had been titled "Crack in World Is Found at Sea." The illustration was less succinctly titled: "A Huge Crack in the Floor of the Oceans Is Traced by Geologists." The article and images were published on February 1, 1957; the former consisted of two illustrations and two short sentences. One of the illustrations was a simple map of the world, with only the names of the continents and the Atlantic, Pacific, and Indian oceans marked. The other was a photo, in black and white, of a grim-looking bespectacled man wearing a dark suit and tie. Under the man's picture it said, "Dr. Maurice Ewing announcing findings yesterday." Under the map it said, "Heavy lines denote a 45,000-mile continuous trench and a shorter one in the Indian Ocean."

On the map, crude dark lines cut down the center of the Atlantic and snake jaggedly all across the world. According to the second article, the crack was twenty miles wide, two miles deep, and had been discovered by "teams of scientists" from Columbia University's Lamont Geological Observatory in "five years of work in various parts of the world." Later, it said that the Earth was "being pulled apart"; it is not a huge leap to understand how the public (including the two women who wrote to Bruce) could have been unnerved by this discovery. To a Mrs. Richards of an undisclosed locale Bruce wrote, "I do not believe that you have any immediate worry. The earth seems to have been 'ripping at the seams' for a long time now (millions of years). Movements of inches a century are considered very fast. Thank you for your interest." "Have no fear," he wrote to a Kathy Dickson of Lincoln Park, Michigan. "The crack has been there a long time. I enclose a description of how we find things in the ocean."

Teams of scientists. How we find things in the ocean. It's true that the process involved many people, but where was Marie in all of this? "Miss Marie Tharp," the *Times* wrote, "cartographer at the Lamont Observatory, had noticed that the locus of a great number of earthquakes in the North and South Atlantic in the past 40 years coincided exactly with the great trench there." The map illustrating the rift valley was not hers, and all quotes in the article came from Dr. Maurice Ewing and Dr. Bruce

Heezen. Neither of them mentioned that they probably wouldn't have seen the rift valley without the help of Miss Marie Tharp.

Marie stayed quiet. For her, the physiographic diagram of the North Atlantic ocean floor was the manifestation of a career that had never been guaranteed. It was unusual that, as a woman, she could call herself a geologist, but it was extraordinary that by 1957 she was one of only a few oceanographic cartographers in the whole world, male or female. It's no wonder that when she began mapping the ocean floor she never, she said, considered anything else, no wonder that she "felt lucky to have a job that was so interesting. Establishing the rift valley and the mid-ocean ridge that went all the way around the world for forty thousand miles—that was something important," she said. "You could only do that once. You can't find anything bigger than that, at least on this planet." So while it certainly would have been nice to get equal public billing with Doc and Bruce, she had only to look at her map to feel a sense of accomplishment, to see the difference between what they had contributed and what she had.

Marie's 1957 physiographic diagram, published as an accompaniment to a *Bell System Technical Journal* paper authored by Bruce and a Bell scientist, was delicate and graceful. It was missing some of the features that would later grace it, but it was a reflection of what she had come to understand, during five years of data analysis, to be true. A ridge treading willowy down the middle of the Northern Atlantic, the rift cut smoothly down its length. Smooth abyssal plains white and blank but for the occasional number noting a depth. Steep islands like craggy churchless steeples. The diagram was drawn from what can be called an oblique perspective—or a bird's-eye view. If something was there it was because Marie had found the pattern in the data, because she had laid her pen to the paper and built up the ocean floor's features stroke by stroke, tiny lines accumulating into something huge.

Pointillists show the shimmer of tree leaves moving in a breeze by covering a canvas with different-colored dots; Marie showed the high-density texture of the seafloor by inking overlapping layers of abbreviated lines (some parallel, some knitted and tangled) onto her paper. Get your face close to the map and all the sharp peaks, like tiny little mountains repeated, look just like the surface of the ocean: peaks and valleys instead of crests and troughs, like a pen-and-ink drawing of a stretch of choppy sea.

It had not been easy. By 1975 Bruce would say, when asked, that "what people think the bottom of the ocean looks like, what most scientists and what most informed laymen think it looks like, is what Marie thinks it looks like." But this was in retrospect; most features were on that original North Atlantic map because she'd had to fight with Bruce to get them there. To convince him, Marie had to show him the original sounding records, the earthquake data, show him the profiles she'd drawn, the various sketches she'd done and the ship tracks, too.

To their contemporaries, Marie and Bruce were known for being stubborn and possessed of impressive tempers. Stories abound in which Marie hurled paperweights or Bruce took an electric eraser to weeks of her work, in which shouting matches about what went where and what to put where there weren't any data lasted several hours. But even in these early arguments there's evidence that Marie and Bruce tempered each other. Marie, for example, wanted to fill in blank spaces with shipwrecks and mermaids and sea monsters, an imaginative allusion to maps of old and a candid admission that there was a great deal they did not know. Bruce, for his part, finessed her idea's sentiment. When she finished drawing it, Marie's first physiographic diagram had the legend blocked in at the bottom, dead center. It was where the Northern Atlantic met the Southern Atlantic—one of those areas for which there were no data—a thousand-plus miles covered up by official business.

In 1955 Bruce had submitted a paper to the Geological Society of America titled "Flat-topped Atlantis, Cruiser, and Great Meteor Seamounts." Doc was the paper's second author, and the data on which it was based had come from one of their National Geographic cruises.

One of the paper's reviewers was Harry Hammond Hess, chairman of Princeton University's geology department; the Geological Society of America rejected the paper in 1956, including with its letter a copy of Hess's feedback. "This paper is poorly written with respect to organization and reasoning," Hess began. He referred to the paper's various types of data as "scraps of information." Those scraps included the products of Lamont engineering innovations such as the ocean-bottom camera (photographs) and the precision depth recorder (sounding records), as well as the cores, seismic profiles, and measurements that were beginning to reveal the strength and direction of the ocean floor's magnetization. "There was a time when information on the seafloor was so rare that the publication of such an agglomeration had value," Hess's letter continued. "I think that era is over." Hess was overly optimistic. Even today, only about 5 percent of the ocean floor has been studied in any detail; in 1956, when Hess wrote those words, it was a fraction of 1 percent.

Near the middle of his rejection letter Hess began a paragraph with the word *finally*, despite the fact that he was only just getting started. "Finally," he said, "the last two pages under the heading of 'Discussion' are exasperating. I am fond of outrageous hypotheses. I think they deserve more than a page of treatment. [But] these are merely outrageous without justification by reasoning." And then he arrived at what he really wanted to say. "Basically I am objecting to the authors' philosophy of research of which this paper is an outward manifestation." He allowed that not everyone needed to follow his own, different philosophy. He noted his "high regard" for the authors and recognized the "great advances in geophysical work at sea" made by Doc and his students. "Nevertheless," Hess said, "I am highly critical of the type of data collecting and geological interpretation which this same group has been doing. A vast amount of energy is going into rushing about the ocean collecting everything possible in the way of data . . . The critical facts necessary to solve any one problem are not clearly in mind before starting out . . . Rather than think the problem through to the point of recognizing the critical experiment or experiments, things are thrown together in a variety of ways in hopes that a fortunate combination will lead to a solution."

These words are echoing in Bruce's head two years later, in 1957, as he finishes giving his continuous rift valley lecture to a group of faculty and students gathered in Princeton's Guyot Hall. He takes a sip of water, looks down at his jumbled notes, removes his glasses. They're all quick gestures, but by the time he places his glasses on the lectern, the smattering of polite applause has already petered out. Most of the audience, unable to understand the impact that the discovery of a worldwide rift system will have on the future of geology, had been bored while Bruce was speaking. Now they're avoiding his gaze; for a moment the dim room is silent but for the sounds of a woman's clicking heels filtering in from the hall.

And then Harry Hess, still chairman of Princeton's geology department, rises to his feet. He rolls forward onto his toes and catches hold of

A very young Marie in her father's surveying truck, early 1920s. *(Image courtesy of Robert Brunke)*

Marie during her university years, mid-1940s. *(Image courtesy of the Lamont-Doherty Earth Observatory)*

A posed Marie pretending to work on the physiographic diagram of the North Atlantic Ocean in Lamont Hall. Sounding records are visible to the left of the diagram, one of the globe prototypes that she and Bruce Heezen constructed sits in the middle, and an enlarged version of her six North Atlantic profiles is propped in the corner. Late 1950s. *(Image courtesy of the Lamont-Doherty Earth Observatory)*

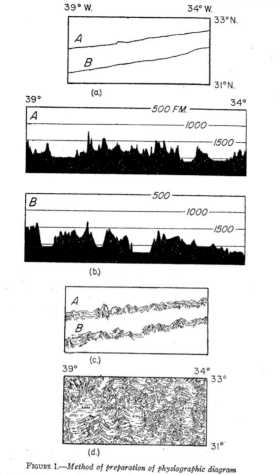

An excerpt from B. C. Heezen, M. Tharp, and M. Ewing's monograph *The Floors of the Oceans: I. The North Atlantic,* published in 1959 by the Geological Society of America. *(Image courtesy of the Geological Society of America)*

FIGURE 1.—*Method of preparation of physiographic diagram*

(a) Positions of sounding lines (A, B) are plotted on chart; (b) Soundings are plotted as profiles (A, B) at 40:1 vertical exaggeration; (c) Features shown on profiles (A, B) are sketched on chart along tracks; (d) After all available sounding profiles are sketched the remaining unsounded areas are filled in by extrapolating and interpolating trends observed in a succession of profiles.

Close-up of the 1961 South Atlantic physiographic diagram, showing the Equatorial Mid-Ocean Canyon off the coast of Brazil. The Fernando de Noronha Rocks visible in the foreground are now known as the Fernando de Noronha Ridge. *(Image courtesy of Marie Tharp Maps)*

Physiographic diagram of the northern part of the Atlantic Ocean. This map was published in the September 1957 issue of the *Bell System Technical Journal* and accompanied the article "Oceanographic Information for Engineering Submarine Cable Systems," written by Bruce Hezeen and C. H. Elmendorf. Note the legend at bottom center, covering up a portion of the ocean floor for which Marie and Bruce had little data. *(Image courtesy of Marie Tharp Maps)*

The physiographic diagram of the South Atlantic Ocean, published by the Geological Society of America in 1961. In the top half of the map, note the fracture zones intersecting the Mid-Atlantic Ridge. *(Image courtesy of Marie Tharp Maps)*

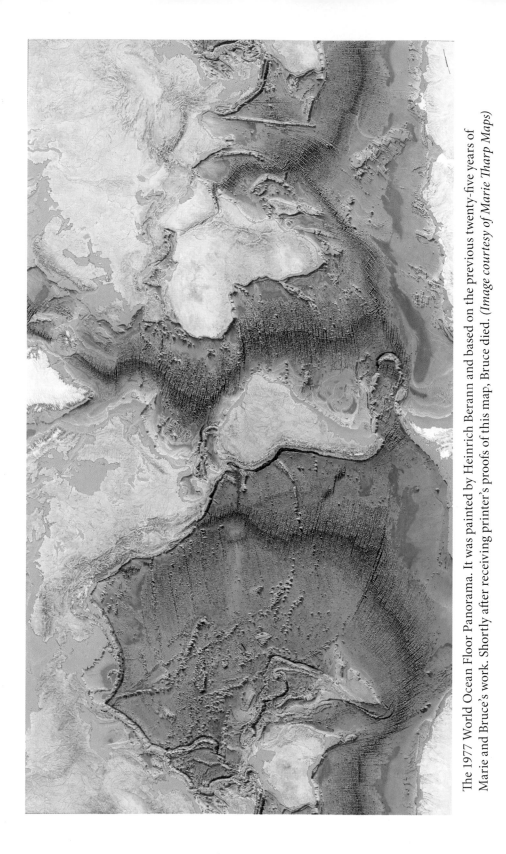

The 1977 World Ocean Floor Panorama. It was painted by Heinrich Berann and based on the previous twenty-five years of Marie and Bruce's work. Shortly after receiving printer's proofs of this map, Bruce died. *(Image courtesy of Marie Tharp Maps)*

Marie and Bruce having one of their tamer discussions in front of the physiographic diagram of the South Atlantic. Early to mid-1960s. *(Image courtesy of the Lamont-Doherty Earth Observatory)*

Marie's Naval Oceanographic Office (NOO) identification badge. It was issued in 1968, when she began working for the NOO, after "The Harassment" resulted in her firing from Lamont. *(Image courtesy of Robert Brunke)*

Nº ● 9676

U.S. Naval Oceanographic Office

M THARP

Marie smoking a cigarette at Bruce's house in Piermont, New York. The South Atlantic physiographic diagram is on the wall behind her and the *New York Times Book Review* is beside her. Mid-1960s. *(Image courtesy of the Library of Congress)*

Marie and Bruce having cocktails. The inscription on the back of the photo reads "World's Fair 1965." *(Image courtesy of the Library of Congress)*

Marie working on the physiographic diagram of the Indian Ocean in Lamont's Oceanography Building. Sounding record are visible beneath her elbows and propped on a ledge in front of her. Mid-1960s. *(Image courtesy of the Lamont-Doherty Earth Observatory)*

Marie and Bruce standing in front of the Lamont research vessel *Vema* in the early 1970s. At the beginning of her career, Marie was prevented from going to sea because women on ships were considered bad luck; she wasn't allowed on the *Vema* until after Doc left Lamont. *(Image courtesy of the Lamont-Doherty Earth Observatory)*

Marie in working-vacation mode. On their extensive travels, Marie and Bruce visited geological sites, surveyed land from the windows of planes, and met with their vast network of international colleagues. This photo was likely taken in the late 1960s or early 1970s. *(Image courtesy of the Lamont-Doherty Earth Observatory)*

The many faces of Marie. Sometime in the 1970s. *(Image courtesy of the Library of Congress)*

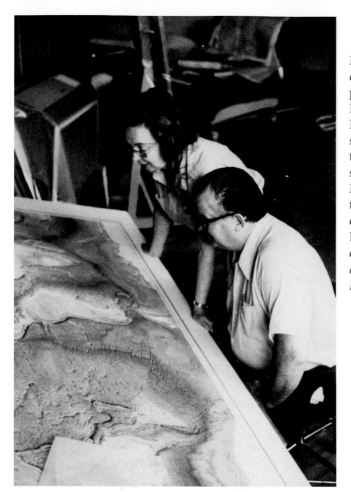

Marie and Bruce examining the in-progress World Ocean Floor Panorama at Heinrich Berann's studio in Austria. Note that Berann has used shading to darken the Mid-Atlantic Ridge in the Atlantic and Indian oceans but not yet in the Pacific. Probably 1976 or 1977. *(Image courtesy of the Lamont-Doherty Earth Observatory)*

Marie with Inky III. Robert Brunke took this photo of them at Bruce's house, shortly after Bruce's 1977 death. *(Image courtesy of Robert Brunke)*

his blazer's lapels, the way some men will thread their thumbs through belt loops or suspenders. In that time, the tightly packed text of Hess's rejection letter flashes before Bruce's eyes and his heart kicks into high gear; he suppresses an urge to bolt. Young man, says Hess, all intense stare and imposing ears. You have shaken the foundations of geology.

This is an intellectual about-face for Hess; he's not publicly casti-gating Bruce—far from it. *You have shaken the foundations of geology*, Bruce repeats in his head. It takes a while for the words to sink in—for Bruce and for the audience. Shaken the foundations of geology? If this were a movie, Bruce would look over both shoulders to make sure Hess wasn't addressing someone standing behind him. Here he looks down at the globe balanced on the edge of the lectern as if it could provide an answer. He and Marie had been using globes like it for years—painting the generalized patterns of the ocean floor onto different globes in blacks, blues, grays, and browns, brushing dark colors over the tasteful pastels already there.

Red had always been reserved for the rift valley that Bruce has just lectured about, the discovery of which Hess apparently thinks has shaken the foundations of geology. Hess and Bruce are the only two men stand-ing in the room; everyone else is still sitting down, still trying to recall what Bruce had said and figure out why their chairman thinks it's so important. Hess was a naval officer in World War II; he's the head of a 103-year-old department of geoscience. Bruce only just received his doc-torate that year and is a research associate at a nine-year-old geophysical observatory. It's not exactly an even match, but they're both seeing red and wondering the same thing: how the hell did that rift get there?

CHAPTER 13

MARIE'S FATHER DIED IN THE FIRST WEEK OF JANUARY 1959. In the decade leading up to his death, Marie went home at every holiday and summer break, driving the same route she took when she ran away from Lamont. Doing, she said, "a room a year" of the farmhouse, which meant that every time she was home she would pick a room, paint it, make curtains, and buy new linens and furniture for it—a touch of the domestic arts she probably didn't have a chance to express in her New York apartments. When her father died, she kept his overcoat, a blue flannel that had been chewed through by moths. She fixed it up the way she'd fixed up the farmhouse: patched the holes with colored thread, had the whole thing tailored into a skirt she'd wear for the next few decades, wide swaths of blue rehabilitated with bright shades. Her father had worn it, which meant that wearing it was like pulling some remnant of him close, even though she didn't need it in order to be reminded just how much he had influenced her.

A few weeks later Marie's apartment house on Broadway in Nyack burned down. "On the evening of Jan 19, 1959 the apartment where I lived burned up. I woke and saw flames eating at the ceiling, quickly decided this was no place for me, grabbed my coat and left," she wrote. "Seconds later the whole building collapsed in the blaze. Three elderly women burned up. I lost all my personal belongings." Except, perhaps, for her father's coat: it survived the fire to be worn for decades more, so it must have been what she grabbed and put on over her nightgown. Needless to say, Marie didn't make it in to work the next day; it's a testament to the closeness that had already developed between them that she ended up at Bruce's door, that he guided his dazed partner into his apartment, replaced her father's coat with his bathrobe, and told her to get some rest.

Marie's father didn't get to see the Geological Society of America present, in April and as part of its "Special Papers" series, his daughter's work on the North Atlantic ocean floor. It was called *The Floors of the Oceans: I. The North Atlantic*, and its authors were listed as Bruce C. Heezen, Marie Tharp, and Maurice Ewing—Marie's first official author credit. It was a slim book, bound in forest green fabric with gold letters, and it included the most up-to-date version of their map, as well as many other pull-out diagrams and charts illustrating their data—a monograph, which was quite an honor. If you happen to get your hands on a copy, the pages will be the color of milky tea, the back will have a block of fold-out pages printed on crinkly paper, and a copy of the revised North Atlantic physiographic diagram will be tucked behind them. The first thing you will read, after the title and copyright pages, after the dedication to the man who made the "Special Papers" series financially possible, is an epigraph from the famed nineteenth-century oceanographer M. F. Maury.

"Could the waters of the Atlantic be drawn off, so as to expose to view this great sea gash, which separates continents, and extends from the Arctic to the Antarctic, it would present a scene the most rugged, grand, and imposing. The very ribs of the solid earth, with the foundations of the sea, would be brought into light, and we should have presented to us at one view the empty cradle of the ocean." The quote cuts off here, and notes that Maury is the author, and that the words can be found in his 1855 *The Physical Geography of the Sea*. In Maury's book, though, the sentence is slightly different: ". . . we should have presented to us at one view, *in* [italics mine] the empty cradle of the ocean, a thousand fearful wrecks, with that dreadful array of dead man's skulls, great anchors, heaps of pearl, and inestimable stones which, in the dreamer's eye, lie scattered on the bottom of the sea, making it hideous with sights of ugly death." Maury's book is filled with such descriptive language; if I had been Marie or Bruce, I would have had a hard time choosing a quote from him to use as my epigraph. I know how much they liked Maury's quote—Bruce repeated it when he appeared on a *CBS News* special in 1964, wanted to call the autobiography he was working on before he died *In the Cradle of the Ocean*, and several of their other publications included the same quote from Maury. What with the great anchors, pearls, and skulls, I can only guess how much Marie, who wanted to put mermaids and ship-wrecks on their maps, liked Maury's words.

When *The Floors of the Oceans* was released, the world was outer space crazy. In 1957 the USSR launched *Sputnik* and put a dog into orbit; in 1958 the U.S. government launched its first artificial satellite, and by 1959 it had hired Doc to develop a seismograph that could be landed on the moon. In 1959 the movies *The Angry Red Planet, Battle in Outer Space*, and *Plan 9 from Outer Space* were released. People had already been pre-sented with a picture of what outer space (and the aliens who apparently resided there) looked like. It was, then, important to trigger their interest in inner space, too. *Imagine*, Marie and Bruce's inclusion of the Maury quote seems to say, *something giant, rugged, and imposing—something exciting and mysterious right here on Earth—and we will tell you how we found and mapped it.*

The text, describing their tools, process, and conclusions, is more than a hundred pages long. In it, they divided the ocean floor of the North Atlantic into three structural provinces for the first time: the continental margins, including (from land to sea) the continental shelves, slopes, and rises—which had been systematically sounded by Doc back in 1935. Where the continental rise ends, ocean basins begin. They're just what they sound like: wide-open basins occasionally punctuated by seamounts (the term for underwater mountains whose peaks don't break the water's surface) and islands—including, in some places, the abyssal plains that were first identified by Doc. There was the Mid-Oceanic Ridge, the con-tinuous median ridge that runs around the Earth for about forty thou-sand miles. And finally, the book offered a description of the rift running down the ridge's center—the first time Marie and Bruce extensively wrote about the feature they themselves discovered. They described, in detail, the topographical and structural makeup of each of the three provinces, using as proof a combination of photographs, gravity, magnetic and seis-mic data, cores, and dredges—again for the first time in print.

Perhaps most important, in light of what they were asserting and how they made their conclusions, they repeatedly noted that although their data were sparse, their methods were reliable. "Between sounding profiles the relief is speculative, based on extrapolation of trends noted in the profiles," they wrote in the first paragraph of the abstract. "The preparation of a marine physiographic diagram requires the author to postulate the patterns and trends of the relief on the basis of cross sections and then to portray this interpretation in the diagram," they wrote early on the fourth page. "After all available sounding profiles are sketched, the remaining unsounded areas are filled in by extrapolating and interpolating trends observed in a succession of profiles," they wrote in figure 1, entitled "Method of Preparation of Physiographic Diagram."

Despite this directness, the thousands of geologists who initially saw the map thought its visual representation of the ocean floor unfair. "They not only said it wasn't fair," Marie said, "they said it was a bunch of lies." British oceanographer Anthony Laughton objected to the scarcity of data used in the production of the map and even said that other ship tracks from the period didn't show the rift at all. As early as 1957 Henry William "Bill" Menard, of the Scripps Institution of Oceanography, expressed his concern about a worldwide rift to Bruce in a letter (sent about a month after the discovery was announced in the *New York Times*), saying, "I have been increasingly distressed to read one account after another in the press and magazines of this fabulous rift two miles deep, 20 miles wide and 40,000 miles long. I had to say to more than one reporter that I believed you were misquoted because I knew no soundings existed to support such a continuous rift in the South Pacific and Indian oceans." And even as late as September 1960, Menard would write to Bruce, "I regret to say that I still cannot see your median rift as a prominent and reasonably continuous feature."

In a 1961 review of *The Floors of the Oceans: I. The North Atlantic*, appearing in the *Journal du Conseil*, the publication of the International Council for the Exploration of the Sea, Marie's named is misspelled as "Tharpe," some of her "suggestions" are called "brave," and the author says that it is "not surprising that some of the authors' syntheses may not be completely acceptable." Nevertheless, he says, "the paper is a stimulating and attractive account of fact and interpretation which will probably be the basis of future geological work in the Atlantic and elsewhere for some time."

A later review of the monograph, this one in the *Geographical Review*, recognized it as a "brilliant compilation of much of the information from the North Atlantic" and said that the authors "presented a farsighted interpretation of its meaning." The choice to represent the ocean floor as a physiographic diagram is called "ingenious," and the author points out that the diagram is "essential for the full understanding of the text." For the author of this review, Marie's method of hypothesizing is understood as a necessity—"in places there are still considerable gaps where information is meager," he writes, "and here there has been intelligent interpolation." And instead of focusing on what isn't there, the author looks forward to the future, when Lamont "and these authors will make an equally vast contribution to the solution of the uncertainties of ocean structure that still exist." In the last sentence of the review, the author offers the highest praise possible: "This special paper and the associated physiographic diagram are essential to all students of the ocean floor."

These early, conflicting appraisals of Marie and Bruce's monograph were the first, but by no means the last, in a long series of clashing opinions of Marie's work. And here's another long-lasting conflict revealed by the publication of *The Floors of the Oceans*: one evening when Marie was leaving Lamont, on her way to take the inked-up physiographic diagram of the North Atlantic to the printer, Doc appeared. He'd gotten word that she and Bruce had not included his name on the monograph or the map; didn't they realize, Doc asked Marie, that their work was based on years of data that had been collected at his discretion, using his ship time and instruments? As a concession, Bruce would write years later, they agreed to put his name on the monograph, but not the map; in order to establish his independence as a scientist, Bruce would have to distance at least some of his work from Doc's. If doing that caused tension, so be it.

BRUCE'S FATHER DIED a few months after Marie's, in July 1959. Bruce had never wanted to follow in his father's footsteps. In fact, he loathed the very basics of his father's life—the turkey farm, the small Iowan community, an unhappy marriage to a woman who dominated both their lives—a feeling that made their father-son relationship uneasy. Between the Smithsonian Institution Archives, where Bruce's papers (mostly concerning the scientific work he did separate from Marie) reside, and the

Heezen-Tharp Collection at the Library of Congress, there are hundreds upon hundreds of letters to Bruce from his mother, most of them fat little envelopes colored the washed-out blue of the autumn sky. Each line of her spidery script presses against the one above it, cramped as if trying to escape off the top of the page. Little of the contents is vital. The weather is good, the weather is bad, the turkey farm is doing okay, do you have a winter coat, are you eating your vegetables, when are you coming home? Gossip about neighbors, newspaper clippings about high blood pressure. And, his mother asks him in nearly every letter, when are you going to find a nice girl to marry? Bruce's father only managed to cram notes to Bruce onto the ends of a handful of his wife's letters to Bruce. "Button up your overcoat, take good care of yourself, you belong to us. Much love, Dad," wrote Charles on a letter dated November 23, 1948.

When his father died, Bruce returned to Iowa to take care of his mother. It was summer, and he stayed about a month before returning to New York. Upon his return, he had his first heart attack. He spent three weeks in the hospital, where Marie visited him, bringing with her the usual letters from his mother, who'd eventually outlive Bruce and two more husbands.

Bruce recovered from his heart attack—just in time for the International Oceanographic Congress, the first of its kind. Its purpose was to "provide a common meeting ground for all sciences concerned with the oceans and the organisms contained in them . . . devoted to the fundamentals of the marine sciences rather than to their applications." The five fundamentals were the history, the boundaries, the deep sea, dynamics of organic and inorganic substance, and the marine life regime. Bruce was set to present thirteen papers; he wasn't going to let a weak heart stop him.

In order to visualize the physical aspects of the United Nations in which the 1959 International Oceanographic Congress took place, I always think of Hitchcock's *North by Northwest* (released that year), in which Cary Grant's character is accused of a murder he didn't commit. The murder takes place inside the United Nations, but before it occurs there's a beautiful shot of the building in Manhattan: the vast gray rectangle, its face broken by a grid of windows, rows of brightly colored flags arrayed before it. The interior has wall-to-wall carpeting and the furniture is all jewel-toned, squat, and square.

There were several heavy hitters at the International Oceanographic Congress, including Doc and Harry Hess. Sir Edward "Teddy" Bullard of Cambridge is probably my favorite peripheral scientist here, partly because he wrote an article titled "The Emergence of Plate Tectonics: A Personal View," in which he spoke candidly about the emotions involved in scientific endeavor: "To think the whole subject through again when one is no longer young is not easy and involves admitting a partially misspent youth . . . Clearly it is more prudent to keep quiet, to be a moderate defender of orthodoxy, or to maintain that all is doubtful, sit on the fence, and wait in statesmanlike ambiguity for more data." And partly because in Naomi Oreskes's book *Plate Tectonics: An Insider's History of the Modern Theory of the Earth*, there's a picture of him at thirty, naked and sitting on some volcanic rocks by the sea, a pith helmet covering his head, a crooked arm blocking his manly bits from view, his front teeth sticking out like a rabbit's. Also, his middle name was Crisp.

There's Roger Revelle, too, the president of the International Oceanographic Congress and director of the Scripps Institution of Oceanography. But the big news in the New York papers from that period was the arrival of Jacques Cousteau, and discussion of the rift and its relation to continental drift. "Some 800 scientists from East and West were told here today that they seemed to be drifting apart—not politically, but geographically," a *New York Times* article began on September 1; "at this opening session of the International Oceanographic Congress, support came for what has long been regarded as a highly controversial theory . . . [an idea that] has been viewed in the United States with a jaundiced eye." The article was accompanied by the same map the *Times* had run in 1957, the one that caused nervous women to contact Bruce. A *New York Herald Tribune* article quoted Bullard as telling the IOC's delegates that he had "fallen off the fence on the side of continental drift" and that the shift was "going on right before our eyes." "The continents are breaking apart and oceans are taking form," Revelle was quoted saying in the same article.

But: "Dr. Ewing indicated he was not completely convinced that continents do shift their positions," the *Tribune* said. The *Times* quoted Doc saying that rift valleys "generally run down the middle of ocean basins, as though associated with tension that might be responsible for the formation of the basins themselves." He didn't, the article pointedly noted, come out in favor of continental drift. Which means that he wasn't mak-

ing the same direct connection between the rift valley and drifting continents as some of the other scientists—including Marie and Bruce—in
attendance at the IOC.

Marie had been saying for years that she thought the rift looked tensional, meaning that it had been formed as the result of two pieces of the
Earth's crust moving away from each other. She, however, was not considered to be one of the heavy hitters at the IOC. In fact, she wasn't a
hitter at all. She attended, but I don't think she was invited to speak
because she isn't listed as an author on any of the articles published in the
voluminous compilation *Oceanography; Invited Lectures Presented at the
International Oceanographic Congress Held in New York, 31 August to 12
September 1959.*

Bruce took the idea of drifting continents and ran with it, receiving a
lot of attention for the papers he presented. By September 8, the ninth
day of the conference, the *New York Herald Tribune* carried the headline
"Earth Seen Expanding Like Ripening Orange," based on Bruce's explanation for how the rift was formed. He called it the "expanding earth
theory": not only were continents in motion, but the planet they rested
on was growing, too.

"Dr. Bruce C. Heezen of Columbia University has stirred up his fellow oceanographers with an 'outrageous hypothesis,'" the *Tribune* article
began. "The earth, says the thirty-six year-old research associate, has been
expanding over the millennia as if it were a slowly ripening orange." That
simile is not quite correct, for Bruce said that the continents had been dis-
placed as the Earth expanded, as if a deflated basketball had been dunked
in plaster, allowed to harden, and inflated—its shell cracking, the pieces
moving away from one another as the ball expanded. With this hypothesis, Bruce was staking a claim, offering an explanation for how he
thought the rift valley had been formed. Such an explanation was not
obvious simply by looking at the map of the ocean floor. You could accept
the rift valley as pictured and reach a different conclusion about how
it had gotten there, but you could not accept Bruce's expanding Earth
hypothesis without believing in the existence of the rift valley. The rift
valley hypothesis, in other words, was bold—and the expanding Earth
hypothesis was bolder.

"All week long the delegates at the International Oceanographic
Congress meeting here pondered on Dr. Heezen's speculations," the

Tribune article continued. "One said: 'It explains all the facts beautifully, but I can't believe it. Do you believe it, Dr. Heezen?' Another, in a major speech today, commented: 'We know so little about the problem of the continents we should not reject even the idea of an expanding earth.' Another simply cried: 'Impossible.'"

While scientists at the IOC were more skeptical of Bruce's hypothesis than of the rift valley depicted on Marie's physiographic diagram, there were still some who thought that she'd taken her extrapolation and inter-polation too far—those who thought the rift did not exist, or at least wasn't as extensive as her maps claimed. Jacques Cousteau had been skeptical of the rift valley since the year before the IOC meeting, when Bruce gave him a copy of the physiographic diagram at a conference in France. Cousteau had tacked it to a wall in the mess hall of his famed ship, the *Calypso*, so he could study it, and when the time came for the IOC, he decided he'd prove Marie and Bruce wrong while crossing the Atlantic, filming the ocean floor with the *Troika* (the "photo sled" apparatus he had designed) on his way to New York. Except instead of proving them wrong, he proved them right. "Just as they were reaching the crest of the Ridge," Bruce said, "they found this marvelous valley appear just where it was supposed to be at the point shown on our chart. At which point they turned around and went back and dragged the *Troika* across it again."

"It is likely," said a bulletin published in *Science* magazine six months before the IOC, "that films, either technical or semipopular, which do not illustrate a particular paper, will be shown in the evenings." And so, one evening after the presentations were done, Cousteau showed his film of the rift valley.

This evening is the only time Marie and Cousteau meet. Imagine a hotel ballroom with plush patterned carpet. Fill it with chairs—not in rows, but in clusters, kind of askew. Fill the chairs with scientists, also askew. They're just back from having descended on various steak houses around the city, stomachs full and cheeks rosy. Many martinis have been consumed.

Imagine Marie in all of this: she's one of the few women in a room filled by male scientists from all over the world. Whiz along the floor, zip-ping between metal chair legs and buffed oxfords, skimming the creased woolen corners of pants cuffs sticking out perpendicular from skinny ankles, grays and browns and blues and blacks, laced leather shoes all the same. And then there is Marie, her shoes not so very different, but different nonetheless. Black leather, a short heel, a ladylike exposure of the top of a stocking-covered foot. Ankles crossed and toe tapping. Her wrists are crossed in her lap, her tweed skirt itches, her feet feel pinched, and she's got a bobby pin poking into her scalp, but she smiles at Bruce and the other men sitting in her cluster of chairs all the same.

Imagine her turn her face away from them and toward the front of the room: there's Cousteau, wearing his signature red knit cap. She watches him; he doesn't exactly fit in either. Much thinner than most of the other scientists, wearing a turtleneck under his suit jacket instead of a button-down. He clears his throat. Marie stops tapping her toe.

Gentlemen, Cousteau says. The scientists are a little drunk. They take some time to quiet down, maybe aren't exactly amenable to this interloper whose movies speak directly to the public—in the same way they're maybe not exactly amenable to Marie and her map, which explicitly reveals the ocean floor's features, including the rift valley she discovered.

Gentlemen, Cousteau says again, and when he continues everyone knows he's about to talk about the rift. No one looks at Marie. I did not believe, he says, his eyes sweeping the audience. I did not believe that the map of the North Atlantic recently published by Lamont could possibly be right. I did not believe that the Mid-Atlantic Rift pictured on it could possibly be continuous. Too complete a story, I thought, from too little information. But it is there, Cousteau says. His eyes find Marie's. It is true, he says.

The room goes dark, the projector begins whirring, and a black-and-white 3, 2, 1 flickers onto the screen. There it is: the ocean floor, beachy beneath water thick with dead plankton suspended like snowflakes. Some eels. The appearance of a sea star prompts a hoot from a biologist at the back of the room. But then a darkness emerges in the distance, and as the *Troika* approaches the darkness takes shape, turns into a ridge. This is Marie's first glimpse of something she's been imagining for seven years, something she transformed from soundings to profiles, from profiles to the physiographic diagram that everyone in the room has seen—the diagram that prompted Cousteau to make this film.

On the screen the ridge looks like a big black mountain with ooze creeping down its side. The camera scales it, climbing up and up until it's clear that it has reached the summit—there's nothing but water at the top of the frame. And then the camera starts coming down the other side and you can see into the rift valley as far as the camera lights will reach, see the hardly touched pillows of young lava with barely any sediment on top of them. Marie knows, just like everyone in the room knows, that if the Mid-Atlantic Ridge had split down the middle as shown on her map, rifted, the other half of it has to be ahead.

When the other half of the Mid-Atlantic Ridge materializes out of the dark water on the screen, the shot is a twin of the scene they'd seen moments before. There's a collective intake of breath. Maybe it's because it's the end of the day and they're secretly tired of the academic mumbling they had to listen to all day. Maybe it's because they're a little tipsy. The scientists are surprised—even though Cousteau's introduction pretty much told them what they were about to see, even though Marie's map had done the same before this evening. The film has made the rift a very real fact whose existence must be explained. Because of this, there are shouts for an encore viewing; the reel is rewound and restarted. But Marie has seen all she needs to see. And she's said—without saying a word—all she needs to say.

I don't know what Marie and Cousteau spoke of that night. Marie said that she "enjoyed" her only meeting with Cousteau and recalled his screening, but she never specifically mentioned what she talked about with the man who'd captured on film what she'd captured on paper. But the event has historical weight, despite the missing dialogue. If only for that night, if only for that hour, Cousteau and Marie converged: Cousteau's film was an argument for Marie's map, and Marie's map was an argument for her beliefs. The Earth's plates were moving, and while she didn't know why or how, she did know that the men around her were going to have to catch up.

Part Three

Maybe I don't get your meaning—but I like mine.

—Georgia O'Keeffe

*I*N 1960 HARRY HESS BEGAN CIRCULATING A PAPER TITLED "History of Ocean Basins" among his colleagues. Early on in his introduction (which did not appear in print until 1962, as part of *Petrologic Studies*, a multiauthor volume), Hess says he's writing an "essay in geopoetry." "The birth of the oceans," began Hess, "is a matter of conjecture, the subsequent history is obscure, and the present structure is just beginning to be understood. Fascinating speculation on these subjects has been plentiful, but not much of it predating the last decade"—wait for it—"holds water."

Hess's real objective was to present a hypothesis describing the mechanism by which the continents move across the Earth's surface and, in doing so, to assert his belief that the continents did actually move. Rather than assume the permanence of the Earth's crust, Hess proposed that old crust was being recycled just as new crust was being formed, and that it was able to do this because it floated on the Earth's viscous upper mantle. There are intricacies to his explanation, but probably the most important parts had to do with explaining how convection currents (which had been theorized as a possible mechanism for continental drift decades before) contributed to the tenet of plate tectonics now called seafloor spreading.

You can see the circular motion of convection currents if you set a pot of water to boil on the stove: the liquid closest to the heat source warms first and then bubbles up toward the surface, cools off a bit, and then sinks back down to the bottom to be reheated. Hess hypothesized that the Earth's viscous mantle did this—with the Earth's plates passively carried along on the ride. The idea was not new. As early as 1929 the British geologist Arthur Holmes had proposed convection as a possible mechanism of continental drift, and he continued to refine his idea, which had continents being moved along a flowing conveyor belt–like mantle, even including a chapter on it in his 1944 *Principles of Physical Geology*. By 1960, others (mostly in England, where drift was more acceptable) were thinking about convection currents as a real possibility.

As for seafloor spreading, Hess hypothesized that the Earth's plates rest on top of a semiliquid layer. Because that semiliquid layer is undergoing convection, the ocean floor moves, pulling apart at ridges and rifts (such as the rift in the Mid-Atlantic Ridge), carrying the continents along with it. The plates eventually encounter each other again—crashing. But they don't just crash. One plate, Hess proposed, is actually forced beneath another, where it melts, getting recycled back into the Earth's mantle. This accounts for all the extra crust produced by seafloor spreading, a problem that had confounded drift supporters for decades.

The year 1960 is popularly accepted as the beginning of the revolution that swept geology and oceanography (and portions of other -ologies) up in its wake, the year in which it became clear that existing explanations for the formation of the Earth's surface no longer held. In his book *The Ocean of Truth: A Personal History of Global Tectonics*, H. W. Menard (the Scripps geologist who wrote to Bruce in 1957 to say he hadn't been able to find the rift valley in the Pacific and did not believe that it was worldwide) wrote that 1960 was the beginning of a decade "characterized by the chaos that precedes general acceptance of a theory." The theory that would be accepted was plate tectonics, and because of the chaos Menard described it's easy to draw a straight line that begins at present and extends backward to Hess—his "History of Ocean Basins" was published precisely when the chaos began to grow.

The starting point may have been abrupt—a year, a man, a paper—but the genesis was not. By 1960, Hess was the head of the geology department at Princeton, with a long CV packed with distinguished publications. And the circulated manuscript wasn't just some dog-eared sheaf of papers passed from the hands of one awed geologist to another. It was what has been called "elaborately presented": a spiral-bound progress report for the Office of Naval Research.

What factors made "History of Ocean Basins" possible? More than anything else, the paper is a synthesis of many different types of data—sediment measurements from cores, seismic refraction studies, paleomagnetism—the kinds of information Hess called "scraps of information" in his hotly worded rejection of Bruce's paper five years before. These were the same scraps that had led to the discovery of the rift whose existence Hess claimed had "shaken the foundations of geology," a world-circling rift valley that he now claimed was where the Earth's plates separated.

It's not totally objectionable that Hess did an about-face; rather, his move shows evidence of a progressive mind. But the way he went about his business also shows a careless disregard for citation—for giving credit where credit was due. While he did cite an article about the expanding Earth theory that Bruce had published in the *Scientific American* earlier that year (and presented in 1959 at the International Oceanographic Congress), he did not cite Marie's map, which synthesized all the "scraps" of information Doc and his students had been collecting for the past few decades, a map whose contents very well could have served as an illustration of Hess's "essay in geopoetry" if not for the fact that they predated the essay by several years. At a very basic level there simply was nothing else he could have looked at to get a detailed picture of the ocean floor, and there was no question that the idea of a worldwide rift had originated with Marie and Bruce; it would have been impossible for him to develop a theory about a global process that happened to take place in rift valleys without knowing that those valleys existed.

Hess's choice not to cite Marie's physiographic diagram or Heezen, Tharp, and Ewing's North Atlantic monograph—and to cite only Bruce's independently authored *Scientific American* article—was disingenuous. *Scientific American* was not peer-reviewed (and therefore not taken as seriously as journals that were); the Heezen, Tharp, and Ewing monograph was part of the "Special Paper" series published by no less than the Geological Society of America. For Bruce and Doc, Hess's failure to cite them would have been temporarily infuriating; they both published papers nearly continuously and received much attention for doing so. But Marie was devoted to the mapping work, work that took up nearly 100 percent of her time—and the discovery was hers more than theirs anyway.

Today Hess is considered one of the founders of plate tectonics; he gets whole chapters in history books that often also feature Doc and Bruce in starring roles. Marie usually gets a sentence of credit alongside her map. Sometimes she gets a page or two of recognition for her work in revealing the ocean floor or appears to narrate Bruce's legacy, but it stops there: her maps left disconnected from the seminal papers that transformed plate tectonics from a hypothesis to a theory.

CHAPTER 15

*I*N THE FALL OF 1961 THE GEOLOGICAL SOCIETY OF AMER-
ica published Marie and Bruce's second physiographic diagram.
This diagram showed the South Atlantic Ocean, included the Caribbean
and Scotia seas, and the eastern margin of the South Pacific Ocean.
Marie spent four years (from 1957, when she finished the North Atlantic,
until 1961) drawing the floors of these oceans, which had never been
done before; it took her only ten months to re-create the land masses surrounding the oceans, all of which had been well documented before.
When preparing these diagrams, Marie followed the same method she'd
used when drawing the North Atlantic: plotting profiles, examining
adjacent tracks for trends and regional characteristics, sketching the
relief of the terrain along the profiles, and filling in blank areas by
extrapolating and interpolating.

In July 1961, while the physiographic diagram of the South Atlantic
Ocean was in the process of being printed at the William and Heintz
Map Corporation in Washington, D.C., Marie wrote three letters to Bruce.
These letters show how deeply invested she was in what happened to her
work when she was finished drawing. After making a trip to D.C. to meet
with the printers, she went to Ohio, where her brother had carried on at
the farm in Bellefontaine after their father's death.

"Dear Bruce," she wrote on July 3, "I thought I would write you a letter about my adventures in Washington with the thought that it might save on your telephone bill." Bruce had just returned from Russia, a guest of the Academy of Sciences, and Marie wrote that she had waited until she was sure he was "back safe and sound."

"I left Piermont Monday, June 19 about 5:30 p.m. and arrived at William & Heintz next day about 1 p.m.," she wrote, "having spent the nite at a Mobil somewhere between Phila. and Baltimore. Fortunately, both Mr. Heintz & his son were there—the son showed me all around the plant—really a wonderful setup." On her tour, Marie got to see printing presses and a camera as "big as a room," none of which would be used on her map because it was, she repeatedly mentioned to Bruce, "too big." "I didn't see the actual outfits they did use on our map—but there was also a huge pie-shaped vat that they pour the colored inks in & whirl around to make the color proofs."

The printers, Marie told Bruce, had made up a blue-ink print of the South Atlantic map for her to review. All the ocean floor's texture had been transferred to a metal plate in order to make a negative, but Marie deemed the print made from it too pale—a disappointing result from four years of work. So she retouched the whole thing, took a "steel point which must have been used for 20 years or so" and etched the grooves deeper, thousands of miniature valleys in which blue ink would pool instead of water. She fixed a mistake this way, too. The Shag Rocks, a group of islands west of the Falkland Islands, were blurry, and the printer "offered to splice a piece in the negative and I expect they could have done it perfectly," she wrote. "But I went ahead, scratching in more lines on the negative & the next day still scratching."

There were also, she said, some mistakes with the markings of degrees along the border and concerning the legend she "suggested that Columbia University be set in smaller type." The big black Old English typeface "seemed a little overpowering," so they reduced it by about one-third. "It looked much better." And then there was the matter of the words *Lamont Geological Observatory.* "I also *wish* I had suggested that [they] be moved down a 1/8 inch from our names—just for proportion's sake—but I didn't." The map's contrast worried her the most. "I do hope you will give this matter of contrast your particular attention. I should be crushed to death if it is a washed out print . . . honest to goodness it's worth another trip to Washington to see the contrast of the print before a color proof is made ... I guess this is enuff for now." She signed off with the words, "Love Marie."

Her second letter, dated July 25, 1961, and sent from Bellefontaine, begins much like the first: she is worried about Bruce's phone bill reaching "astronomical proportions." She is "flabbergasted" to hear that the new oceanography building on the Lamont campus is almost done. "Excuse this writing but my hand is stiff from painting. I am doing the inside hall—changing dark doors to yellow. On rainy days I paint inside & when it quits raining for two days in a row I do windows outdoors." There follows some discussion of the lakes in the Andes. "They should not be solid blue or green or edged in green. If they do turn out any of the above ways I think the best thing would be to call up Mr. Heintz and have his boy paint out the color overlay & print the damn lakes in yellow."

The paragraphs that follow all use the word *also*: "I also hope you like." "I should also like to remind you." "Also I should like to know." "Also if this guy." "I am also happy to hear your little model is working out so well"—she was referring here to a globe of the world's ocean floors with raised relief that Bruce was trying to make. "Have you yet gotten a hold of some dental wax or softer material for final details? ... Somehow I would like to be back helping you. It's very lonely here. Well, keep me posted & write to me. Love Marie."

Marie never mentioned, in her letters from July 1961, all the new features that she had exposed for the first time in her map of the South Atlantic. What would she have said anyway? Also I should like to point out that we showed the Equatorial Mid-Ocean Canyon, which debauches into the Pernambuco Abyssal Plain, for the first time? Also I should like to note that we showed the Ameghino Canyon, off the coast of Argentina, and the submarine canyon of the Orange River, off the coast of South Africa? Also I should like to remind you that we discovered the Romanche and Chain fracture zones? Bruce didn't need to know these things, but in order to know the importance of her work, we do.

Although there were others shown on the South Atlantic map, the Romanche and Chain fracture zones were the largest. A fracture zone is a place where a ridge is offset. If you were to draw a vertical line on a sheet of paper (representing the ridge), tear the sheet in half along the horizontal axis (the tear being the fracture zone), then put the sheet back together so that the line still ran vertical on both sheets but did not line up, you'd have a simplified model of a fracture zone. Marie depicted fracture zones for the first time in the Atlantic Ocean, but they'd been discovered in 1955, in the Pacific, by Menard. In a 1960 *Science* paper, he called them "broad welts" with "very long straight faults" running parallel through each of their centers.

It was not just in her private letters that Marie refrained from verbalizing her accomplishments. Specific features are mentioned throughout the text that accompanies the South Atlantic physiographic diagrams, but their existence is not interpreted, their significance not elaborated upon. That may have been because, as Marie and Bruce wrote in the first sentence of that text, a monograph on the South Atlantic (like the one produced on the North Atlantic), "treating the nomenclature and the morphological, geological, and geophysical characteristics of the area included in the diagram [was] planned for publication by the Society in 1962."

Such a publication would have expanded on the diagrams, but a book-length treatise on the South Atlantic never appeared, so the "informal note" on the back of the South Atlantic physiographic diagram remains Marie and Bruce's only official report on the South Atlantic as a whole. In the note, there is no bravado, no inflated language, just the confident communication of their map's basics. Not only do they acknowledge a need for more data, writing that they would "be pleased to receive older soundings which may have been overlooked" and that they "welcome information concerning proposed or recently completed expeditions in the area," but they're also transparent about how the need for more data affected their final product, resulting in alterations—some canyons, they write, "had to be omitted because of the small scale of the diagram"—extrapolations, and possible mistakes. "The reader will appreciate the difficulty of drawing," they wrote, concerning mistakes, "and may anticipate the regions where errors may be large by studying the distribution of sounding lines on the [provided] track chart and comparing this with the physiographic diagram."

Did their readers actually appreciate the difficulty of drawing? In 1961 reviews of the North Atlantic diagram were just coming out; the reviewers did not necessarily appreciate the difficulty. In 1961 Menard, who was studying the Pacific Ocean floor but not creating physiographic diagrams with the data, was still writing letters to Bruce in which he said he could not find the rift valley in his surveys of the Pacific. Some people called the physiographic diagrams "hen scratching." A research ship captain once told Bruce that he noticed "people don't have nice things to say about your diagrams, but I notice they always have a copy in their cabin and they spend an awful lot of time looking at it."

Marie and Bruce's maps were nearly invisible if you looked at the lists of citations that appeared at the end of scholarly papers (as Marie later put it, "no one would reference maps)," but that didn't mean they weren't provocative: people talked about them. To the extent that, in a 1961 article, Doc and Bruce felt compelled to formalize their differing opinions about the formation of the rift Marie discovered. To do so, they offered what Menard, in his book, called an "unusual joint statement," a statement that publicly hinted at an increasing tension between Bruce and Doc— about theory, about Bruce's behavior and work, about things both petty and meaningful. "The present authors have concluded that the rifted-mid-oceanic ridge is dominated by extensional deformation (Heezen, Tharp, and Ewing, 1959)," Doc and Bruce wrote in their joint statement. "However, they each favor a different primary mechanism of the deformation and differ in their estimates of the amount of extension indicated. Ewing (Ewing and Ewing, 1959) favors a mechanism drawn by mantle convection currents, while Heezen (1959) believes that the extension results primarily from the internal expansion of the earth." Marie's thoughts on the primary mechanism of deformation were conspicuously absent. The results, however, were this: as their relationship with Doc grew first distant and then hostile, Marie and Bruce's bond became stronger, and the assumption was that she, too, believed in expansion, that her beliefs were identical to her partner's.

I HAVE IN front of me a photocopy of two newspaper clippings from the July 13, 1962, edition of the *Morgunbladid*, an Icelandic daily. In one clipping, Marie and Bruce look like movie stars, the photo like something snapped by a paparazzo. The amount of space that separates their bodies is just enough to prevent misinterpretation: they are not a couple. Or, perhaps, they don't want the viewer to think they're a couple.

Between them is a broad stone staircase leading up to a building. Bruce's most notable features are a wide tie and a big white square name tag on his lapel. Marie is shown in three-quarter profile. She is not facing

Bruce and large sunglasses cover her eyes. Her cheekbones are prominent, her lips rouged, her coat open, and her hands are in her pockets. She's wearing a multistrand necklace whose beads have gone all pixilated and unidentifiable in the photocopy. Her hair skims the top of her collar. It looks the same in the second clipping, which shows the back of her head and a sliver of the side of her face, looking on as Bruce smiles at another man, his right arm extended as if they're shaking hands.

Bruce went to Iceland at least three times, possibly many more. Submarine cruises in the Northern Atlantic likely launched from there, and he went on many of those. I know he went in 1960 because in my files I have a letter he wrote to Menard about his "excursion" after a conference in Helsinki, where, he noted, the papers were "fair but [not] sensational." His second trip there was with Marie, in the summer of 1962, so that they could give a paper on the submarine foundation of Iceland and the possible land connections.

Iceland's rocky terrain is "literally," wrote Marie in her unpublished "Opus," "a geologist's paradise." In a 1971 book Bruce coauthored with former student Charles Hollister, titled *The Face of the Deep*, he noted that a visit to Iceland was a necessity for any submarine geologist, for it is there that one can "examine features of the earth's suboceanic crust nowhere else exposed above the waves." Because Iceland is part of the Mid-Atlantic Ridge, it's cleaved (like the rest of the ridge) down its center by the Mid-Atlantic Rift Valley. It lies atop the plume that formed it, an upwelling of magma from deep within the Earth's mantle that hardened when it reached open air. Proxy for what lies beneath the oceans.

They rent a Cessna for twenty-eight dollars, fly up into the clear cloudless summer sky. Sunlight bounds off the airplane's skin and temporarily blinds them. When their eyes finally adjust, things look strange and new, all of it amplified by the exhilaration of being aloft, proportions and relationships set askew. Air like the sea, insistent on their skin. Headsets like avocado halves, one covering each ear so they can hear each other talk. The low corduroy buzz of the engine. Marie's fingerprints on the window like curls of smoke. Bruce's forehead free of creases, gone smooth as a shark belly. He's unfurrowed his brow, he's excited for her to see this land.

The ground they're flying a few hundred feet above is familiar. It looks like one of Marie's physiographic diagrams, only three-dimensional and in full color: real instead of a pen-and-ink drawing. Bruce takes pictures while Marie takes in the land, the structures she's been drawing and thinking about for the past decade exposed to her for the first time. She's getting a true bird's-eye view of the Earth's surface instead of having to imagine it on her own.

They're all eyes, translating. Things from their everyday lives are rendered fantastic, huge or tiny, it's hard to tell, mundane objects carousing with features that belong on the ocean floor. The grass is so green it's chartreuse, the faraway uneven patches scaled down to lichen size and creeping over stones. Stands of pines like fuzzy tufts of moss. Solid streams of three-thousand-year-old black lava. Steaming hot springs resemble ladles of consommé. Volcanic cones have nearly perfect circles scooped out of their tops—some with glassy turquoise water pooled in their depressions, some dented like fedoras and covered with plants. A glacial lagoon is a punch bowl scattered with floating chunks of ice. Beehive-shaped hornitos, which form when lava is forced up through the cooling surface of a flow, accumulate vertically around a hollow center. Boulders piled against seaside cliffs like marbles in a cigar box. Cave openings like belly buttons. Look at that, Marie says over and over again, without turning to look at him. I know, he says, knowing just what she wants him to photograph.

Marie sketches without looking down. She captures textures, patterns, and small shapes, details too small to ever be picked up by the precision depth recorder that measures the ocean floor rift. As time passes, her pages fill up with these swatches of the Earth's surface. Vegetation nubby like an old wool sweater. Spread-out lava floes, some cracked as dry elbow skin, some round and intricate as the leaves of a liverwort plant. Coastal sand arranged by receding waves, marbled like the endpapers of an antique book. Her pencil flying across the pages, Bruce's finger on the shutter release, their necks craned and faces close to the windows.

The structure they're most interested in is the rift valley. It comes ashore in the south and extends north through the countryside, sinking into the Greenland Sea at the northernmost part of the country. They tell the pilot to zigzag over it, the way Bruce tells a ship's captain to zigzag over an oceanic rift. High up in the air they can see more of the rift spread out beneath them; closer to the ground they can see smaller crevices. In some places it's hundreds of meters wide, speckled with houses and

striped by streams; in others it's hardly a meter wide, walls nearly vertical, lumpy and rough and different shades of gray. In one place, an interrupted river falls over the edge, creating a waterfall. In another, its walls
are blocky and columnar, sort of like listing castle walls. Each view is a
treat, a taste of the impossible. Because short of parting the seas, drain-
ing the oceans, no one will ever get to see comparable expanses of the
actual rift on the ocean floor, get to see it in such panoramic detail.

The sun is close to the horizon when they come back in the evening.
When it gets there it will stay, not fully set, for a few short hours until it
rises again; pure darkness doesn't occur this close to the solstice. Instead,
oranges and golds color the mountains and fill the cabin of the plane.
So they rest, put down the camera and notebook. Marie smiles wide. The
feeling she has is similar to what she felt after Cousteau showed his film
at the Oceanographic Congress. Work paying off, hypotheses proven,
intuitions confirmed. It was right to draw the rift the way she had; it was
right to have made it a world-encircling feature even though they didn't
have soundings everywhere; it was right to have returned to Lamont
after she quit. She looks at Bruce, his body twisted to look out the window, a palm on his thigh, an arm bent, his shoulder tucked up near his
ear as he pushes himself up close to the window. It was right to keep working with him.

They don't talk. They sit quiet and content next to each other, flying
back toward Reykjavík and looking down at the earth. I wonder if Marie
tried to conjure this day on the day she got the news that Bruce had died.
The circumstances were similar—Iceland, late June—and thus the leap
would have been small. Time looped over on itself, the present knotted to
the past, opposing emotions united. Or if the memories all ganged up on
her in a chaotic swirl, inks in a vat, blending until they were the correct
shade.

CHAPTER 16

THE CONCEPTS DESCRIBED BY THE TERMS *CONTINENTAL drift* and *plate tectonics* are not the same. *Plate tectonics* describes a much more sophisticated and complete theory that evolved from continental drift. When Wegener proposed continental drift in the teens and twenties, he offered proof that he could see and describe: the fit of the continental shelves, the similarities of species and fossils on both sides of the Atlantic, the similarity of the geologic record. He was right when he said that these facts, compounded, offered proof that the Earth's surface was made up of plates that moved. By the mid-1960s, however, scientists had developed tools that had the ability to collect previously invisible data. They used these data to construct hypotheses that allowed them to move beyond continental drift, forming the basis for the theory now referred to as plate tectonics—which not only asserts that the Earth's surface is composed of moving plates, but also describes where, when, and why those plates move.

Scientists had been using magnetometers, which are instruments that can be towed behind ships to record the strength and direction of the ocean floor's magnetic field, since the 1940s. Such measurements were possible because the ocean floor is composed of basalt, a volcanic rock rich in iron and the highly magnetic mineral magnetite. As basalt cools, it "records" the Earth's magnetic field. By the 1950s scientists knew that the Earth's crust exhibited erratic magnetism—rocks from some places were strongly magnetic, others weak; some were positive, some negative. There didn't seem to be any rhyme or reason to it—Lamont, which towed a magnetometer on every cruise, had picked up strong magnetism over the Mid-Atlantic Rift but had not ventured a guess as to why—until scientists found that the seafloor off the coast of California exhibited magnetic stripes. The stripes ran parallel to one another and the coast and were irregular, with patterning like a zebra skin. But instead of alternating between black and white (and being visible to the eye), the stripes alternated between positive and negative polarization—invisible until the magnetometer revealed the pattern.

The pattern's significance remained mysterious until September 1963, when *Nature* published a paper connecting the phenomenon to Hess's seafloor spreading hypothesis. It was called "Magnetic Anomalies over Oceanic Ridges," and authored by Drummond Hoyle Matthews and Frederick John Vine. It used Harry Hess's seafloor spreading hypothesis and periodic magnetic reversals of the Earth's poles to explain the magnetic striping of the seafloor. Fifteen years later, Teddy "Crisp" Bullard, by then a professor at Cambridge, described Vine and Matthews's hypothesis by saying that if, as they asserted, a "strip of new ocean floor was continually being formed" in the rift valley, it "would provide a double tape recording of the intensity and the reversals of the Earth's magnetic field."

Vine and Matthews's paper wasn't the first to recognize this information. A paper written by another man—arguing that the seafloor spreads at ridge crests and the Earth's magnetic field reverses itself—had in fact already been rejected by *Nature* and the *Journal of Geophysical Research*. The author was Lawrence Morley, a professor at the University of Toronto, and he'd completed his paper before Vine began his. But Vine hadn't seen Morley's manuscript or heard about his ideas—as Bill Menard wrote in *The Ocean of Truth*, his history of the development of plate tectonics, "the year 1963 clearly was a time when the stage was set for a conceptual leap forward."

The stage was set, but the audience was not exactly receptive. Morley's paper, after all, had been rejected; the editor at the *Journal of Geophysical Research* wrote him to say that it was more suitable for discussion at a cocktail party than publication. In his book, Menard offers a list of the immediate reactions to the published Vine-Matthews hypothesis: another Cambridge professor said that for a whole year and a half after its publication, he "never took the Vine-Matthews hypothesis seriously"; Cambridge's 1963 annual report from the geology department did not mention the hypothesis as one of the year's achievements; and one American professor called it "rather ridiculous." And a year later, the American scientist Gordon MacDonald, a member of the National Academy of Sciences and of President Johnson's Scientific Advisory Committee, published a paper in *Science* that obstinately refuted continental drift. Isostasy, MacDonald wrote, prevails.

Further evidence for what was still being referred to as continental drift was presented in March 1964, when a symposium addressing it was convened at the Royal Society of London. In attendance were many of the Americans who had already pledged their varying levels of allegiance to continental drift: Hess, Heezen, Menard. British physicist Sir Patrick Blackett gave the symposium's introductory remarks, saying that in geology "a highly simplified model which can explain a large number of observed facts is invaluable, especially when it suggests new observations." He was not referring to Marie and Bruce's maps, which could have been described the same way, but to good old Teddy "Crisp" Bullard et al., who had brought to the symposium a different breed of maps: ones produced with the help of a "digital" computer. Using the fixed point (or Euler's— pronounced "oiler's") theorem, which says that "any displacement . . . of a continent may be considered as a rigid rotation about a vertical axis through some point on the surface of the earth," they were able to show how well the continents around the Atlantic Ocean fit together.

More discoveries followed. In 1965 a scientist named John Tuzo Wilson published a paper in *Nature* titled "A New Class of Faults and Their Bearing on Continental Drift." It said that what Marie and Bruce had called fracture zones on their 1961 South Atlantic diagram were actually "transform faults": places where plates grind horizontally past each other. The most helpful description of the appearance of transform faults I've encountered comes not from Wilson, but from *The Mapmakers*, a book published in the 1980s by a *New York Times* science writer named John Noble Wilford. He uses the Mid-Atlantic Ridge as an example, writing that "every few hundred kilometers the ridge is severed and shifted some-what by a deep fault, producing an effect much like a long French loaf that has been sliced and then moved so that the slices no longer match up."

By 1965, scientists were starting to describe the generalized move-ment of the Earth's plates that had been named "Bullard's fit" and two of the three types of localized plate movement. There were Wilson's trans-form faults, which explained the lateral grinding that takes place at cer-tain plate boundaries, such as the San Andreas Fault. And there was what would come to be called the Vine-Matthews-Morley hypothesis, which explained what happened at places where two pieces of the Earth's crust pulled apart from each other, such as the rift valley of the Mid-Atlantic Ridge. Bruce called this rift valley a "monstrous scar," and a "wound that never heals," but it is these types of boundaries, where the Earth rifts and then heals itself, that growth occurs. A scar, after all, is a wound that's been treated improperly, and a wound will refuse to heal for only two reasons: if it's been ignored or if a deeper, more serious issue is at work.

CHAPTER 17

THE STORY OF HOW THE INDIAN OCEAN MAP CAME INTO existence unfolds rather like the plot of a *Mission: Impossible* episode. It's 1961 and Marie is Jim Phelps, diligently working in her office on a map of the Mediterranean ocean floor when the ringing telephone startles her. The male voice on the other end belongs to the Secretary (here played by Brackett Hersey, a Woods Hole scientist), and he asks for Bruce. Marie tells Hersey that Bruce is at sea, puts down her pencil to listen.

The International Indian Ocean Expedition (IIOE) is under way, Hersey tells her, and he's on the planning committee. It's being sponsored by UNESCO; it began in 1959 and will last until 1965. He's sure Marie is aware that almost nothing is known about the Indian Ocean floor. He has no doubt that she is also aware that no map of the Indian Ocean floor exists, as she herself has not drafted one. Expedition, he says, is a bit of a misnomer, as the IIOE will be a huge undertaking. The goal is to have dozens of cruises and international cooperation—with scientists from all over the world working together to advance knowledge and survey the region's food sources in an attempt to solve some of its hunger crises. And while he is, he says, only a member of the planning committee and not its leader, he feels compelled to suggest that she get involved. Her mission, he says, if she chooses to accept it, will be to quickly produce a map of the Indian Ocean floor so that scientists can use it to identify problems and informational gaps.

Interesting, says Marie, as she looks through her office's doorway to the GEBCO charts pasted in the hallway. She leans way over to one side so she can see farther down the hall, to the contours of the Indian Ocean. Then she looks down at the in-progress map of the Mediterranean on her desk; it's a small one as far as oceans go. They agree that the Indian Ocean would be a more exciting project. And as always, Hersey says, you have carte blanche as to your methods and personnel.

In the next scene, Marie flips the clasp on a large leather box. For fun, let's say she's smoking a cigarette and sipping a martini. Inside the box are copies of A. K. Lobeck's 1945 physiographic diagrams of Asia and Australia; the Bartholomew (several generations of men named John who did their own cartography and started making maps beginning in the early nineteenth century) maps of Africa and Asia at a 1:10,000,000 scale; the *Atlas Mira*, a Russian-produced atlas of all the world's continents; and the *Atlas Morskoi*, a Russian-produced atlas of the oceans' currents, temperatures, and other water features. She will use all of these materials as reference in her preparation of the map.

Beneath the maps and books are personnel files. There is, of course, Bruce. She takes a packet that includes a column of black-and-white passport snapshots of him wearing various expressions and hats, as well as his Columbia University student and faculty records, off the top of the file and tosses it onto her desk. There is also what looks like a surveillance photo of Doc and Joe Worzel (now Lamont's assistant director), wearing suits and walking across a lawn at Lamont—she must get permission from Joe before she starts the project, so she tosses that picture on top of Bruce's. There's a student ID card for Howard Foster, the deaf art student who, in 1952, plotted the earthquake epicenters that helped Marie discover the Mid-Atlantic Rift; that goes on the pile, too. There are plastic sleeves with information on Hester Haring, Lucy Franceschini, Allen Lowrie, and Michael Schneck, who all already work for Lamont, and one for Leonard Marier, who will be hired to index the data from institutions all over the world that will begin rapidly accumulating. Finally, she leafs through a stack of applications from high school kids—

mimeographed forms covered with blotchy iris ink and black pen, year-book photos clipped to their corners—and chooses four. This is her team.

Fade to black, cue *Mission: Impossible* theme. The combined sound of silvery trilling woodwinds and a quick-struck triangle tell your heart to pump faster, your brain to pay attention. A hand strikes a match and touches it to a braided white fuse, which sputter-sparks across the still-black scene. The bongo and the brass enter quickly and the heat thrown by the fuse seems to have triggered the movement of a reel, a hash of images beating past in rapid succession, each one a cell packed with activity. There are grad students bent over fathograms and ship logs; there's a tight shot of their red grease pencil markings ringed like lipstick around peaks and valleys; there's a close-up of pale green gridded pages filled with the fathoms they've converted to meters. Cut to Allen Lowrie and Michael Schneck, cast as great submarine detectives, two men on two stools side by side, reading profiles and plotting data and checking PDR records for errors until the entrance of the flute's signature sound catches them like twin left hooks, their heads whipping round for the *da-da-duuuh da-da-duuuh da-duh*, then sinking down behind the upturned high collars of their trench coats.

Leonard Marier's fingers move so quickly through the filing cabinet that flesh blurs with manila, becoming one, becoming faster as the massive stack of profiles races toward the ceiling beside him, fast as a bongo mini-solo. There's Bruce's return from sea, sunlight glinting off the vestigial fins of his convertible as it swings into a parking space at Lamont; there's Bruce nodding and smiling as Marie explains that the team is working hard on the Indian Ocean; there's Bruce's hand on an electric eraser as it shimmies over an area of Marie's sketch that he disagrees with, his erasure interrupted by Marie's hand, releasing a glass paperweight that arcs through the air before smashing into the wall next to his head. Cut to his shocked expression.

Every day, boxes of fathograms covered with stamps from all around the world arrive at Lamont. Bruce's students, squatting on the floor next to unfurled PDR records stretched down the length of an entire hallway of the Oceanography Building, draw stars next to significant depths and write out descriptions of what they think they see. A secretary sneaks a quick smile at a mailman as he loads a few tubes with a preliminary version of Marie's sketch into his truck, and Marie laughs with a Russian scientist who is pointing to a string of nine underwater mountains that should be one—nine crossings over the Ob' Seamount, misinterpreted by Marie as nine crossings over nine separate peaks.

Enter the bass trombones, the melody's darkening pitch matching Doc's mood as he rips one of the preliminary sketches off a wall at Cambridge, where it had been hung at Marie and Bruce's request to solicit suggestions. Bruce watches as Doc slams one fist on his desk and uses the other to wave around a memo about getting his permission before sharing findings. Enter the rainlike sound of the cymbals below the deep brass, not slammed with a mallet but touched lightly with a wire brush. Cue Bruce checking and rechecking profiles and province maps, the condensation of three months of work into a three-second clip, the main constant his big hand, sweeping flat across the diagram, a quarter-sun curve stretching from Madagascar to southern Burma, a way to start the day by touching the work, a way to end the day, too—a hands-on gesture of good-bye.

Now the trumpets return, picking up the *da-da-duuuh da-da-duuuh da-duh* of the refrain. They accompany the arrival of a special delivery, just when Marie and Bruce thought they were done: a notebook filled with hand-copied soundings from the Japanese team arrives, by sea mail no less, just in time to fill in some of the areas for which they had no data. Zoom in on a hand inking in the title block, the letters spelling the names of the forty-five representatives from seven countries who contributed data and the titles of agencies that funded the project—a sign that the map is complete, nearly ready for the world to see.

The cymbals make themselves heard again in the background. Marie and Bruce hop in a car, get out at the Keuffel and Esser printing plant in Long Island. Cue Bruce's hand routing across the map again, smoothing it so he and Marie can tell the printers what they want. Begin bongo roll, each slap of the drum accompanied by a swift close-up of a particular feature never before seen by man: the Indus Cone, the Ninety East Ridge, the Kerguelen Ridge—the tempo swift, the images passing at flip-book speed. Enter the hi-hat as Marie and Bruce clink together tumblers in celebration at the airport, the hi-hat as they sip their drinks, the hi-hat as their plane takes off against a sunset sky, bound for New Delhi by way of London, Athens, and Tehran to present their map to the other participants of the International Indian Ocean Expedition.

*   *   *

THEY GO TO India for the conference but stay for the geology. Bruce had been asked to keynote the weeklong discussion by presenting their newly finished map. What he'd planned as a twenty-minute talk turned into an hour. When that was finished, he and Marie answered question after question, rock stars kept onstage by their fans. The rest of the trip to India is for travel, exploration, and casual research.

Marie gets a spot on the conference-sponsored field trip because some poor Japanese professor got quarantined on arrival, so she and Bruce share an air-conditioned sleeper car to Kalka, the train climbing a steep winding Himalayan incline up to Simla, the old British "summer capital." The field trip is educational; Marie and Bruce get to know the rocks of the area pretty well and the personalities of their fellow scientists even better. The story of how the rocks got there (eight thousand feet above sea level) remains hazy even after the usual examination (photographing, peering down one's nose, chipping away bits with a penknife, rubbing those bits between thumb and forefinger, perhaps touching tongue to resultant powder), for each formation presents the opportunity to argue, to disagree with the local scientists, to exhibit disdain for the extant Indian maps.

They take a bus north to Tattapani with snow falling white against the gray not-shale, against the green of a golf course. Corsages of deep violet and gold have been pinned to the utilitarian coats and sweaters of pick- and mallet-wielding scientists by the lovely wife of the area's managing geologist. Marie watches cold blue water rush down from the mountain peaks to meet the bubbling hot spring water coming up from the ground. Boulders the size of watermelons have been transported from farther inland by the flowing river. A quarry outside of Simla exhibits clear evidence of cross-bedding and penecontemporaneous folding. The trip back to town is made in the moonlight, the headlights' glow contrasting with the pitch emptiness where the road ends in cliffside. Thick snow the next day makes for bad traffic. The people of Simla are trying to save their potatoes from the frost, so the buses are packed—60 percent people, 40 percent potato, which doesn't even account for all the foreigners trying to sightsee.

After the field trip is the actual International Geological Congress, and after that Marie and Bruce are itching to see things on their own. For the most part, they avoid tourist spots, and when they do arrive at such places, they do so very late at night or early in the morning, when they're likely to have to share the space only with guards or the devout and when the light off the rising moon or sun exaggerates the view. They arrive at the Taj Mahal a little after midnight. The moon is three days past full. They grip the grillwork of the gates, look beyond the ironwork to the tomb and its pool. Minarets rise up and down, reflected in the water, their finials like the flames of a double-ended candle. Marble surfaces glow. Trees and bushes flatten to dark silhouettes against the sky. When they return to the Taj early the next morning the sun is rising and the buildings have more dimension and Marie and Bruce get up close to the intricate carvings and mineral inlays on the interior walls, examine them like geological formations.

From New Delhi they fly to Bangkok, where they cross and recross the city by boat, following the canals, hopping out for temples and markets and, on Christmas Eve, to dine with the vice president of the Union Oil Company and his wife. They discuss the drilling prospects in the plateau of northeastern Thailand, whether the geology and distribution will combine favorably for the oil company. They visit with the couple's small pet ape and lizards, attend a candlelight service at the local interdenominational church. They fly from Bangkok to Hong Kong, from Hong Kong to Taipei. On the flight from Bangkok they switch from aisle to window seats so they can study the land as it passes beneath them, comparing the relief of the real Thailand, Laos, and Vietnam to what Marie sketched out on the far right of her physiographic diagram of the Indian Ocean.

Pretty good, Bruce tells her.

Especially considering, says Marie—alluding to how little time she had, how sparse the data for the Asiatic islands had been. Their eyes scan the plains cut by rivers, the rectangular rice paddies. Not very well formed, says Bruce of one mountain range. Rather disordered, Marie murmurs in reply, sketching in further detail on top of her printed diagram.

Scattered, says Bruce, also self-correcting. It's exciting to see these areas for real when they've only ever seen them on maps.

For most of the flight to Taipei, all they can see is the tops of clouds—until close to their destination, when a peak pierces the clouds and they're able to identify it from Marie's diagram. Yushan, says Bruce, I think. Or Xueshan, says Marie, but I can't tell just how far north we are. And then the male half of the tourist couple sitting behind them leans forward to talk to them between the crack in the seat.

Nice map you got there, he says. Bruce turns in his seat. The man's wife nods.

Yushan, says Marie to Bruce without looking at him, definitely. Here, you can see—

Where'd you buy it, the man asks, also addressing Bruce. Think we can get one at the airport newsstand when we land? Bruce stares at him for a moment, blinks. Marie is still looking between her map and the land. The clouds have broken. At thirty-five thousand feet the scale is different, but Marie's sketched features are still confirmed.

We made it, Bruce says.

You made it, the man says. It's less a question and more a notification that he doesn't quite understand. You mean we can't buy it anywhere, his wife asks.

No, Marie tells them. I think we'll be able to see Xueshan soon, she says to Bruce, if the visibility holds. She finally turns in her seat to look at the couple. Unless you're members of the Geological Society of America, she says. Are you members of the Geological Society of America?

In Taipei they stay at the Imperial, which has floors of buffed serpentine, commonly found in oceanic crust.

During their flight to Sydney, they forgo sleep to get a look at an approximately nine-hundred-mile stretch of Australia, catch glimpses of New Zealand far in the distance. The sun rises to reveal the Australian outback, no cultivation, just the grays and browns of the desert, the land so flat that even with the strong shadows of the early morning sun it's hard to see the relief of the low hills and dunes. And the slow-gaining elevation of the Great Dividing Range, rising gently from the desert to the crest, smooth except where there are gum trees. Old worn mountains, Bruce says. They're just tired, Marie says. It is 1965; Marie is forty-five, Bruce forty-one, and they've been mapping the ocean floor for thirteen years.

Two or three hundred miles from Sydney they spot a broad sediment-filled double valley. Two grooves running parallel, except where the valleys are offset twenty or thirty miles by an east–west fracture. In that place it reminds them both of the same thing: an undersea fracture zone, like the Romanche or the Chain. Marie has just enough time to capture it before the clouds come, blocking their view, acting like water, covering the offset so they can only imagine its existence down there.

When they land in Sydney they check in to their hotel, throw on clean clothes, and catch a taxi to the offices of the Australian Hydrographic Service. There, the deputy commander makes a crack about their map. Just don't think it's accurate, is what he says. I don't think the ocean floor looks like that, he adds. Marie and Bruce can understand this; they explain their objective to him, their desire to present as realistic a picture of the ocean floor as possible, using the most up-to-date information they have access to. They tell him about their methodology. They make clear that they are serious, ask if Australia is willing to share its fathograms with them. By the time they leave, it seems they've changed the deputy commander's mind just a little; he lets on that he might send some data, that he'd be open to a Lamont ship visiting in the future.

When they get to their hotel in New Zealand the copies of the Indian Ocean proofs are waiting for them. Marie and Bruce spend the day meeting with various geologists, have a brief dinner with one and his wife, and then take the cable car back to their hotel for a night of work. Bent over the proofs long into the night, they root out typos in the text accompanying the diagram and find, on the diagram itself, one possible mistake, west of Borneo—Bruce thinks he sees an island where an island shouldn't be.

They spend only one day in Fiji because both of them are sick upon arrival. Bruce declares it food poisoning. Marie stays in bed, her day in Fiji spent fevered and claustrophobic under the sheets. Bruce ventures out in the pouring rain to find medicine for them both, tries to see through the sheets of rain falling all around his cab to the countryside beyond, but the visibility is bad and they're on the far and sparsely populated side of the island. He returns to the hotel empty-handed and soaked to the skin. He looks at her sleeping curled body and worries. The next morning, Marie doesn't seem to be getting any better, so they catch the midnight plane to Hawaii.

Despite this mysterious illness (which cleared temporarily—they went from Hawaii to Scripps, in San Diego, before returning to New York), the trip was a success. Worth every penny of the one-way ticket to New Delhi that Lamont paid for, every penny of the rest of the trip that Marie paid for herself. In a way, this trip is a sort of scaled-down version of the larger story of Marie's life, a story filled with such momentum that it pauses only when forces beyond her control exert themselves. Perpetual motion, like a Newton's Cradle with its five silver balls suspended on taut wire Vs that swing—until ball number one is plucked out of the air, held between two fingers, separate from the others, the process forced to a halt.

SHORTLY AFTER MARIE and Bruce returned home, Doc and Worzel urgently requested Bruce's presence. "They informed me," Bruce wrote in a 1970 statement to Columbia University's vice president, "that I would be required to leave Lamont on July 1, 1965, if I did not 'change my ways.' With the exception of the charges that I disobeyed parking regulations and that at certain times my vocabulary offended them, no other charges, specific problems, or instances were indicated. They gravely warned, 'you know what we mean.'" Bruce said he didn't. It's possible that the action was belated retribution for having distributed the preliminary copies of the Indian Ocean physiographic diagrams without Doc's approval, but the true cause is unclear. This marked the beginning of a constant and increasing pressure, exerted by Doc, that Marie and Bruce would come to refer to as The Harassment.

Marie also felt the effects of Doc's displeasure, although somewhat indirectly. As the result of her trip around Asia with Bruce, she received a letter from Joe Worzel (who was Doc's assistant director of Lamont) reprimanding her for charging some of her trip expenses against one of Lamont's National Science Foundation grants. Not all of her expenses for the entire trip—she paid everything after the conference in New Delhi. Such expenses, wrote Worzel, were unjustified unless the individual who'd racked them up had presented a paper at the conference in question and the paper presented was "significant." "Did you, in fact, present such a paper," Worzel asked in his letter. "If not, can you present us with a piece of paper that justifies these travel funds?"

This situation is much more concrete than the one Bruce experienced; there was a purported cause (improper expenses) and an effect (chastisement). In Lamont's defense, Marie had not followed protocol by obtaining permission from Doc (the grantee of the NSF money) before leaving. She readily admits this in her reply to Worzel. However, as indicated by

Worzel's use of the word *paper* five times in two paragraphs, the problem was not so much that Marie did not first obtain Doc's permission but rather that her work, again, was not presented in an acceptable format. That a significant contribution to science could be made in the form of map, that the audience at the conference had been well served by the long question-and-answer session they had with Marie and Bruce, seemed not to occur to him or, by extension, Doc. The physiographic diagram of the Indian Ocean floor, which opened the international discussion that Marie and Bruce traveled to New Delhi to attend, was deemed worthless.

Worzel also ignored how Marie's work (both in the office and in public "presentations") was profoundly affected by her gender. Her gender prevented her from going out on Lamont expeditions, which in turn forced her to collect information about the ocean floor in unconventional ways: studying the relief of Iceland and India, forming a partnership with a man who could go out on ships and was an ace at exchanging data with other scientists. Her gender was the reason she'd been cast as research assistant when she first appeared at Lamont; it was why Doc had turned her over to Bruce back in 1952 when she'd tried to quit her job; it was why all of the work she'd subsequently done had to carry his name and why, of the two of them, Bruce was always the one asked to deliver presentations of their work.

In a box at the Library of Congress, in a file marked "Interdepartmental Correspondence, 1965," inside an envelope marked "Joe Worzel Letter after Trip India," I found almost a dozen different drafts of Marie's carefully worded reply to Worzel. The drafts are each slightly different, tissue-paper-thin sheets of canary yellow paper, crisp and crinkly and marked up with pencil. In them, Marie does not shy from defending herself. "As the Indian Ocean Physiographic Diagram had been my sole project for 2½ years," she wrote in the final draft of her reply, "and as I have been a co-author with Bruce on this series, there was no doubt in my mind that the presentation of this diagram at a discussion meeting justified my trip."

At the meeting, she went on, no formal papers were to be presented. Rather, the meeting "consisted of a week-long discussion punctuated by the informal presentation of material which provided the basis for discussion. Our contribution opened the meeting." That contribution was the Indian Ocean floor physiographic diagram, on which Bruce gave the official, opening talk. When he was done, they "both responded to questions in the long discussion period which followed" and in other discussions throughout the weeklong meeting.

Did Marie, as Worzel asked, present a significant paper? To be precise, no: she did not rise and stand behind a lectern and read from a typescript; Bruce did that. Did she do what she could, considering the restrictions placed on her? Yes: she did the majority of the work on the physiographic diagram, she helped Bruce write the paper, she fielded questions from the audience. Did she have, as Worzel wrote, a "piece of paper that justifie[d]" her travel to the meeting? No: just as there is no official record of the impact of Jacques Cousteau's Mid-Atlantic Rift film at the 1959 International Oceanographic Congress, there's no official record of how Marie's presence at the New Delhi meeting affected her colleagues. There's only her word: "All the subsequent speakers, including the Russians, referred constantly to our diagram," she continued in her letter to Worzel. "Several prominent scientists thanked us for our attendance and contribution." Was her presence at the meeting justified? I suppose the answer to that question depends on your view of Bruce: could he have done what he did without her?

AT THE TIME of this correspondence with Worzel, Marie was sick. The illness she'd experienced in Fiji had come back and turned out to be a form of stomach cancer. During her recovery, Doc agreed to let her work from home. That was something she'd done occasionally in the past, to avoid distractions when facing a hard deadline, but this time the arrangement became permanent; even after she was declared cancer-free by her doctors, Marie never worked on Lamont's campus again. When an interviewer asked her, in 1994, if that was "literally" true, Marie's reply was this: "Well, very infrequently. Just a visitor. I did the Indian Ocean at Lamont and then we went to India and when I came back I never went back. One thing led to another and it was best to stay home."

While her illness was the catalyst for the locational change, working from home wouldn't have been an option had Marie not recently purchased a house big enough to spread out her data and drawings and supplies. In 1962 she'd moved from her small apartment in Nyack to a spacious Dutch colonial she bought for herself in the same town. I wish there was a picture of Marie standing next to her new home at the foot of Washington Avenue, on the western bank of the Hudson. I want to see her smile, her pride in the three stories rising up behind her—because it was not a common thing, in 1962, for a single woman to buy a house, even stranger that it was such a stately home, sitting on such a prime piece of waterfront property. It was not a house bought with money from a divorce, not a house bound for child rearing.

I can only imagine the house based on her words and later pictures and its state when I was there the year after she died: ivy having taken over the façade, braced to the bricks around the front door and bay windows, the wide dormer she added to the third floor like some great thoracic hump. And the weeds, which she said were six feet tall when she moved in, tall thin stalks with paintbrush tips that touched in the breeze.

She had intended it to be a home, just for her. And like all the structures that played an important role in her life, she mapped it, named its individual features. There were nicknames for the different rooms of her house, her cars, her maps, the area next to her house where the trash was kept. An outside sitting area was called Stonehenge. There's no need to imagine the interior, at least not the basics, for Marie mapped it in detail, on big eleven-by-seventeen pieces of paper that I found folded up in a black binder at the Library of Congress.

These maps look a little bit like treasure maps—with slide projectors, luggage closets, and phone tables instead of palm trees, skulls, and gold. There's a map for each floor (basement, main floor, second floor, and third floor/attic). Strange circles, some with Vs inside, some with Xs, some connected by lines, are drawn in on all three floors. At first I thought they showed where, as the 1960s continued, her growing crew of workers sat; I connected these circles to notes in the maps' margins that said "20 heads" or "4 heads east side." But they don't add up, and some are in weird places where no one would ever have sat to work: on a flight of stairs, in the middle of a light table.

So much else of the texture of Marie's daily life is revealed on these maps, though, that the mystery of the circles has come not to matter much. Life and work are unevenly integrated in the drawings, with work shoving life to the fringes. Enter the living room, on the first floor, and go clockwise: window, chest, organ, chair with ottoman, newspaper clippings, table, sofa back pressed against light table to form an island in the center, dining table and chairs, window, tea table, table top (shelf underneath), fireplace, and television. Cross the foyer and enter the library: phone table, current projects, work table, art books, window, stationery, chest, window, light table in center, chairs scattered, flat file filled with previous projects and blank paper.

Go down the basement steps and hang a left: shelves with maps, window, island of three shelves in the center (one with rocks, one with negatives of photostats, one unmarked); pass the door leading to the porch: another island of shelves (reprints and fathograms from the RV *Eltanin*), clothes dryer, window, washing machine, window, sinks; enter bathroom: sink, toilet, bathtub, shelves; exit bathroom. Pass photo dryer, head back toward stairs: wine cellar, grocery store; enter new room: process camera tracks running down center, dehumidifier, light table, glassine envelopes, light, light, vacuum frame, light, window, light, Polaroid film. Exit room, hang a right, pass paint shop: fluorescent light tubes and photo chemicals, light, photostat machine, light, furnace, water heater, electrical parts, window, work bench, refrigerated film strorage, file cabinet, window, sinks; enter developing room: chemicals, film, sinks, telephone.

Back up the stairs to the main floor, up the stairs to the second floor: project conference area in hall, slide projector, closet; enter Red Room: light table, window, map shelf, light table, window, current projects, reference books, profiles, door to porch, light table, atlases, window, island of desks in center, stationery, phone, supplies, Bruce's book, profiles, reference books; enter restroom: toilet, sink, shower; exit restroom to Red Room; exit to hallway, hang a left, pass another restroom, enter Marie's room: Marie's books, window, window, closet, window, Marie's books; exit to hallway, pass magazine shelf, hang a left, enter another room: GEBCO sheets (01005 through 15005) in various file cabinets, phone table, land physiographic diagrams, window, closet, desk, time sheets, stamps pads, light table, and supplies in center. Enter staircase to third floor: files and supplies everywhere, luggage closet at back right. I think you get the point: Marie's work migrated to her house. After 1965 that's where she did all her work.

My photocopies of these maps now occupy a folder tagged with a pink sticky note that reads "Maps." The folder holds the meticulously notated maps of each floor of Marie's house, the maps she drew of the metamorphosis of Lamont's space, and a copy of the map she must have drawn to insert into the invitation to her 1966 submarine geology department "Xmas party"; it also contains ones she didn't draw: one of the Lamont Nature Sanctuary, one of the Lamont Geological Observatory campus, and one of the Oceanography Building, which was added to that campus in 1961. These maps reside together because they show the migration that took place at Lamont beginning in the 1960s: as the number of people who worked there grew, new buildings began to appear on campus.

These maps are stylistically very different, with the one of the Oceanography Building being the sparsest, and the ones of Marie's home being the most densely packed. Marie's home is full of furniture and equipment, but the map of the Oceanography Building is a basic architectural rendering, no more than rectangles subdivided into squares, each square a numbered office. The building was completed in 1962, mainly because, Marie said, JFK used the word *oceanography* in his inauguration speech, which increased government funding levels, including money for Lamont. The tight-knit family that had spent its infancy in the basement of Schermerhorn and its youth in Lamont Hall was spreading out, intellectually and geographically, as the programs of the Lamont Geological Observatory rapidly diversified, specialties begetting subspecialties, subspecialties requiring the construction of new buildings in which to house new people and equipment, a family of pursuits and practitioners rapidly growing.

So what about Doc, the patriarch of it all? After the Oceanography Building was completed in 1962, he was pretty much the only person left working in Lamont Hall. Marie drew a map of this incarnation of "The Big House" and called it "Lamont 1962–1972, Ewing's Inner Institute." It, too, is telling, just like her maps of her home. The first floor still looks pretty public; three-quarters of it is labeled "Library," the rest "Seminar." The second floor is where it gets biased; rooms that Marie and Bruce and others used to inhabit are now labeled "Ewing's Sub[marine] Topo[graphy]," "Ewing's Library," "Ewing's Data Files (Seismology)," "Director's Assistant," and "Director's Office." "We had been one big happy family under one roof," Marie told an interviewer much later in her life. And then they weren't.

CHAPTER 18

*T*HE SECOND INTERNATIONAL OCEANOGRAPHIC CONGRESS took place in Moscow in June 1966. The scene was very different from the First International Oceanographic Congress, which had been held at the United Nations, with its cheerfully modern clean lines and bright colors. At the second IOC the scene was darker: held under the auspices of UNESCO, at Moscow University, the conference was dominated by panels of buffed wood veneer, crown molding, and vast auditoriums fronted by imposing podiums. Pre-event press in the *New York Times* had been restricted to one article (out of a total of three about the whole conference), outlining the Soviet government's refusal to allow a U.S. oceanography ship to travel to Leningrad to participate in the conference, despite being invited by the Soviet Academy of Sciences. The second article was tiny—fewer than a hundred words under the headline "2,000 Oceanographers Meet at World Parley in Russia"—and ended with a tally: "the Americans," noted the *Times*, "will read 180 papers, the Russians 150."

Bruce was one of only three Americans formally invited as a guest of the Soviet Academy. Of the two presentations he gave while there, the one that stood out was on the evidence of reversals of the Earth's magnetic field in submarine cores—information that confirmed Vine, Matthews, and Morley's hypothesis about the evidence of magnetic reversals present on the ocean floor. The pattern of magnetic reversals they'd found on both sides of the rift valley resembled a zebra skin with stripes running along the rift's north–south axis. The stripes in the cores that Bruce spoke about looked like the layers of a child's sand bottle: multihued, horizontal stripes of uneven thickness. In his presentation, Bruce explained the implications of the layers, saying that there was a correlation between the magnetic reversals and the evolution of the Earth's species, causing such a stir that UNESCO's press secretary asked him to give a press conference on the subject the following day. By heading laterally away from the rift valley, Bruce explained during the press conference—holding his hands palms down in front of his chest and moving them apart from each other—and drilling down into the ocean floor, you will encounter the same pattern of magnetic reversals. And when you look at patterns of species' evolution in Earth's history, he said, you'll find that large-scale mutations and extinctions happened around the same time as those magnetic reversals.

The discovery had been made by two graduate students working in the lab of Neil Opdyke, a recent Lamont PhD and colleague of Bruce's. Billy Glass, one of Bruce's students, had recognized the reversal-evolution correlation. One of Opdyke's students, named John Foster, had built the instrument that made the discovery possible. It was called a spinning magnetometer, and it spun core samples of ocean floor sediment so softly that the delicate deep-sea material wasn't destroyed. It also measured the sample's magnetism. Using it, Glass studied core samples from the Antarctic whose faunal record had already been established. Almost immediately he discovered that the organic oozes (including the fossilized remains of small sea creatures) preserved in the cores were strongly magnetized; later he found that magnetic reversals were also present in the cores. That's when it became clear that the discovery was big—and when the number of people who expressed interest in the project doubled.

First there was one of Bruce's former grad students, James Hays, brought in because he was the one who'd originally established the core samples' faunal record. Then there was a postdoctoral researcher named Dragoslav Ninkovic, brought in by Bruce to help. Then, while Glass was on a research trip at sea, Bruce's colleague Opdyke suddenly decided that he was interested in sediment. The way Opdyke saw it, he should be senior author on the paper: after all, without him, the spinner (developed by one of his students) wouldn't exist and neither would the work. This was not unreasonable. Neither was his objecting to his lab being overrun by Bruce's students. Bruce agreed to these conditions. He also, however, stood up for Glass, who'd been a rather despondent grad student looking for a thesis topic until his discovery of the reversal-evolution correlation had gotten him more excited than Bruce had ever seen.

The press conference Bruce gave at the Moscow IOC was for work he did not spearhead, but his decision to make the announcement had been influenced by several factors. Opdyke had made a presentation at the annual American Geophysical Union meeting a few months prior, discussing how the correlation Glass had discovered, using an instrument developed by Foster, could be extended into the North Pacific, an area of the oceans that "belonged" to Ninkovic. This made Glass and Ninkovic extremely nervous that the credit for their discoveries would go to the more senior Opdyke—an anxiety that could only have been compounded when Opdyke approached Bruce before the Moscow conference and forbade him from discussing the discovery. But Bruce had the reputations of others to consider: by announcing all of the names of the people involved in the work, he could ensure they made it into the historical record.

Had Bruce's UNESCO-prompted (and hastily arranged) press conference not been a chaotic mess, this tactic might have worked. He read, in English, from a prepared paper. His words were translated into Russian. There was interference between his English-speaking voice and that of the Russian translator—and loud objections to the incorrect translations by some of the bilingual reporters. Later, both he and the UNESCO press officer were adamant that Bruce named his coauthors while he was at the lectern, that he said the words "Dr. Neil Opdyke, Dr. James Hays, Dr. Dragoslav Ninkovic, Billy Glass and John Foster." But when *Time* magazine ran an article about the discovery, it mentioned only Bruce by name. And in the single article the *New York Times* published about the IOC, Opdyke, Ninkovic, Hays, Glass, and Foster were not mentioned until the third paragraph of a story whose subject was Bruce's claims about magnetic reversals.

By the time Bruce arrives in Austria after a short expedition on Lake Geneva to study turbidity currents, there's a note waiting for him from someone at Lamont. It's clipped to the *New York Times* story; Opdyke and

Hays think, the note says, that Bruce was unfair. Later, while out walking, he happens upon a newsstand. He wants to catch up on the news from home. So he picks up a copy of the June 17 issue of *Time* magazine. He's walking and nonchalantly flipping through the magazine when he sees an article titled "Flipping the Magnetic Field." He stops walking.

"A group of Columbia University scientists has collected evidence . . ." Bruce looks up briefly, sees a bench, and goes to sit down on it. "Working with 32- to 65-ft.-long sediment cores taken from the bottom of the North Pacific, geologist Bruce Heezen and his associates at Columbia's Lamont Geological Observatory . . ." He's horrified. He scans the rest of the article for names of anyone else. Nothing. He closes the magazine, springs up, and rushes down the street looking for a telegraph service.

He's already composing a telegram in his head: "Fossil magnetism study of deep-sea sediment cores was work of Neil Opdyke and John Foster who devised instruments [that] made magnetic measurements . . . Dragoslav Ninkovic, Billy Glass and James Hays who selected cores [and] made mineralogical paleontological studies STOP." The first office has a line; he can't wait. "Principal results were presented by Opdyke at April meeting in Washington but Ninkovic, Opdyke, Heezen, Foster, Moscow report added new North Pacific data STOP." In the second telegraph office he starts scrawling the message to *Time*, beginning with the word *Sir*. "ALL MEMBERS OF TEAM SHARED WORK AND IDEAS MUST SHARE CREDIT STOP." It doesn't matter. The damage is done.

He travels next to London, calling Marie upon his arrival. Not good, she says after he says hello. They're upset, she says. He's calling from a wooden phone booth in the lobby of the hotel. How upset, he asks. Disturbed, she says, I would say disturbed. Doc in particular. She repeats some of the colorful phrases that have been repeated to her over the past few weeks; because she no longer works out of Lamont, nothing is first-hand. Someone knocks on the booth's glass. Bruce ignores it. I sent a tele-gram to *Time*, he tells her, it makes sense: if I had worked that long and been left out—he stops. I should write a letter to the editor and demand that it's printed, he says. You should stay over there, Marie says. The per-son knocks on the glass again. This time Bruce turns around and points at the phone, nearly yanking it out of the wall as he jerks open the booth's door. Trans, he yells in the person's face, Atlantic. I was joking, Marie says. He slams the door. Why don't you send them a cable, too, Marie asks, meaning the angry Lamonters. So he does, despite what he refers to as the considerable expense.

The message he sends at Marie's urging contains more sentiment. "SHOCKED AT RECENT INCORRECT UNFAIR NEWS REPORTS STOP. UPON SEEING TIME MAGAZINE CABLED EDITORS [THE] FOLLOWING MESSAGE," he writes, inserting the text of the telegram from the previous week. "I ALSO CALLED TIME AND URGED THEM IN THE INTERESTS OF FAIR PLAY TO PRINT CABLEGRAM AS A LETTER TO THE EDITOR STOP." Bruce also calls a colleague, on sabbatical at Cambridge, who confirms what Marie said: people are angry. The charges are serious. While Bruce is in London, a petition is being circulated against him at Lamont; only a few signatures are collected and none are from Lamont professors.

By the time he returns to New York Doc has prohibited Bruce from spending any of his grant money for anything—equipment, supplies, service, personnel, travel. Bruce can't be fired because he's had tenure since 1964, but when he goes to Doc's office the afternoon after he returns, Doc lets him have it. Later that night, Bruce reenacts the altercation (complete with an imitation of Doc's voice) while pacing in Marie's living room. The tone, Bruce tells her, was clear from the outset: Doc told him that he should have called for an appointment. So I asked him why he'd taken over my grants, Bruce tells Marie, and he refused to discuss it. Bruce takes a swig of whiskey from a tumbler; Marie is sitting on a couch with her legs folded beneath her. He said I was trying to set up an institute of my own at Lamont. He objected to my cruises on other ships, even though he hasn't let me use Lamont's since '58, Bruce says, his voice rising. He said I shouldn't be doing geology; I should only be doing topography. Bruce has dropped the voice by now; Marie is just watching him and nodding. He told me that I had not only stolen the physiographic diagrams from him, but that I had stolen 90 percent of my scientific work from him, and he presumed I had stolen the rest from others. He was provoking me, Bruce tells Marie, and I stayed quiet. I know what's at stake. He looks at her, takes another swig. I've got an appointment to go back tomorrow.

Without control over his own grants Bruce will not be able to pay anyone's salary—not Marie's, not those of many people now working for Marie, some of whom are trying to stay silent upstairs. Not the grad students. No one. Doc was partly right when he said that Bruce had been trying to create his own little institute inside of Lamont. Along with Marie, Bruce had cultivated a sort of family with himself at the head. He went out and got grants, was the breadwinner on whom a lot depended. And the only person above him was Doc, who controlled the thing Bruce couldn't live without: data. In 1966, due to Doc's obsessive and constant collection of every possible piece of information about the Earth, Lamont had one of the biggest collections of seafloor data in the world.

When Bruce returns to Lamont Hall for his appointment with Doc the next day, Doc isn't there. Bruce waits for almost two hours. He thinks about Hawaii, where he'd been offered directorship of a new geophysical institute. He thinks of Rhode Island, where he and Marie were both offered positions, and even went so far as to look for a place to live. He thinks of D.C., where the navy's Hydrographic Office also offered him something. He thinks of Marie and he thinks of his students. He thinks of the Core lab and the thousands of soundings records that are stored in the buildings on the acres around him. And he thinks of himself, just a few years before, on CBS. The show was called *Tomorrow Was Yesterday*, and they had him surrounded by fog, on a dais that spun him around to face the camera.

We can see the stars, he'd said when Charles Collingwood asked him why, until recently, people had known more about the structure of stars than the oceans. We can see the stars, and the ocean floor is covered, Bruce replied; for the public to believe that the invisible land covered by water is a reality—for that, the world needed Marie, needed Bruce, and needed the data they had access to as Lamonters. That is more important than this. He can make it work. He has to make it work. The phone on Doc's secretary's desk rings. She stops typing, pulls off her earring, listens. But he's here right now, she says. Bruce looks up. Okay, she says into the phone. She replaces the receiver and her earring. That was Doc, she tells Bruce, he says the meeting is canceled.

BRUCE HAD BEEN in Austria to meet Heinrich Berann, the artist who was going to create a painted version of their Indian Ocean diagram for *National Geographic* magazine. The map wasn't just some quarter-page illustration for an article. It was a supplemental map, the kind people had been pulling out and saving for decades, even after the issues themselves were long gone, trashed or recycled after efforts to donate them had been exhausted; *National Geographic* maps were survivors. Outlasting their companion issues, their subscribers, and, often, the borders of the nations they showed, they lived on in shoe boxes across the nation, boxes that probably hadn't been opened in years.

If your family subscribed to *National Geographic* in October 1967, like about six million other American families, the Berann-painted version of Marie and Bruce's Indian Ocean physiographic diagram was in your house. Six million! That circulation is one of the reasons Marie and Bruce agreed to consult with *National Geographic*. Their philosophies lined up: both parties were committed to helping people see images of things that distance, access, and cost prevented them from seeing in person. The ocean floor was all of those things, and Marie and Bruce wanted as many people as possible to see it. As Bruce said a few years before he died, "We've had only one client all these years, and that's the scientific public." Their desire to show the public the ocean floor was so strong that even though *National Geographic* didn't pay Bruce's way the first few times he went to Austria to meet with Berann, he went anyway—the first trip piggybacked on a trip to London and the second was tacked onto his return from Moscow. He and Marie received small consulting fees for their efforts.

The way Marie remembered it, *National Geographic* had found Berann sometime in the 1960s, when a little girl from outside Innsbruck, Austria, wrote to them. The girl said she'd been looking at *National Geographic*'s maps and that, in her opinion, her father could paint much better than they could. Seeing as how, Marie told an interviewer, "the NGS are very sensitive to letters from children," they sent their chief cartographer, Newman Bumstead, straight over to Innsbruck to "case the joint."

Berann had a home and studio in a small town in Lans, where he did what Marie called "serious paintings in the style of Leonardo Da Vinci." He'd been trained as a graphic illustrator as a young man in the 1930s, and had studied sculpture and medical illustration, too—but never cartography. Having grown up in the shadow of the Alps, he'd vowed never to paint them (an aversion similar to, but decidedly weaker than, Bruce's hatred of anything to do with turkey). His natural affinity appears to have been for the fantastic: churning atmospheres filled with intense colors and fog sharpened to points, naked female bodies rendered extreme, flesh formed tight around bones, concavities deep and shadow-filled. But, Marie said, he couldn't make any money with his serious paintings, so he started doing panoramas for Austrian tourist sites, painting his country's mountains and trails so skiers and hikers would know which way was down. By the time his daughter wrote to *National Geographic*, he'd already done panoramas of Cortina, Rome, and his hometown of Innsbruck for the Olympic Winter Games. His relationship with the magazine began in 1964, with two panoramas of the Himalayas.

Classically, a panorama shows a 360-degree view of a landscape, so that a viewer can stand in the center of a room and be surrounded by a simulated picture of a scene. Berann's panoramas also aimed to show large stretches of horizontal distance, but they did more than that. He called his work hybrid: "exact like a map and visual like a photograph, more colorful, clear and three-dimensional than satellite images." His Himalayan panoramas, for example, reduced massive mountains down to magazine size, at the same time emphasizing the mountains' sharp crags, peaks, and contrasting shadows.

The results, particularly with Everest, are strange. Because the mountain extends almost to all four of the paper's edges, the viewer feels close to it. This is disorienting; if you're up close to something and can see all of it at once, either it is small or you are huge—and neither of those is true in this case. Snow covers the mountain, the dirt in the foreground is an unsaturated maroon, the sky deep dusky blue like a blueberry's skin. Indentations run like stripes up the mountain's sides, and the snow catches incompletely on the parts of the mountain that are closest to vertical, leaving maroon earth exposed. With the vertical indentations and the almost-marbled maroon, the surface looks like a scallop shell. Delicate seashell lines superimposed on hard mountain rock—it's this patterning that must have made the powers-that-be at *National Geographic* think Berann was the right man for the ocean floor job.

When painting a panorama, Berann's process was rigorous, but in a different way from Marie's. They both began with planning. In the case of the Indian Ocean Floor Panorama, the planning took place between Berann and Bruce. Color schemes, style, and technique were discussed. The seafloor was the main subject of the panorama; its colors, they decided, should be bright in comparison to those used to depict dry land.

Marie wasn't present during these first meetings, but reflecting on the relationship between herself, Bruce, Berann, and Berann's assistant, Heinz Vielkind, that developed during the ten years they worked together, she realized "that words were not as vital a method of communication as gestures when a scientific project is being presented as an art form." Berann, she wrote in a 1988 letter, "couldn't speak English and Bruce couldn't speak German, but with lots of pointing, waving of arms, ohs and ahs, their communication was established."

The pointing was at Marie's completed physiographic diagram, a pen-and-ink drawing Berann had to transform into a painting that could be understood by the general public. Before he could do that, though, he had to understand it himself—which features needed to be emphasized, which ones could be left out, what textures went where. How, in other words, to "minimize the distortions and distractions of nature," so that the viewer could absorb visual information about the ocean floor (perhaps noting similarities to land features with which they were already familiar) and not simply stare at it agog. Instead of consulting aerial photographs (the way he usually did when working on a panorama) or doing field sketches from a helicopter, Berann had Marie's physiographic diagram to sketch from and Bruce's vision to translate. Luckily, the land scape on her map was alien in location but not in content. As Marie said, Berann's experience painting Alpine panoramas made him "the obvious choice" for the project; "his technique adapted very readily to painting underwater mountains."

Part of Berann's technique involved manipulating projection. On a map, projection is the method used to show the features of the Earth (a sphere) on a sheet of paper (a plane). In the article that accompanied Berann's Indian Ocean Floor Panorama, the author notes that Berann "shows the round earth as flat from east to west, but rolling gently away northwest." This curvature flattens the horizon. In the printed panorama, the sky occupies a strip about an inch wide, glowing aqua near the Earth and darkening toward space. Between it and the ocean floor, which occupies the bottom three-quarters of the panorama, the "vast Asian landmass" is squeezed onto the page, the Ural Mountains tiny bumps rising up from land flat as a vast North American plain. "The over-all view," the article says, "is much as if an astronaut, orbiting far out in space, were to look down upon a world drained of all its water."

"From his painting" the article continues, "jump features of earth's wrinkled face that were unknown a few years ago." This is an effect of exaggeration. When planning and sketching, Berann used an idiosyncratic approach he'd employed in previous panoramas: he exaggerated features meant to attract the viewer's gaze. In the case of the Indian Ocean Floor Panorama, features above sea level are understated; as represented, the 19,340-foot-tall Mt. Kilimanjaro looks about the same size as any of the much smaller underwater mountains. The eye naturally drifts to the visually exciting Mid-Oceanic Ridge.

After getting his detailed drawing approved by Bruce and *National Geographic*'s Newman Bumstead (whose name is printed, on the panorama, after the phrase "conceived of by"), Berann began the final version. He sketched basic landforms onto thick paper using pencil and then began painting, filling in patches from top to bottom. He used, Marie said, a multimedia approach, employing "air brush and frisket, casein-based paints and oil-based paints in an assorted sequence," working through a hole cut in a sheet of tracing paper that protected the rest of the painting. A light wash of paint went down first, basic shapes filled by watery colors. Then Berann tackled the features' textures, consulting the physiographic diagram and, if necessary, collecting details in rawer form, referring to profiles and conversing with Marie and Bruce.

The result, the *National Geographic* article says, in a caption above a Kodachrome of Marie drawing and Bruce standing by with crumpled profile in hand, is "remarkable map painting" that "combines scientific discoveries and an artist's skills." And for the reader whose map was somehow lost before he got to see it, pinched from his mailbox or slipped into a friend's notebook during an afterschool study session, *National Geographic* describes it. "Color," they say, "gives depth to the map: light green for shallow seas and continental shelves; medium blue for sediment covered plateaus and hills of the mid-depths; dark violet-gray for the abyssal plains; darker still for the great trenches. Towering undersea mountains and plunging slopes of this waterless ocean are highlighted as if at sunrise."

On the next page of the article, there's help for the reader who might have been floored by his first confrontation with the Earth's deep recesses: a globe, a shape more easily identifiable as planet Earth than Berann's panorama, with an "open wound" in its skin. "A tremor-racked rift slashes the Indian Ocean Basin, as shown on a National Geographic globe slit by a knife." That the rift could still, in 1967, be described with such violent terms belied a fear not unlike the one projected by the terrified ladies who'd written to Bruce a decade before.

But Berann's panorama was very different from Marie's physiographic diagram—in form and effect. Because it made its way into six million homes, Berann's first panorama of the ocean floor undoubtedly did a much better job at reaching the "general scientific public" whom Bruce said he and Marie had always been trying to reach. It was also simpler to look at. Bruce said that even some marine geologists (those who lacked a "plastic sense") preferred the "frivolous" panoramas to Marie's physiographic diagrams. "The frivolous ones," he said in 1975, "were the ones that stuck." History has borne this out: I've never seen one of Marie's physiographic diagrams displayed, anywhere, but I've often seen Berann's panoramas of the ocean floor displayed and reprinted. After 1967 the public's understanding of the Earth made a giant leap forward. What had been shocking was made popular.

*I*N 1967 THE SITUATION THAT MARIE REFERRED TO AS THE Harassment began to come to a head. It started in October, when *Nature* accepted a paper that Billy Glass and Bruce (along with several other Lamonters) had coauthored. Glass had submitted it first to a group of readers, then gave it to David Ericson, by then a senior staff member at Lamont, who submitted it to *Science*, whose editors rejected it, and then to *Nature*, whose editors accepted it. By doing it that way, Glass made himself a target of Doc's wrath.

Official Lamont policy (stated in a memo originally issued by Doc in September 1963 and reiterated in a December 1964 memo for the staff's "convenience" by Worzel) was that 1) plans for papers were to be discussed with the senior staff member in charge of the research area; 2) approval from two senior research scientists was to be obtained before papers were submitted to publications or conferences; 3) copies of the paper were to be submitted to a Mrs. Weston, who would run down a checklist of various details before submitting the paper to the publication or conference in question; 4) and if the paper was accepted, the authors were promptly to correct and edit them before giving them, again, to Mrs. Weston, who would run down another checklist before turning the final draft over to the publication or conference. Bruce noted that he always followed these "formal rules," except that he submitted "manu-scripts directly and carried on a direct correspondence with the editors." He did things his own way, circumventing Doc in the process, and Glass followed his example.

According to Bruce, after much back-and-forth—Doc calling Glass, Glass talking to Bruce, Bruce writing letters to Doc—Doc summoned Glass and told him to "pack up, vacate his office, and leave Lamont Observatory permanently by the end of that day," just two months before he was to be awarded his doctorate. Eventually Doc relented and Glass got his degree, then hightailed it out of there, scoring a job at NASA. Bruce did not fair so well.

In November 1967, Doc informed Bruce that he was "suspended from the Observatory, that [his] research grants would be administered by another," and that the only thing he was allowed to do during the sus-pension was advise his students. At the end of January 1968, Bruce said, his students and "supporting staff were shown, and asked to sign, a memorandum from [Doc] informing them of [Bruce's] suspension from 'all activities at Lamont except direction of the work of his students.'" At some point during all this, three of Bruce's students went to Columbia's provost to protest Bruce's treatment; they were expelled for a short time for their efforts. The conflict at Lamont happened to coincide with increased student protests against Columbia's involvement in defense research; no one in the administration wanted more trouble, and at the time, it must have seemed as if Lamont's conflicts, all the way out in Pali-sades, were the kind that would disappear if ignored.

Doc followed through on this suspension—unlike the one he'd issued upon Bruce's return from the Moscow conference. He informed Dennis Hayes, who'd only received his doctorate from Columbia in 1966, after studying marine geology with Bruce, that he was to "take responsi-bility for monitoring the contracts and directing the work under them in the submarine topography group." That was Bruce's group.

Doc also removed Bruce's name from National Science Foundation grant GA-580, which Bruce had written and was principal investigator of, preventing him from spending or seeing the expenditures on the account, and named Hayes its principal investigator. Doc did the same on another one of Bruce's sources of funding: Bell Laboratories had con-tracted for Bruce's services ever since he began studying cable breaks for them in the mid-1950s, but after Doc and Hayes visited Bell, "in an effort," Bruce said, "to formulate a plan of work which would enable Lamont to keep the money but would exclude me," all of that changed.

After reluctantly agreeing to the change, and then privately communicating to Bruce that the situation was unsatisfactory, Bell canceled the contract. It seems they realized it made little sense to continue the arrangement without Bruce's expertise. To them it would have been apparent (and confusing) that Doc was denying them the services of a longtime collaborator and expert, and offering in return only those of Hayes, a novice. But it was Bruce who, Hayes would say in an interview years later, "didn't really play the game according to any rules." Bruce was the "renegade," Hayes said, and Ewing the "frustrated," "loveable dictator."

Worzel, Doc's right-hand man, said that Bruce had been a "loner" even before the conflict. "Bruce had by and large kept his own counsel even before this whole thing erupted," he said. After his rather public censuring this stance became even more pronounced—in Marie as well as in Bruce. They'd both been independent (although both were still being paid by Lamont), working best with only each other; after the conflict this independence took on a rebellious edge, affecting their lives and work.

Marie's independence had long comforted her. One year, when she was still a young girl, she kept a short-lived diary. Her resolution (number two) to "keep up" her diary lasted for only twelve days, but a much more telling resolution (number four) appeared in the same list. "Be as independent in every way as possible," she wrote. "More at a later date." She never expounded on this subject, but she did follow through in real life—in high school, college, graduate school, and beyond. Even her involvement with Bruce, their inextricable bond, left her a great deal of space—when he was at sea or traveling to some conference, she was back in South Nyack, running the show.

She'd already been cut off from the goings-on at Lamont when the conflict between Bruce and Doc erupted. She had, after all, been working out of her home for a few years. It was a nice setup, with Bruce bringing her data and materials and some of the people who worked in his department splitting their time between campus and her house; Marie would even visit Bruce there occasionally, creeping up Lamont's drive in her big dark car, emerging from its plush interior clad in the large hats and trailing scarves that had become part of her style.

When Bruce was suspended, everything changed. Marie bought a black standard poodle to guard her house against the Lamont "varmints" and named it Inky, after Bruce's childhood dog. She began referring to Dennis Hayes as "snot nose." She kept her own nose to the grindstone, recalled Worzel, and those on Doc's side of the conflict had access to her work only when it was published for the rest of the world to see. This, of course, infuriated Doc: regarding "the problem of Marie Tharp" refusing to work on Lamont's campus, he wrote to the dean of Columbia College that year, "her present work is done entirely under the supervision of Bruce." While that had been acceptable before (her house like a satellite, a distant outpost department of Lamont), upon Bruce's suspension, it suddenly no longer was. Her house had been transformed into a building under occupation by the resistance—and Marie herself rarely, if ever, visited Lamont's campus.

IT IS LATE January 1968. The sky is gray. Chunks of ice float down the Hudson River, past Marie's house. Inside, radiators clank, their heat fogging the edges of windowpanes. The phone rings. Marie hears it, does not pause. Inky, who's sleeping on the floor beside her, lifts his head off his paws and pricks his ears. Marie is revising the physiographic diagram of the North Atlantic; the first version is, by now, out of print and a lot of data have been collected since it was published nine years ago. The phone is still ringing, but Inky has determined it doesn't require investigation. Marie sighs and keeps drawing; one of the boys should have answered it by now. Bruce isn't there, but there are others who fill the house when he's not—a ragtag group of workers, including the boys from Nyack's Missionary Training Institute who she calls her "missionary boys," people who do the mundane work she used to have to do herself, diligent but often (like now—the phone is still ringing) slow on the draw.

She doesn't trust them with much more than basic tasks, and sometimes assigns two to the same job so she can compare the results. It's not the most efficient way to operate, but it lets her evaluate the boys' intelligence and make sure mistakes don't get carried too far—onto a map, for example. It's also not always the most pleasant way to operate; if the work doesn't compare, if one or both have made obvious mistakes, she fires them—one or both. She hires other kids from town, high school and sometimes college kids, who generally need less supervision than the missionary boys. Often they're kids who don't really fit in with their peers, some with artistic proclivities that make them appear eccentric, some who are in possession of personalities that are just plain strange, some who would never fit in anywhere else. Many of them fit in here perfectly, revolving around a nucleus that consists of Marie, Bruce, and the maps.

She looks up from her work, annoyed that no one has answered the phone yet. But there—the ringing finally stops. After waiting a beat to see if it's for her, she looks back down at her work, touches pen to paper. And then hears her name being bellowed up the stairwell. She looks up from her work again, out through a circle she's cleared in the window fog so she can see the river below. She rests her pen on a crumpled tissue, slides her stocking feet into slippers, and walks to the hall phone. Inky follows, lies down at her feet. When she has the receiver partway to her ear, she covers it and shouts down the stairs that she's got it, waits to hear the clatter of the other extension being hung up before she speaks.

Hello, she says, Marie Tharp. Hello, says a man's voice on the other end. This is Dr. Ewing. Which is not a good thing. She hasn't spoken to him for—it's hard to say how long it's been. She tucks the hand that's not holding the phone into the crook of the arm that is. I trust you're well, he says. Downstairs she can hear the boys rolling their chairs across the living room floor, the rattle of casters followed by short cries of pain: they're having, she can tell, a rubber-band fight. I am, she says. Working hard, you know me. Indeed, Doc says. That's why I've called. Oh, she asks. She sits down in the chair next to the telephone table, picks up a pen, and starts doodling on a notepad that has her name printed in the top margin of each sheet.

Doc tells her he's going to cut to the chase. There are many here, he says, referring to Lamont, who feel it would be better for you to return to working at Lamont. Physically, he adds. And why is that, she asks. The original circumstances that led to such an arrangement, Doc asks her, they've changed, correct? I assume you're no longer recovering from a surgery that took place in 1965? Yes, she says, right, but there are other factors. Fewer distractions here than at Lamont, she says. A crash and a loud expletive sound from downstairs; Inky raises his head and looks at Marie. Doc clears his throat, starts listing reasons why she should be back there.

It is inappropriate, for example, that she's been amassing and, furthermore, hoarding data at her house. She knows the data belong to Lamont, he tells her. She knows that said data need to be accounted for by the agencies that granted the money for their collection, he tells her. He does not go so far to as to use the word *ungrateful*, as in he gave her her start and now she's repaying him by being an uncooperative, ungrateful little—if it's about the data, she asks him, I can have my boys make copies and get the originals back to Lamont.

One of the boys sticks his head around the bend in the stairway. Uh, he says with a pained expression, Marie? She waves him away with her pen. It is not, Doc says, just about the data. As you well know. As Bruce well knows. Oh yes, she asks, what else? I'm sure you know his status here right now, Doc says. Which is really just a veiled threat at her own status—what Doc gave he can take away. Marie has access only to what Bruce has access to, and what he doesn't have she can't have either. And so what, she asks, you want me to come back to work at Lamont? That's it? And what about all my people, she asks, referring to her workers—the townies, the missionary boys. I'm afraid, Doc says, we don't have room for all that here. But I'm happy to make arrangements for the move. Men and trucks, you let me know a date.

Outside, the Hudson is icing over again. Each morning Coast Guard boats called cutters run up and down it, clearing the river of ice to keep shipping lanes open. By the evening, its surface is a shell, a thin crust of ice on top of the flowing water.

In fact, Doc says, I insist that I make arrangements for the move. Our men, our vehicles. She's still silent, staring. The date, he asks her again. Inky puts his paws on her lap, raising his body up to see what she's looking at. It's not convenient right now, she says. I'm revising the North Atlantic, and everything is a mess. Of course, Doc says. I won't pack everything up in the middle of it and disrupt my work, she says. She looks through the doorway into her office, considers her progress on the map spread out on her drafting table. I might be finished by the middle of next month, she says. Fine, Doc says, I'll renew your appointment for the month of February. But your status beyond that—that's contingent on the move. So let's agree to talk in a few weeks.

Oh, and Marie? Doc adds casually. Dr. Hayes looks forward to having you on his team, too. I don't know if you've heard, Doc slips in before hanging up, but we're happy to have him directing the submarine topography group now. Marie slams the phone into the cradle. Inky gives her a look and trots over to the dog door that leads out to the porch, goes outside. Marie tears the paper she was doodling on off the pad, crumples it, and throws it against the wall.

She doesn't know what else to do, so she follows Inky outside, passing through her office and out a human-size door. Marie doesn't notice the cold as she stands facing out toward the river, leaning up against the porch's railing. If it were a little narrower it could be called a widow's walk and if a whole range of things were different, she might be a wife, worrying over her husband's return. She isn't Bruce's wife, but he's due for dinner soon and she wants to be ready; she pulls her sweater tight around her body and goes back inside. Inky follows. Good boy, she calls back, her voice distracted.

CHAPTER 20

*T*ODAY YOU CAN GO TO A LIBRARY, WANDER INTO THE CHIL-dren's room, and pluck a picture book off the shelf that will explain to you the workings of the theory we now understand as plate tectonics. In 1967, though, that theory was a series of hypotheses backed by data sets from scientists all over the world—unnamed, impressive but discon-nected, and only starting to be understood by practitioners in the field. "To visualize what 1967 and 1968 were going to be like for geologists," Bill Menard wrote in the last chapter of his book about the plate tec-tonics revolution, "one can hardly do better than contemplate the class-room." In the winter of 1967, he wrote, graduate students sitting in their very first marine geology classes at Scripps (the oldest oceanography pro-gram in the country and Menard's home institution) were not privy to the usual introductory formalities. A syllabus was not handed out. The professor did not make academic small talk. Instead, he went straight to the blackboard and started drawing pictures. That was the only way to do it. The old information didn't, as Harry Hess might have put it, hold water, and the new information was so new that it existed only in the pages of journals and in the minds of the scientists making the discoveries.

By January 1967, scientists were pretty certain that the Earth's surface was separated into pieces and that those pieces interacted at their boundaries. The first type of boundary, what we now call a divergent plate boundary, was discovered and drawn by Marie in 1952 (the Mid-Atlantic Ridge system with a rift valley running down its center), had its mechanics (which came to be called seafloor spreading) hypothesized eight years later by Harry Hess, and was confirmed two years after that by Vine, Matthews, and Morley (when they discovered the seafloor's pattern of magnetic reversals). The second type of boundary was what we now call a transform boundary. First discovered and drawn by Marie in 1961 (pictured on her South Atlantic physiographic diagram and described as a "fracture zone" in the accompanying text), the transform boundary was renamed and described four years later by J. Tuzo Wilson, when he noted that the edges of plates on the ocean floor grind past each other.

What scientists did not understand in the spring 1967 academic semester was the third type of boundary: what we now call a convergent plate boundary. Hess hypothesized this type of plate boundary back in 1960, explaining that if mid-oceanic ridges were spreading, then some crust, somewhere, would have to be recycled back into the Earth. He called the areas where plates converged "jaw crushers." When two plates meet, he said, they crash, and one is forced beneath the other. According to Hess, this happens because one of the plates is 1) denser, 2) older, and 3) taller than the other. The details of this concept, however, were unclear. Precisely how and where the Earth's surface changed to accommodate this new material remained largely unanswered—until the 1967 American Geophysical Union meeting, at which Lamonters Jack Oliver and Brian Isacks gave a paper that explained convergent plate boundaries.

In their paper, Oliver and Isacks said they'd found proof of "large-scale thrusting phenomena" in the South Pacific: a place where the top 60 miles of the Earth's surface (including the Earth's crust and the upper portion of its mantle; they called this the "lithosphere") were thrust to depths of about 450 miles. This thrusting motion, in which one plate is forced beneath another (converging), is called subduction. Among the results of subduction are island arcs such as Fiji and Tonga, curving chains of islands formed by magma that escaped and accumulated during the process, and deep-sea trenches, of which the Mariana Trench is probably the most famous.

To picture how the Mariana Trench was formed (and how a convergent plate boundary works) think of the game Rock, Paper, Scissors. You choose paper, your friend chooses rock. The thin and light piece of paper covers the dense and heavy rock—but instead of clasping your friend's fist as you normally would to show you've won the game, both of you stretch out your arms, hands with palms facing the floor and fingers pointing at each other. Your rock friend is the Pacific plate. You are the Mariana plate. You are light, young, thin and if you were actually lying on the ocean floor some magma would be bubbling up between you and the plate behind you, shoving you toward the Pacific plate. As you move slowly toward your friend, your hand begins to slide over his, the pads of your fingers skimming his nails, rubbing his knuckles, then his wrist, his forearm and shoulder, traveling slowly up his body. Your friend, in turn, will melt as he subducts beneath you, mixing back into the Earth's mantle. Eventually he will disappear.

The paper on convergent plate boundaries presented by Oliver and Isacks at the 1967 AGU conference was important, but it was another paper presented there that Menard would later call "the foundation for all subsequent work on ancient plate tectonics." It was written by a young scientist named William Jason Morgan, who had earned his PhD in physics at Princeton in 1964 and joined the faculty there immediately after. The paper he presented at the AGU conference was called "Rises, Trenches, Great Faults, and Crustal Blocks," and in it Morgan made four important points. The first was that the Earth's surface is "made of a number of rigid crustal blocks." The second was that these blocks interacted at their boundaries: where they diverged (such as at the Mid-Atlantic Ridge), converged (such as at the Mariana Trench), or transformed (such as at the Romanche and Chain fracture zones). The third point was that there is "no distortion of any kind within a given block": that distortion (features such as faults, trenches, or ridges) could occur only at one of the three types of boundaries. Morgan's fourth point was that the blocks moved relative to one another: a movement of one would cause movement in another. With these points, he'd united the hypotheses of the previous few years.

Morgan's paper had two important precursors, both published in 1965: Bullard's paper on the fit of the continents and Wilson's transform fault paper. In their paper, Bullard and his coauthors had been concerned with producing "the facts about the geometric fit of the continental edges."

They looked only at the fit of the continents around the Atlantic Ocean—notably, along the continental slope, and not the coastlines. And they provided a mathematical explanation for how the continents had moved—using Euler's fixed-point theorem, which says that "any displacement of a spherical surface over itself leaves one point fixed." Wilson's paper presented the idea of a transform boundary and argued that the Earth's surface contained a series of these "mobile belts." Mobile belts, he said, "are not isolated," but are "connected into a continuous network . . . about the Earth which divide the surface into several large rigid plates."

To understand why Morgan's paper is so frequently praised as the granddaddy of plate tectonics, you have to understand the limitations of both Bullard's and Wilson's papers. Bullard and Wilson both argued for the movement of the Earth's crust. Bullard, however, was transparent in his assertion that he was interested in studying only the fit of the edges of the continents ringing the Atlantic Ocean, ignoring the remaining 83 percent of the Earth's crust (the rest of the continents and all of the ocean floor). And Wilson's model, which did account for the Earth's entire surface (continental and oceanic crust), ignored the ways in which the movements of the Earth's plates were affected because they took place on a sphere. The question left unanswered by both of their papers, then, was this: If one considered the Earth's spherical surface as consisting of a series of plates, fit tight together like puzzle pieces, how could their movements be explained?

Morgan's paper addressed that question from the outset. His methodology and the implications of the work are addressed in the first sentence of his introduction: "a geometrical framework with which to describe present day continental drift is presented here," he wrote. By combining Wilson's notion of a continuous network of moving plates with Bullard's application of Euler's fixed-point theorem, and bringing the ideas of divergent and convergent boundaries into the fold, Morgan presented a unified understanding of how the Earth's surface worked. His paper didn't stop there. He tested his hypothesis and offered concrete numbers: the poles (or fixed points) around which some of the Earth's blocks rotated, and the rates by which they spread apart from each other.

Morgan's "Rises, Trenches, Great Faults, and Crustal Blocks," which appeared in the March 1968 issue of the *Journal of Geophysical Research*, is one of the most frequently cited papers in the history of geology. His prepublication presentation of the same material at the American Geophysical Union's annual meeting the previous spring had not fared so well. He was scheduled to present a paper on magnetic anomalies (which were, by then, old hat) just before lunch. Few were interested, so few attended. As a result, it would take nearly a year—until the publication of a slightly revised version in the *Journal of Geophysical Research*—for everyone else to catch up.

Even Menard, who had chaired the AGU session at which Morgan presented, did not remember hearing the delivery of the paper he later said was possibly the most important one ever written in geology. "I not only did not remember hearing Jason's famous talk," Menard wrote; "I didn't remember presiding over the session."

What he did remember was the extent to which Bruce's political troubles at Lamont appeared to have excluded him from direct participation in the unfolding revolution: Bruce had complimented his friend Menard's presentation, saying that it was "just the kind of analysis" he would have done himself if he had "not been forbidden to use the Lamont data." Instead, Bruce had presented an important (but minor within the context of the rest of the conference) paper with his student Billy Glass. It was on tektites, the small glass rocks they'd discovered could serve as markers of magnetic reversals, an extension of the work that had gotten Bruce in trouble after the Moscow conference.

MARIE DID NOT finish her revision of the North Atlantic physiographic diagram in February 1968, as she'd told Doc she might. She and Bruce had a lot going on in the beginning of that year. She was working on the revision, they were dealing with The Harassment, and they had embarked on another partnership with *National Geographic*: in February they both traveled to Austria to work with Heinrich Berann on a panorama of the Atlantic Ocean floor—part of the reason why Bruce wanted Marie to revise the North Atlantic was so that they'd be able to provide Berann with the most up-to-date topographic data.

The map supplement that would appear in the June 1968 issue was a double: a portrait showing "the visible face of the Atlantic and the lands around it" on one side and an "unseen panorama [of] the Atlantic Ocean Floor" on the other. This was a new endeavor for *National Geographic*.

Its publication of Berann's Indian Ocean Floor Panorama the previous year had, the editors said, "won acclaim from geographers," which might have been why they decided to go a step further with the Atlantic. "Publication of this first such double map," they wrote, "represents a milestone in the Society's long association with oceanographic study, and adds new dimension in ocean mapping." The new dimension being, presumably, Berann's translation of the "finely detailed diagram" of "geophysicists Dr. Bruce C. Heezen and Miss Marie Tharp," diagrams that had been made possible partly by *National Geographic*'s support, in the late 1940s, of the "first precise mapping" of the ocean floor.

The roughly six million subscribers who received their copies of the Atlantic supplement must have found it more familiar than the Indian Ocean Floor Panorama. Mostly because the area was closer to them geographically: the "visible face of the Atlantic" was a picture that they'd been seeing on walls and in books their whole lives. The Atlantic Ocean at center, framed by North and South America on the left, Europe and Africa on the right, Greenland poking in at the top. Even the colors on this side of the map would have been comforting: pastel purple, pink, orange, yellow, and green outlining states and countries, bright red stars marking capitals, the ocean awash in baby blue. This side, then, primed people for the other, where the familiar shapes of continents provided context for the unfamiliar colors and features of the ocean floor.

Whereas Berann had painted the Indian Ocean Floor Panorama from a perspective that showed the Earth curving away from the viewer, the ocean floor huge in the foreground and Asia compressed into the background, the perspective he employed when painting the Atlantic Ocean floor makes the viewer feel high above the Earth, floating in space and looking straight down. The perspective (the same as most maps used in the United States) is familiar—so familiar that it almost seems like a non-perspective, as if Berann had not allowed subjectivity to creep into his creation, as if it were possible to float in space with a camera that could see through thousands of feet of water, snapping a series of photographs from which to draw. *National Geographic* did what it could to make that association for the reader, giving more than half a page to a photo taken by a satellite 22,300 miles above the Earth, showing the continents and the Atlantic, partially obscured by clouds and trapped on a circular globe, positioned the way Berann had painted them.

National Geographic was ready to say that the continents' "shelf edges match like jigsaw pieces" and allude to Bullard's paper, which it said had shown the fit of the continental shelves to be so perfect as to "all but rule out chance." It offered diagrams showing the mechanics of seafloor spreading and transform faults without actually referring to them as such. But it did not explain how all of these new hypotheses were coming together to help scientists understand how the Earth's surface had been formed—or hint that a revolution was growing out of that new understanding. It was a curious move; the *National Geographic* could have lauded the new theory of the Earth not only with an illustrative map, but also with the first short history of what would soon be referred to as plate tectonics—a sort of family tree of hypotheses, with Wegener at the top and Marie, Hess, and Bullard as his outgrowth.

The timing would have been perfect: just after Marie and Bruce returned from helping Berann with the Atlantic Ocean Panorama (and therefore when its accompanying article was being written), Jason Morgan's "Rises, Trenches, Great Faults, and Crustal Blocks" was published in the March 15, 1968, issue of the *Journal of Geophysical Research*. With that paper, Menard wrote, "the revolution was over," and "the flowering of geology could begin."

$\mathcal{B}$Y APRIL 1968, MARIE AND BRUCE APPEARED TO BE OPER-
ating under the faulty presumption that their problems with Doc
might disappear if ignored. They were provoked repeatedly, and repeatedly they did not respond—or rather, they responded with provocative
inaction. On April 8, Bruce was called into the office of Grayson Kirk,
Columbia University's president, who pointed out that, because of his suspension, which excluded him from accessing any of his grant money and
from doing anything but advise his students, it would be impractical for
him to remain at Lamont. Kirk was happy to "use his good offices in
obtaining a position" for Bruce. He was happy to arrange for the copying
of Bruce's files and documents. He welcomed suggestions and comments
on "the Lamont problem." In response, Bruce wrote a letter with some suggestions and comments, but did not send it—or agree to anything. The
next week he received a follow-up letter from Kirk implying that he had
agreed to leave. "I pondered what to do, not wanting to precipitate a show-
down," Bruce wrote to Columbia's vice president, Polykarp Kusch, in a
twenty-page narrative of the period written after the fact.

On April 19, 1968, Marie received a letter from Doc. It was cc'd to
Worzel (still Lamont's assistant director) and Dennis Hayes. In it Doc

summarized their conversation of January 25 and said he'd been disappointed that Marie hadn't been in touch since. His next sentence, then, is a little confusing: Dr. Hayes, he says, "informed him" that Marie said she needed one more week to finish the North Atlantic before making the disruptive move; in order for Doc to know this Marie would had to have been in touch with Dr. Hayes in the three months since her conversation with Doc. "I expect that it is not ever going to be really convenient," he wrote to her. "Therefore I think the only way to do it is to set a deadline and hold to it." She could count on Hayes to help her get "resettled," Doc said in closing; she had only to let him know what she needed for the move on April 29 and 30. She did not respond.

Several weeks later, Hayes called Marie to discuss the move. In passing, wrote Bruce in his 1970 letter to Vice President Kusch, Hayes mentioned to Marie that he "did not know if she had received her check." In fact, Marie hadn't noticed that not only had she not been paid for May, but she'd also not been paid for April. That's when she and Bruce started taking Hayes seriously. The move to suspend Marie's pay had been executed by Doc and communicated by Hayes. That Doc had chosen to pass such a powerful piece of information through someone he knew Marie and Bruce did not acknowledge as a serious presence was an insult.

Marie's refusal to comply with Doc's requests and Bruce's refusal to resign sent a similarly insulting message to Doc: with their inaction, they communicated to Doc that they did not respect his authority. And until Doc suspended Marie's pay, it had been a stalemate; they'd figured out ways to work around Doc's wrath. Marie often referred to "midnight requisitions," in which Bruce and his students used Lamont computers and made copies of data during the wee hours of night. "Restriction," she said astutely, "was a form of harassment." Back then, though, such a form of harassment had not scared her. Her firing did. And even though Bruce would assuage things for her almost immediately, securing her employment with the Naval Oceanographic Office within thirty-six hours, her perception of the threat took on monstrous proportions. "I kept the house locked," she told a journalist in 1975. "I didn't have anyone to talk to and I just didn't think I wanted them to take Bruce's project away from him." She paused here. "From me." How could they do that, the journalist asked her, over and over. "If I left things lying around," she answered, "they'd just come in and take it away." I don't have a tape of that interview, but even the transcript reveals more emotion than I've ever heard or read Marie express.

It was abundantly clear to everyone that the real fight was between Doc and Bruce, that Doc was using Marie to get to Bruce. I don't know what Marie was thinking during all of this, but I know some of the possibilities. Without him, she would not be worth firing; without him, she would not be fired; without him, she wouldn't have her work, and without her work, she'd be a different person entirely. These options strip her of power.

But there's another possibility, a possibility it took me a long time to realize. Doc had taken from Bruce as much as he could, waiting to fire Marie until she was the last thing left to take. And Bruce said himself that he could "only regard the withholding of Miss Tharp's salary as another instance in the effort to press me to leave Lamont." If he hadn't been able to replace her salary by getting her the Naval Oceanographic Office job, he would have been forced to resign from Lamont, to find a job elsewhere and "ask [Marie] to accompany" him. The possibility is that, by 1968, Bruce knew he needed Marie just as much as she needed him. As William Palmstrom, *National Geographic* magazine's chief of "geographic art," wrote to her around the same time, regarding the work she'd done to help Berann prepare the panorama of the Atlantic Ocean for the magazine, "I am sure that Dr. Heezen doesn't know what he would do without you and, looking back on this project, we feel the same way."

In June of that year Bruce received a second letter from President Kirk, asking when his salary should be terminated. "I then replied that I had not resigned," wrote Bruce in his 1970 letter to Vice President Kusch, "and did not intend to." Instead, he called a lawyer and drafted a letter to the American Association of University Professors. This happened immediately before he and Marie were scheduled to leave on a four-month-long U.S. Navy–sponsored expedition in the Atlantic Ocean on a new navy research vessel called the *Kane*. So when Bruce heard, on June 26 and through a secretary loyal to his cause, that Doc was about to send him a letter asking him "to vacate or be vacated," he absconded in the night, "to avoid a confrontation" that might "jeopardize [his] participation in the cruise." He left his office intact.

Marie and Bruce left for the *Kane* cruise earlier than planned, and with less preparation. As a result, when they arrived in Bermuda to rendezvous with their ship, they were missing materials and equipment. They borrowed some from a colleague running a Lamont outpost in Bermuda. Other than that, the trip had nothing to do with Lamont—a good thing, since Bruce's status as an employee of Columbia University was tenuous. Fortunately, his navy connections were strong. He'd made sure Marie was salaried and had a "special passport" from them, and he was directing the *Kane* cruise as part of a new U.S. Naval Oceanographic Office–funded program called GOFAR, or Global Ocean Floor Analysis and Research.

By June 26, Marie had already directly addressed the confrontation Bruce was avoiding. On June 21, she drafted what appears to be a tardy reply to Doc's letter of April 19. "As you know, Bruce and I have worked as a team on deep sea physiography for over sixteen years," the letter began, with a bang, "and have chosen this work as the principal activity of our lives. During approximately half of these years I have sought peace and quiet in order to better apply myself to the work." Marie is replying to more than Doc's request for her to return to Lamont, which she deems an out-of-the-blue restriction; she's also defending her team. In her letter, she uses the words *we*, *our*, and *us* far more often than she uses the word *I*. "Do you wish us to stop our studies and stop publishing our physiographic diagrams," she asks Doc near the end of her first paragraph. In her second paragraph she tells him that she is "very grateful" for his "vigorous and successful efforts to provide adequate financial support for Lamont's expeditions" and for the "many successful programs" he established.

And then she jumps back in time, identifying what she sees as the original cause for the breakdown in relations. "In regard to our work, and as I discussed with you in the Summer of 1957, when you requested that your name be added to our first diagram [in the Lamont parking lot], Bruce and I strongly believe that the only fair authorship of our physiographic diagrams is that which we have used." The agreement, "made in deference" to Doc, was that his name would appear only on *The Floors of the Ocean* series, the Geological Society of America–sponsored series of monographs that still wasn't, as of 1968, a series. The only one that had appeared was the North Atlantic. "We would wish that we could continue this series as planned," Marie writes, implying Doc's lack of cooperation.

And then she pulls out all the stops. "I think I can with due modesty," she writes, "point out that our work has proved useful to scientific and Naval problems and has been extremely well received. In the past 10 years approximately 50 million copies of our diagrams have carried Lamont's name." The fifty million might be an exaggeration—the precise total is hard to determine—but not by much. There were the replicas of the physiographic diagrams that had been produced and printed by the *New York Times* in the pages of its newspaper, replicas that appeared in *Time*, reprints in textbooks, and there was, of course, the massive circulation of the two *National Geographic* issues. "I cannot believe that our contribution has been an insignificant factor in obtaining further support for Lamont's ship programs." This would have been a particularly prickly sentence: Bruce had been on only one Lamont cruise since 1958 and Marie hadn't been on any. Due to Doc's restrictions, neither of them had been able to directly reap the benefits of that support.

"I wish to continue our work," Marie writes.

> I would like to continue at Columbia. But now you have stopped my salary and have forced me to work without compensation on our present study. Despite such strange tactics we will not grant you authorship on our diagrams. But we would be glad to continue including your name as author on the Floors of the Ocean series. This would, of course, mean that you would have to allow me to receive a salary, and that you would release the funds of our department, that you would allow Bruce and I to submit proposals for further support and that if received, such funds would not be diverted to other work or withheld.

These words are the clearest articulations I've seen in which either Bruce or Marie communicated directly with Doc concerning their problems. In private, Marie might have been anxious and afraid, but not so much that she was publicly cowed. She sent Doc the letter by registered mail, from Bermuda, on June 27.

It is July 1968, morning, and Marie and Bruce are aboard the *Kane*, heading east in the Atlantic Ocean from Bermuda to Dakar. It's the *Kane*'s maiden research voyage, and her objective during this four-month expedition is to survey, for the navy, several fracture zones to try to determine just what route and through what epochs of time the North American continent drifted away from Europe and Africa. Bruce is the chief scientist, but also along for the ride are dozens of other scientists and students from MIT, Catholic University, University of Wisconsin, Columbia, and Cornell. Bruce has just written these words, describing the *Kane* and her objective, on a yellow legal pad. He reads them out loud to Marie, who's bent over a drafting table working on her new physiographic diagram of the Pacific Ocean.

Epochs, he asks her, do you think I should say "periods of time" instead? Nope. She answers quickly, her eyes jumping to his face, scanning it to judge his reaction: none. He's deep in composition mode, working on an article for the *Saturday Review*. He starts writing again: after the theoretical work of Morgan, what's left is the collection of data relating to seafloor spreading, fracture zones, and subduction zones, the interpretation and reinterpretation of data in an attempt to determine the exact paths of the Earth's plates.

They're in one of Marie's two onboard laboratories. In the other lab she's revising (still) the North Atlantic physiographic diagram. The lab they're in now is actually on the ship's deck, right behind the bridge (or control center), and it's where Marie works on a new map: a physiographic diagram of the Pacific Ocean floor. The data she's working from are spread out as much as is possible in what they call the Pacific lab, sounding records and bottom photographs and core diagrams overlapping one another and her in-progress diagram, pens, pencils, erasers, masking tape, and the rest of her usual supplies scattered about on a desk top.

Marie tugs on the end of a profile that Bruce's legal pad is resting on top of, trying to adjust it without him noticing, but he does anyway. He grunts, and she returns her hand to where it was previously resting, somewhere along North America's East Coast. Bruce, in turn, shifts the orientation of the pad without looking at her, his pencil staying on the paper. He hasn't told Marie, but the article begins with her: sixteen years ago, says the longhand on a sheet of paper he's already torn off the pad and stowed in his cabin, a Michigan land surveyor's daughter, Miss Marie Tharp, was charting the floor of the North Atlantic Ocean from soundings made by ships at sea.

Marie and Bruce should probably be in the slightly bigger "Atlantic" lab, but they're supposed to be multitasking and talking about the Pacific diagram, which is along on the trip out of necessity—it needs to be finished so they can start working with Berann on a third panorama for *National Geographic* magazine. The other lab is filled with the profiles and data Marie needs to finish her revision of the North Atlantic Ocean Floor physiographic diagram. Between the two projects in the two labs, she's currently mapping about one-third of the Earth's surface. Neither one of them has really slept in days; although they physically escaped the tension at Lamont, Doc still managed to reach them at sea. The previous day, Bruce had been handed a message from Doc that had been radioed to the ship. "MAIL ADDRESSED HEEZEN ACCUMULATING STOP," the message had read. "PROPOSE SCREEN PROCESS OBSERVATORY PART THEN FORWARD PERSONAL STOP REQUEST SCHEDULE DATES ADDRESSES OR ALTERNATE SUGGESTION STOP EWING SENDS."

Bruce and Marie haven't replied. Their work, as always, continues.

It's taken her some time to get used to drawing at sea. Of course she doesn't try when the weather is bad. She doesn't get seasick, but with the ship pitching and rolling in a storm it's hard enough to keep her body perched on her stool, let alone keep her arm and hand steady so that her fingers can guide her pencil across the paper. She tried once—ankles wrapped around the legs of the stool, clutching the table with one hand and a pencil with the other—until the rolling got so bad that she had to lunge to grab jars of pencils and bottles of ink when they started sliding toward the edge of the table. Rain lashing at the windows, the bodies of men in slickers blurred yellow behind the glass, Bruce bursting into the lab with his hood up and glasses fogged, the wind slamming the door out of his grasp and against the wall, bringing in a gust of rain and ocean spray. She reacted by heaving herself up onto the table and into a protective sprawl over her map. Now she works only when the movement of the ship is gentle, when her own movements can compensate for the ship's.

Marie's bent over her map, inking in an area of the Western Pacific that's studded with tiny seamounts. Lately she's been working with her glasses pushed down on her nose, looking over them rather than through them. Her eyes mostly rest on the map, occasionally darting back and forth between it and a sounding record she's spread out across the northernmost portion of the Atlantic Ocean floor. Bruce is bent over his article, writing about the sounds of the ship at work, the constant high-pitched pings and lower-pitched chirps, the thunderous underwater explosions separated by eight-second intervals—sounds generated so they'll bounce off the ocean floor (or the Earth beneath the ocean floor) and give the scientists aboard the ship a picture of the topography and content of that part of the Earth's crust. At night, he writes, the spark that ignites the explosives illumines the ship's stern with a blue light. During the day, streams of ascending air bubbles break the sea surface. For sixteen years they've been together—they could have a kid learning to drive, starting to think about college, a kid they're worrying will reach eighteen before the Vietnam War ends. Instead they've produced maps.

This maiden voyage of the 289-foot-long *Kane* is actually quite a big deal, making Bruce, as chief scientist of the expedition, a big deal by extension. It's a role he's used to by now. He gets to direct where the ship goes, what she does, what her priorities are—and because Marie is his partner, those decisions are (unofficially) partly hers. The decision to start revising the North Atlantic map, even though the Pacific map was already under way, has been less so: Bruce proclaimed the necessity of the switch, and she acquiesced, which is how she's come to be sitting on the *Kane*, with two labs going at once, helping him direct the ship to the places on their North Atlantic map that she filled in using interpolation more than a decade before—particularly a fracture zone they've been calling "Scarp D" since they discovered it two years before. Scarp D is an example of what Tuzo Wilson deemed a transform fault, a concave curving crack intersecting and offsetting the Mid-Atlantic Ridge, a feature whose boundaries Marie and Bruce want to concretely establish.

The *Kane*'s echo sounder is more precise than anything they've ever worked with before. It's already shown them that the floor of the rift valley is much rougher than they thought—lacy rather than smooth. The ship also has an IBM computer, which means that data can be processed practically in real time. As the ship steams along collecting data, scientists take turns coding the information into numbers understandable to the computer. They need not wait several months for the processing to be done onshore before taking the next step in an experiment.

Instead of watching for danger up ahead in the form of ships or icebergs, the scientific watch on board monitors the constant stream of data being spit out by the ship's instruments. There's a cage of sensors that gets lowered into the water so that it can measure temperature, salinity, sound velocity, and ambient light. There's a magnetometer, trailing on a long wire from the ship's stern, which measures and records changes from positive to negative polarization of magnetism in the rocks it passes above. And there are the various sounding devices, which make those pings and chirps Bruce is writing about, also trailing on long wires. Right now they're traveling above Scarp D, sounding it and trying to find the places where it intersects with the Mid-Atlantic Rift Valley. They already know that Scarp D offset the rift by about ninety miles, which means that there are two places of intersection—a western point, where the rift valley extends down from the north and hits Scarp D, and an eastern point, where the rift extends up from the south and hits the scarp—with ninety miles of offset in between. The person who's been keeping scientific watch knocks on the door. It looks, he says, like they've located the southwestern intersection of the rift and the scarp. You should probably come look at the sounding record.

When Marie and Bruce get to the sounding lab they go straight to the sounder. Marie bends to pick up the record unfurling from it. They examine it together, Bruce's eyes on Marie's finger as it traces the grainy black of the seafloor stretching across the scroll. She touches the places where, a short while before, the ship crossed over a depth of twenty thousand feet, where the floor made a brief slow climb, and where it abruptly rose sixteen thousand feet in one sheer cliff—that sharp rise is Scarp D. They don't even have to talk about it. Bruce leaves for the bridge to tell the captain they need to stop the ship so they can make some more observations of the area.

He wants to collect some core samples, take some photographs, gather as much information about the area as they can before they leave. The coring tube comes up from the floor of the fracture with fresh crystalline rock—giant crystals that require long periods of cooling and may be, Bruce writes in his article during a moment of downtime, from the Earth's mantle and not its crust. Rocks that many have often tried (and failed) to obtain. This is exciting; several more days pass without sleep. They dredge in an attempt to get a bigger piece of the crystalline rock, but the basket just keeps coming up filled with volcanic mud—nothing that might be from the mantle, he writes. Just the kind of thing they've all been finding for years, more evidence of volcanic activity.

Marie works around the clock on her maps, drawing her way across two oceans while the ship is paused. She and Bruce consult—he travels between the immediate present and her offices, which are focused on the distant past—and she helps him plan the ship's work. She is not, however, a part of the scientific watch. Bruce thinks she's more valuable working on the maps and helping him plan. He doesn't want her hovering around watching data streams or monitoring the various sampling attempts. She gets a little more sleep than he as a result.

When it looks like they've wrung all of the data they can out of the area, Marie and Bruce replot a course for the ship. They'll continue zigging and zagging over Scarp D, east toward Dakar, Marie tells the captain. Bruce has already collapsed into bed, so her North Atlantic lab is empty and dark when she returns to it. She flips the light switch next to the door, lets her body relax slightly into solitude. There is her map, spread out on the table. She crosses the room and stands looking down at it.

This physiographic diagram is already substantially different from her 1959 version: right now she's working on the portion of the ocean floor that used to be covered up with a big rectangular legend. Already she's been able to fill in the smooth floor of the rift valley with a rougher texture. She's been shifting the angle at which Scarp D intersects the rift valley; it's not perpendicular, but the action is akin to straightening a frame hanging on a wall—lift one end slightly and the other goes lower. With more precise boundaries of Scarp D (and other fracture zones) cor-related to the magnetic orientation of its rocks, they should be able to figure out the rate at which North America traveled away from Africa.

Looking at the map is still a curious sensation—like being able to see through thousands of feet of water, space collapsing so that the ocean floor is close and the world she lives in is far away. This revision has made time collapse, too. Her current process is different from when she first mapped the North Atlantic, and she's still aware of the ghostly presence of her former self, as if time has folded up like an accordion, making her two selves touch.

One floor below her, Bruce has just been roused from sleep by the scientist on watch. The fracture, the scientist says through his door, is lost. We need help finding it again. Bruce sits up, swings his legs over the side of his bunk. Lost? he barks. Yes, says the scientist. Bruce rests there for a minute, hunched over and trying to wake up. He feels old. He also feels similar to Marie—not only is he working on revising the North

Atlantic diagram with her, but this area of the ocean is where, in 1947, he went on his first cruise. Back then they had to stop the ship constantly if they wanted to take measurements. Now measurements are taken automatically and constantly, the ship stopping only when there's something particularly interesting or, like now, a problem. And he's the one who decides when to stop the ship, a consolation for the impotence that Doc imposed upon him at Lamont. He gets up and makes his way through hallways to the sounding lab, carrying his insecurity with him, feeling along the way that he might bump into his twenty-seven-year-old self rounding a corner.

The *Kane*'s maiden voyage was successful; Scarp D was found, lost, and then found again. Marie and Bruce discovered three new seamounts (and eliminated a phantom one) for the map, collected more details on the Senegal Submarine Canyon, mapped a small abyssal plain within the Cape Verdes, and modified the boundaries of the Sierra Leone Abyssal Plain. By the time they arrived at Dakar, their eastern destination, all of their data were processed and plotted, the first time an oceanographic expedition ever accomplished such a feat. They bought a map of the "Ville de Dakar," the kind of city map that folds up on itself and into a bifold cardboard cover, a map dominated by robin's egg blue and crimson and sea foam green. On the trip back to the States, they gave a naval captain a tour of the *Kane* and hosted a documentary film crew. All in all, Marie wrote many years later, "the revisions in the topography resulting from the cruise on the *Kane* were more extensive than any of the [other] cruises Bruce and I were ever on."

The trip was not all excitement and discovery. Waiting for them at the U.S. Defense Attaché Office in Dakar was a letter from Doc. It was addressed to Marie, but like most things Doc addressed to her, it was also meant partly for Bruce. In it, he said that he by no means wanted Marie to stop her work on the physiographic diagrams, that he was proud of her work. He repeated that if she were to continue to work for Lamont, she could not continue to do her work at home and would have to "completely alter [her] attitude." He said he was confident, however, that it would be "simple" for her to "find ample support elsewhere." And then he said something that, like Marie's statement about the number of copies of her maps in circulation, was open to interpretation. "I am sure," he wrote, that not having access to Lamont's data would be "no serious problem."

Lamont's data bank was Doc's pride; he knew perfectly well that Marie and Bruce would have left long ago if not for it, and knew that these data were the reason they were still fighting.

Doc's tone changed after that, and he noted that her letter appeared to "hinge" on a misapprehension that he wanted his name on the physiographic diagrams. That, Doc wrote, was not the case. "You say that in 1957 you agreed, in deference to me, to include my name as an author of *The Floors of the Ocean*." During that academic year, he continued, Bruce had just received his doctorate and Marie was a "promising, but fairly junior" employee. "To speak so condescendingly of my role in the work done during those years displays a grave misconception, since you know perfectly well that I organized, planned, and participated in all phases of the work which led to Dr. Heezen and you doing the actual preparation of that book." This is true; just as without Marie's work it wouldn't have been possible for Hess, Vine, Matthews, Morley, Bullard, or Morgan et al. to develop the theories that were the building blocks of plate tectonics; without Doc's obsessive collection of deep-sea data, without his building of Lamont, Marie's work would not have been possible.

No reply, if written, exists in the archive of Marie's and Bruce's papers. When I came across their map of Dakar, it was folded so that only one quadrant of the city was exposed, as if it had been used just last week, the trip—and the hurt—fresh.

*T*HE HARASSMENT GOT WORSE BEFORE IT GOT BETTER. ON December 10, 1969, Harriett Ewing (Doc's wife and secretary), acting under what she described as verbal and written authorization from Doc, his assistant director Worzel, and Dennis Hayes (the new head of the submarine topography group), had the Lamont building and grounds crew remove the locked door of room 204B, formerly Marie's office, from its hinges. Room 204B could be accessed only through Bruce's office, which was itself locked. Room 204B still contained many of Marie's belongings and various pieces of furniture, data, and objects belonging to Bruce and his students.

"You cannot possibly believe that it is proper under any circumstance to dump the contents of a man's office without warning into a corridor, whether he be professor, student, or technician," Bruce wrote in a memo to a Lamont administrator almost two weeks after the incident. Months later the contents of that office were still in the hall, Bruce having refused, on principle, to move them. "The assignment of office space cannot be taken as an isolated action, but must be considered in connection with the long series of harassments which have hindered my work, disrupted my research and teaching functions, and had other grave effects."

Indeed, the harassments certainly hindered the work and research of both Bruce and Marie, but the whole situation did the same for Doc. "I am of the view," Columbia's vice president wrote to Doc in April 1969, "that formal actions with regard to the Heezen matter can be damaging to the University and to [Lamont]." He went on to urge caution, noting that Doc's wish to fire the tenured Bruce could "result in a future for Lamont considerably less bright than its distinguished past." He told Doc to explore all options and, if he still felt that the situation could not be mended, to prepare a "bill of particulars" that included clearly outlined examples of substantive charges. From what he knew of the situation, the vice president wrote, "charges of substance, if they exist, are buried in a welter of records of annoyance, frustration, and irritation."

And then there was this, near the end of the vice president's letter: "While I admire and respect a civilized urbanity of conduct, insolence to the Director is not, I think, actionable. . . . For all of Heezen's difficulties, it has not been proposed that he is other than a good scientist, heavily immersed in science, with an above par record of supervising the research of Ph.D. candidates." Against this veiled advice, formal actions were initiated by Lamont's executive committee—which was headed by Doc. Throughout 1970, various committees consisting of men from Lamont and the highest echelons of Columbia tried, in countless meetings and drafts of memoranda, to decide what was to be done about what they called the Heezen Affair.

On April 6, 1970, Doc sent Bruce a letter saying that it was his "belief" that the suspension in place since November 10, 1967, "would be lifted." That said, it was unclear just who had won the battle between Doc and Bruce. In keeping his job, Bruce had scored an oedipal victory over Doc, effectively rendering his former mentor administratively impotent. But while the constraints on Marie and Bruce loosened, restraints remained even after Bruce's suspension was officially lifted. "For the time being," Doc wrote to Bruce, "you will not be appointed any administrative duties. Dennis Hayes will continue to direct the submarine topography program."

Maybe the true winner was Doc, who'd bruised his ego but emerged with the spoils. After all, in not having administrative duties or control of the submarine topography program, Bruce's position was considerably diminished. And if Marie was Bruce's heart, Doc still had it clutched in his raised fist—the ruling of Columbia's administration did not extend to Marie, so Doc refused to rehire her, knowing that he could hurt Bruce in the process. Look back at Marie and Bruce's body of work and the scars are obvious: Doc left his mark by preventing Bruce from going out on Lamont ships, from submitting grant applications under Lamont's name, and from directly accessing the Lamont data that they needed to create their physiographic diagrams.

But Bruce had managed to circumvent much of this. Other than the midnight requisitions, he'd collected data about the ocean floor by getting involved with the U.S. Naval Oceanographic Office, a connection that had begun in the mid-1960s, led to Marie's employment with them when Doc fired her in 1968, and, eventually, to the navy consulting Bruce when it began planning the construction of new dual-use submersibles and submarines (submarines and submersibles not being the same—submersibles are much smaller and dexterous than submarines, but unlike submarines they're dependent on larger surface ships for supplies and long-distance travel). The plan was to use the new boats for defense purposes first and scientific purposes second. By sending them out on research missions, the crews would be kept, as Bruce put it, "up to snuff," and scientists would be able to get an "intimate feeling for the [ocean] bottom environment."

Bruce's first "eyeball view" of the ocean floor had left an "indelible impression" on his mind. After an acquaintance and fellow scientist invited him to go on several dives with him in the Jacques Cousteau–designed submersible *Deep Star 4000*, Bruce was hooked. The experience, he said, was as vivid as if he were standing "in the bottom of a gully or on the top of a sand dune" simply observing nature. Not quite the same as having sand in your face or water flowing around your feet, he continued, "because you're encased in this ball looking out, but you have a feeling of the process which is so vivid that it is difficult to translate into scientific terms." In exchange for first-person glimpses of the ocean floor, Bruce had to accept that his collection of information would be at "a rate several orders of magnitude lower" than he was accustomed to. The surface vessels he'd spent time on during his career (first those of Lamont, then of the navy and of other universities) may have been thousands of meters from the ocean floor, but their instruments were unequaled in efficiency and sophistication.

The timing was perfect, for by the beginning of the 1970s Marie had, either in her physiographic diagrams or in sketches for Berann's *National Geographic* paintings, mapped nearly all of Earth's ocean floors. For most of her career, her firsthand glimpses of the ocean floor (in photographic form) were static—like studying a dancer's movements with only a strobe lighting the stage. Her future, however, lay in revision, in the refinement of textures and the precise boundaries of features—tasks readily served by Bruce's new eyeball views.

Marie and Bruce grew closer then. Despite Bruce's temper, despite the constraints and anxieties imposed upon them by The Harassment, they had proven their loyalty to each other. They'd also found so many ways to work around the obstructions Doc placed in their paths that they seemed to be the better for it. In addition to the new types of observations Bruce was engaging in, and to Marie's having worked her way across nearly all of the ocean floor, they had a fruitful relationship with *National Geographic* and the U.S. Navy, had appeared on television and in documentary films, and had served as educational consultants for materials that were being developed to teach children about the new concept of plate tectonics.

And Bruce had finally written a book. Coauthored with his former student Charles "Charlie" Hollister (who later mentored Robert Ballard, celebrity oceanographer and discoverer of the *Titanic*'s wreck), the book was titled *The Face of the Deep*, and was what they referred to as "an illustrated natural history." With more than five hundred photographs of the ocean floor spread out over 650 pages, it was a major accomplishment, especially considering the stress under which it had been produced; Hollister moved on to Woods Hole after earning his PhD from Columbia in 1967, but he and Bruce began the book at Lamont during the height of The Harassment. In an interview conducted during the mid-1990s, Marie said that during the period "Hollister learned how to finagle photographs." The book's illustration credits include AT&T, Bell, Duke University, Scripps, Woods Hole, the navy, NATO, the National Science Foundation, the United Kingdom's National Institute of Oceanography, Canada's Bedford Institute of Oceanography, and the USSR's National Academy of Sciences. The Soviets, Marie said in that interview, were more forthcoming than Doc's Lamont.

Billed as "the first compilation of its kind," *The Face of the Deep* illustrates "life in the abyss": what the book's editor at Oxford University Press deemed a "dark, bitter, cold world" where "tiny marine creatures are nourished by deep-sea sediment," "volcanic upheavals" take place, and "two hundred million years of evolution" are recorded. Seafloor! Abyss! A dark cold world previously hidden from the public! Crack the book and this tone might sound slightly off: the photos are in gray scale, many of them showing gunk and sediment of various particle sizes, photos spectacular mostly for their context. Compared to the Technicolor deep-sea creatures that grace the pages of today's books and magazines, creatures with exciting names such as Fanfin seadevil and Dumbo jellyfish, *The Face of the Deep* might be disappointing, like showing up for the trapeze act and having to watch grade-school tumblers instead.

That was not the case in 1971, when it was published. Its authors aimed to eliminate jargon in order to speak to the same "general scientific public" that had been Bruce and Marie's target audience for all of their physiographic diagrams and *National Geographic* panoramas. The emphasis, like that of the maps, was on the visual: to use photographs and diagrams to take the reader on a "visual armchair journey through the abyssal world." The text was meant as a "verbal accompaniment," not intended to be read alone. And the book was successful. Reviews (and there were many) almost unanimously praised its accessibility and magnificence.

"The photographs are, of course," said one reviewer, "brilliant," but the majority of reviewers applauded the lively, evocative, poetic text. Bruce and Hollister had managed to overcome what Bruce called the difficulty of "translat[ing] into scientific terms" the "visual character" of the ocean floor. They were even nominated, along with Norman Mailer, John McPhee, and E. O. Wilson, for the science category of the 1971 National Book Award. Much of the book's success was due, I think, to its multifaceted approach. In addition to text, photos, and maps, the book included diagrams of the instruments used to study the ocean floor. Carefully captioned sketches of underwater cameras and submersibles helped readers understand how, in spite of darkness, intense pressure, and murky water, the book's photos had been collected. There was even a poem presumably written by Bruce and/or Hollister: "The Sea, our sea, thou great and glorious sea / Yield up thy secrets to our weak and fumbling band," it began. "Honors, titles and epithets are but empty words for joy of teaching, joy of learning / Joy at the instants of revelation are our life's real rewards."

On the flip side of the poem page was a picture of an unidentified Marie working on a physiographic diagram. Even though she wasn't listed as an author of *The Face of the Deep*, her presence bookends the text: the photo of her is on the last page of the book's body, and the preface is signed with Bruce and Charlie's initials and the words "beside the Tappan Zee." Marie's house, next to the Hudson and slightly upriver from the Tappan Zee Bridge, was where they did much of their work. If the book itself gives off what Bruce might have called a vivid impression, it is one highly influenced by Marie and her belief in the power of images.

Doc is not mentioned outside of the illustration credits. In the third sentence of the book, however, Bruce and Charlie write that their "study began in 1947 when one of us led a minor expedition which obtained two hundred photographs and bottom samples of the continental shelf and continental slope off New England." It was Bruce—the expedition was his first, the *Atlantis* cruise that Doc invited him to join during their fateful first meeting at the University of Iowa—and the camera he used during that expedition (and many others in the years that followed) was one that had originally been designed by Doc. In other words, Bruce's career had been made possible by Doc—a fact that Bruce was well aware of. "My dear Dr. Ewing," Bruce wrote in a letter at the time, "I have asked my publishers to send you a galley proof of the text of my forthcoming book." He and Charlie had started work on the book seven years prior, he said near the letter's opening, and "planned to dedicate the work to you, a plan which subsequent events made quite impossible."

In the rest of the letter, Bruce detailed all the ways in which they had planned to acknowledge, allude to, and quote Doc—but hadn't. "We have not praised you in any way in this book," Bruce wrote. "Let us hope that in the future we shall be able to resume our former position of mutual admiration," he wrote in closing. "Sincerely yours, Bruce." The former admiration was never restored. Doc resigned as director of Lamont in 1972, taking Worzel with him to Texas, where he founded a new division of Earth and planetary sciences at the University of Texas at Galveston's Marine Biomedical Institute. It wasn't an official retirement, but it may as well have been.

After Doc left Lamont, any external restraints left over from The

Harassment vanished. What remained were the habits Marie and Bruce had settled into. Constraint had conditioned them, and in examining the post-Harassment period of their lives, it's clear that the constraints freed them to focus on details, too, the way a sonnet's structured form can offer a poet freedom to focus on imagery and language. Marie continued working from home, but was rehired as a Lamont employee. Bruce was allowed on Lamont ships again, but he continued to spend the majority of his seafaring time on the ships of other institutions, and on underwater vessels.

Sometime in the early 1970s, the navy finally completed work on the super-secret amphibious research and reconnaissance submarine that Bruce had helped to plan. It was called the *NR-1* and was powered by a miniature nuclear reactor. It could stay on the ocean floor for weeks at a time, had cost $100 million to build, was forty-four meters long, and could carry ten crew members and two scientists. Bruce and Charlie Hollister were chosen as the first scientists on board, partly because, as Lee Vyborny and Don Davis, the authors of 2004's *Dark Waters: An Insider's Account of the NR-1, the Cold War's Undercover Nuclear Sub*, wrote, "they were already famous and did not need to write a book."

Despite their previous submersible work, on their first *NR-1* voyage, Bruce and Charlie were "like two kids with a new toy," the sub's skipper said. The sub's observation deck was a tiny space, with just enough room for two men to lie on their stomachs, heads propped on elbows, looking out through the *NR-1*'s three four-inch portholes like little boys enthralled by their first glimpse of television. As the *NR-1* "threaded into canyons," "crawled along the sedimentary floor," and flew over seamounts, Bruce and Charlie grew glum—and then grumpy. In just a short amount of time on the *NR-1* they realized that they would have to "go back and rethink" much of what they'd recently written in their book.

By that point, Bruce was content with his "wide reputation," which meant that he didn't "have to look very hard at every project to make sure that [he got] some publicity out of it." He was "gaga over the deep," and so he became, *Dark Waters* notes, "a particularly frequent and favorite rider," influencing the small boat and crew with his "loud shirts," "friendly personality," and ability to turn the *NR-1* into a "nuclear-powered delicatessen" when he came on board with "strings of preserved sausages, sweetbreads, canned delicacies, and jars of treats that he stuffed into any crevasse he could find and hung from overhead pipes and cables." All of these habits tempered some of the difficulties and inconveniences—stale air and tightly rationed water; sleeping in shifts; one small table, one old airline oven to heat up frozen dinners, and one toilet—of life on a nuclear submarine in the 1970s.

Somewhere on my hard drive is a file of photos I scanned at the Library of Congress. In it is an image of a page from one of Marie's photo albums. It's just a scan, but I can remember the exact feeling of the sleeve's glossy clear plastic, smooth but for the rough-sealed seams that provided boundaries for the photos. There are five on the page, three horizontal and two vertical: a sequence of shots of Bruce getting into a submersible. What's remarkable about these pictures is the joy they show—Bruce, it's clear, has softened. Just as the years he spent on his father's farm during World War II drained some of the cockiness out of him, the end of The Harassment and the beginning of a new type of work let him settle, relax. He's only just reached his fifties, but he looks older in his thick-rimmed glasses, with his thinning straight-combed hair lifted up haphazard in the wind.

In the first picture he stands with his hands on the sub's back, his checkered button-down absorbing the sun that makes the bare muscled limbs of the young men facing him glow. In the second picture he has come around closer to the sub's narrow hatch, and a few of the young men have, too, their profiles revealing virile beards and the tight stretch of cutoffs across broad tanned thighs. For the third picture the photographer has zoomed in on Bruce, who's sitting balanced on the hatch's rim, the thickness of his torso contrasting with the position of his hand, caught midair and delicate, fingertips reaching to steady. In the fourth picture he's knee-deep down the hatch, belly hanging down while one of the young men holds a headset up and ready for him. And in the fifth picture his head hangs down toward his chest, giving the impression that he might not make it at all, his mass too great to get much farther in.

When I first discovered these pictures, I could feel an urgency in them, as if they marked the point at which Marie and Bruce knew they were no longer young—Bruce wanting to spend as much time as possible directly observing the ocean floor, Marie's maps getting ever more detailed as a result—this knowledge like a shift in the air, the sky gone green and still before a summer thunderstorm, when all the people and animals hurry home. These moments are not the actual storm but the expectation of it, when you remember all the storms you've been through before and are able to say the words *of course, I know what is coming*: fate always catches up, presents itself as a sentence or gesture that falls perfectly into place, the brick completing the path that leads to the end.

CHAPTER 23

O F ALL THE THINGS I'VE COME TO LOVE ABOUT MARIE, one I'm particularly fond of is her idiosyncratic organizational method. Some might not consider it a form of organization at all. There are those who might view Marie's tendency to treat some things with meticulous care and leave others chaotic as sheer archival mayhem. In the 1950s and '60s, for example, she put together binders filled with clippings about the work of people at Lamont and science stories that interested her, but that dropped off as she grew older—replaced, I believe, by binders filled with correspondence. These binders were labeled according to subject or event, and only after they were thus grouped were they chronologically ordered. The people with whom she corresponded a great deal received their own binders, with Bruce's mother and Marie's brother, Jim, winning on the bulk front.

Marie did not compile similarly organized scrapbooks of her travels and experiences. She saved what appears to be a good deal of the paper items that passed through her life. She saved news articles and letters, she saved greeting cards and notes written on the backs of envelopes, old identification cards, postcards, contracts, invitations, pamphlets and brochures, bills, receipts, address books and datebooks, photographs, drawings, memos, labels, flattened boxes. She saved a lot, and she did not necessarily discriminate when organizing it. A good example of this is a box at the Library of Congress marked "Marie Tharp, House Library, 'Gold' File Cabinet 1/7, Drawer 2/4."

This box was not directly filled by Marie, was probably packed by one of the Tharpophiles after she'd died, but it was filled from a drawer that had been filled by her. In it were four binders, each one at least two inches thick, containing assorted versions of the document Marie called her "Opus." There was also a manila envelope marked "Connecticut 1973 BCH & MT," which held brochures for various hotels, the Winchester Gun Museum, the John Tarrant Kenney Hitchcock Museum, the Old New-Gate Prison and Copper Mine, and a small catalogue of homes for sale in the area. There was another manila envelope, this one marked "Europe 1972 BCH & MT," which included postcards from all across western Europe. Also in the envelope was an invitation to a party (addressed to both Marie and Bruce, at Lamont) at the Park Avenue home of a Ms. Elizabeth Moxley, at which Mr. Salvador Dalí was to be the honored guest. I can imagine Marie deep in conversation with Dalí; he was, I think, just her type.

In another box, marked "BCH travels," were many things that related to Bruce's travels in the 1950s and '60s, but also many things that did not. There was, for example, a 1972 calendar with bloodred plastic binding and the words "Heinz Hall for the Performing Arts" and "Pittsburgh Cultural Trust" embossed in gold on its front. The only events written on the entire calendar, on three separate days, were "sprayed Inky for fleas," "spent the day at B. He moved bedroom," and "big truck came down to pick up one chair. Called Danielle." Also in that box was a file marked "Things BCH & MT did together," which contained just two things: a pamphlet for the Metropolitan Museum of Art's September 1970 to January 1971 exhibit on the sculpture of Middle America and a folded sheet of paper explaining handwriting analysis.

I also came across, again and again, a series of documents that Marie and Bruce had produced for a man named John Lear. The documents were mostly interview transcripts and letters. Lear had been the science editor of the *Saturday Review* in the 1960s and '70s, and during that time, he broke stories on the dangers of fluoride in drinking water, the Robertson Panel report on UFOs, and the emerging theories of plate tectonics.

He wanted, in fact tried, to write a book about Marie. In a flurry of letters dated between 1974 and 1978 he gave her lists of questions to answer. He saw parallels between her and Rosalind Franklin (a biophysicist who was the first to capture images of DNA's structure), even sent Marie a Xeroxed copy of Ann Sayre's book *Rosalind Franklin and DNA*, with notes such as "pertinent here is Marie's story of the telegram she got from Ewing after her flight to Ohio" and "it would be interesting to know her identity, her feelings, her fate" jotted in the margins.

"Compare to Marie," he scribbled.

"Compare with plate tectonics."

"Compare to Ewing-Tharp row on the maps."

On June 9, 1975, Lear seemed to think that he understood the basics of Marie's story and had only to wait for her to fill in some small gaps. "Only the remainder of this month and the months of July and August remain for me to complete my book on your work and its consequences. It would be most helpful to me if you could somehow find the time to answer the following questions." On February 23, 1976, in the letter that accompanied the excerpt of the Franklin book, he was still waiting. "I hope to write you a longer note later today to delineate some of the very large holes that still remain in my story. Bruce has been a very gratifying source of information," Lear wrote. Bruce had been recording countless tapes and sending them off to Lear, who responded with a "Thanks!" and noted that the tapes were "pelting" him "like snowballs." But there were holes in the story, Lear wrote, that only Marie could fill. "It must be clear to both of you that I have no intention to slight Bruce in pressing you for your responses. He is a major character in the book but you are the main character. As a writer, I just can't escape the consequences of that fact."

About the same time that John Lear started earnestly pursuing the idea of writing Marie's biography, Doc died. He'd had a stroke at his home in Galveston and was in a coma for six days before dying on May 5, 1974. During those six days, his wife, Harriett, said, the nurses shaved him so well that it looked like he'd done it himself and was just sleeping, comfortable amid a tangle of monitoring equipment, the constant beep of his heart monitor like sonar pings, the read on the digital display like the peaks and valleys of a fathogram. He was being kept alive, the electricity gone from his brain. The doctor repeated this to Harriett every day. At first she couldn't get it through her head; then she wouldn't get it through her head. Until she did: finally went home, she said, and then they disconnected him.

A funeral was held in Texas, and then Doc's body was flown back to Palisades and buried in the Rockland Cemetery, close to Lamont. Marie remembered being in the car with Bruce as they drove up the hilly road leading to the cemetery, remembered the crowd clustered around the grave, the Ewing children sobbing and Harriett clad in a pink raincoat and tam. Harriett seemed, Marie wrote, to "sigh with relief after the brief words of the service were over."

Marie and Bruce must have been relieved, too. In all of the materials they prepared for John Lear—hundreds of pages of letters written by Marie, each line of her loopy scrawl filling two lines on the yellow legal pads she favored; more than two dozen tapes that Bruce recorded, some by himself and in response to Lear's questions, some with all three of them in dialogue—it's obvious that Lear had a hard time getting them to speak in detail about The Harassment. Bruce told him that they weren't keen on reopening wounds only recently healed and as a result the transcripts are both voluminous and secretive. The materials' magnitude alone suggests that Marie and Bruce revealed a great deal; considering that these materials were supposed to include details about a period more than two decades long, it wasn't that much.

"I wasn't here. I couldn't feel those things you felt," Lear said to Marie in one of the transcripts, trying to figure out why she'd refused to work on the Lamont campus after she got back from India, why she'd refused to let Doc come to her house to see her work, why she was so afraid at the time. He tried flattery: "From what you tell me, you must have had reason for feeling this way. It didn't come out of the air. You didn't just invent it. There must have been things that happened." He tried humility: "There are just big gaps in the story from my point of view . . . and I don't know enough to know why you were so careful. My job as a reporter is to have enough facts to feel that I can feel exactly as you do as of a given time." He tried good cop: "I haven't wanted to hurt you or Bruce at any time." He tried tough love: "You probably wonder why in the hell am I tormenting you about these things and the answer is I've got to have these things . . . I've got to have the answers to these questions. Who am I going to ask, if not you?"

The answer to that was Bruce. They were a shrewd team, those two, deftly passing questions to each other that they then only selectively answered. At times they were candid. On at least one occasion Bruce referred to the situation with Doc as "one big stinking mass of bullshit politics." Marie laughed. "You realize I can't print something like that," John Lear said, and Bruce went on to use some more colorful language, and John Lear again tried to steer him back toward the topic at hand, but Bruce would have none of it. He was what you might call a talker. Marie, for her part, was more direct in her written replies to Lear, but even then she could be short. If, for example, she felt he was mistaken, she said so. When she felt she'd already adequately answered a question, she simply referred him back to her previous statement. "If you look back at the [reverse] of some of the Lamont bulletins I already sent you, particularly those of the early 1960s . . ." "You asked the various steps in making a chart. I presume you mean a physiographic diagram. You state that I have already told you that I begin with actual soundings, taken by ocean-ographic research vessels, but you state that after that you are lost. I refer you to the little green book that Bruce and I wrote, called *The Floors of the Oceans,* and in the early part of the first chapter you will find a brief description of how we proceed. Before I try to explain the whole thing from scratch, I suggest you read that over so you might be able to ask a more specific question."

It was not that Marie refused outright to provide long explanations for complicated matters. She was just reticent. Things she viewed as private were not discussed in detail: Lear's request for her to provide motivation for her feelings toward Doc was ignored, and when Lear asked her to narrate her childhood, he received just ten pages dealing with the first twenty years of her life. It was a stalemate: the gaps in Marie's story remained and Lear never wrote his book, unable to part with any of his protagonist's story if he couldn't tell it all.

What I think John Lear failed to understand was that in order to write about Marie he would have to apply the credo that had been influencing her life and work for decades. "Processes," she said, referring to how the Earth's movements created the ocean floor's topography, "do not cease to exist with the last available sounding track. They carry on until the next set of parameters presents itself." She and Bruce never would have been able to offer views of the ocean floor to the public solely on the basis of the hard data—that's why she hypothesized to fill in the gaps. Or to look at it from another perspective: when Bruce started doing his submersible work, getting as close as humanly possible to the ocean floor, he realized that proximity didn't magically solve all the problems distance had presented. Each informed the other, and you had to study both in order to solve the puzzle.

BY THE MID-1970s, Marie's house on Washington Avenue in Nyack was also the workplace of a devoted crew, some of whom occasionally lived there, many of whom became the founders of multigenerational lines of Tharpophiles, a complex constellation of people who orbited Marie until she died, people she hired to tackle a huge range of tasks and often took under her wing.

Robert Brunke started working for Marie in 1972, after his older brothers had vacated their positions. "They weren't really scientifically minded," Brunke said. "But I say that with a grain of salt: my first job when I got down there was to empty the trash and clean the Inky porch." (Habitually too engrossed in her work to remember to let Inky out, she'd had a dog door installed that led out to the second-story porch. There, Inky would do his thing and then Brunke would come along every so often and sweep everything off into the Hudson.) "Marie always loved to begin with that story whenever she was telling people about me," Brunke said. "She was always like, 'Oh, he started off—' and you gotta get her voice. Probably all the people you talk to have replicated the voice," he told me. The voice, as he called it, was high-pitched, breathy, and wavering—sort of the audio equivalent of hand-wringing. "She's like, 'Oh, Bobby started out cleaning the Inky porch.' I mean we'd be talking to professional people at a conference and I'd be like, 'Oh great, this is the way I started out.'"

By all accounts, working at the Nyack house was fun, everyone with his own little nest of a work space, the perimeters of which were constantly being breached by rubber bands shot by coworkers. There was the time they taped up someone's entire doorway, leaving him stuck in his office; the time Brunke mistakenly whacked Marie with a map tube (he turned one way and the length of the tube went the other), smacking her in the head so she went sprawling onto the couch. How when she got up, she fired him, which was what she did when anyone who worked for her did even the tiniest thing against her wishes: "You're fired, you're fired, you're fired! And don't ever come back," she'd say to the offender, who was usually not surprised. "You'd get fired maybe twice a week," Brunke said, "but it never lasted." After some silence had passed she'd ask what time he was coming in the next day.

Marie's house was, I've concluded, a haven for misfits; enthusiasts who passionately collected—comics, records, books, antiques—were the ones who truly thrived there. I think it must have been something about how their minds were wired, a predilection for systematic and repetitive examination that working for Marie cultivated. Because the ones who really fit in down at the bottom of Washington Avenue got to work on maps, plotting and crunching numbers and doing photographic reduction and reproductions. She didn't care that when Brunke moved into her basement he brought along his dozens of crates of records—before that he'd actually lived in her yard, camped out in a tent.

Any encouragement to fit in came from Bruce. He'd barrel down Marie's curving gravel driveway at "sixty or seventy miles per hour," Brunke recalled, and if the workers had been goofing off when they heard his tires squeal they'd scramble back to their desks. Whereas Marie was known to tell them to do something and be content to let them finish lunch first, Bruce laid down the law: do what she said, or else. "While it was work time, it was serious as hell and he didn't take any garbage at all," Brunke said, "but after five o'clock it was like you'd flick this switch." Bruce and Marie would pour drinks and Bruce would sit lecturing Brunke "for hours and hours on why I shouldn't be a marine biologist and I should be a geologist instead. When I went to school he actually got me some interviews at the University of Rhode Island." Over the course of his career, Bruce had to make concessions, and long ago he'd decided to make intimidation the dominating characteristic of his public persona— only in private, or with those he trusted, was he generous.

Marie did not make concessions naturally. She cared for what she cared for and didn't give a damn about the rest. She never did concede to Doc, and continued revealing the ocean floor to the public through her physiographic diagrams and work with Berann—even though her contributions to the ever-growing theory of plate tectonics were largely ignored. What concessions she did make were small, and made mostly to Bruce. If they had to attend a black-tie event, for example, Bruce would send Alma Kesner, one of the Lamont secretaries, over to Marie's house early to "pick her up," code for trying to tamp down some of Marie's quirkier wardrobe decisions.

"Let me see your feet," Alma would say when she arrived, and Marie would gather up the skirt of her evening gown to reveal the sneakers she wore with everything. Or she might arrive to find Marie in a tailored skirt slit up to her knee, a man's shirt, and oxfords or tennis shoes on her feet. When Alma objected, Marie would tell her that she didn't "go in for the looks" of what people were wearing. "I look for intelligence," she said. Alma remembered that before Bruce started sending her in to intervene, Marie would be off on her own talking to a million people, not caring what she looked like, not considering that others might judge her differently from how she judged them. Once Alma got her into fancy shoes, after remarking that it was possible to be intelligent and look nice, too, Marie thanked her. "I don't know what I'd do without you," she'd tell Alma as they surrendered their jackets at the party, which was really like saying the same to Bruce.

*I*N 1974 MARIE AND BRUCE WERE WORKING WITH BERANN to produce what would be their last panorama for *National Geographic* magazine. It showed the area around Antarctica, and would be published in the National Geographic Society's 1975 *Atlas of the World* instead of as a supplement to the magazine. The end of the relationship between Marie and Bruce and *National Geographic* signaled not only the extent to which the ocean floor had been enfolded into American culture, but also what Marie referred to as the "philosophical difference" that she and Bruce had with *National Geographic*. She and Bruce had come to believe that the world's oceans were all part of one interconnected system. The NGS recognized, she said, five discrete oceans: the Atlantic, the Pacific, the Indian, the Arctic, and the area around Antarctica. Some of those areas had been depicted and then revealed in the pages of *National Geographic*'s various publications, all while a revolution involving the floors of the oceans was taking place. But by the mid-1970s the revolution was over.

The job was over, too. The NGS never extended the funding for a World Ocean Floor Panorama to Marie and Bruce, who'd dreamt of working on a project that would visually express their philosophy of a one-ocean world. When they decided they'd waited long enough, they approached their friend Brackett Hersey at the U.S. Office of Naval Research, asking him if the ONR would be interested in funding such a project. He was, Marie wrote, "amenable," which meant that in 1974 she and Bruce began planning what would be their final project together.

It was also their biggest project together: huge and important for a couple who had spent most of their professional lives mapping the world's individual oceans; huge and important for the general public, who'd seen only pieces of the ocean floor; and huge and important for the science of plate tectonics, which had rapidly progressed during the twenty-plus years that had passed since Marie and Bruce's first physiographic diagram was published. Since then, geologists had been producing new theories and subdividing the field into smaller specialties—all without a comprehensive picture of their subject. They could, of course, have gone through their files and pulled Marie's published physiographic diagrams (revised and original North Atlantic, South Atlantic, Indian, and Western Pacific), Berann's panoramas (Indian, Atlantic, Pacific, Mediterranean, Arctic), the GEBCO contours, and the assorted smaller-scale depictions of the ocean floor that others had made in recent years. They could, if they so desired, have pushed together several large drafting tables or cleared out a room to piece together a whole-planet picture—but how much better to have Marie Tharp and Bruce Heezen undertake the project?

ONR was paying, but decisions regarding color separation, printing press dimensions, paper stock, scale, boundaries—things that *National Geographic* had previously taken care of—were now entirely up to them. To get an idea of the constraints they would have to deal with, they pored over books about the printing trade. To get an idea of what the map would look like printed at different sizes, they made huge photographic reproductions of the separate maps and pieced them together, weighing the benefits of larger size against the costs of overseas shipping. They decided on a press (the Mueller Color Plate Company of Milwaukee, Wisconsin) and a layout (the panorama would have a twenty-degree overlap, with a column the width of Western Australia, stretching from Siberia to Antarctica, repeated on its left and right sides). And they submitted a formal proposal to the ONR, which approved it in 1974, setting the project in motion.

In Austria, Berann constructed a special table for the project. It was large enough for the whole unstretched canvas, which was six and a half feet wide and four feet tall; had a tabletop that could tilt vertically like an easel or lie parallel to the floor; and was low enough that Berann would be able to sit in front of it during the several years the project would consume. With the table tilted vertically, Heinz Vielkind, Berann's assistant, projected transparencies of the most recent GEBCO charts onto the canvas, its surface illuminated as his pencil traced out the continents' dark shorelines. After that, he painted the oceans blue, a base layer that temporarily left all landmasses white.

Next, Vielkind worked from sketches periodically delivered by Bruce (who would make eight trips to Austria throughout the duration of the project, often tagging them onto the ends or beginnings of research cruises) to fill in these vast blank spaces. The sketches were from Marie, based on data she and her assistants had gathered from her own previous work, the GEBCO charts, and a copy of a six-volume catalogue of the world's active volcanoes. Like all the previous panoramas and Marie's physiographic diagrams, the goal was to make the eye gravitate toward the Earth's most dynamic features. Land above sea level was painted in "subdued" tones, generally meant to retreat from the eye unless the land was seismically active (volcanic islands and terrestrial rift valleys, for example, were given a reddish hue).

Certain panoramas—parts of the ones previously published by *National Geographic*, plus the Mediterranean, which had been published by a German magazine—were "still essentially acceptable" because they were based on data that had not been challenged or significantly added to. Marie also sketched from her own physiographic diagrams. Some of these, such as the Western Pacific, were quite recent, and so needed few changes. Others, such as the northern- and southernmost portions of the North Atlantic, were outdated, and required revision. Marie assigned to Robert Bodnar, her "chief assistant" (who also happened to be the poor soul who was once trapped in his office in Marie's house when his coworkers taped his door completely closed), the "monumental task of annotating profiles and abstracting significant depths"—precisely the tasks that she had undertaken when beginning her very first physiographic diagram. Bodnar drew from the Lamont profiler records and data from Scripps, Woods Hole, the U.S. Navy, and Russian, French, English, and German sources. "These profiles," she said, "served as the basis for initial studies in new areas and revisions in previously mapped areas."

While no one else was doing anything like Marie's large, scientifically precise, and accessible physiographic diagrams, other specialists in deep-sea topography were making increasingly detailed contour charts. There was Anthony Laughton of Great Britain's National Institute of Oceanography, Jacqueline Mammerickx and Robert Fisher of Scripps, and Gleb Udintsev of the Soviet Academy of Sciences' Institute of Oceanography. This work, by "far-flung colleagues," was "undoubtedly of high quality and scientifically valid," Marie said; it was where she started when she needed to get a feel for the topography of the few locations she'd never mapped. Bruce, however, "preferred that we evaluate and check and if necessary modify [the contours with] our own Lamont data and methods." Lamont, despite The Harrassment, was still the epitome of quality.

The other specialists' contour maps were very useful in that Marie didn't have to start from scratch—but they had limitations. "A contour map, even one of the best," she said, "may be thought of as a great white sheet laid over the terrain." Marie wanted the general public to be able to see texture on the ocean floor, and when looking at a contour map, she said, a viewer could not "differentiate the smooth from the rough areas"; contour maps showed regional patterns and the shapes of large features, but lost the details of texture. With her physiographic diagrams, she could give viewers the wide-ranging information of a contour map and the textures she knew were key to triggering their imaginations—both of which were necessary to understand the ocean floor and its processes. And since Bruce had started bringing back observations and photographs from deep-sea vehicles, she'd been able to show the ocean floor in ever more detail.

Marie never just took someone else's contour and translated it, wholesale, into a physiographic diagram. Rather, she sent it on a vast process of examination and overhaul in which her workers, each with a different role, tinkered with its content, one person scanning it for the boundaries of ridges, seamounts, and trenches, another converting these observations into profiles, another augmenting those profiles with depths from Lamont fathograms, another adding depths from spot soundings—her house a veritable cartographic assembly line. Her own physiographic diagrams were revamped in a similar fashion, the only difference being that instead of starting with a contour, some assigned person began where Marie had in 1952, confronting rolls of new sounding records that had to be converted into peak- and valley-revealing profiles. At the end of the line was Marie, to whom the extremely detailed new profiles were handed off, ready to be sketched into three-dimensional existence, sketches that were headed for something even bigger: the World Ocean Floor Panorama, a map of the Earth that would show, all at once and for the first time, the 70 percent of its surface that was hidden by water.

IT'S EARLY MAY 1977, at Berann's house in Austria, and a yellow lined legal pad rests on the nightstand between the beds where Marie and Bruce sleep. The corners of its cardboard back have gone soft and flexible, and the majority of the pages have been used. Most of them are still attached to the pad, folded back over the bound edge, so many that their bulk prevents the pad from lying flat. The pages contain notes and lists—notes documenting some of Marie and Bruce's reasoning for the more inferential features on the World Ocean Floor Panorama, lists of things that need to be fixed during their last few days of work with Berann—reminders he'd jotted down throughout the day and as he and Marie spoke quietly in the dark before falling asleep.

The pad belongs to Bruce. Buried deep within the sheaf of folded pages is one that's different from the others: an outline, in pencil, some scribbles in Bruce's hand that Marie will later refer to as "the birthday poem." "It is 1977," begins Bruce's note to himself. "I am 53. I have 12 years until I retire (if I am lucky). This is not very much time to:

1. Complete my life work (whatever that is)
2. Enjoy life's rewards (all simple kinds)
3. Pack away in case I beat the actual odds.

"Thus each period should be carefully and <u>seriously planned</u> to obtain maximum rewards in #1, #2, #3.

A. It would give me great personal satisfaction to write another master work (I must do it).
B. It would give me great personal satisfaction to complete a still more detailed view of the earth on a Marie-BCH map (we must do it).

C. It is necessary to maintain certain monetary support to be able to do the above. This is the sticky wicket.

"I. The subject cannot be much different than our life's work, i.e. not enough time, not enough residual talent, too much resistance." A Roman numeral two is penciled in after this, but the space beside it is blank, a line on a page Marie doesn't know about stuck in between all the ones she does.

In the morning there's the hustle and bustle of morning rituals. They make their beds; they put on their glasses. Marie holds bobby pins between her teeth before using them to secure the hair she's piled on top of her head. She does it without looking, watching Bruce in the mirror as he pulls the sides of his shirt out like wings before buttoning them over his big belly, letting her eyes meet his and smiling. Before they leave the guest room Bruce picks up his legal pad and looks at the notes from the previous night. Lot to do before next week, he says, leading the way down the stairs. They'll be leaving to fly back to America then. I know, Marie says. A lot, Bruce says, the second word a punch. I know, she says again, imitating his inflection, reaching up to smooth the back of his sleep-rumpled hair and tucking her own under a hat.

In the kitchen Marie goes straight to Heinrich's wife and kisses both her cheeks. They each say good morning in the other's native tongue. All of them—Marie, Bruce, Berann, his wife, and Berann's assistant, Heinz Vielkind—have known each other for seven years now, long enough to develop a German-English pidgin that works just fine, especially when combined with lots of gestures and pointing.

Even though the group does less verbal communicating than they would if they had a language in common, the tendency to hit sensory over-load in Berann's studio is high. The four of them—Berann's wife steers clear of the work process—enter the studio and stand in front of the huge panorama spread out flat on the drafting table. Marie leans across it to turn on the industrial lamp that extends over the table, bathing the work surface in extra light. The four stand still for a moment. The map alone is overwhelming, with intricate craggy textures painted onto large swaths of washed-out cerulean, contrasting with the warm tones of the continents, contrasting with the flat black stripes of the border, the whole room thick with the smell of paint and mineral spirits and coffee, the sounds of breakfast dishes being washed drifting in from the kitchen. Berann's paintings are everywhere, unframed ones leaning in stacks against the walls, some on easels, some in thick rococo frames, all the canvases filled with swirling tempestuous skies.

The quartet's clothing, too, is a riot of layer and pattern. Berann has on a brightly embroidered fur-trimmed vest, and the cardigan Bruce has put on over his shirt is striped black and white with zigzags and dots; the short kimono sleeves of Marie's Navajo-patterned shift poke out into the space around her, the dark-tipped points of fur on her white Cossack hat do the same; Vielkind, with only a bit of white collar poking out from his a solid black sweater, is a single lithe column of calm. Together, they're a dream team of oceanographic cartography.

Then Berann inhales deeply and claps his hands together and they're all suddenly animate. He takes his place on his drafting stool in front of the table. Bruce puts on his reading glasses and consults the notepad he's had tucked under his arm. Marie looks over his shoulder at the list of tasks they compiled the night before. Drifts, she says. He nods, repeats the word. Vielkind is already bent over the map, using a thin-tipped brush to apply yet another coat of brilliant white paint to some of the ocean floor's more prominent peaks. Drifts, Berann says, okay. He pauses, a pained look on his face. Where? When Marie and Bruce arrived almost two weeks ago, the panorama was nearly finished, with only a few nearly blank spots for which Berann and Vielkind needed input.

Since then Berann and Vielkind have been making anywhere from thirty to seventy changes on the panorama every day, as well as filling in the blank areas. The days are packed with fast-paced highlighting (what Vielkind is doing right now), shadowing (which Berann does with what Marie refers to as his "eyebrow pencil"), airbrushing (to give the seismically active Mid-Oceanic Ridge a reddish tinge), and, even this late in the game, the painting of new features. Today, it's drifts: large peaked sediment deposits formed by deep-ocean currents. Bruce and Charlie Hollister had given them a more specific name (contourites) back in 1972, but Bruce still just calls them drifts. Because that's what they resemble—sort of like large-scale sand dunes in real life, on the map they're little more than collections of pale brushstrokes atop the base layer blue. A few of them will make their debut here.

By dinnertime Berann looks drained. Under Marie and Bruce's direction, he's been propelling himself around the panorama for hours.

Marie has her face up close to the map, just about even with the Bering Sea. She's examining the Bowers Ridge, a flat-topped submerged ridge with a fetal curl, its head resting on the Aleutian Islands, a narrower nearby ridge and chain of seamounts forming a cord that connects it to Russia's Kamchatka Peninsula. Vielkind is working a few feet south, still highlighting. All is silent, but for the occasional sound of Berann's airbrush, which sends a diffuse spray of atomized red onto the Mid-Oceanic Ridge—the plum color that has resulted from this has not, according to Marie and Bruce, achieved perfectly uniform application yet.

Bruce hasn't demanded any more changes from Berann and Vielkind since that morning's drift directive. Right now he's sunk into a chair across from the panorama, studying it intently with his hands clasped on top of his stomach. Marie straightens; she's been bent over, peering at the map for some time. I think, she starts to say. Berann lifts his finger from the airbrush's trigger and looks up at her. Please, Mary, he says—this is what he always calls her—please, no more changes. Oh I know, she says, and plops onto a stool on the opposite side of the drafting table. I was just going to say that I think everything looks good. She meets Bruce's gaze. I think you're right, he says. Someone had to declare it first, but just like that—they're done.

After Berann and Vielkind finish the spots they're working on, they roll a huge humidifier into the studio and turn it on. Over the next twenty-four hours it will raise the room's humidity, allowing the lightly glued canvas of the panorama to be detached from the drafting table. After that, they'll wait for the paint to dry, then carefully roll up the map, a sheet of acetate covering its surface. For now they celebrate. Bruce snaps photos of the map from every conceivable angle, with the team arranged around it in every possible configuration. Champagne is located. When the group bursts into the kitchen to find flutes to drink it out of, they startle Berann's wife, who couldn't hear them over the sound of her electric mixer, beating cake icing into stiff white peaks. Bruce has his arm around Marie's waist and they're both grinning as Berann grabs his wife and waltzes her around the kitchen, accompanied by the sounds of the still-running mixer and the pop and fizz the champagne makes when Vielkind opens it.

By the end of the evening the camera is being passed around to everyone. Bruce seems to have an unlimited store of film and flashbulbs, is always able to pull a new roll out of one of his pockets after rummaging around long enough, or heave himself out of the dining nook to go upstairs for new bulbs, the crackled old ones piling up on his notepad on the counter, the light of the new ones reflecting off the red oak paneling, catching the shine of Marie's auburn hair, some of it falling down over her shoulder, her fur hat removed. Bruce catches a good shot of Marie in profile, her mouth open wide, waiting for Berann to feed her a forkful of cake. As the night wears on, they begin to snap photos indiscriminately, forgetting to focus the camera's lens but never forgetting their master-work in the dampening studio, getting closer to the point where it can be detached.

On the flight back to New York Marie and Bruce persuade a steward-ess to let them stow the cardboard tube holding the map in a corner of the galley. Every hour one of them gets up to check on it. The map, they ask each other, panicked until they make visual contact—when they debark, when they pause in the airport so one of them can use a restroom, when they pile into a cab at the airport and exit it later at Marie's house. It's precious, and they're cautious. After a quick stop in Nyack to drop off lug-gage and get a night of sleep, they get on another plane, this one to the printer in Milwaukee.

Their stay there is also short, just long enough to discuss and con-firm the plans they'd agreed upon months before. And to let the map go. It's not easy. They're attached. But they do it with only a little bit of back-tracking: what perhaps began as nervous chatter over coffee in the air-port becomes a serious discussion of the map's scale. Think of how long it took him, Marie says, referring to the black border Berann had inked in around the panorama, a border that lay outside of the boundaries of the printer's largest plate. What I don't understand, Bruce says, pulling his notepad out from his briefcase, is how we overlooked this.

In the end, they decide to reduce the map slightly, bringing it in at a scale of 1:23,360,300, and when the proof (a one-off copy of the printer's reproduction of the original panorama) arrives a few weeks later, it still isn't perfect. So Bruce pulls his notepad out again to draft a letter to the printer. As for the colors, he writes, they're too red and too limey green on the land, too turgid on the seas. They write instead of calling because Bruce hates large phone bills—and anyway, there's no reason to rush.

Part Four

The Feet, mechanical, go round—

Of Ground, or Air, or Ought—

A Wooden way

Regardless grown,

A Quartz contentment, like a stone—

—EMILY DICKINSON, excerpt from "After great pain,
a formal feeling comes"

CHAPTER 25

*T*HE TEXTBOOKS AND WEBSITES THAT DRYLY NARRATE THE life and times of the Earth mostly have to do with just one-eighth of that life. One-eighth. That's seven-eighths we know almost nothing about: four billion years, a number nearly impossible to grasp. It's hard to conceive of something that huge, so somewhere along the line, someone came up with the idea of using a single calendar year to walk people through the passage of time on Earth. If a whole 365-day-long year equals the total age of the Earth, then each unit of time—seconds, minutes, hours, days, weeks, months—represents a discrete period in the Earth's history.

It's like this: you find an old discarded datebook somewhere. Maybe it's yours; you found it wedged in a closet corner. Or maybe it's someone else's; they're gone and it's up to you to decide which of their belongings to keep. Either way, you open it up, dust it off, and start flipping through it. At first, there's just blank page after blank page. By the tail end of February, a doodle of a prokaryote (a single-cell organism lacking a nucleus and membrane-bound organs) appears in one of the squares where notes such as "cardiologist @ 3 p.m." would normally be scrawled. By the second week of May there's a drawing of a single-celled eukaryote, complete with a nucleus and some squiggle-filled organelles. Drawings of different types of single-celled eukaryotes begin to appear: some blue-green algae, some choanoflagellates that resemble sperm cells sporting dog cone collars turned backward.

By the beginning of June the eukaryotes start to congregate, forming multicellular organisms such as *Grypania spiralis*. Long and thin and loosely coiled, they hang like vines on the borders of late June days. Other organisms appear. The bilateral *Vernanimalcula guizhouena*, proudly flaunting specialized tissues: a mouth, a gut, an anus. More and more living things pile up, filling the pages, a tumultuous mass of densely packed lines that, by November 15, blot out nearly all of the white space on the pages. This is the dawn of the Cambrian explosion. Trilobites, shrimp, scorpions, oh my!

By November 24 animals and plants have taken hold on land.

Dinosaurs, December 27.

Flowers, December 30.

Primates, December 31.

Humans arrive on Earth at four minutes to midnight on New Year's Eve. That means that on December 31 there's a very tiny (four minutes out of the possible 1,440) drawing of a man crammed into the bottom right corner. Minuscule ears of GMO corn and Labradoodles and pluots, mules and zorses and tangelos are packed like germs into the crook of his right arm. You'd need a microscope to see these things, just like you'd need a microscope to see that the tiny drawing of a man is not solid gray, but includes organs and nervous and vascular systems. He has a heart, he has a brain. They're both still—this is a drawing, after all. But if he were suddenly animated? The clutter of life around him cleared, a submarine sketched into the scene, a crimson smudge added to make his heart glow red, his cartoon body climbing down the hatch of the docked sub, blood pumping through arteries, capillaries, and veins. And his jerky fast movements as he settles in on board, stowing his bags as the ship travels out to sea, eating at the mess table, the ship descending through darkness to the seafloor, going down into the observation compartment, staring out at the illuminated ocean bottom and taking notes and speaking into the microphone of a Dictaphone and then stopping—his mouth open, eyes open, microphone in hand, heart stopped. Bruce, says the man sitting beside him. Body dragged up to the main deck, men crowding around, shirt ripped open, chest exposed, CPR delivered, glances exchanged, CPR duty transferred, wristwatch consulted, death declared.

On the geologic calendar all of recorded history takes place during the last four seconds of New Year's Eve. 12:59:56, 12:59:57, 12:59:58, 12:59:59. When scaled down, everything humans know about anything, everything we love, everything we've made—condensed into four seconds. We come and go in the amount of time it takes to uncap a bottle of water and take a sip, sign on the dotted line, or fasten a seat belt. Because we have to shrink and streamline history even to attempt an understanding of the Earth's vast time line, we end up crammed into a period of time just as hard to grasp as the four billion plus years we started with. Things such as proximity and proportion get totally messed up, with everyone way closer, way more equal than they ever were in real life. And so we must make a choice. Either let history remain incomprehensibly huge and domineering or shrink it down, sift out the choice bits, and allow for some distortion.

In her writings and interviews, Marie repeated the bare facts of Bruce's death over and over: who, what, where, and when strung up like beads, passed through her hands so many times the pattern worried off, a version of the truth she trimmed to ensure its survival. "*On June 21, 1977, Bruce Heezen died suddenly of a heart attack in a submarine near the Reykjanes Ridge. I was on the research ship* Discovery *studying the Ridge from above. We had recently completed work on our world ocean floor panorama and each had proofs with us on our respective boats. Bruce was 53 years old.*" Although bare, this version of the story is undeniably dramatic: thirty years of work and companionship finished in pretty much one instant; it's the version she told most often. But how did you feel, an interviewer with a concerned voice might have asked Marie, when everything you cared about was gone?

How do you answer such a question?

Well, as she got older she changed the tale a little, alterations that hint at her feelings. Sometimes she told people she was back at home in New York when it happened. Other times she didn't mention the proofs. Once, she said that Bruce had hacked off only the North Atlantic section of the proof to take with him on the *NR-1*, left the rest at home. People tell me that she had quite a sense of humor and so some days I imagine her saying *Bruce who?* when asked about his death. The truth, though, is as she said it was. *On June 21, 1977, Bruce Heezen died suddenly of a heart attack in a submarine near the Reykjanes Ridge. I was on the research ship* Discovery *studying the Ridge from above. We had recently completed work on our world ocean floor panorama and each had proofs with us on our respective boats. Bruce was 53 years old.* So yes, about Bruce's death there are basic facts and small spoken untruths and details of movement from point A to point B. As for why they all exist, I guess all I can say is that Marie knew the value of a good story. She knew the impact of trauma and drama and so she suppressed the reality of her grief, tried to redirect interest toward the events and not her reactions to them, tried to exert control in whatever way she could.

Because if June 21, 1977, and the days that followed had not been so utterly devastating, so rife with narrative perfection, she wouldn't have had to explain how she recovered, wouldn't have had to admit that maybe she hadn't, that maybe a mind capable of conceiving of tens of thousands of miles of land hidden under meters and meters of water simply could not deal with a world without just one man and a map to work on together. If June 21, 1977, had not so distinctly marked the end of one era of her life and the beginning of another, she wouldn't have had to talk about how the final thirty years of her life were spent silently cataloging the middle thirty years, filing papers and maps and letters and books and folders and photographs and all manner of all things relating to that map and that man and her life with them, so that when she was gone someone else could sketch them out, each leading into the next, a very long story she had forced past the boundaries of her own imagination.

On June 21, 1977, Bruce Heezen died suddenly of a heart attack in a submarine near the Reykjanes Ridge. I was on the Discovery *studying the Ridge from above. We had recently completed work on our world ocean floor panorama and each had proofs with us on our respective boats. Bruce was 53 years old.* These words are an ending, but also a kind of beginning. After all, the Reykjanes Ridge was in the Northern Atlantic, the place where they began their work in 1952. And for Marie, Bruce's life—and death—was constantly present in her own life until she died. Like a tornado surging toward a metropolis on a radar screen it had a precise end point, rushing forward in vivid color only to stop abruptly, dead in its tracks, reappearing at its origin to trace out the exact same path again and again. Take a look at *that,* Marie would say each time, pointing at the storm behind her.

And then there's me. I'm not a part of the story of Bruce's death, but I'm the one who's here. When I look up from the screen of my laptop it is

Marie's face I see: in my office dozens of Maries stare out at me. When I close my eyes I see her face, too, a collection of shifting hollows and slopes.

If I could dream of her, I would. I'd dream of waking up, and of her being there in a chair waiting for me like some Ghost of Christmas Past. "Finally," she'd exclaim, jumping up to take my hand. She would already know about me, so I wouldn't have to waste any time explaining anything, and her presence would be a kind of blessing. It's true that I've talked to her before: sometimes I'll aim an "I'm sorry!" skyward after a particularly bad day of writer's block; I've also been known to mutter the words "Oh, Marie" under my breath when I run into a particularly infuriating hole in the middle of a manuscript at the Library of Congress—but this time she would answer.

And so, with the time I had with her, I'd ask her about Bruce's death. Not how she felt, because I know she'd hate that question, but what she did. For a shape instead of a texture, movements of feet instead of mind, a region instead of states—a map showing her grief in oblique perspective. In my dream she would answer—talk and talk and talk—and I'd hope that I could remember it all when I woke up for real.

$\mathcal{B}$RUCE'S DEPARTURE IS CAPTURED ON FILM. A MOVIE CAM-
era follows him as his yellow shirt disappears down the *NR-1*'s red
conning tower. Through the hatch, down the tower. Down a river, under
a bridge, out to sea. The film will be called *Chasms Beneath the Sea*, and
in it Bruce is supposed to guide viewers through the history and importance of marine geology. Instead, the directors will be forced to use a
combination of live shots from previous cruises, photo stills, drawings,
archival films, and a cast of supporting scientists in an attempt to make
up for the loss of their leading man. Marie will watch the film over and
over after she receives a copy of it in the mail sometime after Bruce's
death. She watches it so often that it becomes the chorus of her days, its
soundtrack becoming the soundtrack of her memories, its scenes and
songs looping around her own memories, threads tied like rings round
fingers, ways to remember what happened.

They'd set sail six days before, Bruce on the *NR-1* out of Reykjavík,
Marie leaving from Barry, Wales, on the *Discovery*. One above water, one
below. It's early morning on June 21, 1977, and she leans on the rail of her
ship, watching the frothy trail that the hulk of a ship kicks up in its wake.
Somewhere far beneath and north of her the *NR-1* glides smoothly
through dark deep water. The weather is good, the sea is calm.

Her ship faces the open sea. Marie is hopeful; she's not been on so many cruises that she sees them as routine. For example, she still loves the instant the land disappears from view, a moment she's found actually happens more than once. Like watching a balloon float higher and higher, it might only seem vanished, swallowed into clear blue sky—but if she looks away and then quickly back, to the spot where her eyes last saw land, she can discern it again. And she loves the feeling of a sounding record fresh from the fathometer, the thermal paper smooth and still warm with the ocean floor's topography. She loves, too, wondering what Bruce is doing—if he's staring out a porthole at structures she knows by heart, if he's stirring coffee with a metal spoon and thinking only about what he would see that day.

She lets herself daydream. Floating in these moments, she imagines herself somewhere beneath the surface of the ocean, watching a submarine descend through layers of water penetrated less and less by the sun; she slowly sinks with it. The only light comes from the submarine itself, spotlights illuminating unfocused circles of water, minute plants and animals swirling like specks of dust in the sun, dotted lines of rivets puncturing the broad dull walls of the sub, wheels waiting to touch down on the seafloor. When she swims closer the walls go translucent like theatrical scrims, the submarine lit from within. She swims closer still and peers into the ship, its inner machinery and crew visible but indistinct, an animated diorama crammed with clusters of knobs and valves, columns of small screens, thickets of pipes, and men in jumpsuits making adjustments. There are four bunk beds. There is one oven. There is one toilet. There are twelve men, and one of them is Bruce.

And then the NR-1 comes to rest on the ocean bottom, sediment rising up in clouds to block her view. She doesn't hear much either: not the slosh of water or the sound of her own heartbeat in her ears. But she does hear the NR-1's sonar, a beat and then a rest, like a tennis ball repeatedly served and waiting to be returned. When she thinks of herself in the moments before Bruce's death, this is what she hears. This is what she replays. As if she might find a misplaced beat, an audio component to Bruce's death. Maybe his heart released a ping when it stopped, a signal so she could calculate the distance separating them. Maybe there were tympanis, maybe there were cymbals—only she wasn't paying close enough attention to notice them at the time?

The sediment has settled. The *NR-1* rests on the ocean floor in front of her. But Bruce is not a part of it anymore, not really. His body is now just a body. Men ring him. A few kneel and try to revive him. Most are standing and watching. Around them are the walls of the ship. Around that is water; interrupting the water is land; together they make up the Earth, which is itself surrounded by space and stars and planets and comets and other massive entities infinitely extending, the place where Bruce's body rests now just a location: a latitude, a longitude, a depth. A dot. He's data, meaningless without context.

"On June 21, 1977, Bruce Heezen died suddenly of a heart attack in a submarine near the Reykjanes Ridge. I was on the *Discovery* studying the Ridge from above. We had recently completed work on our World Ocean Floor Panorama and each had proofs with us on our respective boats. Bruce was 53 years old," Marie said.

"He up and died," she said in an interview almost twenty years later. "I don't really know why it had to be Bruce instead of me."

HERE'S WHAT MARIE doesn't say about the day Bruce died: the call came over the radio and she was given the news. She was told that Bruce's body was being taken to the *NR-1*'s support ship, the *Sunbird*; from there it was going to be airlifted to the U.S. Air Force base in Keflavík. Someone asked her if she wanted to get to back to dry land right away. Someone asked her if she wanted to meet the body.

The call came over the radio and she said she wanted to return to Iceland and then the *Discovery* pulled up all of its equipment, ceased operation.

The man on the radio had referred to Bruce by his name only once, so that she got the idea, and then as *the body* or *it*. As in *the body is en route to Keflavík* or *the body is on a helicopter flying above the North Atlantic right now*. She had turned and looked at the men in the communications room, said no, that can't be right.

The boys from Lamont who were on the *Sunbird* said they were continuing on. That Bruce would want them to carry out the mission. That they were sorry. About that time, Bruce's body was placed in the *Sunbird*'s freezer. His Rolex may or may not have been stolen off his wrist.

The men on the *Discovery* said that it would take four days to reach land in Reykjavík. Four days of waiting, four days of smaller journeys. She went to her cabin. She put on a clean dress, took it off. She got into bed, let herself be calmed by the gently rocking sea. People knocked on her door to check on her. She made her way through corridors. Up and down ladders. Her arms lifting a blanket to wrap it around her body. Hours counted. The opening and closing of her eyes. Because Bruce died on the summer solstice, and they were so far north, the sun did not fully set. For most of the night it sat sullen above the horizon, twilight even for the three hours that it dropped from sight. The days had been getting shorter but they seemed, from the *Discovery*, as if they had been getting longer. Four days—and what then?

WHEN MARIE DOCKED in Reykjavík Charlie Hollister was there to meet her. He had rented a small plane and together they flew up into the air so that they could see Iceland's rift valley. It was a kind gesture, an attempt to get her mind off the circumstances. He hoped her attention would be grabbed by the land's jagged exposed valleys, that the crags and weathered boulders would snatch her out of grief. He watched her as they flew.

Her face was pointed at the window; Iceland was still pretty much the same as when she and Bruce were there in 1962. The fields green, the rocks gray, the sky blue, and clouds white. The sea shining like a shallow burnished bowl beyond it all. The rift valley was wider by a few inches and there were more houses than before, everything only slightly different, just enough to ghost the passing land, a double exposure—the past imprinted on top of the present.

But no Bruce.

She had to keep reminding herself.

The plane moved forward. She stayed still inside of it. It was, for her, the perfect place to be, a gray area where she could easily substitute the past for the present, fall for a trick of the eye: look away and then back and there was Bruce, sitting beside her, snapping pictures. They still had new discoveries to make together.

*I*N BRUCE'S KITCHEN THERE'S AN OPEN BAG OF KLEEN KITTY cat litter on the counter next to the stove. A pair of pruning shears. Dirty plates stacked three and four deep, a pressure cooker, a crock pot, an electric can opener, and a brass vase holding several stems of lilies. In the living room there's an open can of Welch's grape soda on a table, a lamp with a crooked shade in front of a galley proof of the World Ocean Floor Panorama that's been taped to the wall, a statuette of the mythical character Leda, and a fully inflated blowfish hanging from the ceiling. In the bathroom there's a comb on the radiator, a plant on the floor, and a framed print of Botticelli's *Birth of Venus* on the wall.

And, in a bed upstairs, there's Marie. For one single second before she opens her eyes she forgets that Bruce is dead. It's July 1, 1977, the day after Bruce's memorial service at Lamont, a few days after his funeral in Iowa. Of the funeral she remembers little; there were black clothes and flowers, and she'd had to deal with Bruce's hysterical mother, who had insisted that Bruce be buried next to his father rather than in the plot he had purchased for himself in Nyack, next to Marie's.

A fan slowly oscillates at the foot of the bed, blowing air onto Marie's face and sending strands of hair back and forth across her forehead. Every so often she blinks, but for the most part her body remains still under a shaggy blanket that looks like a piece of unrolled sod. She lies on her back and stares into Bruce's open closet, where his clothes hang slack inside dry-cleaning bags. She lies on her side and stares at the pale curtains on the windows that billow occasionally, closes her eyes when the light filtering through them grows bright. She does not cry. She ignores the ringing telephone.

The room goes Technicolor orange when the sun starts to set, like it's trapped in some massive Chinese lantern. Marie gets up. The robe she pulls on sticks to her hot skin. She pulls it tight anyway, and grasps the handrail as she makes her way down the stairs and into the kitchen. The phone rings. Vapor clouds swirl around her face when she opens the freezer to get the coffee. She dumps yesterday's damp grounds out of the percolator, gives it a cursory rinse before scooping new grounds into it and turning a flame on under it. The kitchen table holds a scattering of papers, which Marie pushes into a pile while she waits for the coffee. When it's done, she tucks the papers under her arm, pours some coffee, and heads outside.

In a box near the front door are bouquets and wreaths that have collapsed onto each other after a day in the heat. A trail of envelopes creeps antlike from under the gate that leads to the road. She ignores them and goes behind the house, where she sits, watching the Hudson while she drinks her coffee. The papers beside her glow in the dying light. Eventually she picks them up and starts to read. "We are gathered here today," Manik Talwani's introduction began, "to pay tribute to the memory of our friend and colleague Bruce Heezen." At the Lamont memorial the day before the sky had been a perfect clear blue, the Hudson sparkled in the distance, and Marie had watched the service take place against a backdrop of the massive pines she'd watched grow, decades before, from the window of her office. One by one men went up to the podium— colleagues, students, friends—and told the gathered audience things that she already knew.

Bruce's death, Manik said, was "tragic." "Even among other distinguished oceanographers he was a towering figure," one who valued and understood answers that seemed to other scientists like nonanswers. Bruce could be "stubborn and sometimes frightening," Bill Ryan said, "warm, friendly, charming, and infuriating all in the course of five minutes. From my personal vantage point, it was his visionary approach and not his anger that thrust us into the action." One could either be "impressed" or "disgusted" by Bruce and the physical evidence of his extraordinary curiosity—"pockets bulging with objects picked up weeks in the past and a desk and bookcase filled with a vast variety of rare cruise reports, encyclopedias in foreign languages, privately printed books and journals dating back more than five decades . . . maps, charts, and manuscripts piled on his desk and every available table top or cabinet. I used to wonder," Ryan wrote, "if this was how he learned to become a stratigrapher." "It was as though," Marcus Langseth said, "this library mind of his provided a tapestry of past experiences, not only from his own life, but from those of his friends and even people he had only read about, into which his own existence was woven."

By the time Marie gets to the last eulogy, the sky is almost black. The river in front of her blends into it and the house behind her is dark. Cars occasionally speed by on the road beyond the house. Mosquitoes buzz and fireflies hang in the air, their lights like hardened amber holding them. Before she goes back to bed, she thinks about what Kenneth Hunkins said it was like to be on a submarine with Bruce. "I made two dives with Brue in the NR-1," he'd said at the memorial. "The difficulties of observing, photographing, note taking, and sleeping in this confined space were compensated by the excitement of what we saw when flying above the seafloor. Time goes by fast on the bottom." He'd talked about how they'd each had to lie prone, each glued to a porthole taking photographs, each taking notes—Bruce, of course, with his tape recorder, Hunkins with paper and pencil. He said that sometimes they traveled in silence, emerging after a run into the lighted crew area to discuss what they'd seen, to try to understand it and make a strategy for the next descent.

It is dark now. It is late. There are few cars and Marie can hear the river lapping at the wall. She's staring at the dark, stuck on the part about the submarine flying above the seafloor, Bruce lying on his belly inside of it. But then the submarine thins, dissolves like a candy shell. His body sheds its clothes. This is where he'll remain for her: Bruce as a fish, as a whale or a shark, swimming along the ocean bottom, Bruce with his fingers trailing through the sand, alert and observant, collecting information for the future.

Part Five

And though you fade from earthly sight,

declare to the silent earth: I flow.

To the rushing water say: I am.

—RAINER MARIA RILKE, *Sonnets to Orpheus,*
Part II, Sonnet 29

*T*HE CONDOLENCE MESSAGES MARIE RECEIVED AFTER Bruce's death fill a thick blue linen binder at the Library of Congress. There are notes that arrived tucked into bouquets, large greeting cards, telegrams, handwritten phone messages, longhand letters, typed letters, and a few of Marie's replies. Most of them are from the days just following Bruce's death. They are remarkably consistent. No one questioned the extent of Marie's personal loss; she wasn't married to Bruce but the people expressing their condolences addressed her as if she had been: with Bruce's death she became a widow. One friend wrote to Marie about her own experience of losing her husband. "After the first few days—no one comes unless they want something—and you are alone." She told her to take it easy and remember that she had friends, sentiments that the women writing to Marie expressed repeatedly.

More often than not, the men mentioned Bruce's professional contributions. In a cable sent to Lamont, the navy's chief of research, Rear Admiral Robert K. Geiger, said that Bruce had been a real friend and shipmate, that "HIS RESEARCH HAS BEEN OF ENORMOUS VALUE TO THE NAVY AND THE COUNTRY." "Science will miss him," wrote Bill Menard, one of Bruce's oldest colleagues and friends; "I will miss him." John Knauss, of the University of Rhode Island, wrote that Marie and Bruce were "a magnificent team" who together had "produced some of the most exciting charts the world has ever seen. Few are given the opportunity for such personal immortality."

"It is difficult to accept that the long partnership of Heezen and Tharp has come to an end," Knauss wrote elsewhere in his letter, echoing a sentiment Marie had already been feeling. "I feel as if my life has just been cut in two," she wrote in response to one of the other condolence letters. In a way, though, she did not let her partnership with Bruce end upon his passing. Until her own death in 2006 Marie actively mourned and defended Bruce—her way, perhaps, of soothing the pain that came with quickly learning her value as single entity, not part of the Heezen-Tharp package.

"PLEASE PASS MARIE THARP," said a cable sent to Lamont from the General Bathymetric Chart of the Oceans' (GEBCO) Guiding Committee secretary Desmond Scott. "PLEASE ACCEPT SINCERE CONDOLENCES DEATH BRUCE HEEZEN STOP HIS WORK IN WHICH YOU PARTICIPATED SO FULLY [WAS] SUPREME IN ITS FIELD AND SURELY WILL ENDURE THE TEST OF TIME." This cable was sent a week after Bruce's death. Less than a year later, though, it became clear that Marie's participation in the GEBCO's endeavors would not endure for long at all.

IT'S LATE APRIL 1978 and Marie is standing in a conference room in Ottawa filled with other people who study the ocean floor. They're the members of the GEBCO Guiding Committee, gathered to discuss the next edition of the chart. Some have bowed their heads and closed their eyes. Some are praying, but all have risen and all are observing a moment of silence in Bruce's memory.

Marie is there because Bruce is not; he usually represented them at such meetings and she's trying to complete everything he'd been working toward before he died. That includes, she assumes, taking over the coordination of several sheets of the chart's fifth edition (which will show the entire ocean floor on eighteen sheets), work that Bruce had committed himself to. She's also brought along a proof of the World Ocean Floor Panorama (WOFP; the map itself was done but she and her workers were still labeling features with names and depths) to make sure the names on her map match the ones officially recognized by the GEBCO committee.

Things start off well. There's the moment of silence (appreciation that she feels by proxy) and a crush of people inspecting the WOFP. Someone suggests naming a seamount in the South Atlantic after Bruce: the Heezen Ridge. She smiles at the thought and imagines Bruce doing the same, wide cheeks rising to meet the crinkles around his eyes, they're sitting in her living room and he's saying the words *Heezen Ridge* to her, the word *Ridge* rising slightly at the end, almost a question, and he's taking a sip of the drink she made him and asking her where she wants to go to celebrate—no. No. She's in Ottawa, by herself, and the meeting is moving quickly; somehow she's back in her chair with a stack of freshly typed and mimeographed minutes in her hands, close to instantaneous records of the morning's events that still reek of ink. Robert Fisher, she reads off one of the papers in front of her, has been nominated to replace Bruce on the GEBCO Guiding Committee. He's from Scripps. He's not Marie.

And then it's well into the next day and Marie is back in the same chair, in the same conference room, her pile of the meeting's minutes growing. Open in front of her is a binder filled with inventories and lists and descriptions of the progress her team has made on Bruce's sheets since he died, the originals of reports that the GEBCO steering committee began requesting after waiting what they must have determined was a respectful amount of time for Marie to absorb the shock of Bruce's death. After receiving the reports they'd started suggesting that one sheet after another be reassigned to various people, and Marie had replied in one letter after another that she was willing and happy to keep all of Bruce's assignments, letters from which she's reading to them right now, reiterating her abilities and enthusiasm out loud: her efforts to keep the project up and running without Bruce, the amount of time and money that have already been spent on the sheets, some of which, she says, are nearly completed.

I believe, she says, it is the privilege of the coordinator to select his co-coordinator, and in that official capacity Bruce selected me as co-coordinator of sheet 5.16. Sheet 5.16 was in the South Atlantic. The room is dead quiet. People exchange glances. Then the committee's chairman says, I've offered to accept responsibility for that sheet. This is news to Marie. She fidgets with the clasp of one of her bracelets. Inhales. Flips to a different section of her binder. Sheet 5.13, then. Let me update you on

that, she says. In 1961 Bruce and I showed that— One of the men inter-
rupts her by saying her name. We've given 5.13 to Dennis Hayes.

Marie flips to another section of her binder. Okay, she says, 5.18, the
Southern Pacific. No, a voice says, we've assigned that to Ellen Herron and
Jacqueline. 5.07—no. 5.08—why don't you take that, someone asks her.
I've already submitted a revised project document to the National Science
Foundation to process that data, she tells them. But sheet 5.08 covers the
Northern Atlantic, an area with a huge amount of data that Bruce had
only tentatively agreed to work on; it was the only area she'd come to the
meeting prepared to give up, simply because working on it would have
been so time-consuming—and because Bruce had died there.

Marie doesn't really want sheet 5.08, so Dr. Laughton and Dr. Johnson
are invited to assume the sheet's supervision. She listens as the chairman
directs them to attempt to locate what he refers to as a suitable scientist
to act as the sheet's coordinator. Later, they offer her sheets 5.10 and 5.14,
which she accepts, even though they're the areas—north and south of
Australia—about which she knows the least.

The rest of the meeting passes in a haze, much of the work she'd been
expecting to be occupied by for the next few years disappearing. And
then she's shaking the hands of her colleagues, many of them younger
than she, none of whom stood up for her. She's smiling when they com-
pliment the WOFP; she's gathering up her binders and the meeting minutes, which recorded her loss in real time; she's going back to her hotel
room and calling in the changes to the map, telling Bruce's former secretary, among other things, to note that the name denoting the "Heezen
Group" of seamounts should be removed and that the "Heezen Ridge"
should be added, telling her the news, telling her that she's traveling on
to London but that she'll be back soon, even though there's not much to
come back to. Don't talk like that, the secretary says.

Some time after Marie got back home from London, a GEBCO committee member came to her house and took the in-progress maps, data,
and contours for the sheets whose coordination had been transferred to
other scientists—"it was forcibly stolen," was how Marie put it, decades
later—leaving her without Bruce and without the work they'd chosen for
their futures. There was nothing she could do. "I am not," she wrote a short
time later, "the nincompoop I have been made out to be." "I was crushed
and crushed and crushed," she said in an interview many years after that.

She completed the two sheets over which she retained control but "the circumstances attending their completion," she wrote, "were more in keeping with episodes found in TV soap operas rather than the minimum rationale expected of the scientific community."

ON MAY 22, 1978, Marie wrote a letter concerning the WOFP to Mr. G. Bellisari, resident representative for the Office of Naval Research at Lamont. "I, Marie Tharp," she wrote, "have been asked to write, (1) a history of the map, (2) the cost of compilations, painting and printing and (3) how it was funded. This map," she continued, referring to the WOFP, "incorporates Bruce Heezen's and my work from former maps over a period of years and I shall have to answer these questions chronologically rather than separately." In fact, she ended up writing two letters. One answered the questions just given, the other detailed the complications that arose after Bruce's death; in both, it seems, she was being asked to defend her work.

In May 1978 the ink on the first printing of the WOFP had only just dried. Marie and Bruce had received the proofs from Mueller nearly a year prior—right before they'd left on their trips to the Northern Atlantic. The proofs were on film, full-color tests that they were meant to check for color fidelity and mistakes. Now those tasks were left for Marie to complete. "I thought that since the map was painted and in the printer's hands there was nothing left to do except get a satisfactory color proof and complete the black plate—that the job was virtually finished," Marie wrote in her 1978 letter to Bellisari. "Little did I know."

In the time that had passed since Bruce died, Marie had seen several sets of color proofs and, with the help of a variety of sources, determined that they were unsatisfactory. "I realized," she wrote, "that color was not my forte." One set of eyes that she borrowed were those of Steve Sagala, a lab technician and photographer at Lamont who'd been helping Bruce for years. He'd taken the last portrait of Bruce, just weeks before Bruce's death, a picture he called the "Buddha Bruce" because he shot it from down low and Bruce rises up from its center. In the picture Bruce is rotund and smiling, Buddha-like, in front of a wall plastered with overlapping copies of his and Marie's maps. Whether it was because of the years Sagala had worked for Bruce, the portrait, or his photographic skills, Marie considered Sagala a kindred spirit. So she took the color proofs of the WOFP up to Lamont and asked him what was wrong with them. He took one look, he said, and realized the issue: the red plate was missing. The result, Sagala remembered, was a "stop the presses" kind of situation. Marie called Mueller Color Plate at once and explained the problem; this was only the first of many times she would issue a declaration to "stop the presses."

The next set of eyes belonged to William Palmstrom, chief of *National Geographic*'s cartographic art division. He stopped by Marie's house and she showed him the next set of proofs, which were hanging on her stairway wall, where they had, she wrote, "evoked a number of unfavorable comments from everybody." So Palmstrom offered the services of Bill Smith, *National Geographic*'s "top color man," and Terry Kryston, its production man, whose guidance allowed Marie to consider the color problem solved.

After this she got two more proofs, which she affectionately called her "Bibles." One was for the names of features and the other was for numbers—depths and heights. She and Bruce had been working on names and numbers long before Bruce died. Several years before, they'd devoted a few weekends to listing the names of all the features they wanted to show on the map, first looking at atlases and extant maps, then going to recently published papers, and finally making up their own names. They'd also chosen an appropriate typeface, one that would be legible from eighteen to twenty-four inches away but would disappear at farther distances, making the map look like a painting. A worker named Suzanne MacDonald grew her fingernails long when she began what Marie called "the long and arduous task" of applying the type to a clear sheet of acetate laid over the map; MacDonald's nails made it easier for her to pick up the tiny sticky letters and place them perfectly (evenly spaced and aligned) on top of a deep-sea feature.

Another team member, named Michael McClellan, worked on numbers. The original plan had been to keep the notation of elevations evenly distributed—on both land and sea. To ensure that, Marie circled in red a selection of ten or twenty numbers per ten-degree square (as if latitude and longitude lines had been extended down into the map from the border, creating a grid of ten-degree squares), and McClellan inked them in on a translucent sheet laid over the WOFP original. The only problem with this method was that when they reduced the layer with the numbers down to the scale at which the WOFP was set to be printed, the numbers and features didn't match up. So McClellan started over, working from a list of features and depths, and locating them on the smaller-scale version of the WOFP.

But Marie didn't like this version when she saw it, either. The numbers were all horizontal, as Bruce had insisted during their many arguments about the subject. She'd always argued that the numbers should follow the features' trends. In her version the multidigit numbers would slant or curve with the terrain, much as they did in her physiographic diagrams, which had always been hand-lettered. In Bruce's the letters would all be straight, as if the ocean floor were a city and each feature had a placard marking its street address. For consistency's sake, he'd also wanted the numbers set in the same type as the names, but Marie had had enough trouble with stick-on type. "They'd fly off into space," she wrote, referring to the individual letters; I imagine them drifting in zero gravity, animated like in some *Sesame Street* segment. "And land on some strange inappropriate feature. I couldn't begin to spot misplaced stick-on numbers." Bruce was gone, and so the numbers were inked by hand.

It turns out that Marie's other instinct was correct, too. When the number sheet with all horizontal numbers was placed atop the color proof, it "looked like a fine mesh screen had been laid on the painting. This," wrote Marie, "would never do." So she and McClellan started over, orienting most numbers in the direction of the trends, leaving the land elevations and seamount depths horizontal. For his troubles, Marie noted in her 1978 letter, "we all voted to give Michael a medal for persistence and patience at a very tedious task." She didn't have a medal, but she did name a "large, isolated" seamount after him.

Once Marie was satisfied with both the number and name sheets, she merged them in order to "spot overprints." These were places where either a depth or a name had to be shifted because they happened to fall at the same place. Some numbers had to be eliminated altogether, and after they were, the black plate (the merged number and name layers) was ready to be proofed. Marie sent it off to Mueller in Milwaukee and waited for the results. When they arrived she took them and the color proof down to Brackett Hersey at the Office of Naval Research so he could examine the results of the project he'd funded. He liked the numbers "so well," Marie wrote, "that he wanted many more." He also wanted a monotone (gray) version of the WOFP. The project was still not finished.

Luckily, to hasten the progress of the WOFP, Marie had hired an unemployed cartographer (and former Ukrainian freedom fighter) named Luba Prokop. She was, Marie wrote, "skilled and conscientious and a delightful person to have around," and it was Prokop who scribed out a ten-degree grid to be printed on the six thousand copies of the map (color and gray) that the navy wanted printed; the grid would not appear on the four thousand copies Marie was having printed to distribute on her own.

And so, after some last-minute adjustments to the gray plate, the WOFP was ready to go to press—but not the press Marie and Bruce had planned on. Mueller, it turned out, had the world's largest reproduction camera, a camera that had been working hard to create the WOFP's color separations for more than a year. But it was Case-Hoyt, in Rochester, New York, that had the world's largest four-color printing press. At seventy-six inches, it was the same size as Mueller's press, except Mueller's was only two-color. The printing job went to Case-Hoyt.

The first copy of the World Ocean Floor Panorama—conceptualized by Marie Tharp and Bruce Heezen, painted by Heinrich Berann with assistance from Heinz Vielkind, and funded by the U.S. Office of Naval Research—rolled off the presses at about 7:00 p.m. on May 17, 1978. Marie, one of the Mueller employees (who was still supervising color separations), and *National Geographic*'s Bill Smith had met at Case-Hoyt early that morning. When the first proof came off the press, Marie thought it was "beautiful, [with] perfect registration and gorgeous colors": a purplish red, an ochre, and a deep grayish blue that somehow made most of the ocean floor look dusty and watery at the same time, so you'd remember what was normally there. Greenland and Antarctica were white. Deep fissures and trenches were filled in with almost-black blue. The United States was slightly to the left of center. Australia was all the way on the left and then repeated its western half again on the right side of the map. The ochre landmasses ripened into orange in the mountains, as if the sun had tanned everything but their snowcapped tips.

The Mid-Oceanic Ridge snaking across the Earth looked like, as Bruce would have said, a monstrous scar. In the Pacific it started at the Baja California Peninsula and sagged down toward the South Pole. In the

Northern Atlantic it curved like a spine, the coccyx almost touching Libe-ria, Iceland like some awful growth, the vertebrae continuing past Green-land and eventually petering off near Siberia. In the Southern Atlantic it was just kind of there, a mountain range running north and south until it was stopped short by another one of its own branches coming in from the east. Together, they formed a Y shape whose concavity cupped Africa and reached up to touch another branch directly east of Madagascar. In the Indian Ocean the Mid-Oceanic Ridge began at the tip of the Arabian Pen-insula, headed south, and then curved around Australia, linking up with itself again, forming a 49,700-mile-long mountain chain. A rift valley ran down the center of the entire range, the feature Marie discovered twenty-six years before, an underwater cleft that caused a shift up above.

But as Marie had said, color wasn't her forte. When that first proof came off the press, Smith instantly deemed the Himalayas too red and the balance of blue uneven from east to west. These problems were fixed, and Marie, Smith, and the Mueller man went out to dinner. They came back, made some more adjustments, and, "in the course of the evening, it developed that Mueller had not made the black plate for the [gridless] 4000 copy printing"—the maps that were to have been for her. It was a long night. The group parted ways at two in the morning, Marie having been instructed to return in the morning to pick up a few dried copies of the WOFP and give the Case-Hoyt people shipping instructions. As if she could have been stopped—she and Bruce had, long before his death, made careful plans for the shipment and eventual possession of the maps.

"Bruce and I opted," she wrote, "for 50 maps to a package as the lamination does add weight. A skid slightly larger than the maps is to be topped with a piece of plywood. Thus two men can carry the plywood with a number of flat packages of maps directly into my basement with-out even having to roll them." To Case-Hoyt she "emphasized that a small truck was necessary to negotiate my driveway, which is steep, curvy, and narrow." She allowed that the navy could handle the arrangements for its six thousand copies on its own.

As she's leaving the Case-Hoyt plant, Marie takes note of the presses, still humming and churning and spinning copies of her work, just as they'd been doing all night. The combined smell of inks is not so much a wave as a breaker, the breeze cast by the machines, the blurring of colors whirring past—if she merges with all the movement she can pretend that Bruce is there beside her. Not too close but not too far, pausing to take in what is and should be a momentous occasion. Pausing for a moment to feel content at all their work before letting worry creep back in.

Case-Hoyt's art director breaks into Marie's daydream. Bruce isn't there. There's really not any future work to worry about. But there are questions to answer: the art director wants to know if he can have her permission to enter the map in the PIA's annual contest. Marie doesn't know what the PIA is, so she asks. Oh, says the art director, surprised. He's got his hands in his pockets and is letting himself be lulled by the presses, too. The Printing Industry of America, he answers. Marie smiles. I'd be delighted, she tells him. If she couldn't quite summon pride on her own behalf she'd have to imagine it, conjure up her many memories of Bruce's ego, give each instance dimension, as if each were a balloon floating—and she could pluck one from the air and hold on to it just long enough to carry her through situations like this.

She tucks the tube containing her half dozen copies of the map under her arm and straightens her back. I trust you'll win your award, she tells the art director, pushing open the industrial door that leads to outside.

IN OCTOBER 1978 Marie and Bruce were awarded the Hubbard Medal from the National Geographic Society. The medal is named after the Society's first president, Gardiner Greene Hubbard, and is its highest award. It's been given only thirty-four times since 1906, to a prestigious group of explorers, researchers, and discoverers. I like to imagine that wherever Marie went after her death she gets on well with the other Hubbard awardees—carousing with the Arctic clique that includes Roald Amundsen, Sir Ernest Shackleton, and Richard Byrd, swapping exciting tales with Anne Morrow Lindbergh and Mary Leakey, the three of them waiting for Jane Goodall to arrive so their numbers can be expanded.

Bruce's medal was accepted by his mother, who was by then on her third marriage and called Esther Dauch. I have a color copy of an eight-by-ten photograph that I think shows part of the awards ceremony: a thick-set man in a black suit, flanked on one side by Marie, holding what appears to be a large square jewelry box in her aging hands, and on the other side by the former Esther Heezen, one of her small arthritic hands disappeared between his much larger ones. Behind the man (Robert E. Doyle, the president of the Society at the time) hangs a flag, curled around a vertical pole, white letters on a blue background spelling out a word that is obscured by the three people in the shot. Only the letters "TIONAL" and, below them, part of a brown stripe are visible. It's the presence of the flag (which fits the description of the Society's flag—three horizontal stripes, the top one blue, the middle one brown, and the bottom one green, each with one word of its name printed on it in white) and the medals (Esther grips what looks to be a wood-mounted medal in the hand that's not shaking the hand of the NGS official) that lead me to believe this is a picture of the Hubbard ceremony. I don't think Marie received any other awards until the 1990s and the stylings in this picture are undeniably 1970s: mustard yellow curtains at their backs, Esther in a brown tweed suit, her hair set and tinted the color of sand.

Marie wears a black, rust, and tan gored skirt she had constructed for her from Bruce's old clothes. Her hair is pinned up but not shellacked like Esther's and a large metal cuff bracelet circles her left wrist. She also looks skeptical. Her eyes, behind her aviator frames, are wide as usual. It's her eyebrows that transform her face: they're thin, but decidedly raised. She's in three-quarter profile, but even from that angle it's clear she's got the right side of her lip raised as well. Not a sneer, just an expression that says she doesn't take what she's looking at very seriously.

This makes sense. Marie and Esther didn't quite get along. The level of discord fluctuated widely, according to the circumstances. They were each other's most direct connection to Bruce, yet there was a long history of antagonism that couldn't be ignored: they were both the most important people in Bruce's life, but Marie was there by choice, Esther by blood. Bruce himself had a lot of antagonism toward his mother even though he was, by all accounts, a mama's boy. He was an only child, and I suppose he felt he had to protect his widowed mother. A few people told me that Esther had always thought Marie wasn't good enough for Bruce, that he'd listened and never officially married her. But in the end, on paper, his estate was split down the middle: half to Marie and half to his mother.

That's not exactly how things worked out, though. The first battle, for example, was won by Esther. Despite her son's wishes to be buried in a plot in Nyack with Marie, his mother succeeded in having him installed in the Heezen plot that had been set aside for her, next to Bruce's father. Esther bristled easily. She also played the Mother Card. "Please can you hurry the closing of the estate," she asked Marie in a letter dated August 13, 1978. "I can only say my dear son would not have wanted it carried on and on." That letter also carried her reply to Marie's good news about the Hubbard Medal. She was, she wrote, thrilled—and wondered if Marie and Bruce had been awarded the medal "as one" or if she might be able to add Bruce's to her "collection."

Marie took a more direct tone. After the Hubbard ceremony she wrote to Esther to say that she hoped she and her husband had arrived home safely. "We did, however, expect to see you afterward," she wrote in the next sentence. "I am puzzled about your concern for the estate. Bruce's estate is in the hands of two highly competent lawyers. I do work to earn my salary," she continued, defending herself to yet another person. "My job is finishing Bruce's projects, and finding money to continue Bruce's projects." In the next paragraph she adopted a different tone, saying, "Sometimes I like to write about Bruce; I think he was a great man." And she closed her letter with a great deal of kindness, reminded Esther that although she had lost her son, she still had peace, joy, and her beauty.

Marie and Esther corresponded a great deal after Bruce died. Marie typed her letters, but Esther often wrote in longhand, and after her letters were typed up by one of the Tharpophiles, all three parts of the correspondence were slipped into cellophane sleeves and inserted into black binders. Marie did this with most of her correspondence, not just Esther's. It's possible, then, to follow the events of her life based on the dozens of binders of her letters that are archived in this way at the Library of Congress: in 1977 she lost Bruce and in 1978 she lost even more than the GEBCO work. "It grieves me greatly to send you the following correspondence," she wrote to Esther on October 30, 1978.

> Within days after Bruce and I received the Hubbard medal, the Office of Naval Research withdrew their support at Lamont. After thirty years they just pulled out. My proposal for future work on maps, particularly to revise the World Ocean Floor Panorama over a period of 3 to 5 years was rejected. My proposal to finish and publish the Physiographic Diagrams was also rejected . . . My salary is guaranteed for a year and that is

all. I have tried to obtain funding from two other sources the past year and have failed. Would you be willing to set aside a fund, say $100,000, for me to revise the World Ocean Floor Panorama over the next 3 to 5 years and finish and publish a series of all of the physiographic diagrams?

"Please help," she wrote in closing, "I would so much like to finish Bruce's work." A postscript to that letter referred to something she'd found among Bruce's things. "It was scribbled on a piece of yellow paper," she wrote. "I call it Bruce's Prophetic Birthday Poem." Its enclosure sent a clear (albeit passive) message to Esther: Bruce had written it just as he and Marie were putting the finishing touches on the World Ocean Floor Panorma with Berann—and just before he died on the *NR-1*. "It would give me great personal satisfaction to complete a still more detailed view of the earth on a Marie-BCH map (we must do it)," he'd written, referring to Marie and himself. But, he continued, "it is necessary to maintain certain monetary support to be able to do the above." And not only that— they had to make the time, find the talent, face what he referred to as "too much resistance," just as they'd been doing throughout their careers.

A revised World Ocean Floor Panorama never appeared, nor did a series of the physiographic diagrams. The money didn't come from Esther or anyone else. As several people told me, no one was willing to place a large bet on a Bruceless Marie. It didn't matter how important her (or their) work had once been. Her time, it seemed, had passed.

*B*Y ALL ACCOUNTS, BRUCE'S OFFICE WAS PHENOMENALLY disorganized. Papers spewed out of file cabinets and onto the floor. Every inch of every flat surface was covered and maps and charts wallpapered the wall. But legend has it that before he left for the submarine cruise on which he died, Bruce cleaned up his office—and went around Lamont saying good-bye to his staff and colleagues. Both acts were voluntary and totally out of the blue, things no one can remember him doing before any other cruise; Bruce was not one for formalities or organization. It was as if, people said, he knew he was going to die. Maybe he wanted to make things easier for Marie, because he knew she would have to deal with whatever he left behind?

Things were not easy. In addition to finishing the World Ocean Floor Panorama, dealing with GEBCO, and having her navy support pulled, Marie had to contend with Lamont evicting Bruce's belongings from the premises. It was not unreasonable. Bruce was gone, space was at a premium, and although I haven't been able to find a written warning, I can't imagine that Marie was not given one. But the move must have echoed The Harassment for an already vulnerable Marie—in different versions of the story, she said that Bruce's belongings were "evacuated," "thrown out," and "removed." No matter the wording of the message, as the executor of his will, she had to deal with almost two decades of collected materials.

"I didn't think that these [things] should go to the dump," she wrote in a letter, "so I took what I could to my house and to Bruce's house and put the rest into storage"—another expense she was incurring with no hope of reimbursement. By 1981, she wrote to Esther Heezen, she had "spent the better part of $100,000" honoring her responsibility and "sacred trust" toward Bruce's projects and papers. She'd also been edged out of her own home: "my house in Nyack is all work space and stored stuff," she wrote in the same letter to Esther. She was living in part of Bruce's house and renting out the other half of it and the parts of her house that weren't filled by the things from Bruce's office.

The early 1980s were trying times. "Several times a day," she wrote, the things Bruce had left behind reminded her of their value, "historically and intrinsically." "I do cherish the opportunity," Marie said, but she was "frustrated by lack of space, lack of help, and lack of money. . . . I do not like how I am treated." Luckily, she was still a Lamont employee, drawing a salary. And she still had small bits of work coming in—nothing with the stature of her physiographic diagrams or panoramas, but work nonetheless.

There was her map business, which she ran out of her home. She had letterhead made up, cream linen paper with her name printed large and brown in a 1950s script. "OCEANOGRAPHIC CARTOGRAPHER," it read beside her name, her address and phone number printed in lowercase letters below. She had matching mailing labels printed up, too, as if she hoped she could brand herself with a new title and logo, be reinvented through the force of stationery. Around the same time she took out an ad in the *New York Times*, on one of the last pages of the Sunday Arts section in late November. The page on which her ad appeared was dominated by an article about *Epimediums*, which the article's author said "are plants you can depend on. They require no coddling, but go on year after year."

The ad itself occupies a tiny space. It's crammed down into the bottom right corner of the page, beneath a header that reads "Shopping Guide" and a collage of ads for such mail-order items as the Squirrel Spoofer ("feed the birds, fool the squirrels"), two different companies' personalized letters from Santa, and Su-ZED Enterprises' Door Stop Alarm ("Protect your home!"). "Ocean Floor Panorama," reads the first line of Marie's ad. "Full color maps by/Bruce C. Heezen, and Marie Tharp." The large version was listed at forty dollars, the smaller version at fifteen, and the address and phone number of "Marie Tharp, cartographer" were printed below. The only ad as small as Marie's was for Flexitron Industries' one-dollar "Miracle 'Smoke-Out'" cigarette extinguisher.

In 1980 Marie began a new collaboration, one that hadn't been initiated by Bruce. The work was with the Educational Materials and Equipment Company, and Marie's contact there was a Thomas McMahon, the company's president. McMahon had seen the World Ocean Floor Panorama and wanted to buy copies and advertise them for sale in his catalogue, which reached thirty-five thousand high schools and colleges. And although the deal was not brokered by Bruce, McMahon had met Bruce years before. Long before he was president of his own company, he'd taken a model of the seafloor that he'd constructed to Bruce's office. Marie wrote that McMahon had been in search of an informed critique and Bruce, "never one to pull his punches, said it resembled more a dish of tapioca pudding than anything else he could think of."

Apparently McMahon recovered from the incident. In addition to the maps, he wanted slides of certain regions of the ocean floor, and texts to match. So, Marie recalled, she "got out the red tape and some of our World Ocean Floor Panoramas and proceeded to outline various oceans, physiographic provinces of the oceans, as well as physiographic land provinces such as major drainage systems which influenced ocean basins." She "roughed in descriptive texts," then enlisted the help of Allen Lowrie, a former Lamont employee who'd moved on to work for the Naval Oceanographic Office. Together they revised what she'd written. In the end, Marie thought the project "turned out very well.... If I live to a really ripe old age my royalties eventually will balance out the $2,500 or so I spent on photographic work, typing and telephone calls," she wrote. "Anyhow, it was a fun project."

She was working on a lot of other projects at the same time, and in 1981 got to see the fruits of her labors. There were the two articles she published in the journal *Marine Geodesy*: one, a review of the documentary in which Bruce was supposed to have starred, called *Chasms Beneath the Sea*; the other, a short article titled "Differential Bathymetry," in which she outlined the technological requirements and applications of ocean floor mapping. "There is at present a notable lack of interest in the usual channels of funding for large scale maps," she wrote near the article's end. "Bluntly then, the need for increased financial support in research and development is one of the most essential requirements for the future of the ocean sciences."

One of Marie's other projects was the Seismicity of the Earth map. This had been in the works since Alvaro Espinosa, a seismologist with the U.S. Geological Survey, paid Marie a visit after the publication of the World Ocean Floor Panorama. He wanted to "overprint" the WOFP with earthquakes, placing dots at the epicenters of all earthquakes that had taken place since 1960. Earthquakes were signified by dots whose shades of red darkened as their points of origin in the Earth's crust deepened. The dots of earthquakes with magnitudes of more than 7.5 were outlined in black; the dots of earthquakes with magnitudes of less than 4.5 on the Richter scale were plain.

The result is a WOFP that looks like someone went after it with a stipple brush, intending to transform it into a pointillist masterpiece, and gave up pretty quickly—the Mid-Oceanic Ridge is clotted so thick with dots that most of them are indistinguishable from one another. "We are all pleased with the quality of the final printing," wrote Marie. And even though others were surprised that the epicenters coincided so well with the rift valleys and trenches on her maps, Marie wrote that she wasn't. After all, she'd been supplementing her sounding data with seismic data from the very beginning. The whole project, including a booklet she wrote with Espinosa's daughter, Rebecca, was funded by the Office of Naval Research.

In the spring of 1981 a book called *The Mapmakers* was published. It was written by a science correspondent for the *New York Times* named John Noble Wilford and included a chapter called "Mountains of the Sea." The chapter was about the continuing "discovery" of the seafloor—from Magellan's 1521 sounding of the Pacific to contemporary times—and said that Marie and Bruce's early maps "projected a new world into human minds, revolutionizing geology and our understanding of the entire planet we live on." Only about three pages, total, of the twenty-seven-page-long chapter were about Marie and Bruce's work, but Marie was delighted anyway. "Here is a review from last Sunday's *New York Times Book Review* section which I thought you might like to read," she wrote to her brother, Jim. With good reason: the review in the *Times*, written by

David McCullough, called the chapter in which Marie appeared "the best chapter in the book—or at least the most arresting." And not only that. McCullough wrote that it was the story of Marie and Bruce's work in the 1950s that most forcefully and memorably brought home the point that the oceans were largely unexplored.

Not one to brag, Marie didn't mention any of this in her letter to Jim. She did, however, want to share a memory with him: of Sunday nights on the farm, the two of them and their father, with "ice cream and the *New York Times* for supper," everyone "happily reading" their favorite section of the paper. She did say that she "never thought anything that [she and Bruce] did would ever be mentioned in the book review section." And in a letter she sent Jim the next month, along with a copy of *The Mapmakers*, she allowed that Wilford had said "some very nice things about me and Bruce."

The year 1982 brought the publication of a book in which Marie was more personally invested. *The Ocean Floor: Bruce C. Heezen Memorial Volume* was edited by R. A. Scrutton and Manik Talwani; the latter had taken over as Lamont's director after Doc left. Marie referred to it simply as the memorial volume; it consisted of articles by Bruce's colleagues and former students, including a heavily edited piece of writing whose original draft Marie referred to as her "Opus." The formal title of the "Opus" was "Mapping the Ocean Floor: 1947–1977," a title that was probably an accurate description of the story contained in the original one-hundred-page piece of writing Marie handed over to Talwani, the complete bibliography of Bruce's thirty years as a scientist that she'd compiled, and the few dozen illustrations she'd collected. It's a curious title, though; for what actually appeared in the memorial volume was a version of her "Opus" that had been "deleted down to 20 pages [and] focused mainly on the development of new concepts of geology."

Marie's article, as published, included eight illustrations and a two-column-long list of references. It did not include her section on the GEBCO. It did not include a translation from French to English of a paper titled "Géologie sous-marine et désplacements des continents" (Continental Displacements) that Bruce had delivered in Nice in 1958, which Marie called "a benchmark paper." It did not include her epilogue or her "comprehensive full page of acknowledgements covering thirty years at Lamont. Also deleted," she wrote, "were my travel-log sections, anecdotes, my general comments on the titans of the Geology Department who had been Bruce's professors at Columbia and the incredible Lamont team of many talents of which Bruce had been a member." It was, in other words, mostly stripped of the details explaining, really and truly, how Marie and Bruce had managed to do what they'd done. The resulting story was largely redundant; scientists, particularly geologists, would already have been familiar with most of its elements; the book's price, and the tone of the rest of its articles, made it inaccessible to the general public to whom the story would have been informative.

Regardless of all this, Marie "really felt" that the "Opus" was something she had to do. "I guess I was overly ambitious in trying to cover all aspects of Bruce's background," she continued. "I now look back at this project as an extended writing course both as to style and content." All told, she spent about $6,000 of her own money on the project and went through a number of extensive revisions of the "Opus." I have photocopies of both the published article version of the "Opus" and a ninety-one-page version of the document, and during my time going through her papers at the Library of Congress, I probably ran into dozens of other versions, some only a few pages shorter, some only a few pages long.

That same year, 1982, Marie learned that she'd also become redundant: Lamont wanted her to take an early retirement. She was sixty-three years old. Not young, but also not the oldest person there by any means. "It is my strong feeling that you should reject early retirement," K. O. Emery, a colleague of Marie and Bruce's who worked at WHOI, wrote to her in a letter. "You have done much for Lamont—so much that you should not oblige them by retiring voluntarily (without putting up a last-ditch stand). Stay with it!" But she didn't. Maybe because she was too busy with projects, maybe because she just didn't have it in her to fight Lamont anymore. Maybe because her brother was dying.

During the years since their father had died, Jim and Marie had stayed in what appears to be close contact, writing at least once a month, sometimes spending holidays together. Jim was Marie's only relative (and she his; he never married), a retired Forest Service worker, farmer, avid hunter, and gun enthusiast. Their correspondence manages to be both tender and gruff, which is due partly, I think, to the frequency with which they use the word *trust*. "I trust you have the good health to enjoy the holiday season," she once wrote to him. "Trust things are going well with you," he wrote to her at the end of a November 1982 letter.

"I am here at St. Pete's Medical Center," that letter began, "for an x-ray treatment of that leg cancer. Things are not going very well. Came in the last week of October & thought I would be here about a week or so." He figured he'd be in the hospital another week after that, and I don't know what occurred (if, for example, he got to go home) between then and February 27, 1983, when he died. But his death certificate said sepsis, the consequence of disseminated lymphosarcoma. I also don't know if Marie was able to visit him in the interim, but I know that she drove out to Iowa for his funeral. Jim had chosen to be buried in Stuart, where he'd grown up with his mother's family, after his mother had died and William, their father, had to move on.

IT IS RAINING in Muscatine, Iowa, and Marie stands in a cemetery with a woman named Marilyn Jackson. Marilyn grew up in Muscatine with Bruce and wrote an article about him for the University of Iowa's alumni magazine a few years back; Marie had wanted to meet her ever since, and Muscatine was on the way back to New York from Jim's funeral in Stuart. Their car is parked behind them on a narrow gravel road, and behind that stands a bare young oak. In front of them is Bruce's grave, between his father's grave on one side and the Heezen family monument on the other. Rain pelts Marie's slicker and the umbrella that she and Marilyn are huddled under. Marie watches it drip steadily off the edges of the umbrella, streams of water like threads, resolving into a kind of mesh, a veil drawn down from the domed umbrella top.

The Heezen monument is a white marble obelisk. It's topped with an urn that's carved from the same type of marble, and a draped cloth is carved into its face. Marie watches water collect in the sculpted folds. She feels the knees of her pants getting soaked and her socks dampen from standing so long on the spongy dead grass. This is the first time she's been to Bruce's grave since his funeral and now that she's here she's not quite sure what to do. She moves forward toward the graves and Marilyn moves with her. Bruce's headstone is a simple granite rectangle set almost flush with the ground, a circle with the outline of a cross carved into it floats near the top, his name centered beneath it, his birth and death dates beneath. That's it.

Marie looks over at the obelisk. Up close, she can see its strangeness. The cloth carved closest to the urn looks nondescript, but the one below it is almost anthropomorphized, its tapered ends clasped together like the hands that emerge from the tier of cloth just below them. She looks up at the carved urn, which now resembles a head. Marilyn is not saying anything. They'd had trouble even finding the grave; the cemetery is so huge that it has its own street names, but there hadn't been anyone at the office to direct them. Marie had relied on her scant six-year-old memories of the funeral and they'd driven around in circles for a long time before ending up here, on 28th Avenue, between Gateway and Peaceful.

Bruce's father's gravestone is stylistically identical to his son's. Between them are baskets filled with pink flowers. There doesn't seem to be much else to do but examine the graves of the other family members in the plot, so Marie slogs over to Bruce's grandparents' and stands looking down at their headstones, which are much taller and have their names carved out in reverse relief.

The day before, Marie had gone looking for Bruce's childhood home. She knew the address and that it sat on the edge of a bluff overlooking the Mississippi River but— again—didn't have a map. So she started at one end of town and drove along the road closest to the bluff's edge until she found herself staring at Smalley Street. She turned the river way. And there, at the end of the dead-end street and partly hidden by huge evergreen trees, was the big yellow home she'd only ever seen in photographs. Marie parked her car across the street and got out, leaving her umbrella behind even though it was raining.

The house was three stories tall and looked to be square. The windows were interestingly spaced. The narrow siding was the color of butter. She thought it might be aluminum, but decided it wasn't after tapping on it lightly with her finger. As she made her way around to the side of the house facing the river, a screened-in veranda came into view. It ran the whole width of the house's front, and just beyond it the wooded bluff dropped off steeply. She leaned forward, trying to see down the hundred feet or so to the railroad tracks where Bruce said he sometimes walked as a child, hunting for interesting flora and fauna. She leaned forward even more, one arm crooked around a rain-slick tree trunk, and could see the lock and dam in the river that Bruce had so often told her about. Marie heard a door open and straightened back up. Can I help you, called a voice from the direction of the veranda. Oh, Marie said, hello. The woman behind the screen didn't reply. I, well, Marie said loudly, a very good friend of mine grew up in this house. His name was Bruce Heezen and I'm Marie Tharp. We mapped the ocean floor. Using sonar. He died and I just thought—

Good grief, interrupted the other woman, come on in from the rain. She held open a door at the top of a small flight of stairs that led down to the yard. You must be soaked. Marie looked down at her body. Her feet squished in her shoes as she walked across the small yard.

On the veranda, Marie and the woman stood across from each other, Marie quietly dripping onto the floor. The woman gave her a smile. You mapped, she asked, the ocean floor? How on earth did you do that? With sonar, Marie said. They looked at each other. The other woman was younger. There were wicker things arranged around the periphery and empty plant hangers hanging from the ceiling. What do you do, Marie asked. Well, the woman said, smiling and folding her arms across her chest, my husband is a dentist here in town and we have a whole gang of kids. She stopped. Where did you say you were from? New York, Marie said. And I should really be going. She backed up. Oh, said the other woman, okay. But didn't you want to see the inside? Marie already had the screen door open. That's all right, she said. I really have to get going. But thank you, she called from the stairs.

In the car, she turned the windshield wipers and defrost on full blast as she executed a many-armed K turn in the narrow street. Despite the weather, she wanted to see Bruce's house from across the river. So she crossed the bridge and drove along the levee, passing neat black fields on her right and the wide brown river on the left. She wasn't able to get a clear view of Bruce's childhood home until she got to a higher elevation.

It was larger than she'd realized when she was on the property. It dominated the western shore. She drove back to her motel then, pulled back the covers on the tightly made bed, and crawled underneath.

"WHEN ABSENCE BECOMES the greatest presence," the author of a column in the Hospice Foundation of America's newsletter advises, "you have transformed the past into the present." The author is Rabbi Earl A. Grollman, and he's responding to a woman whose husband recently died. She's wondering if doing things such as setting a place for her husband at the dinner table and renewing his golf magazine subscription, even though she doesn't golf, means that she's going crazy. Absence is a tacky substance, the rabbi implies—easy to become suspended in, floating among memories instead of the living. He then invokes a quote from the actress Helen Hayes, commenting on her own widowhood: "I was just as crazy as you can be and still be at large." But neither woman, the rabbi maintains, is crazy; he also says that being "inconsistent," "unpredictable," and experiencing "brief periods of irrational feelings and chaotic bewilderment" is normal after the loss of a loved one.

By 1984 Marie's main coping mechanism had all but dried up. "During the past 51 months that Bruce has been gone," Marie wrote to Bruce's mother, Esther, in 1981, "I have really needed to keep busy. Work has been a sort of therapy to keep me from becoming overdepressed." But just three years later the medium-size projects with which she surrounded herself in the first years of the 1980s were finished. She was retired, no more projects were waiting for her attention—and she was still grieving. "Bruce has been gone for 87 months and 5 days," she wrote in a September 1984 letter to Esther.

She was living back at her own house in Nyack by then, had moved out of Bruce's house and into the attic of her own so that she could bring in more income from renting out his entire home. "It is very private and isolated and I love the sound of waves on the beach," she said of her new living quarters, at the top of her house on the Hudson's banks. The rest of her house consisted of storage and rooms for boarders. It was also work space, but the work had changed. If, in the years just after Bruce's death, her work had shrunk in volume and consequence, it changed again toward the middle of the 1980s. The shift was directional: instead of working on projects that described the present (the GEBCO sheets) and future (her articles in *Marine Geodesy*), Marie's attention became increasingly directed toward the past. If her talents for seeing deep down into the oceans were no longer appreciated, she would focus on a time when they were.

She was still running Marie Tharp Maps, which was wholly focused on distributing things she'd created in the past. There was still the occasional request to reprint one of her maps in a textbook; in 1986 a Russian version of the novel *The Hunt for Red October* even had one printed on its endpapers. Most of her time and money were spent on what she called the Bruce Project. The storage spaces holding Bruce's things became what she called Sorting Centers, the people who had previously been helping her with cartographic work now occupied by a vast archival project, their salaries paid out of the income Marie had from her Columbia pension, the money she received granting reprint rights for the maps, and small rental fees she collected from boarders in her house and tenants in Bruce's house.

Her goal was to get the Smithsonian Institution Archives to accept Bruce's papers—letters, books, audio logs, films he took while on submersibles, slides, and maps—many of the things that had been evicted from Lamont after he died. It was not a simple matter of tossing it all into boxes and sending it down to D.C.; imagine having saved the majority of papers that passed through your hands (business and personal) over a thirty-year period; then imagine a stranger trying to make sense of them. No, the organization of Bruce's things was something only Marie could do, a kind of maintenance, a grooming of his legacy through collation, binding, transcribing, and alphabetizing.

It took years but it paid off in the end; the Bruce C. Heezen Papers are now a part of the Personal Papers and Special Collections division at the Smithsonian Institution Archives. Copies of his complete bibliography, consisting of nearly a dozen volumes, bound in maroon leather with titles stamped in gold, were distributed to a number of oceanographic institutions all over the world. Some of Bruce's collections of professional journals were sold to dealers; some were sent to developing nations, where they would hopefully inspire a new generation of oceanographers. And the collection of sounding sheets from the nineteen countries associated with GEBCO that he'd amassed over the years were sent out to the National Geophysical Data Center in Boulder, Colorado.

Shortly after the Bruce Project swung into high gear, Bill Menard (Bruce's friend and fellow marine geologist) called on Marie at her house. Like Marie, he was working on a retrospective project—a book called *The Ocean of Truth: A Personal History of Global Tectonics*. It would be the first book about the plate tectonics revolution written by a direct participant with an inside perspective.

Menard felt that the recent revolution "merited a history that had not been written," so he collected his own papers—the Menard Project, one might say—and talked to his friends and colleagues who had also been participants. That included Marie. He visited her at the end of May and beginning of June and asked her what she referred to as "some very direct questions." The questions concerned two things: the causes and effects of the rift between Bruce and Doc, and Bruce's behind-the-scenes feelings about continental drift. In the book, then, Marie appears mostly as an accessory, offering small but substantial insights. She dominates page 201, an oceanographic Mona Lisa, even though she appears in only one of its sentences. "Marie Tharp smiled when she mentioned 'midnight requisitions' during this period," the sentence says, referring to the times during The Harassment when members of the Heezen-Tharp camp would sneak into Lamont to use the computers and data that had been deemed off-limits by Doc.

The Ocean of Truth is dedicated to "the memory of Teddy ['Crisp'] Bullard and Harry [Hess], the two Maurices [Ewing and Hill], and Bruce [Heezen], and the good health of those who remember." "For most of us," the first sentence of Menard's book reads, "except historians, it is fatal to look back." If you believe in magical thinking, you might say that Menard believed a little too much in the fatality of looking back. Although he'd originally planned for the book to follow the revolution into the 1980s, it ends after the seminal events of 1968; Menard discovered that he had terminal cancer, spent some of the last days of his life propped up in his hospital bed, laboring over galley sheets of his book, until his pain made it impossible to continue. He died before the book was published.

I don't think Marie would have professed a belief in the fatality of looking back. If anything, she would have said that it sustained her, for as the years passed by she continued to immerse herself in the past. In 1986, the year Menard's book was published, she and her friend Henry Frankel published the article "Mappers of the Deep" in *Natural History*. The article is written in the first person, from Marie's perspective, and begins by noting how little was known about the ocean floor just a few decades before. She leads the reader through a capsule history of sounding the oceans and gives short biographies of Bruce and herself before moving on to a detailed description of her discovery of the Mid-Atlantic Rift Valley and drawing of the North Atlantic physiographic diagram; the article ends shortly after a narrative description of the rift valley film that Cousteau screened at the 1959 International Oceanographic Congress.

The same month that the *Natural History* article appeared, Frankel published another piece of writing in which he defended the import of Marie's work. In the pages of *Eos*, the American Geophysical Union's weekly newspaper, he reviewed Robert Muir Wood's *The Dark Side of the Earth*. The book, Frankel said, had "a dark side." Some of the "factual mistakes," he wrote, "are just annoying, others are more serious." He classifies Wood's treatment of Marie as falling on the "less serious" end of the spectrum, but also sounds particularly distressed by it. "[Wood] tells us in the preface that 'the reader will find' that there are 'no women in this history.' Not only were there women involved, albeit far too few, but Wood even mentions one of them, namely oceanographic cartographer Marie Tharp. Perhaps he thinks her contribution was not important," Frankel wrote before explaining what her contribution was.

After their *Natural History* article came out Frankel wrote to tell Marie that New York University had ordered 1,500 copies to give to their freshmen. "I'm writing," he added, "to push you a little about working on your book outline." The book he was referring to was tentatively titled *Bruce Heezen, Mapper of the Deep: A Scientific Biography*, and Frankel tried to assuage any fears Marie might have had about not being able to do it on her own. She had written, he reminded her, the original first draft of the *Natural History* article and "about 15 additional first drafts." He'd made suggestions about what to cover, done some editing, rewriting, and revisions—and Marie had done "the real hard work." "You know how to tell a story," Frankel wrote, and she wouldn't really be alone in her endeavor. Bruce was absent in body but not spirit.

Every Tharpophile has a favorite Marie story. It's possible that by spending so much time around her they acquired a knack for storytelling, but it's also possible that a common love of stories is part of what made the Tharpophiles appreciate Marie at first sight—and kept them around for the long haul. There are several stories that fall into a category that I'll call the Classics. These stories have been repeated to me by several Tharpophiles. They soften their voices and smile during their recitations. They shake their heads—the remains of decades-old disbelief—and qualify their stories by calling them kooky or weird or eccentric. But they also encourage me to see the stories not as proof that Marie was crazy but, rather, uniquely and delightfully charming.

The largest subgenre in the Classics is probably Cooking. Marie loved food. She loved to cook, she loved to eat, she loved feeding her friends and workers. She would often, I'm told, wake early to spend the whole morning preparing a multicourse meal (once, it was a full Thanksgiving dinner, totally out of season) and go Martha Stewart on the table, creating elaborate centerpieces and making place cards—all by lunchtime. For Marie, there was no need for a special occasion such as a birthday or holiday: these days were special because she said so.

Another of Marie's cooking quirks involved experimentation. This one appears to tug particularly hard at the hearts of the Tharpophiles. According to them, some days it was as if Marie were possessed, inhabited by a spirit who compelled her to cook no matter what. Create! the spirit said, and she did: "Chicken Jell-O, anyone?" Marie would call out to her workers from the kitchen. Substitute! the spirit said, and she did. No rice in the pantry—try Rice Krispies, countered her imagination. No American cheese in the fridge—try cottage cheese, she'd think, ecstatic at the possibility of a culinary discovery.

There's another subgenre of Classics known as Hospital stories, but which can be more precisely categorized as Medical stories. Most of these take place in the early 1990s, when Marie was in her seventh decade of life and her health started to decline. Like many older women, she relished the attention she received from male doctors; unlike many older ladies, she did not shy away from letting these doctors know how much she enjoyed their attention.

There was the time she escaped from the hospital, an anecdote recounted by nearly every Tharpophile I met. Some placed it shortly before her death, others as much as a decade before; it could have been a stay for hip or knee replacement. Either way, it involved two things about which Marie felt strongly: food and personal freedom. The most detailed accounts of this tale involve her getting hungry at an off hour; she called a nurse, told her she was hungry. You have to wait, the nurse told her, meals are served only at certain times. But I'm hungry, Marie said. When presented with a piece of information she did not like, Marie seems to have had trouble integrating it into her understanding of reality; if she didn't like what she heard, it certainly couldn't be true.

So Marie put her clothes on, presumably unhooking herself first from the various monitoring devices to which she was attached, and then walked across the street to have herself a meal at the diner. Once the hospital staff realized she was gone, they went berserk, called Marie's house, and got one of the Tharpophiles and asked if Marie was there. Confused, the Tharpophile asked if she wasn't in their care. We've lost her, the hospital representative had to say, which of course was not as surprising to the Tharpophile as to the representative. The hospital started looking for her and the Tharpophiles joined in and no one found her until she wandered back on her own, put her hospital gown back on, and got into bed.

There are also the Gardening stories. They are more a collection of anecdotes, ranging from harebrained to charming, including Marie asking some of her workers to dig a drain that would magically manage to drain water up instead of down. There was the time she took Big John, a Tharpophile I never met, up to the state park to find some new ferns. They were digging the ferns up when a ranger approached them and asked (understandably) what they thought they were doing; Marie (characteristically) asked what about their digging up the ferns was wrong. In the autumn and winter she would "plant" brightly colored silk flowers in the fallen leaves and snow covering her property. By all accounts, Marie loved to garden. It was a passion she hadn't had time for when Bruce was alive, and she got to indulge it when he died.

Lastly, there are the stories that can be collected under the heading of Clothing/Personal Style. Each of the Tharpophiles made sure I knew that Marie had worn Bruce's clothing. A local seamstress named Jean Shenkman had conducted the conversions, cutting Bruce's pants into wide strips and piecing them together into gored skirts, making Bruce's button-down dress shirts more feminine and casual, hemming them and adding flourishes here and there with embroidery and cord. When Marie's brother died, Marie took to wearing his old jumpsuits and fatigues; before that, she'd been buying them from the army surplus store, a habit that happened to coincide with both the Iranian hostage crisis and her need to travel down to Washington, D.C., to arrange for the transfer of Bruce's papers to the Smithsonian, resulting in her being mistaken for a terrorist—and frisked.

As she aged, Marie's application of makeup became significantly more idiosyncratic. She favored bright shades: nail polish with glitter, purple eyeliner, and red lips and cheeks. Her shoe choices, however, changed only after much outside encouragement. When she moved to New York in the 1940s, she had almost exclusively worn black orthotic shoes. They were heavy and clunky and had a lot to do with why, later, she came to favor her skirts so long that they skimmed the ground, hiding her shoes from sight. Then, at one point, she began wearing what she called "space shoes," which were marginally more attractive than her old orthotics, and was crushed when the store from which she bought them went out of business. In the 1990s she was given a pair of Nikes as a gift. "They're so light," she's said to have exclaimed. If she'd been younger she might have kicked up her heels; as it was, she settled into their comfort with zeal, wearing her new sneakers everywhere.

DURING A ONE-WEEK period in September 1994, the Society of Woman Geographers (SWG) and a joint effort between Columbia University and the American Institute of Physics (CU-AIP) sent interviewers to Marie's house to begin recording her memories. Not since John Lear tried to write his biography of Marie had anyone asked her such detailed questions—or listened so carefully to her answers. But Lear had given up on that book more than a decade before, making the arrival of Ronald Doel (working for the CU-AIP project) first, and then Helen Shepherd (from the SWG) a veritable shower of attention—something to which Marie was unaccustomed.

"I know that you were born in Ypsilanti, in Michigan, but I don't know about your parents or your early home life," Doel began his interview by saying. "I wonder if you could tell me who your parents were, and what they did?" "How far back do you want me to go, sir," Marie replied, laughing. Then she turned shy: "I don't want to take up time on something you don't want to know about." Doel reassured her that he really did want to hear what she had to say. Marie's first session (between 1994 and 1997 there are two others with him and an additional two interviews with his associate Tanya Levin) with Doel is survey-like. In 56 pages it covers the period from Marie's birth up to the 1959 International Oceanographic Congress, where Jacques Cousteau showed his film of the Mid-Atlantic Rift, and ends with the recorded arrival of lunch. The rest of what I've come to call the Doel Sessions (another 114 pages) provide context for and detail about Marie's work; an additional 87 pages of interview conducted by Tanya Levin do the same, but cover much of the same territory as Doel.

By the time Shepherd arrived, one week after Doel's first 1994 visit, Marie was interviewing like an old pro. When asked again about her very early life, Marie began with her birth date and place, telling Shepherd that Ypsilanti is eight miles from Ann Arbor and that, when she was born, "there were no built-up things between Ypsilanti and Ann Arbor. I was born there because that was my mother's home, and she went home to have me." Then she pretty much dove into a genealogical history of the

Tharps, formerly the Thorps. The change in spelling, she said, had come about after the Thorps "beat up the British" during the Revolutionary War and were "so proud that they thought they would proclaim their independence by changing the spelling from Thorp to Tharp."

Marie and the SWG's Helen Shepherd had five sessions together. Four took place in the last months of 1994; the last took place in 1997. (In 1996 the SWG honored Marie with an outstanding achievement award.) The frequency and proximity of their meetings contributed, I think, to the tone of the interviews. Of the 434 transcribed pages, nearly 300 pages are devoted to Marie's life before Lamont—the childhood she spent moving with the seasons, the loss of her mother, her college and graduate school years. This information provides context for her later work, revealing the details of the idiosyncratic education that made her perfectly suited to map the ocean floor. Peppered between these stories are anecdotes about the men she lost during her life: mostly about Bruce, but also about her father and brother. Whenever the topic of discussion is tangentially related, she brings it back to them. By letting her follow these digressions—about her childhood, about the men in her life—Shepherd gave Marie the opportunity to do something she'd never done before: she got to tell the story of how her history had influenced her present.

When, back in 1975, John Lear tried to extract information from Marie about her early life, she had been reticent, as though she couldn't envision a story about herself that did not give equal treatment to Bruce. Twenty years later, however, she could.

Time had passed, and events had not progressed as she might have hoped. The history of plate tectonics had been recorded with little attention paid to Bruce and even less to her. The result was that her innovations, contributions, and motivations were misunderstood, even to friends and colleagues who should have known better. In 1983, for example, she responded to a friend and former colleague who had apparently defined her as someone who was content to follow and be "abused to meet [other's] dreams." "I did not feel abused," Marie wrote in rebuttal. "I felt I was very fortunate to be doing something that was challenging." Then she got rolling. "You were a member of our team for some years some time ago. But I was there some years before you—in fact I was there so long ago that there was this thing called no women in any jobs at all except teacher, nurse, and secretary." She could, she wrote, backtrack even further and tell him about how, as a child, she used to go out into the field with her soil surveyor father, an unthinkable activity for a young girl in the 1920s.

Three years later, in a 1986 letter to Henry Frankel, Marie still felt misunderstood. "The continuing lack of references to our work is annoying," she wrote. In 1994, when Doel and Shepherd first appeared, things were no better; perhaps by then Marie was fed up—ready to set the record straight. So she told her story. Throughout the 1990s she talked to Doel, Shepherd, and Tanya Levin, and in her correspondence with authors who wanted to write about her she tried to outline the role she'd played in the development of modern earth science.

There was, for example, Richard Ellis, famed marine conservationist, journalist, and painter of oceanic fauna, who also managed to downplay Marie's contributions. Ellis mailed Marie a chapter from his manuscript for what became *Deep Atlantic: Life, Death, and Exploration in the Abyss* and Marie replied, opening her letter graciously by complimenting his style of writing—it was "vividly descriptive, colored and dynamic," she wrote. However, she continued, "I am in a state of SHOCK to see my life's work attributed to someone called Wiseman [who had studied oceanic ridges, but only postulated the presence of the rift Marie discovered, in the Indian and Arabian oceans before World War II] in 1933. Nor do I like to see a perpetuation of the trivial or belittling observation such as me being 'startled at what I had mindlessly drawn.' Sometimes I have seen words such as these used to show how badly women scientists have been treated." She then took Ellis to task via his time line, getting all the way to 1961 before she really let loose.

That was the year her physiographic diagram of the South Atlantic was published, a physiographic diagram that illustrated, she wrote, "the rectilinear pattern of the Rift Valley offset by the fracture zones of the Mid-Oceanic Ridge." Marie rarely used technical language; her tone here indicates her anger in much the same way a mother's invocation of a child's full name—first, middle, last—indicates her displeasure. She did not, Marie implied by using words such as *rectilinear* and *offset*, mindlessly draw anything; for her efforts, she appears very briefly in the published version of Ellis's *Deep Atlantic: Life, Death, and Exploration in the Abyss*.

Marie was not actively pursuing fame. All of these people had come to her. She obliged because she wanted credit where credit was due, but she approached getting recognition for her contributions in the same way that she had revealed the topography of the ocean floor: she put the information out in the open, available for people to see and read, and let them draw their own conclusions.

CHAPTER 31

O N CAPITOL HILL IN WASHINGTON, D.C., THERE ARE THREE
Library of Congress buildings. The oldest is the Jefferson Building,
famous for its cupola, which is embellished with bronze and marble and
stained glass. The newest of these, the Madison Building, was constructed
in 1981 and is pretty much the opposite design-wise. It's a giant receptacle,
a rectangle full of smooth gray planes and hard angles evenly spaced, and
in its basement is the Geography and Map Division—ninety thousand
square feet of maps, atlases, and globes bathed in fluorescent light. This is
where the Heezen-Tharp Collection has lived since 1995, forty-seven thousand pieces and counting, in various states of organization.

Marie's relationship with the Library of Congress began in the spring
of 1994, when the Geography and Map Division's Jim Flatness visited
her South Nyack home. Flatness knew about her accomplishments—
the World Ocean Floor Panorama, the physiographic diagrams—and
wanted to see the state of her papers. Even though Marie had given the
bulk of Bruce's papers to the Smithsonian Institution Archives, her house
was still packed with thirty years of materials. There were the pieces
she and Bruce used to produce their maps, including sounding sheets,
fathograms, nautical charts, ship tracks, cruise logs, profiles; photographs

of the ocean floor; diagrams of cores; and notebooks and files filled with atmospheric, water, seismic, gravity, magnetic, and cable break data.

There were the pieces that resulted from their studying all those materials: contours; preliminary versions of physiographic diagrams; province maps Marie had drawn by hand, with rifts, abyssal plains, continental shelves, and other basic features rendered in different colors; sketches of various stages of the maps on tracing paper, acetate, and ozalid paper; the prototypes of globes that Marie and Bruce crafted, including the globe that prompted Harry Hess to declare that Bruce had "shaken the foundations of geology" at his 1959 Princeton lecture; hundreds of publications and drafts of publications; briefing materials they used when giving presentations; and all of Marie and Bruce's published physiographic diagrams and panoramas. And then there were the personal items: letters and postcards to and from Marie and Bruce; files and notebooks filled with Bruce's high school and college work; journals and datebooks from both of them; photos and slides from vacations; receipts and pamphlets; the audio Bruce and Marie recorded for John Lear. Marie kept pretty much every imaginable form of recording—paper or otherwise—a person could accumulate in life, and it was all mixed up together.

The Library of Congress and Marie worked out an arrangement that was mutually beneficial; Marie would begin sorting and sending the things that were jam-packed into her three-story house, and the Library of Congress would organize them and develop a user's guide in the process. That way, the items Marie and Bruce struggled to collect over the years would be easily accessible to future generations of geologists, cartographers, and historians.

The transfer began in early 1995. Marie and the Tharpophiles who were working for her at the time (including Lex Reibestein and Debbie Bartolotta, who would both work for Marie until her death) packed the materials into "crates, boxes, file cabinets, and large metal vertical storage map containers." Then Marie accompanied the materials on their journey to D.C., in a battered old cargo van, with a Tharpophile named Peter Esmay. The maps had been packed with characteristic Marie flair. They'd first been rolled. Then the ones that weren't already labeled had round multicolor tags or sticky notes attached to them. After that they were placed in tall plastic garbage cans. The cans themselves were labeled, each one with a wooden tomato stake tall enough for a few words about the can's subject matter to be written on it and still stick out above the maps. The van would roll up to the Library's loading dock—there were several trips like this—and Marie would ease herself out of the van's cab, ready to get to work.

Back in the stacks of the Geography and Map Division, a man named Gary North was in charge of organizing Marie's materials. North had retired from his post as assistant chief of national mapping programs for the U.S. Geological Survey and been hired by the Library in 1997 to process what would become the Heezen-Tharp Collection. Along with Marie and a rotating cast of staff members from the division, he set to unpacking and identifying the items. No matter the container—file cabinet, box, garbage can—the oldest round tags, some of which had been clinging valiantly to their maps and sketches and charts since being attached decades before, had fallen off. The bottoms of the containers, then, were littered with tags, the papers they'd once identified also orphaned. These papers and tags had to be reunited, which meant that during each one of Marie's trips down to the Library, materials were unrolled and laid out on large tables and flat files so that she could confirm the guesses that others had made. According to Gary, Marie would sometimes end up horizontal, too—tired from travel and the fast-paced review of her life's work, she'd climb onto one of the nearby tables and take a nap, her Nike-clad feet poking out from the folds of her flowered skirts.

Gary and Marie became good friends. The process, Gary told me, was like turning on an old faucet. When he'd call her on the telephone to ask a question about a particular piece of the collection, Marie would give short answers in a soft voice. But as he kept her talking, the trickle of information would turn into a stream, so that by the time they hung up Gary would have been flooded with stories—some of them only tangentially related to the thing he'd called about. And then, a week later, a package from Marie would arrive in the mail: a thick black binder filled with documents relating to whatever they'd discussed, a hard-copy appendix to what she'd already shared with him. These binders were everywhere in the Heezen-Tharp Collection.

One of the largest binders Marie sent Gary was in response to a set of questions he mailed her in advance of an interview they were going to tape for the Library. He would be the interviewer, but the taping part made Marie nervous, so Gary gave her the questions in advance. In return, ten days before they were to meet up at the Library, in late November 1997, he received a box of giant binders filled with Marie's answers and supporting documents.

You can see one of those binders in the resulting video. It lies open in front of Gary, who sits at a table positioned in front of a copy of Marie's World Ocean Floor Panorama. Marie sits off to the side of the table, playing guest to his Letterman. Her hands are folded on her lap and her shoulders are hunched toward each other as if she's trying to shield her heart. Watching this video in a cubby at the Library before I met Gary and heard his stories about Marie, I was struck by how timid she looked—not at all what I expected after reading her salty accounts of life with Bruce and their maps. Her voice wavered, her hair was a fuzzy halo around her head, and her eyebrows were drawn on with an exaggerated curve. Here was an old lady, not the headstrong and beautiful woman I'd seen captured, in various states of development, on thousands of pages and in hundreds of pictures by and about her.

Gary and Marie covered the usual bases—her childhood, her father the soil surveyor, college and grad school, her appearance in Schermerhorn Hall, meeting Bruce, starting to map the ocean floor, Jacques Cousteau, *National Geographic*, expeditions, The Harassment, the *NR-1*—and at the end of the interview, Gary asked her in a kind voice to talk "a little about Bruce and what happened to him." "Oh," Marie replied. "So many things happened to him." She smiled at her lap. "Have we used up our time?" she asked Gary, who urged her gently on, toward the subject of Bruce and his unfortunate end in the *NR-1*.

In 1997, the same year Gary and Marie recorded their video interview, Marie received two substantial honors from the Library of Congress. The first was from the Geography and Map Division's Philip Lee Phillips Society, a national organization formed to help further public understanding of cartography and grow the Library's collection; they named Marie one of the four greatest cartographers of the twentieth century. The second was part of the Library's celebration of the one hundredth anniversary of the Jefferson Building. The building had been restored for the occasion, and to mark its reopening, the Library put up an exhibit called *American Treasures from the Library of Congress*.

Marie's work was included in that exhibit, and Gary remembered accompanying her to the opening night gala. It was attended by President Bill Clinton. Marie was in a wheelchair (so as not to overexert herself), wearing one of her fantastical outfits. Gary wheeled her past the exhibit's treasures: among them, the original rough draft of the Declaration of Independence, the contents of Abraham Lincoln's pockets the night he was assassinated, maps drawn by George Washington when he was a surveyor, the first motion picture, the Emancipation Proclamation, and pages from Lewis and Clark's journals. That collection alone would have been amazing for Marie to see firsthand, and she later said that the Great Hall, in which it was housed, was "by far the most beautiful room I had ever seen in my life." But also there, amid all of those treasures, was one of her maps of the ocean floor.

Gary said Marie started to cry when she saw it. She looked up at him and asked, in her soft voice, "How did it all happen?" They stayed awhile in front of her work, which was finally hanging with worthy peers. While the formally attired guests at that night's function might not have taken much note of the eccentrically dressed older woman in the wheelchair, they did notice her work, stood before it in awe or recognition; whether they were seeing it for the first time or remembered it as a relative of a map they had unfolded from between the pages of *National Geographic* magazine decades before, they knew they were in the presence of something great. "I wish," Marie told Gary that night, "that Papa and Bruce could see it."

IN 1997 MARIE wrote a letter to Joe Worzel to see if he might be able to fund what she called her "unfinished projects." She was having, she said, "serious financial problems" since she'd been forced to retire from Lamont. Marie thought Worzel was in a position to help her because he was the president of the Palisades Geophysical Institute, Inc., a private company founded by some Lamonters back in the 1960s, when, in response to student protests, Columbia restricted the amount of defense money its departments could accept. Marie's unfinished projects included, she wrote, labeling and sorting maps for archiving at the Library of Congress; collecting and having sets of Bruce's complete bibliography bound; collecting her thousands of slides and organizing them so that they could be transferred to video; and sorting and labeling photographs.

The bad blood that existed between them during The Harassment was almost entirely absent, manifesting itself only slightly, in the form of Marie gently reminding Worzel that she was worthy of attention. "By the way," she wrote near the end of the letter, "last month I was deeply honored down at the Library of Congress." "And guess what," she asked after telling him a little about the *American Treasures* exhibit, "one of the cases housed a work sheet of mine, and a small plaque of our World Ocean Floor Panorama and a most cogent and flattering text describing our work of the past fifty years. I certainly am flattered to be associated with Lewis & Clark and other trailblazers . . . with this honor I have an added incentive to finish my various unfinished projects."

"Do come over and visit me," she wrote in closing, showing him that she wasn't the same person with whom he'd silently battled so long ago. "The place is open for inspection." Worzel might have visited her, but I don't think he was in a position to fund her various unfinished projects. This illustrated her situation pretty well: she had created an American treasure, was herself a living treasure, but neither distinction was going to pay the bills.

Nor were some of the other accolades she was collecting. There was, she wrote in her letter to Worzel, a young man named David Lawrence "attempting to write" a book about her. In 1999 he published an article in a cartography magazine called *Mercator's World*; that same year, Rutgers University Press acquired his manuscript "Upheaval from the Abyss: Ocean Floor Mapping and the Earth Science Revolution." In his proposal for that book he wrote about his desire to unite the stories of ocean floor exploration and mapping with the story of the earth science revolution; other books, he wrote, had addressed these subjects, but none brought them together—and none of them gave adequate attention to Marie. One of the books he referenced was Robert Kunzig's *The Restless Sea*, published that year (and the next, under the title *Mapping the Deep*).

Kunzig's book did indeed reference Marie, more than any other book had to date. "Marie Tharp receives visitors these days in a room that is about ten feet away from the Hudson River at its widest and most oceanic point," began his third chapter. "Part living room, part bedroom, and part explorer's den," he continued, "the room is decorated with globes large and small, with African masks and oil seascapes, with stacks of books and papers and assorted mementos, and, most noticeably, with photographs of

Bruce Heezen." But, Lawrence wrote in his proposal, Kunzig's book was, "unfortunately, marred by mistakes, misinterpretation of some of the facts and repeated statements disparaging Tharp's work." One of them being, perhaps, Kunzig's assertion that while Marie had discovered the Mid-Atlantic Rift, only "Heezen understood what it meant."

Regarding this and other statements in *The Restless Sea/Mapping the Deep*, Lawrence went on to say in his proposal for "Upheaval from the Abyss" that "the record should be corrected." Indeed. But while in that proposal Lawrence writes that Marie "knew what she saw," he never elucidates the details. In the end, she appears on fewer than two dozen pages, having gone from a star Lawrence was going to resurrect to someone who'd played, at best, a supporting role.

Lawrence wrote in his book that Marie "remains relatively unknown today, to some extent a result of her unrelenting efforts to keep Heezen's memory alive in the decades since his death." It's true that Marie's efforts to keep Bruce's memory alive consumed her, but she also spent a lot of time trying to tell the whole story of their work together—including explaining her own contributions. Getting attention for Bruce, in other words, did not mean robbing herself of credit. On the contrary. Read her publications carefully (her chapter in the Bruce Heezen memorial volume and her 1986 *Natural History* article with Henry Frankel) and you can see her creating boundaries, drawing distinctions between the roles she and Bruce played. She had changed her tack: with Bruce gone, she was holding the light; without her he had no hope of posthumously shining, and in curating Bruce's life she was also curating her own.

In 1999 Marie received the Mary Sears Women Pioneers in Oceanography award from the Woods Hole Oceanographic Institute (WHOI). It recognized Marie's "significant contribution to her field." Among Marie's papers at the Library of Congress is a binder filled with the greetings she received from friends and colleagues upon receipt of the award, the tangible equivalent of the television show *This Is Your Life*. One letter is from Heinrich Berann and his family. "Your spirit, your laughing, your work, your personality is still present here," Berann wrote. "We remember the Manhattans, the Fernet, the meals in the garden . . . And we remember the discussions and the good time[s] with Bruce and we appreciate so much your work." Another letter is from Debra Shenkman, the daughter of Marie's seamstress Jean. Debra's first job out of college was working for

Marie, who became a mentor to her. In her letter to Marie, Debra wrote that one of her fond memories was of going to the Cooper Hewitt National Design Museum to see the World Ocean Floor Panorama, which was hanging there as part of an exhibit on maps. She, like Berann, recalled lively dinner discussions.

A third letter is from Gail Matthews, who had been sent, by Bruce, to join the crew working at Marie's house back in the 1980s. The first day they met, Gail wrote, Marie's flaming red hair was piled atop her head and she was wearing a cast on her foot. She needed to buy warm clothes for an expedition to Antarctica; Gail accompanied her to Manhattan, and Marie talked her into buying "a fake fur so eccentric" that Gail's three-year-old cousin gave it a name. Marie's life and work were lived in the spirit of what Aristotle called "likely impossibility," Gail wrote, which "is always preferable to an unconvincing possibility." She made a list of examples of Marie's "own way of doing things": In Marie's "magnificent garden, silk flowers sprout up through the snow. All her poodles have been named Inky—even the most recent *white* one. And Bruce's old house down the river has been lovingly and meticulously maintained these past 22 years since his death."

Nearly all of the letters in this binder talk about Marie as both a friend and colleague, mentioning how, in addition to her unrivaled scientific abilities, she was possessed of a personality that was fun and kind and eccentric. Although she hadn't been able to practice her science in recent years, and the same eccentricity that some loved had gotten her in trouble at Lamont, those combined traits were the ones that made those who knew her love her. By 2001 the emotions surrounding The Harassment had faded for both Marie and Lamont. That year Lamont also honored her, giving her the first Lamont Heritage Award. Marie was eighty-one years old. Bruce had been gone for twenty-four years, Doc for twenty-seven, and the event that precipitated The Harrassment—Bruce's press conference at the Moscow International Oceanographic Congress—had occurred thirty-five years before.

As early as 1984, Marie wrote, "I feel I can view the Lamont phase of my life somewhat more objectively. It was a great team of many diverse talents. It took a firm, determined—if harsh and unfair—director like Ewing to pull [together] these diverse elements of instruments, research vessels, and people to solve significant problems of the world's oceans."

In 1996 she called Doc "a great man" for having collected so much data about the ocean floor in such a short period of time. (She was, however, still bitter about select issues: "What was Ewing's view about women in the scientific fields," an interviewer asked her in 1997. "I think he hated their guts," Marie replied.) But being honored by Lamont helped her feel vindicated. As did her inclusion in the book *Twelve Perspectives on the First Fifty Years* that Columbia University Press published in celebration of Lamont's fiftieth anniversary.

Gary North told me that Marie cherished the physical award Lamont presented to her. The rock that formed its bulk had been dug up from beneath the campus's surface and then had a hollow carved into it. The hollow, which held a slice of a core from the northern Mid-Atlantic Ridge, was covered by a piece of glass onto which was etched the portion of the ridge that the core was taken from. The award represented where her work started and where Bruce's ended; its creation showed that Lamont finally recognized her discovery. As she said in the final sentences of her essay in the *Twelve Perspectives* book, "establishing the rift valley and the mid-ocean ridge that went all the way around the world for 40,000 miles—that was something important. You could only do that once. You can't find anything bigger than that, at least on this planet."

MARIE'S DEATH, ON August 23, 2006, was unattended. It seems that she had been sick for some time, but as with many of the most important subjects in her life, she stayed silent about her illness.

At the time, there were four main Tharpophiles in Marie's life. Debbie Bartolotta (whose mother, Marian Dollar, had worked for Marie for years, typing and transcribing many of the documents that made their way to the Library of Congress), Kerri Connolly, Lex Reibestein, and Fiona Schiano-Yacopino. Most of them were at Marie's house every day. Fiona, however, went to Florida for a short trip at the beginning of August. When she got back, Marie looked as if she had a little flu. Fiona was concerned. We should get you to the doctor, she told Marie, who replied that a couple who lived in the next town knew she was sick and were going to take her to a specialist in Manhattan.

The two halves of this couple are something of a controversy in the circle of Tharpophiles. There are those who say that they're bad news—

who claim that, in the 1990s, they put pressure on Marie to fire (for real) the other Tharpophiles so that they could take control of her finances, that after doing so they embezzled enough money from her to put their kids through college. While it's true that both Debbie and Lex went through a hiatus at that time, and that Marie was indeed prone to making donations to a curious collection of causes (the NRA, Planned Parenthood) and people (an "inventor" who lived up the street, a cast of outsiders she took into her home as boarders), in the years he spent going through Marie's papers, Gary North was never able to find evidence that this couple took advantage of Marie's financial situation.

Either way, the couple arrived the next day to take Marie to the New York specialist and, Fiona said, she didn't return. Fiona couldn't reach the couple. A whole day passed like that. The night passed, and the next morning came. Fiona, Debbie, Lex, and Kerri were in a panic. They called every hospital in Manhattan. Eventually they found Marie in the last place they thought she would be, in the Nyack hospital, just miles away. She was alone, and she was quarantined; she'd been dropped off very ill, and her lungs were in such bad shape that the doctors thought she had a virulent infectious disease.

The Tharpophiles were shocked, to say the least. True, the last they saw her she'd looked under the weather, but this? When they finally got to see her (after Debbie and Kerri proved that they had medical power of attorney) they found her confused and disoriented and scared, which was totally out of character. They took turns staying with her while the doctors did their tests. They had to wear masks; they held her hands and turned on her favorite television shows.

Fiona and Kerri were holding Marie's hands when the doctor came into the room to tell them what was wrong with her. Debbie tried to steer the doctor into the hall, and Fiona and Kerri chattered away, trying to distract Marie. Neither the doctor nor Marie would have it, though. She needs to hear this, the doctor told them. Be quiet, Marie told Kerri. Am I going to die, she asked. You have advanced lung cancer, the doctor said. It had spread throughout her body, and the only thing left to do was manage her pain.

Marie was in the hospital for about two weeks. The Tharpophiles continued to take turns staying with her during the day. And then one night the hospital called them. Marie had taken a turn for the worse and the nurses had had to start her on morphine. For cancer patients, morphine is the beginning of the end; Marie never regained consciousness after that. But they kept talking to her, kept turning on the news (her favorite) so she could listen to it, moistened her lips and mouth with swabs dipped in ice water. "We didn't even have the time to catch up with her," Fiona said.

Many medical practitioners believe that the terminally ill choose when to die. Marie, an intensely private woman throughout her life, died alone, at night, after all her visitors were gone. The *New York Times* obituary appeared three days later:

> Marie Tharp, an oceanographic cartographer whose work in the 1950's, 60's and 70's helped throw into relief—literally—the largely uncharted landscape of the world's ocean floor, died on Wednesday in Nyack, N.Y.
>
> The cause was cancer, according to the Lamont-Doherty Earth Observatory of Columbia University, which announced the death. Ms. Tharp was a researcher at the observatory from 1948 until her retirement in 1982.
>
> With her colleague Bruce C. Heezen (pronounced HAY-zen), Ms. Tharp compiled the first comprehensive map of the entire ocean bottom, illuminating a hidden world of rifts and valleys, volcanic ranges stretching for thousands of miles and mountain peaks taller than Everest . . .
>
> In the revised edition of his book "The Mapmakers" (Knopf, 2000), John Noble Wilford, a science reporter for *The New York Times,* described their achievement this way: "Like other pioneering maps, the one by Heezen and Tharp is not complete and not always completely accurate. It is, nonetheless, one of the most remarkable achievements in modern cartography."

CHAPTER 32

I DISCOVERED MARIE IN THE FIRST HOURS OF THE FIRST day of 2007. I'd been on the East Coast visiting my family and friends for the holidays and when I returned home to Iowa City, Marie was still with me. She was still with when me I began teaching and taking classes of my own, still with me as I started trying to write about other subjects. She wouldn't go away, but she also would not yield—researching her online brought up the same few articles and interviews, most of which repeated the same stories that had appeared in the *Times*; going to the library proved even more unsatisfying.

In a 1968 *Harper's Magazine* article called "Notes on Writing a Novel," John Fowles describes how he began writing *The French Lieutenant's Woman*. "It started," he wrote, "as a visual image. A woman stands at the end of a deserted quay and stares out to sea." Like the information about Marie's life that I'd gleaned, the woman in Fowles's image was "obviously mysterious," and "vaguely romantic . . . an outcast." By the spring of 2007 none of my other writing mattered; like the image of the solitary woman on the quay, Marie "soon came to make the previously planned work seem the intrusive element in my life." At the end of my first year in graduate school in Iowa, I looked up at a scrap of paper I had tacked above my desk, onto which I'd copied a sentence from Fowles's *Harper's* essay. "Follow the accident, fear the fixed plan—that is the rule," it said. So I did.

"I'M HERE," I shouted, leaning out the open car window and waving. It was January in New York but the day had gotten warm, reaching seventy degrees sometime before lunch. I was a couple of hours late, had gotten lost because I hadn't confirmed my Google Maps directions to Marie's house in South Nyack with a real person. It was 2008; the sun was beginning to set.

Gary North came out of the turquoise front door to wave as I pulled in behind a gigantic Dumpster; I'd been introduced to him the week before, on my second trip to visit the Heezen-Tharp Collection at the Library of Congress. There were two other men out on the porch: one who stood with his arms crossed, grinning and shaking his head, and a stocky man in a dress shirt and shiny shoes. They blocked the doorway of Marie's house at first, a tableau of graying hair against worn stone, but then rearranged themselves into a more welcoming formation. As I grabbed my things, stuffing a camera, notebook, voice recorder, and pens into the pockets of my jacket, I saw the stocky man go inside and come back out with a medium-size box, which he carried to his car. Later, Gary told me that he was a book dealer, come to buy the books that were worth something. "I guess we thought he'd take more," he said. When I got to the porch I shook hands with Gary and he introduced me to the grinner, who turned out to be Lex, a Tharpophile to whom I'd spoken on the phone but never met. He and Gary both looked dusty and exhausted; Marie's house had been sold, and this was their final day to clean it out.

Inside, Gary went back to deciding what would be saved and sent to the Library. I peeked in after him. He was perched on a short stool in the center of the living room. The room was still crammed with stuff, even though it had to be completely clear by noon the next day: boxes of papers everywhere, stacks of paintings and prints popping out of picture frames, a box filled with dozens of keys, a box filled with china, some African shields, a jar of black-strap molasses, a small marble sculpture of the mythical character Leda, rolled-up posters, lamps, maps, an overturned box of slides, a filing cabinet. "You missed the human skulls," Gary called out to me in the foyer, "someone came earlier to take them." I could hear footsteps up above, the sounds of heavy things being moved, wood creaking. The place smelled musty.

I turned back to Lex, who was standing next to the staircase leading to the second floor. His hands were on his hips as he tilted his face and chest up toward the ceiling. "It's really just a shell now. It used to be this kind of magical castle—that's what we used to call it—she had created this wonderful place that you could escape to, but now . . ." He straightened his body and sighed. "Oh well."

My tour of the house with Lex kept getting interrupted by people coming to take things. Or his phone would ring and he'd look at me apologetically and then go into the next room to beg the person on the other end to take, say, Marie's drafting table. He was already taking her light table; the drafting table was too big to fit in his apartment, none of the other Tharpophiles wanted it, and the house had to be emptied of all of Marie's things by the next day. "Please," he said over and over, "otherwise it's gonna end up at the dump."

I did everything gingerly in those first hours at Marie's, softening my tread as I followed Lex around, getting my face up close to examine things but not placing my fingers on their surfaces. I left papers stacked and books closed, took pictures with my digital camera of black-and-white snapshots strewn about the floor, sniffed loads of dust into my nose and then sneezed to discharge it. All around me things were changing—different people moving different items out of the house—yet I felt as if there were something that had to be preserved, an imprint of Marie that might have remained, even though people had been sifting through it all since she died the year before. I tried to see everything so that it wouldn't be forgotten, refused to touch any of it so as to not disturb her pattern and replace it with my own.

The rooms of the house seemed as if they'd been painted according to a code that only Marie had known. The front door, for example, was turquoise, the door to the basement was coral, the carpet in the office on the second floor was bloodred damask, and the kitchen was tiled in yellow. A bathroom on the second floor had rainbow colored tiles. The concrete floor in the basement was painted purple. There were walls of marbled-patterned mirrors everywhere on the first floor, a small room in the basement filled with the silk flowers Marie used to plant in the snow, a small bathroom off the kitchen separated only by a yellow curtain patterned with ducks, and a widow's walk on the second floor looking out over the Tappan Zee Bridge. Once, when Lex had to disappear for a moment, a rotund man with snowy muttonchop sideburns (who'd been introduced to me earlier as "muscle") sidled up to me as I was taking pictures of the top half of a wall papered with ducks. "Whole house used to be like that," he said, looking up, his hands shoved in his pockets. "Covered with ducks?" I asked. "Well, no, although that bay window out there in the living room had so many decoys in it that it looked like a little pond." He paused, both of us looking up at the glossy pictures of gadwalls, wood ducks, and mallards Marie had cut out of old calendars. "Seems to me someone told me once that her brother liked hunting ducks, I think. Or anyway the house was plastered with pictures like that, whole walls, floor to ceiling. We just took it all down this morning."

There were other things that had already disappeared. Layers of oriental rugs scraped up from the floor, a thronelike leopard-print couch from which Marie had held forth in her later years, row and rows of handmade dresses hanging from piping in the basement. When we got to the top of the staircase leading to the second floor, Lex stopped for a moment and stared at a space on the wall. There were nail holes there, and two rectangles that stood out bright and white from the dinginess of the rest of the wall. "Hey Gary," Lex shouted, "you know where those portraits got to? The sketches of Marie and Bruce that were hanging together here?" There was a pause, a shuffle, and then Gary's head appeared at the bottom. He furrowed his brow. "I don't know," he said. "Didn't we just take those down this morning?"

Lex rubbed his chin and we turned into the suite of rooms facing the river on the second floor, toward the wall into which Marie had a doggy door installed "so that the Inkys could go out onto the widow's walk to do their business." "Plural?" I asked; back then I thought there had been only one Inky. Lex nodded as we walked into the next room. "Black standard poodles. When one would die she'd just name the new one the same thing and bury the old one out front. There were four, or three, depending who you ask." The last one was white, he told me, which had caused some controversy among the Tharpophiles; there were those who thought it wrong to call a white dog Inky.

We were standing in front of a large black-and-white photo of Bruce that was hanging next to Marie's drafting table. His brow was furrowed.

He looked as if he were staring into the sun on the deck of a ship. Catty-corner from his picture on the wall hung a modern map of the ocean floor. Its colors were mostly primary, so supersaturated that they seemed about to leap off the wall and splash Bruce in the face. I snapped a picture of the scene and turned back to Lex just as his phone rang again. He closed his eyes for a moment as if very tired. He held up a finger, sort of turned up the corners of his mouth like he wanted to smile, and answered the phone.

Gary came into the room then, a light blue envelope in his hand. He held it open for me. "Look at this," he said, watching my face. I looked inside and saw a hank of light brown hair curled up in the bottom. I wanted to touch it. It was shiny, as if it might have been snipped from someone's head the day before, but still I assumed it was Marie's. "One of Bruce's girlfriends," Gary said. We held each other's gaze for a beat and then Gary shook his head. We both found other things that night and since that Marie must have seen, things that proved Bruce had not been as faithful to Marie as she'd been to him. I pointed to the photos on the floor. "You see these yet?" He nodded. "Mmm-hm. I'm trying to make my way up here but   " I picked up a tin box that had been resting on one of the filing cabinets and opened it, thumbing through the thick manila cards. "It's a time line," I said. "All the events in their lives on index cards. She arranged them by year." I pulled out the card for June 1977, just a single card among probably a hundred, with a single sentence in shaky pencil writing noting that Bruce had died. "That'll be useful to research-ers at the Library," I said. He nodded and put the box back on the filing cabinet; I never saw it again.

When I first arrived, Marie's house didn't seem to be emptying so much as redistributing its contents in a vast new layer: sediment kicked up and allowed to settle down again. But things got more urgent as evening turned to night. It was a race to save what we could, and we all bustled around, sifting through the mess, trying to decide what would become his-tory and what would become trash. For a while I watched Gary sort things in the living room—a plaque of the *NR-1* that had been taken down off the wall, photographs and slides from vacations, file folders filled with busi-ness correspondence, binders filled with things she wrote, a few pieces of furniture—the things she had kept for so long.

And then all of the people who had been working so hard since I arrived started to disappear. Lex stopped loading a van so he could run home to check on his aging mother; muttonchops was his ride. Fiona, who had inherited Marie's map business in the will, had been clearing stuff out of one of the offices on the second floor; she left after dragging a half dozen black garbage bags down the stairs by their necks. Others appeared: a man in fatigues with stringy gray hair and open wounds on his hands showed up and asked if there were any old issues of the Geological Society's newsletters left. We found a few somewhere. A couple dressed in jeans and sweatshirts showed up and Gary unfolded himself from his stool to talk to them, sighing as his long legs straightened like wings.

When they left, it was just us, Gary busy trying to save what he could, me pacing circles round him as I ate the cold piece of pizza he'd insisted on. As I chewed, he told me how Marie had moved into the living room in her later years, had set up the leopard-print couch in the middle of the room where she worked, watched television, and slept. I nodded. I had known that already: a while back I'd found a picture of her propped up on a mountain of pillows on a leopard-print couch, in what looked like this room, in an article in the same German oceanography magazine that had described her and Bruce as *Liebespaar*.

While listening to Gary I looked at the papers he was going through, trying to read what they said from a few feet away, wanting to make sure that nothing useful was getting thrown away. When he fell silent we stayed that way for a while, him sorting and me watching. It startled me when he spoke again. "You can take some things if you want, you know," he said. He's a very tall man and so even though he was seated our faces were at almost the same level. His eyes were tired and the papers he held in both hands drooped toward the floor. "As long as you don't think it's something the Library would want." He gestured to an empty box. "Just fill up a box." I stared at him for a moment. "Go on," he said.

I dug in then, set aside certain things for Gary to take to the Library and chose others for myself. I took two binders filled with copies of transcriptions of the tapes Bruce had made for John Lear; one cigar box filled with letters people had written to Marie's brother, another filled with envelopes containing letters people had written to Marie when she was in Ann Arbor and Tulsa; Bruce's copy of A. K. Lobeck's 1939 book *Geomorphology*; a few snapshots of a man I now know was Marie's ex-husband. I'd go into the living room, where Gary was perched again, and show him something that I thought the Library should have and he'd say "okay" and exhale at the same time. Or he'd come into the room where I was elbow-deep in some box, hold something up, and press it into my dusty hands. "You should take this," he'd say. Once, it was a one of Marie's famous binders, filled with notes she'd handwritten on yellow lined paper.

Eventually I had to use the bathroom, and everyone in the house—Lex and his friend had returned by now—was scattered around the first floor, so I had to sort of call out to ask where it was. "Well," the guy with the mut-tonchops said as he walked up to me, "we've just been using the bath-room off the kitchen." He pulled a curtain printed with ducks to the side and pointed at a toilet. "But since you're a lady . . ." He winked at me and I followed him up the stairs to the second floor, to a door that I hadn't noticed in the back of the house. It was white. He opened it and flicked a light switch. A warm glow filled the stairway. "There she is," he said, pointing up the stairs. "Used to be where Marie lived, before she moved down to the living room. The room on the river side was where she slept." She had slept in a round bed, he told me, but that had also been taken out of the house earlier in the day, two semicircles dragged down the stairs to a waiting truck. I smiled at him and put the cap on my pen, closed the door behind me, and went up the white stairs.

The ceiling was slanted. At the short end of the room was a claw-foot bathtub. A strip of plaid vinyl curtain covered the long, low window that stretched along the bottom of the wall. The toilet sat beside a stacked washer and dryer. When I was done using it, I tried to see into the other rooms. The light at the top of the stairs illuminated Marie's old bedroom a little, just enough so that I could see to walk around in it. The carpet was filled with green swirls, each one a different shade. The swirls looked like little whirlpools and were made of long thin crescent shapes that curved toward a dark point in the center. I tried to sketch the pattern, be a good reporter, but ended up completely hypnotized, as if I were on my own little raft, bobbing on seas getting rougher, seas that would assuredly swallow me up.

When I drove away from Marie's house that night, I had two boxes of her things in the trunk of my rental car. I was staying with a friend in Philadelphia between my trip to the Library of Congress and the one I'd just taken to New York, and when I got back to her house I placed the boxes at the foot of my bed. They stayed there while I slept, like baby animals that needed to be kept warm. The next day, when I had to drop them off at the post office to ship them to my own house in Iowa City, I had a hard time parting with them. When the woman behind the counter started asking me the usual questions, I found I didn't know how to answer.

"Fragile, liquid, or perishable?" she asked. Define fragile, I said; we determined that the contents were not fragile. Then I tried to insure the boxes. "For how much?" she asked. I wasn't sure, I told her; it's the letters and photographs and writings of a scientist, actually probably one of the most important scientists of the twentieth century. So a lot, I said. "Can't insure something unless you can prove how much it's worth," she said. "But it's priceless," I said. "Can you prove it," she asked, and I couldn't, so I settled for delivery confirmation and, for less than two dollars, received two slips of paper printed with long strings of numbers that I still have, tucked away in a box. That was when I became a Tharpophile.

CHAPTER 33

*P*ROFESSIONALLY, WALTER H. F. SMITH IS ABOUT THE CLOS-
est you'll come to a present-day Marie. He's one half of Smith and
Sandwell, famous among oceanographers, geologists, geographers, geophysicists, and sundry other subspecies of scientists for the Smith and
Sandwell map of the ocean floor. The Smith and Sandwell is not one map
but many; the first version appeared in 1997, with new versions following
the advances of the technology used to collect information about the
ocean floor.

One of the technologies Smith and Sandwell used is the satellite
altimeter. Due to gravity, the Earth's surface is not perfectly spherical. In
places where there's a large feature on the ocean floor, such as the Mid-
Atlantic Ridge or the Mariana Trench, the ocean surface deviates—bumps
where there are mountains, dips where there are valleys. The satellite
altimeter takes advantage of these imperfections. A very simplified explanation of what the altimeter does goes something like this: a satellite with
advanced radar capabilities is launched; as the satellite orbits the Earth, it
bounces electromagnetic waves (or radar—different from sonar, which
uses sound waves) off the surface of the ocean; a computer then analyzes
the data, mapping out the subtle bumps and dips of the ocean's surface.

Smith and Sandwell's maps also use data collected by multibeam echo sounders, which are more advanced versions of the precision depth recorders used in Marie and Bruce's day. Instead of sending out just one ping and listening for its return, the multibeam sounder sends out several at once, a fan of pulses that measures a wider area of the ocean floor. The resulting image is wider when compared with ones created using technologies of the past, but in relation to the rest of the ocean floor it's still thin—now scientists collect data in ribbons instead of threads.

Both of these types of measurement probably appear to be easy fixes compared with the sounding methods Marie and Bruce relied on. It seems like a simple matter of completing the task: go forth and measure! the leaders of the world's countries cry in unison, their science advisors hastily directing the writing of outsize checks, and it will be done. But that is not the case. Although multibeam sounders and satellite altimeters collect more information faster—and do it rather automatically, thus increasing the quantity of information about the ocean floor that we can look at—there are several problems. Only very large features can be picked up by the satellites, and the multibeam sounder can collect data only from the relatively narrow "ribbon" strips. Maps made using satellite data look good when you view the whole planet or large regions, but draw closer and the picture you see is blurry.

Marie had a copy of the Smith and Sandwell map hanging above her living room fireplace. "I only wish that Bruce were here to observe how well their map . . . agrees with our map," she wrote in a letter to an acquaintance. The maps have something else in common: they're both incomplete. Like the precision depth recorders with which Marie and Bruce were working, the multibeam echosounders need to be on top of the areas being sounded. There's no quick fix. But instead of extrapolating like Marie, Smith and Sandwell filled in the blanks with data collected by the satellite altimeter. The result is a more accurate map, one with much of the subjectivity removed.

Without the extra- and interpolation, without the vertical exaggeration and highlighting and all the other methods employed by Marie (and later Berann) to help the public understand that there was a world hidden under all that water, the ocean floor looks very different. When I asked Walter Smith where his map diverged most from Marie's—where, in other words, she made mistakes—he said that the most glaring error was in the Pacific. In all her maps the texture of the Mid-Oceanic Ridge looks like alligator skin. As if the ridge were a reptile with all but its spine sub-merged. That texture is true in the Atlantic Ocean; in the Pacific, how-ever, the flanks of the ridge are much smoother. But Marie extrapolated the Atlantic's texture all over the Earth, didn't have enough data satura-tion in the Pacific to know she was wrong.

"Even if it's wrong," Smith said, "it's still beautiful." And it gave people a picture of a place that many of them had never considered before. "We can't underestimate the role her maps played in helping people visualize the features of plate tectonics." That revolution, he said, "could not have happened without a lot of people being able to see the features she drew." Her work, then, was exactly what was needed at the time. "The start," Smith said, "of seeing our planet in a whole new way."

Despite the new technologies, we haven't moved much past that start-ing stage. Even today, only about 10 percent of the ocean floor has been surveyed using multibeam sonar; in other words only about 10 percent of the ocean floor has been studied in any detail. This lack of information about the ocean floor means that scientists have mapped Venus, the Earth's moon, and Mars in more detail (with several thousand, 1,000, and 250 times more detail, respectively) than Earth. We know less, period, about our own planet than we do about those places. The U.S. Naval Research Laboratory published a study in 2004 estimating that it would take two hundred ship years to completely map the ocean floor in detail—one ship two hundred years, twenty ships ten years, or one hundred ships two years.

In Marie and Bruce's day a scientist could get ship time and go out and explore, not knowing what he was going to find, just to do it. "I keep my ships at sea," Doc had said, and he meant it. As long as data were con-stantly being collected, he was content; as long as the conclusions he and his men produced helped the granting agencies and companies, they were content. Today, Smith told me, "the era of exploration is over." Sci-entists have to write convincing proposals that account for how every penny and moment on a ship will be spent, which essentially means that they have to predict what will happen while they're at sea. Without the time and money for exploration, there's little space for discovery. Research vessels return to the same places again and again, building expeditions around those places because they can be described in proposals. Lack of funding results in less data and fewer discoveries, which results in less public interest; in a *New Yorker* cartoon much circulated among ocean-ographers and geologists, a woman chatting with her friends in a genteel sitting room says, "I don't know why I don't care about the bottom of the ocean, but I don't."

That was 1983. In 2009 Google released Google Ocean, which used data from agencies all over the world to give users a view of the ocean floor—the first truly publicly accessible picture since Marie's 1977 World Ocean Floor Panorama. It was a big leap. Much of the data came from Smith and Sandwell, but Google was unhappy with all of the blurry areas of the ocean floor, Smith said. The company wanted to fill in the blank areas, the way Marie had done so many years before.

But times have changed, and so have the stakes. Climate change, for example, is greatly affected by the shape and texture of the ocean floor. If the public doesn't know how much work there is to be done to create a complete picture of it, they won't understand why such projects should be funded, so Smith told Google it was important to release the map with the blurry areas intact. "I wanted people to see what we don't know," he said. "I wanted children to be able to see how much more is left for them to discover." Google eventually agreed, and to satisfy its users' imaginations the staff did something that would have made Marie proud: they included a layer in their program called the "Marie Tharp Historical Map," which, when turned on, wraps the World Ocean Floor Panorama around the Earth. As her *Times* obituary said about that map, it is "not always complete and not always accurate." But "it is, nonetheless, one of the most remarkable achievements in cartography."

THE DEAL TO make the World Ocean Floor Panorama a part of Google Earth was negotiated by Fiona Schiano-Yacopino, the Tharpophile who inherited Marie Tharp Maps. "She would have been so excited to see the map like that," Fiona said, which partly explains why she decided to go through with the deal, even though Marie Tharp Maps didn't (and doesn't) receive compensation from Google. Usually, whenever someone wants to use any of Marie's maps they have to get permission from Fiona and pay a fee to reprint it—something that still happens quite often. The WOFP appears in textbooks and people contact Fiona looking to buy prints of it to hang on their walls. Sometimes it even appears on television, Fiona said. She'll be watching the National Geographic or Discovery channels with her children and there it will be, on a show she forgot she gave permission to use it. She loves when this happens; it's a chance to be reminded of Marie's effect on the world.

I visited Fiona two years after we all spent that day in Marie's house trying to get it cleared out. Marie Tharp Maps now operates out of an artists' warehouse space, what's left of the work that used to be spread out over the four floors of Marie's house packed into a studio. It was raining and cold the day we met, the weather the exact opposite of what it was when I went to Marie's house. Our footsteps echoed in the halls of the warehouse and the only indication that anyone else was in the building was the occasional clanging of the freight elevator. Fiona had heard that Lex was renting space in the warehouse, too, she told me as she unlocked the door to her studio, but she'd never seen him there. That's kind of how it had been with all of the Tharpophiles: after Marie died they all went their separate ways. Marie, and her house, had been holding them all together.

Fiona's studio had to it a bit of what I'd come to understand as the Marie vibe. There were, of course, maps everywhere—rolled in cardboard tubes, stacked and wrapped in brown paper, spread out on flat surfaces. There was a bronze bust of Papa Tharp that Marie sculpted for a continuing education art class she took at Columbia. There were boxes in various stages of distintegration and a few pieces of antique furniture. The furniture, Fiona said, had been her own father's. He'd passed away shortly after Marie. We talked about how to decide what to keep after someone dies and Fiona admitted that she felt a little foolish that she was the one who ended up with the business—she'd started working for Marie only in 2004; had no experience with cartography, oceanography, or geology; and had spent less time working with her than any of the others. When talking with her, though, it was easy to see why Marie had chosen her.

Fiona called Marie "a true explorer." In her old age, this meant that Marie was constantly itching to get Fiona to take her on car trips—any way she could. Small ailments required trips to the doctor, going to Dunkin' Donuts was a ritual. Fiona also always tried to think of more exciting things to do. One of Marie's doctors was in Manhattan, for example, right across from the Metropolitan Museum, so Fiona would make sure Marie scheduled the earliest possible appointment with the doctor, leaving lots of time for the museum. They'd spend the whole day there, Fiona wheeling her through the entire thing, Marie marveling at the art and being exhausted for a whole week after.

Fiona told me a story about how, at one point, water began pooling at the base of Marie's driveway. They had to call someone to come and dig a giant hole for drainage. "It was a huge hole," she said, "and I had to get there extra early because if I didn't, Marie would be out of the house first thing in the morning to look at the hole. Toes on the edge. She *needed* to look in," Fiona said. The plumber did not take kindly to this and told Marie so, but Marie ignored him. "I told him, 'She's not just some old lady, don't expect her to listen to you,'" Fiona remembered. Marie ignored them both. "I caught a glimmer that day of something I hadn't seen before. She was rebellious! She didn't care for the rules that other people thought should apply."

We talked about Lamont and how much Marie had been hurt by The Harassment. We talked about the obstacles she'd faced as a woman in a man's field, we talked about her love of her work and how it outweighed her desire to be recognized, and about what the act of putting on Bruce's clothing meant. I got distracted then, imagined the first time Marie had done that after he died, standing naked in his dark bedroom after having slept through the day, slipping her legs into a pair of his pants and belting their huge waist around her smaller one, slipping one of his shirts off a hanger and over her skin, switching on a lamp so she could see herself in his mirror, the light shining on her as she dressed.

The story Fiona started next jerked me back to attention. She told it as I sat on her father's settee and the rain pelted the safety glass of the room's single window. Not too long before Marie died, Fiona told me, someone contacted Marie on the phone and told her that they needed to make a decision about where the Atlantic Ocean ended and the Indian Ocean began. Fiona couldn't remember who it was, and it might have been the Indian and Pacific oceans, but neither of those details really matter. What matters is the enthusiasm with which Marie threw herself into the task.

"We had to go into the red room"—the red-carpeted room on the second floor of Marie's house that had been her office—"and I had to sweep out everything and clear off everything because she was in there on a daily basis now. We had to get a piece of vellum and put it over her map and tape it all down. Because she decided that she was going to rewrite where the borders of those oceans were. I remember she said 'draw a line that follows this. Come on!'" Fiona had gotten up and was pointing to a place on the World Ocean Floor Panorama. "And I said 'just any line, Marie?' And she said 'yes, I want to see what you think, where you think the boundaries are.' So I did something—I drew it—just a straight line. Totally at random, not having ever been able to understand what I was doing.

"And she said 'no, no, no. Erase it. Let's do it again.' And she was literally just erasing my line, wiping it off and having me do it again. Until she finally decided that that was where it went. As we did that she wanted me to start relabeling everything. She had me redraw the entire map out on the vellum, to follow her lines."

"You traced over the entire thing?" I asked Fiona.

"The entire thing," she said. "How long did that take," I asked. "Weeks and weeks." And she was sitting there with you? "Oh yeah." She couldn't do it, she couldn't draw anymore? "Her hand wasn't steady. I knew she wanted my steady hand, that I really couldn't have been anything more than a steady hand. But I was having fun.

"It was entire days in the red room and she wanted me there early and she wanted me to stay later and I had to walk her up the stairs and we set up a comfy seat for her. I brought up cushions and really got her comfortable in there because it was too hard for her to stand at the map table for long periods of time. She would sit and I would bring her things to eat or drink up there. She was completely immersed. I think someone just asked her a quick question about where the division of the oceans happens. But she took it on as a project and when it was done she had me wrap it up and mail it to this person."

Was there a response, I asked.

"No, not that I know. I don't think they wanted all that we gave them. But she took it on and I'm sure all this information came flooding back to her. I'm sure that in her mind she had drawn the boundary, was just going over and over it. All the information that had gotten her here. Because I could see the way her mind was working. The way she was talking. She would talk for twenty minutes straight. It was fascinating. She was literally reignited, she was so excited—I could almost picture what it must have been like years and years before when she was her mad scientist self: so obsessed and completely focused on what she was doing. I felt like I was watching a piece of history. Even if it turned out to be for no good reason or the person who asked the question didn't need all that information, *she* needed to put that information out there, in some way, and that was really what mattered."

"BEFORE YOU STUDY Zen," a proverb from that tradition says, "a mountain is a mountain. After you study Zen, a mountain is no longer just a mountain. When you finally understand Zen, a mountain is a mountain again." It used to be that when I looked at a rock all I saw was a rock—a thing that the sole of my sandal could scoop under my foot to annoy me, something to pick up and skip over water till it sank, something to build with, something to throw. Now, though, because of Marie, I peer down at rocks when I walk a trail or beach. It's hard not pick them all up, weigh myself down for a day, a month, a lifetime, sink into the telling of each one's story. Because each rock carries on its face its own autobiography, ready to be deciphered.

Let me tell you the story of just one rock. The rock is called Pangaea, and it was a huge rock, a supercontinent that existed 250 million years ago, one huge continent surrounded by one huge sea called Panthalassa. To be a supercontinent is to be alone—the only dry land on Earth. But Pangaea had predecessors—Pannotia before it, and Rodinia before that—which means that by the time Pangaea began its pre-division grumblings, Earth had already been through several periods of continental attachment and separation. The roots of the word *Pangaea* mean "entire earth"; the events that took place during the 250 million years Pangaea spent separating are part of the story of how the Earth came to look the way it does today. And the movements are still taking place, even though most of us don't notice them: at about the same rate your fingernails grow, pieces of Pangaea are converging and diverging all across the Earth.

Those are the words we currently use to tell the story of Pangaea, but as we collect more information about the Earth's past, the words and the story will probably change. There are lots of ways to keep history alive, and telling stories is only one of them.

The word *letter* doesn't do justice to the volume of material with which one could apparently be bombarded, by post, after asking Marie a question about her past. I'm told that she would initially respond with a letter, but that such a letter was often followed by a long list of enclosures and accompanied by thick packets of documents that had been stapled or packed into binders; Marie loved the accumulatory effect of the appendix. As she saw it, letter plus appendix equaled whole story; when she sent off these packages she was turning the facts over to the receivers, letting them mark the texts in solitude, leaving room for their imaginations to be snagged by the lines they read.

As I wrote this book I tried to imagine that I was writing a very long letter to Marie. It always was a strange letter, though. Or maybe not: when I think about how this book is at once to Marie, about Marie, for Marie—and sometimes even, in a way, *by* Marie—I think it might just be a love letter, the boundary between author and subject gone fluid. So here's an appendix I think you would have appreciated, Marie, the resources you left behind mingling with those I discovered on my own.

The notes that follow feature a selection of the sources I found invaluable while writing, with special care taken to list those materials available to the public. It is by no means a complete list. While writing, I made an attempt to draw the bulk of my information from primary sources contemporary to Marie—letters, drafts of papers, scrapbooks, journals, photographs—most of which are a part of the Heezen-Tharp Collection (HTC) in the Geography and Map Division at the Library of Congress, the Bruce C. Heezen Papers (BCHP) at the Smithsonian Institution Archives, and the Maurice Ewing Papers, 1912, 1925–1974 (MEP) at the University of Texas at Austin's Dolph Briscoe Center for American History. I also drew from contemporary secondary sources such as newspaper articles, reviews, and textbooks.

Of the sources Marie left behind, by far the most useful were the interviews she granted throughout her life. Three interviewers in particular deserve special mention: Ronald Doel, John Lear, and Helen Shepherd. Doel (and Tanya Levin) interviewed Marie several times as part of a joint effort between Columbia University's Oral History Research Office and the American Institute of Physics' Center for the History of Physics (CU-AIP); these transcripts are available online through the website of the AIP. The interview conducted by Helen Shepherd was sponsored by the Society of Woman Geographers (SWG) and is accessible only at its Washington, D.C., headquarters or in the HTC.

The transcripts of the tapes that Marie and Bruce made with John Lear reside in the HTC—as do countless other personal and work-related treasures that once belonged to Marie and Bruce. When I began researching this book, the HTC was housed at the Geography and Map Division (GMD) in the Library of Congress's Madison Building in downtown Washington, D.C. As I write these notes, the personal papers are still housed there; the data and sketches and drafts of maps Marie used in her work are now housed off-site, accessible only by prior arrangement with the GMD.

Marie's friends, employees, and colleagues relayed countless stories and anecdotes to me. I thought about these stories constantly when writing about the personalities and settings that appear in this book; not all of the people I interviewed appear by name in the text or these notes, but without their help this portrait would have been impossible.

Four books were indispensable in helping me understand the histories of geology and plate tectonics. The first is John McPhee's *Annals of the Former World*, an omnibus chronicling the history of modern geology that earns delight and respect from scientists and nonscientists alike. The second and third are *The Rejection of Continental Drift: Theory and Method in American Earth Science* and *Plate Tectonics: An Insider's History of the Modern Theory of the Earth*; the first was written by science historian Naomi Oreskes, the second was edited by her. The last is Henry William Menard's *The Ocean of Truth*, which brought to life, with great detail and analysis, the pursuits of the scientists studying the Earth in the 1940s, '50s, and '60s.

While I have tried not to list these transcripts and books too repeatedly in the notes that follow, the reader can assume I consulted them in nearly every chapter—to create time lines, clarify, refute, and try to absorb the background and emotions of the moments I was striving to depict.

Finally, a word of explanation regarding this book's "imagined" scenes: told in the present tense, these sections are just as heavily researched as the rest of the book. In other words, I took my lead from Marie, going from "the known to the unknown," using my knowledge of the events and people in question to interpolate and extrapolate. So while I invented some of the dialogue and incidental details (such as what people were wearing, interior decoration, physical movements), all of the situations and interactions in the imagined scenes are based on actual occurrences.

A note on distance: in her writings, Marie almost always referred to the Mid-Oceanic Ridge (MOR) as 40,000 miles long. That's a good approximate figure for the continuous portion of the MOR, but the reader should note that the entire thing, not continuous, runs 49,700 miles. In general, I've used the length that Marie used herself—except when quoting from a source that used a different number.

Part One

CHAPTER 1

The information about Bruce's grave and childhood home in Muscatine, Iowa, comes from a trip I took there in October 2008.

The copy of A. K. Lobeck's *Geomorphology* that I have on my bookshelf is a 1939 printing. My copy belonged to Bruce, and there's one of his bookplates on the inside cover—a pointillist picture of a ship with billowing sails on cresting waves—and his name is scrawled on the flyleaf. The other assorted ephemera I refer to all came directly from Marie's house.

The information about Marie's childhood comes from four main sources: her SWG interviews; a short narrative she wrote about her childhood that's now part of the HTC; an unpublished document titled "Chronology of William Edgar Tharp's Career as a Soil Surveyor, c. 1904–1935," written by Lex Reibestein in the winter of 2003 and now part of the HTC; and a letter she wrote in "reply to John Lear's letter of Dec. 4." The photographs that I refer to (of Marie as a child, of Marie and Bruce relaxing) are also part of the HTC.

CHAPTER 2

Of the cited reasons for the rejection of Alfred Wegener's continental drift hypothesis, one most often mentioned is that Wegener argued that the continents around the Atlantic had matching shorelines—not a tailored fit by any means. In her January 1976 *Geology* article titled "Alfred Wegener's Reconstruction of Pangea," Ellen Drake translates a 1910 letter from Wegener to his wife, Else, in which he says that "the fit should be made at the margin of the continental slope in the deep sea." This translation is markedly different from the previous ones that had Wegener arguing for a shoreline fit.

History contains many examples of people noticing the congruity of the continents (including Benjamin Franklin), but the examples I cite appear in John McPhee's *Annals of the Former World*. For more information on Thomas Dick, see Alan Goodacre's letter from the November 28, 1991, issue of *Nature*; for more information on Ortelius, see James Romm's article "A New Forerunner for Continental Drift," from the February 3, 1994, issue of *Nature*.

Whether Wegener actually attended the 1926 American Association of Petroleum Geologists (AAPG) meeting is somewhat up in the air, but one of the sources that puts him at the meeting is a 2001 issue of the AAPG's *Explorer* magazine; the chapter discussing Wegener is subtitled "Calm Before the Storm."

To read more about the opposition to Wegener (or for a colorful yet meticulous history of the earth science revolution), see Edward Bullard's May 1975 article, "The Emergence of Plate Tectonics: A Personal View," published in the *Annual Review of Earth and Planetary Sciences*.

CHAPTER 3

The information about Marie's childhood that I consulted for this chapter comes from the same sources as chapter 1, with the addition of one more unpublished and untitled document from the HTC: another narrative Marie wrote about the years before her mother died, with some of the stories she told John Lear expanded.

Marie's story about her father taking a picture of her next to a tree comes from one of her CU-AIP interviews; her stories about skating with Quava Hart and her first glimpse of mountains come from the childhood narrative she wrote for John Lear.

CHAPTER 4

My information about the PG girls comes from Marie's interviews and one particularly detailed letter written to her on January 7, 1997, by fellow PG girl Helen Foster, who went on to have a long career as a research geologist with the U.S. Geological Survey.

To learn more about what students were being taught—and confused by—in American geology classes in the 1940s, turn to Naomi Oreskes's *The Rejection of Continental Drift*. While writing, I surveyed a variety of textbooks from the period in order to understand the rhetoric their authors used when talking about the formation of the Earth's surface. One of those books was *Outlines of Physical Geology*, authored by Chester R. Longwell, Alfred Knopf, and Richard F. Flint. Phillip Lake and R. H. Rastall's *Textbook of Geology*, published in the United Kingdom, was also helpful.

To understand the ideological atmosphere of the University of Michigan's Department of Geology while Marie was there, see the article "Our Shrinking Globe," written by then-department chair Kenneth Landes and published in the March 1952 issue of the *Geological Society of America Bulletin*.

CHAPTER 5

For a basic history of ocean floor mapping and early sounding methods, see the chapter "Mountains of the Sea" in John Noble Wilford's *The Mapmakers*. For a detailed, poetic, and often philosophical treatment of nineteenth-century oceanography, see Matthew Fontaine Maury's 1855 *Physical Geography of the Sea*.

The *Report on the Scientific Results of the Voyage of the H.M.S. Challenger During the Years 1873–76* is readily available online. And while the *New York Times* articles I mention in the text offer amusing contemporary portraits of Prince Albert I, a more serious perspective on the Monaco-based International Hydrographic Organization (called the International Hydrographic Bureau until 1970), which still produces the General Bathymetric Chart of the Oceans (GEBCO), can be found in *The History of GEBCO, 1903–2003: The 100-Year Story of the General Bathymetric Chart of the Oceans*.

Many other *New York Times* articles from the 1920s gave me contemporary views of the emerging technologies that enabled the growth of oceanography. Information concerning the *Meteor* cruise comes from the article "Merz and the 'Meteor' Expedition," which appeared in the July 1926 issue of the *The Geographical Journal*. A history of the development of sounding technology can be found in Sabine Höhler's article "A Sound Survey: The Technological Perception of Ocean Depth, 1850–1930," originally presented at a conference titled "Transforming Spaces: The Topological Turn in Technology Studies" and held in March 2002 at the University of Technology in Darmstadt, Germany. For a more chronological breakdown with a focus on early American seafloor exploration, see oceanexplorer.noaa.gov/history/history.html.

For more academic perspectives on the development of American oceanographic institutions in the early twentieth century, see Rexmond Canning Cochrane's *The National Academy of Sciences, First Hundred Years: 1863–1963*, and Susan Schlee's *The Edge of an Unfamiliar World* and *On Almost Any Wind*.

CHAPTER 6

Concerning Marie's marriage: Gary North told me first. Subsequent interviews with other Tharpophiles confirmed his story, although it's clear that many of them thought they were keeping their knowledge a secret from the others. The story about Marie and David's lack of cohabitation; how they would travel to meet each other at bus stations while they were living apart; and that the impetus for divorce came from Marie all come from North.

A copy of Marie and David Flanagan's marriage certificate is part of the HTC, as are many envelopes with "Marie Flanagan" written on them in her handwriting, David's U.S. Air Force immunization record, and photographs of them together. The notes that Marie scrawled on yellow paper concerning the "survival" of her marriage are part of the HTC.

I based the outdoor portion of the scene about Marie's first trip to Schermerhorn Hall on my own experiences as a young person on Columbia University's Morningside Heights campus: the inscription above the doorway, the uneven bricks, the way the air seems to crackle with wealth and intelligence. My physical descriptions of Marie are based on photographs of her from the period, and the story of the Geological Society secretary telling her "we ain't got no room for file clerks" comes from one of Marie's CU-AIP interviews with Doel. When creating this scene I tried to think about what Manhattan would have been like for a headstrong but imaginative young woman who had spent most of her life west of the Mississippi—thus a glimpse of one of her daydreams, a set of images to which I imagined she might naturally turn in order to keep her mind occupied while waiting.

CHAPTER 7

If you do a quick online search to try to find out the penetration depth of light in water, you'll probably find that many sources say two hundred meters. I placed the number much lower because of an exchange I had with Walter Smith, a NOAA geophysicist; he said he's seen the two-hundred-meter allusion floating around the Internet but, "in reality, nearly all sunlight is extinguished within a few tens of meters" from the ocean's surface.

My main source of information on Maurice "Doc" Ewing's pre-Columbia years was the one and only biography ever written about him—published in 1974, authored by William Wertenbaker, and titled *The Floor of the Sea*. My personal copy of *The Floor of the Sea* is a discard from the Huntington Beach High School Media Center. Stamped on the front flyleaf are the words "OBSOLETE" and "NO LONGER THE PROPERTY OF HBHS LIBRARY"; the off-white paper of the flyleaf has printed on it, in teal ink, a portion of Marie's revised North Atlantic physiographic diagram.

Other information about Doc's years at Lehigh University, Woods Hole, and the first years spent in the basement of Schermerhorn Hall comes from Worzel's chapter in the book *Lamont-Doherty Earth Observatory: Twelve Perspectives on the First Fifty Years (1949–1999)*.

The quote expressing how the majority of the scientific community felt about the seafloor (i.e., that they had no feelings) is from the book *The Oceans*, published in 1942, authored by Scripps head Harald U. Sverdrup, Martin W. Johnson, and Richard H. Fleming—and considered the first modern oceanography textbook.

The information about Bruce's first meeting with Doc is repeated in many places, including in a document in the HTC titled "BCH on BCH" or, in other words, "Bruce on Bruce." It's a transcript of one of the tapes Bruce made for John Lear. The anecdote about

Bruce's childhood solemnity came from an October 2008 interview I conducted with Marilyn Jackson, who grew up with Bruce in Muscatine.

The scene of Marie returning to Schermerhorn Hall to talk with Doc after he returned from the sea is based on a document Marie wrote. It's on file in the HTC—just a few pages written on a typewriter with the word *Schermerhorn* typed in all caps across the top of the first page. Information about the setup of the geophysical lab also came from Worzel's chapter in the *Twelve Perspectives* book, including how cramped and noisy the space was. Marie mentions the question Doc posed to her when they first met—"Can you draft?"—in one of her SWG interview sessions. While writing, I tried to imagine what it would have felt like for Marie to wait weeks for Doc to return, all her education and intelligence so far unutilized, roiling and accumulating pressure within her, so that when she was asked to speak it all came tumbling out.

Part Two

CHAPTER 8

Information about the people and setting of Schermerhorn Hall came from the same sources consulted in the last chapter of part 1, with one addition: Marie's CU-AIP interviews with Ron Doel contain many addendums—sections of written text that were spliced into the body of the interview, in which Marie elaborated upon some of the subjects that she didn't fully explain while talking to Doel. I based my physical description of her on a photo from the HTC that shows her walking down a Manhattan street. Whether one can actually walk to the Cloisters from Columbia's Morningside Heights campus during lunch is doubtful and most certainly depends on the length of the lunch break. Marie says that she did, so I've taken her at her word.

The first *National Geographic* magazine article I refer to, "Exploring the Mid-Atlantic Ridge," is from the September 1948 issue of the magazine; the second article is titled "New Discoveries on the Mid-Atlantic Ridge" and appeared in the November 1949 issue. Both bear Doc's name.

Bruce's hatred of turkey was discussed in Enrico Bonatti's "Oedipus, Turkeys, and a Revolution in the Earth Sciences," published in the *International Journal of Earth Sciences* in May 2007; that distaste was mentioned to me by the Tharpophiles as well. Information about early deep-sea cameras comes from the 1971 book *The Face of the Deep*, written by Bruce and his former student Charles Hollister. The power supply problems on mid-century oceanographic cruises, which caused the fathometer to turn off when another source demanded energy, were mentioned by Marie in both her CU-AIP and SWG interviews.

I have a file on my computer called "First Looks," which lists all the ways in which Marie and Bruce described their initial meeting. The first one I quote is from Marie's SWG interview; the second is from what Marie referred to as her "Opus" (formally titled "Mapping the Ocean Floor 1952–1977"), which is on file in the HTC; the third is from Marie's article in Lamont's *Twelve Perspectives* book; the fourth is from one of her CU-AIP interviews with Doel; the fifth is from a letter Bruce wrote to John Lear and is also on file in the HTC; the last is from a videorecording made (and kept on file in the HTC) by the Library of Congress, in which Gary North sat down with Marie and they spoke about her work and life.

CHAPTER 9

The information about the geophysical lab's move comes from Worzel's chapter in the *Twelve Perspectives* book and the Wertenbaker biography of Doc. I found the maps Marie drew of the various configurations of Lamont Hall in a binder of her papers that is part of the HTC. Her stories about the early days that the group spent working in Lamont Hall come from a variety of sources, including the CU-AIP and SWG interviews and the "Schermerhorn" document on file in the HTC. The details about the crystal chandeliers and birds painted on the walls of Lamont Hall's dining room come from the Wertenbaker biography of Doc.

Laurence Kulp's involvement in the Atomic Energy Commission–sponsored "Project Sunshine" has been well documented: a *New York Times* article published on February 8, 1957, announced that the project, whose goal was to investigate how much radiation nuclear bomb tests had been spreading, concluded that the strontium-90 levels in "more than 500 autopsy samples" were safe; a February 18, 1957, article in *Time* magazine also addressed the project. A 1995 final report issued by President Clinton's Advisory Committee on Human Radiation Experiments acknowledged that Project Sunshine did obtain bone samples without consent and had investigated the possibility of "body snatching."

A long passage in one of Marie's handwritten letters to John Lear, dated November 19, 1975, describes Alma and Harold Smith. A document titled "Profile of a Scientist: Bruce Heezen" tells the story of when its author, Ray Edwards, first met Bruce in Lamont Hall, tossling a mattress down on the floor of John Ewing's office and going right to sleep.

To imagine what might have prompted Marie to quit Lamont in 1952 and drive back to her father's farm in Ohio, I consulted the CU-AIP and SWG interviews. Marie talks at length about the farm in the SWG interview, so I found that transcript to be particularly helpful when describing the farm's appearance and depicting the rhythms of her father and brother's days.

CHAPTER 10

I consulted three main sources when re-creating the scene in which Marie and Bruce look at fathograms together for the first time: a 1986 *Natural History* article titled "Mappers of the Deep" that Marie coauthored with science historian Henry Frankel; Marie's contribution to Lamont's *Twelve Perspectives* book, titled "Connect the Dots: Mapping the Seafloor and Discovering the Mid-Ocean Ridge"; and an undated letter she wrote in response to a letter John Lear had written to her on September 19, 1975.

It's in this letter to John Lear that Marie talks about the differences between what she and Bruce were hoping to find. Details about how she spliced together the various ship tracks and the size of paper she used also come from this letter. For an outside perspective on Marie and Bruce's process when making this first physiographic diagram, see Cathy Barton's article "Marie Tharp, Oceanographic Cartographer, and Her Contributions to the Revolution in the Earth Sciences," which appeared in the 2002 book *The Earth Inside and Out: Some Major Contributions to Geology in the Twentieth Century*.

In the aforementioned 1975 letter to John Lear, Marie says she saw notches in all six of the first profiles of the North Atlantic ocean floor; in the 1986 article she wrote with Henry Frankel, she says she saw the notch only in the top (or northernmost) three profiles. I chose to go with the number she gave John Lear because the statement had been made closer to the event in question—fewer years had passed, leaving less opportunity for time to take its toll on her memory. I've also referred to Marie's statement that it took six weeks to do the initial work of plotting and splicing, but in other places she says it took her eight weeks.

Much more can be said about the *Meteor* expedition than I had room for. Captain Albert Theberge, Jr. (retired), of the NOAA Central Library, drew my attention to Gunter Dietrich's 1938 paper; Walter H. F. Smith, a geophysicist with NOAA, helped me interpret the Dietrich paper. While Marie and Bruce were well aware of the *Meteor* expedition, there's no way of knowing if they saw this particular article. Based on conversations I've had with Smith, it seems that Dietrich's vocabulary only hints at a rift. Dietrich described the patterns he was able to pick out as a "series of approximately parallel trains of undulations rising from the ocean bottom"; the words *trains* and *undulations* imply a belief in compression, which would have been more in line with theories that claimed the Earth was shrinking like a raisin in the heat of the sun. If he had, like Marie, used the loaded terms *rift* or *tensional*, his paper would have implied that areas formerly united had separated. Marie used the word *rift* because she explicitly correlated the crack she'd found with seismic activity; Dietrich did no such thing.

CHAPTER 11

Bruce and Doc's "Turbidity Currents and Submarine Slumps, and the 1929 Grand Banks Earthquake" was published in the December 1952 issue of the *American Journal of Science*. The information about Bruce's relationship with Bell Labs and his work on cable breaks comes from a transcript of tape "24B," which Bruce recorded for John Lear.

Marie's descriptions of transferring ship tracks and profiles onto the navy and GEBCO charts come from her various interviews, letters to John Lear, her 1986 *Natural History* article, and her chapter in Lamont's *Twelve Perspectives* book. Her comments about Lobeck, and the decision she and Bruce made to create a physiographic diagram, come from her "Opus."

The details of Bruce's work on cable breaks come from tape "24B" (just mentioned), and his assertion of the difference between the type of work being done by Foster and Marie comes from a December 5, 1975, letter to John Lear that is on file in the HTC.

I include several versions of the story of how the correlation between the rift valley and the earthquake epicenters was discovered. The first comes from a transcription of a tape "titled BCH Reply to John Lear December 5"; the second comes from a letter Marie wrote to John Lear that is undated but that begins with the words "this is in reply to your letter of September 19, 1975"; the third is from Marie's "Opus." Also note: when discussing this discovery, Marie was always careful to acknowledge that Beno Gutenberg and Charles F. Richter had noticed the correlation of earthquake epicenters and the path of the Mid-Atlantic Ridge in the 1940s.

Marie's comments about contours versus physiographic diagrams come from her "Opus." Further explanation of Lobeck's method and hachuring in general come from Cathy Barton's article in *The Earth Inside and Out*.

Bruce's "except what I gave her" comment comes from the transcript of tape "09B" made for John Lear. Bruce's journal is also part of the HTC; the entry I quote is dated January 23, 1954. Marie's "I had no feelings" comment, and her thoughts about Bruce's upbringing and his "other girlfriends," all come from her SWG interview. The *Mare* article I refer to is from issue number 47 (December 2004). Lia Hörmann's article, "Das Gesticht Der Tieffe," was published in *Tirolerin* in January 1996; the letter she wrote to Marie that included her translation of that article into English is dated February 21, 1996, and is on file in the HTC.

CHAPTER 12

H. W. Menard's *The Ocean of Truth* provides a detailed narrative chronology of the publications that came out of Lamont in such quick succession in the latter half of the 1950s. Ewing and Heezen's "Some Problems of Antarctic Submarine Geology" paper was published in 1956 in *Antarctica in the International Geophysical Year: Based on a Symposium on the Antarctic*, which was the first volume of the American Geophysical Union's *Geophysical Monograph Series*. It's important to note that this paper again credits the earthquake epicenter work of Gutenberg and Richter; it also notes that a median rift valley is visible on separate profiles by Stocks (after the *Meteor*'s South Atlantic expedition), Hill (in the Mid-Atlantic Ridge), and Wiseman and Sewell (in the Arabian Sea).

All scientific discoveries build upon the discoveries that came before them; nothing happens in a vacuum. In the history of science there are what are called paradigm shifts (see Thomas Kuhn's 1962 *The Structure of Scientific Revolutions*), or times when the known facts seem to come together and then explode previously held beliefs. Marie was the first to assert the presence of a rift valley that was 1) worldwide and 2) seismically active. So while there was work before her that noted rifts in several different oceans, no one made the leap—using hypothesis and inter- and extrapolation—that it was both continuous and the site of tectonic motion. I've come to think of Marie and her early work as the neck of an hourglass: information and data funneled down to her, were confined for a historical instant in her magnificent and uniquely educated mind, then shot back out into the wide world below.

The interviews of Charles Officer (and his wife, Trixie) and John and Betty Ewing were conducted as part of the same joint CU-AIP effort that resulted in Marie's interviews; both are available through the AIP website.

The letters that Bruce received from a public fearful of a dismantling Earth are in the BCHP at the Smithsonian Institution Archives. The *New York Times*'s coverage of the announcement of the rift valley appeared in the February 1, 1957, edition of the paper. Marie's comments about her job and discovery appear in her 1997 filmed interview with Gary North and her chapter in Lamont's *Twelve Perspectives* book. Marie's 1957 physiographic diagram of the North Atlantic Ocean accompanied the paper "Oceanographic Information for Engineering Submarine Cable Systems," written by C. H. Elmendorf and Bruce, and published in the September 1957 issue of the *Bell System Technical Journal*. Bruce's comment about how most people's understanding of the ocean floor's topography came from Marie is in a December 10, 1975, letter to John Lear that is part of the HTC. Stories of Marie and Bruce's legendary fights come from various Tharpophiles.

Bruce's cover letter for the submission of the paper "The Flat-topped Atlantic, Cruiser, and Great Meteor Seamounts" (by him, Doc, David B. Ericson, and C. R. Bentley) to the Geological Society of America (GSA) was written on December 25, 1955; the GSA's response was written by H. R. Aldrich on March 20, 1956, and was accompanied by

Hess's undated rejection letter; all are on file in the HTC. The story of Hess's declaration that Bruce had "shaken the foundations of geology" is recounted in many places, among them Marie's "Opus," her chapter in Lamont's *Twelve Perspectives* book, and the article "Hess's Geological Revolution" in *The Best of PAW: 100 Years of Princeton Alumni Weekly*.

CHAPTER 13

Information about the fire at Marie's apartment comes from a document she wrote that is stored in a binder in the HTC marked "NGS and Marie's Lawsuit," and a CU-AIP interview with Alma Kesner, who was a secretary at Lamont during Marie's time there.

B. C. Heezen, M. Tharp, and M. Ewing's *The Floors of the Ocean: I. The North Atlantic* was the GSA's Special Paper 65 and was published in 1959. In one of her CU-AIP interviews with Tanya Levin, Marie estimates the number of scientists who saw the North Atlantic physiographic diagram at thirty to forty thousand; in their July 2006 *Journal of Historical Geography* article "Extending Modern Cartography to the Ocean Depths: Military Patronage, Cold War Priorities, and the Heezen-Tharp Mapping Project, 1952–1959," Ronald Doel, Tanya Levin, and Mason Marker refer to a letter (on file in the BCHP) that British oceanographer Anthony Laughton wrote to Bruce on January 27, 1958, in which Laughton "expressed concern that Heezen and Tharp had drawn a continuous valley through the Mid-Atlantic Ridge when so few data points existed." Menard's letters to Bruce were written on March 20, 1957, and September 14, 1960, and are on file in the HTC.

A. H. Stride's review of Special Paper 65 appeared in the March 1960 issue of *Journal du Conseil*; M. N. Hill's review appeared in the January 1961 issue of the *Geographical Review*. In an addendum to a January 1, 1970, letter to Columbia University vice president Polykarp Kusch, Bruce wrote that "in June of 1956, when Miss Tharp was leaving Lamont en route to the printer in Baltimore, Dr. Ewing stopped her and asked to have his name added as author." This letter is part of the HTC.

The description and announcement of the 1959 International Oceanographic Congress appeared in the May 16, 1958, issue of *Science* magazine; further information about the IOC appeared in the March 27, 1959, issue of the same magazine. Sir Edward "Teddy" Bullard's article "The Emergence of Plate Tectonics: A Personal View" appeared in 1975's *Annual Review of Earth and Planetary Sciences*.

Most of the newspaper coverage of the IOC that I quote from was part of a scrapbook of Marie's marked "First Oceanographic News Clippings 1959," which is part of the HTC. Marie described Cousteau's skepticism in her *Natural History* article. Bruce's comment about Cousteau dragging the *Troika* across the Mid-Atlantic Ridge comes from tape "15B" for John Lear. The *Science* magazine bulletin about the screening of films at the IOC appeared in the March 27, 1959, issue.

Marie briefly mentions "meeting" Cousteau in an undated reply to John Lear's letter of September 19, 1975, and section 9A of her addendum to one of the CU-AIP interviews; Bruce paraphrases what Cousteau said when presenting his film of the rift in the transcript of tape "15B." In her *Natural History* article, Marie says that in Cousteau's film, "the great black cliffs of the rift valley, sprinkled with white glob [*Globigerina*] ooze, loomed up through the blue-green water." To re-create what the film must have looked like I also consulted stills of the ocean floor that were taken around the same time (some of which appear in Bruce's 1971 book *The Face of the Deep*).

Part Three

CHAPTER 14

Harry Hess's "History of the Ocean Basins" was published in November 1962 as part of the book *Petrologic Studies: A Volume to Honor A. F. Buddington*. Information about its pre-press circulation came from Menard's *The Ocean of Truth*. Bruce's *Scientific American* article titled "The Rift in the Ocean Floor" appeared in the October 1960 issue of the magazine.

CHAPTER 15

The Geological Society of America published the "Physiographic Diagram of the South Atlantic, the Caribbean, the Scotia Sea and the Eastern Margin of the South Pacific Ocean," authored by B. C. Heezen and M. Tharp, in 1961. Marie's letters to Bruce about the printing of that map are part of the HTC. Information about some of the features that were shown on the South Atlantic comes from Marie's "Opus." Menard's paper "The East Pacific Rise" was published in the December 9, 1960, issue of *Science* magazine.

Bruce's comment that people referred to Marie's maps as "hen scratching" came from the transcript of tape "08B," which is part of the HTC. His quoting of the ship captain who relayed people's negative reactions to the physiographic diagrams appears in his reply to John Lear's letter of December 10, 1975, which is also part of the HTC. Bruce and Doc's "unusual joint statement" appeared in the paper "The Mid-Oceanic Ridge and Its Extension Through the Arctic Basin," which was published in *Geology of the Arctic* in 1961.

The clippings from the *Morgunbladid* that I reference were a part of one of Marie's scrapbooks that are now on file in the HTC. Bruce's letter to Menard was written on August 20, 1960; Marie talks about the motivations for their summer 1962 trip in a letter she wrote in response to John Lear's letter of September 19, 1975; both are part of the HTC. Her "Opus" is the source of many of the details that I used to reconstruct their Cessna flight. As I was writing, I spent a lot of time looking at aerial photographs of Iceland, trying to pick out the features and textures of the landscape I thought would have caught her attention—things that she might have found useful when creating her early physiographic diagrams.

CHAPTER 16

R. G. Mason wrote about the magnetic lineations I refer to in his 1958 paper "A Magnetic Survey off the West Coast of the United States Between Latitudes 32° and 36°N, Longitudes 121° and 128°W," published in the *Geophysical Journal of the Royal Astronomical Society*. The August 1961 issue of the *Geological Society of America Bulletin* held two papers concerning the lineations: Ronald G. Mason and Arthur D. Raff's "Magnetic Survey off the West Coast of North America, 32° N. Latitude to 42° N. Latitude," and Arthur D. Raff and Ronald G. Mason's "Magnetic Survey Off the West Coast of North America, 40° N. Latitude to 52° N. Latitude." Bullard used the "double tape recording" simile in his paper "The Emergence of Plate Tectonics," and Menard discussed the timing and reception of Vine, Matthews, and Morley's papers in *The Ocean of Truth*.

"The Fit of the Continents Around the Atlantic," by Edward Bullard, J. E. Everett, and A. Gilbert Smith, was published in the October 25, 1965, issue of the *Philosophical*

Transactions of the Royal Society of London. John Tuzo Wilson's "A New Class of Faults and Their Bearing on Continental Drift" appeared in the July 24, 1965, issue of *Nature.*

CHAPTER 17

Based on Marie's comments in the transcript of a tape she made titled "Marie Indian Ocean Conversation with John Lear," and a table Bruce compiled titled "Published Physiographic Diagrams of the Ocean Floor Resulting from Our Research," it appears that work on the Indian Ocean physiographic diagram began in 1961; the former document is from the HTC; the latter is from the MEP.

The list of extant maps and diagrams that Marie and Bruce referred to when beginning their Indian Ocean map is from the back of that physiographic diagram, which was published by the GSA in 1964 as "Physiographic Diagram of the Indian Ocean, the Red Sea, the South China Sea, the Sulu Sea, and the Celebes Sea." Marie lists the people who worked on the Indian Ocean diagram with her in a long, handwritten, and undated letter to John Lear. She wrote in her "Opus" about Bruce's students stretching PDR records down the hall, the Ob' Seamount, the arrival of the hand-copied soundings from Japan, and her and Bruce's trip to the Keuffel and Esser printing plant in Long Island. Of all the features Marie named, it's the Roo Rise in the Indian Ocean that's my favorite: a note in the *GEBCO Gazetteer of Undersea Feature Names* (which lists, among other things, feature names, their latitudes and longitudes, and histories) says that this rise was named "by Marie Tharp in memory of the 'Winnie the Pooh' personage."

In order to reconstruct Marie and Bruce's travels through Asia and the South Pacific, I consulted Bruce's detailed narrative of the trip, a 158-page document stored in a green cardboard binder labeled "Trip to India, Taiwan, Australia, New Zealand and Scripps—December 1964, January 1965," which is part of the HTC.

There are copies of Worzel's May 28, 1965, letter to Marie about her travel expenses in both the HTC and MEP; Marie's response to his letter is dated June 14, 1965, and is part of the HTC. Gary North told me that Marie was diagnosed with stomach cancer during that time in an interview I did with him in July 2010.

Many of the Tharpophiles told me about Marie's propensity for naming the structures of her home and its surrounding property. I heard about "Stonehenge" from them, and Marie refers to it as that in the transcript of tape "BCH08A," which is part of the HTC. All of the maps that I refer to in this section are also on file in the HTC. Marie talks about how JFK's 1962 speech brought a lot of money to Lamont and how the dynamic shifted drastically after the construction of the Oceanography building in her SWG interview.

CHAPTER 18

Pre-event press coverage of the Second International Oceanographic Congress, held in Moscow in 1966, comes from the May 20 and May 31 editions of the *New York Times.* The following documents were the basis for my understanding of what took place in Moscow (and the context for the altercation): Menard's *The Ocean of Truth*; a memo from Doc to Bruce dated December 19, 1966; a July 11, 1966, letter to then vice president of Columbia University L. H. Chamberlain from Sally Swing Shelley, UNESCO's information officer; and several narratives Bruce wrote about the event that are part of the HTC, including a handwritten one in a small green vinyl notebook with "II International Oceanographic Congress, Moscow 1966" imprinted on its cover. The articles that caused such ire at Lamont were the *New York Times*'s "Evolution Linked to Magnetic Field," published in the June 2, 1966, edition of the paper, and "Geophysics: Flipping the Magnetic Field," from the June 17, 1966, edition of *Time* magazine.

Marie talks about the job offers from Hawaii, Rhode Island, and the navy in her CU-AIP interviews. Bruce appeared on CBS's *Tomorrow Was Yesterday*, hosted by Charles Collingwood, on January 15, 1964; a transcript of that appearance is on file in the BCHP.

Marie's recollection of how *National Geographic* found Heinrich Berann came from her CU-AIP interviews. Further information about Berann's work and education comes from his official website, www.berann.com, which is maintained by one of his grandsons, and from U.S. National Park Service cartographer Tom Patterson's paper "A View from on High: Heinrich Berann's Panoramas and Landscape Visualization Techniques for the U.S. National Park Service," published in the Spring 2000 issue of *Cartographic Perspectives*. Marie wrote about the development of the relationship between herself, Bruce, Berann, and Vielkind in a May 16, 1988, letter to A. A. Meyerhoff. Bruce's comment about the "frivolous" maps came from tape "BCH08B," which is part of the HTC.

CHAPTER 19

There are many bundles of documents marked "Harassment" in the HTC. Particularly useful were Bruce's January 1, 1970, letter to Columbia University's vice president at the time, Polykarp Kusch, and a single-spaced twenty-page accompanying narrative of the period; the transcript of tape "BCH13A," subtitled "Administrative Committee of Columbia University Harassment Meeting, December 30, 1970," which Bruce recorded the same day as that meeting; and a December 14, 1970, draft of a letter, also to Polykarp Kusch, which began "you have requested that I prepare a memorandum stating my objections to certain rulings at Lamont . . ."

To get a look at the situation from the "other side's" perspective, I consulted hundreds of documents from the MEP. I also quoted from interviews with Dennis E. Hayes and J. Lamar Worzel that were conducted as part of the CU-AIP oral history project.

Marie's short-lived diary from her youth is on file in the HTC. She referred to Dennis Hayes as "snot nose" in both writings and interviews. According to an April 19, 1968, letter from Doc to Marie, their phone conversation about when Marie would return to Lamont's campus took place on January 25, 1968. That letter is part of the HTC, but there are a half dozen additional letters in the MEP addressing the situation.

CHAPTER 20

Jack Oliver's chapter, "Earthquake Seismology in the Plate Tectonics Revolution," in Naomi Oreskes's book *Plate Tectonics: An Insider's History of the Modern Theory of the Earth*, helped me understand the discoveries scientists were making that led to the development of the idea of convergent plate boundaries. B. Isacks, J. Oliver, and L. Sykes's "Seismology and the New Global Tectonics" appeared in the September 15, 1968, issue of the *Journal of Geophysical Research*.

William Jason Morgan's "Rises, Trenches, Great Faults, and Crustal Blocks" was first presented at the 1967 American Geophysical Union meeting and later published, in a slightly different form, in the March 15, 1968, issue of the *Journal of Geophysical Research*. Contextual information for this paper came from Bullard's "The Emergence of Plate Tectonics," and Wilson's "A New Class of Faults and Their Bearing on Continental Drift";

also useful was the GSA's Special Paper 388: a 2005 monograph titled *Plates, Plumes, and Paradigms*, and edited by Gillian R. Foulger, James H. Natland, and Dean C. Presnall. Menard's recollection of that 1967 meeting and Bruce's impact (or lack thereof) there came from *The Ocean of Truth*.

Marie and Bruce's Berann-painted Atlantic Ocean Panorama appeared in the June 1968 issue of *National Geographic* magazine.

CHAPTER 21

Marie refers to "midnight requisitions" in Menard's *The Ocean of Truth*. Bruce discusses securing a position for Marie with the Office of Oceanographic Research in his reply to John Lear's letter of December 5, 1975. William Palmstrom's letter to Marie is dated May 8, 1968, and is part of the HTC. Marie's June 21, 1968, letter to Doc is part of the HTC; Doc's copy of the letter and the dated envelope in which it arrived are part of the MEP.

In order to reconstruct Marie and Bruce's summer 1968 expedition on the *Kane*, I consulted the following documents: "200,000,000 Years Under the Sea: The Voyage of the U.S.N.S. 'Kane,'" written by Bruce and published in the September 7, 1968, issue of the *Saturday Review*; a memo dated July 19, 1968, written by Doc and copied to Dennis Hayes and Leah Miras (Bruce's secretary), in which Doc includes the text of the message he radioed to the *Kane*; Marie's recollections of that cruise in her "Opus"; and Doc's July 19, 1968, letter addressed to Marie in care of the U.S. Defense Attaché in Dakar. The last three documents are part of the MEP; I found the map of Dakar at Marie's house during my January 2008 visit there.

CHAPTER 22

Harriett's narrative of the events of December 10, 1969, when she instructed Lamont maintenance workers to remove the door of Marie's former office, can be found in a packet of several "interdepartmental memos" dated December 10 and 17, 1969, and on file in the MEP. Bruce's letter to Lamont administrator H. J. Dorman is dated December 23, 1969, and is on file in the HTC. Columbia University's vice president Polykarp Kusch wrote his letter to Doc advising caution on April 4, 1969. That and the letter in which Doc tells Bruce that he believes the suspension has been lifted are both part of the MEP.

Bruce discusses his submersible work and the genesis of the 1971 book *The Face of the Deep* in the transcript of tape "22A," which is on file in the HTC. J. D. Woods reviewed *The Face of the Deep* in the October 1973 issue of *The Geographical Journal*. Bruce's letter to Doc detailing all the ways he was not going to be thanked in the acknowledgments of *The Face of the Deep* was dictated onto tape "BCH27A"; its transcript is on file in the HTC.

Information about the *NR-1* comes from Lee Vyborny and Don Davis's 2004 *Dark Waters: An Insider's Account of the NR-1, the Cold War's Undercover Nuclear Sub* and a 1999 Department of the Naval Sea Command booklet titled *NR-1 Submarine: Nuclear Powered Research and Ocean Engineering Vehicle* (text from the 1992 edition can be accessed via www.nr-1-book.com).

CHAPTER 23

Information about Doc's final days comes from a CU-AIP interview that Ronald Doel conducted with Doc's widow, Harriett (Ewing) Greene. Marie's comments about the funeral are an addendum to the transcript of tape "05BM"; she subtitled that transcript "Bruce

Reminiscing About Dr. Ewing After His Death," and labeled her appendix "Notes by Marie Tharp on Dr. Ewing's death (April 21, 1985)"; the full document is on file in the HTC.

The quotes in which John Lear tries to get Marie to expound upon why she stopped working on Lamont's campus are from a transcript marked "Indian Ocean Marie Conversation with John Lear." In the same section, I refer to tape "08A" and Marie's reply to John Lear's letter of September 19, 1975. Her comments about the constant pace of the Earth's processes come from her "Opus."

Many of the details about the work environment of Marie's house in the 1970s came from my interview with Robert Brunke on August 20, 2009. The quotes from Alma Kesner are part of her CU-AIP interview with Ronald Doel.

CHAPTER 24

Marie spoke about the "philosophical differences" she and Bruce had with *National Geographic* in her SWG interview. Information about the ONR's funding of the World Ocean Floor Panorama, the work Marie and Bruce did to prepare materials for the panorama, and how Berann and Vielkind used those materials to paint the panorama comes from Marie's "Opus" and her May 22, 1978, letter to G. Bellisari, the ONR's resident representative at Lamont. The Bellisari letter and a May 16, 1988, letter to A. A. Meyerhoff, in which she wrote about Berann and Vielkind's process, are part of the HTC.

To reconstruct Marie and Bruce's final trip to Austria to work on the panorama, I consulted the documents mentioned in the previous paragraph. I also spent a lot of time studying a cache of photographs taken at the time (currently on file in the HTC), which showed me the clothes the group was wearing, the clutter of Berann's studio, and the ensuing revelry. Multiple copies of Bruce's "Birthday Poem" are scattered throughout the HTC; while I did dramatize its presence in Bruce's notebook during this trip, Marie says that he wrote it on his birthday, in April, and their Austria trip was in May; she notes repeatedly that she wasn't aware of the poem's existence until after Bruce's death.

Part Four

CHAPTERS 25 AND 26

Marie made mention of Bruce's death in nearly every interview she granted and article she wrote. He was a constant, even after he was gone. What is perhaps more interesting is the unfixed nature of her memories of the time before and after he passed. I know she was on the *Discovery*, because the cruise report for that expedition still exists: "I.O.S. [Institute of Oceanographic Sciences] Cruise Report No. 60" details the personnel, path, and activities of *Discovery* cruise 84, which was at sea from June 15 to July 28. But even among the people who were part of what I'll call the Heezen-Tharp entourage (their colleagues, their employees, the people who became Tharpophiles), there was no consensus about where Marie was when Bruce died.

In what the authors of "Cruise Report No. 60" refer to as the "Narrative" section, one paragraph and one sentence dispassionately describe what happened on June 21, 1977: "the survey . . . was only partly completed when news came of Professor B. C. Heezen's untimely death, and it was necessary to break off the survey to take Marie Tharp, his assistant and colleague, to Iceland to fly back to the U.S.A."

Marie published a "technical note" in a 1981 issue (volume 5, number 1) of the journal *Marine Geodesy*. The "note" was titled "Exploring the Deep Ocean Bottom: Chasms Beneath the Sea," and Marie begins by writing that "the Oceanographer of the Navy has provided us with a heroic documentary of the sea, an epic of courage, vision and tragedy." I turned to this piece of writing for many of the details that appear in chapter 26.

My descriptions of the *NR-1* are drawn from the book *Dark Waters* and an online account written by Gene Carl Feldman and titled "Take a Dive on the NR-1," both of which include maps of the sub. Part of the JASON Project, which connects scientists and researchers with students and provides teachers with science curricula, the Feldman article includes many photographs of the interior and exterior of the *NR-1*; you can even listen to the sound of the sub's sonar system sending out pings. Kenneth Hunkins, a Lamont research scientist, also told me stories about what it was like to be down in the sub with Bruce. Several sources mentioned having heard that Bruce's Rolex was stolen off his body while it was in the *Sunbird*'s freezer.

Marie's emotions at the time are captured in her letters. She wrote the words "I don't really know why it had to be Bruce instead of me" in a February 7, 1978, letter to Gail Matthews, one of the people who worked for her in the mid-1970s. And in a July 18, 1977, reply to a condolence letter written by M. L. Lindquist of the National Academy of Sciences, Marie wrote the following: "I was very fortunate to be at sea when I heard the news of Bruce's death. The sea was unusually calm and as we sped homeward I literally felt as if I were [being] rocked in the cradle of the deep. But I did wonder how I could derive such solace from the sea which had finally claimed Bruce as its very own."

CHAPTER 27

My descriptions of the interior of Bruce's house come from a series of black-and-white eight-by-ten photos taken by Robert Brunke shortly after Bruce's death; they're on file in the HTC. My description of the exterior of the house comes from my own visit there, with Lex Reibestein, in July 2008.

All of the eulogies I quote are in an old black binder I was given the day I spent at Marie's house. It contained photocopies of the eulogies written by Manik Talwani, Bill Ryan, Marcus Langseth, and Kenneth Hunkins. The description of the setting and weather of the memorial service for Bruce held at Lamont comes from a July 25, 1977, letter Marie wrote to David Needham that is on file in the HTC.

Part Five

CHAPTER 28

My reconstruction of the April 1978 GEBCO meeting is based on a variety of documents, including three authored by Marie and on file in the HTC. Of these three documents, all are undated and untitled and only one deals at length with the events of the meeting. I also consulted *The History of GEBCO 1903–2003* and the "Summary Report of the 1978 GEBCO Guiding Committee Meeting," both of which are available online.

Marie's letters to G. Bellisari, in which she describes getting the WOFP ready for press, are part of the HTC. Other information about putting the finishing touches on the

WOFP comes from my interviews with Steve Sagala (in October 2008) and Suzanne MacDonald (in July 2009).

Information about the Hubbard Medal came from the National Geographic Society; particularly helpful was an article written by Cathy Hunter, of the NGS Archives Division, describing the ceremony. The picture of Marie, Robert E. Doyle, and Esther Dauch (Bruce's mother) that I describe is a color copy of a photo that was tucked into one of the binders given to me when I visited Marie's house. The correspondence of Marie and Esther is profuse and on file in the HTC; many of the Tharpophiles told me how Marie assigned them the task of typing up Esther's handwritten letters and placing the originals and typed versions in sleeves, which were then inserted, facing each other, into black binders.

CHAPTER 29

Marie's comments about the removal of Bruce's things from Lamont come from several letters on file in the HTC and one untitled document in which she narrated her loss of funding following Bruce's death, also on file in the HTC. Most of Marie's outgoing letters were written on the stationery I describe in this chapter.

The *New York Times* ad appeared in the November 25, 1979, edition. The information about the projects Marie completed in the early 1980s comes from an undated document she wrote titled "Completed Projects." It's on file in the HTC and details, project by project, her work and financial investment. She wrote two "technical notes" for the first issue of volume 5 of the journal *Marine Geodesy*: the aforementioned "Chasms of the Deep" review, and another article, titled "Differential Bathymetry."

The Seismicity of the Earth: 1960–1980 map was published in 1982; its authors are listed as Alvaro F. Espinosa, Wilbur Rinehart, and Marie Tharp. John Noble Wilford's 1981 book *The Mapmakers* was reprinted in 2000; that's the version I quote from in the text. The David McCullough *New York Times* review of Wilford's book was published on May 3, 1981. The correspondence between Marie and her brother (about the publication of *The Mapmakers* and Jim's health) that I reference is on file in the HTC, as is Marie's "Opus."

To reconstruct Marie's trip to Muscatine following her brother's funeral in Stuart, Iowa, I consulted several documents from the HTC, including a September 10, 1984, letter she wrote to some of Bruce's relatives in Holland (with whom she'd stayed in touch after Bruce's death) and a May 16, 1983, letter to Bruce's mother. These documents, and a single typed paragraph also on file in the HTC, gave a vivid description of Marie's trip—full of rain and colors. I based my description on Marie's, with one addition: her interaction with the lady of the house on Smalley Avenue comes purely from my imagination, an attempt to show yet another way in which Marie might have been startled from her reverie.

When I first began writing this book, I happened to live about an hour away from Muscatine—hence my visit to Marilyn Jackson and her husband in their assisted-living facility in October 2008. I drove and Marilyn guided me around town to all the places that were key to Bruce's childhood. After I dropped them off, I retraced the steps Marie took in February 1983, looking for Bruce's grave. Bruce, it seems, is one of the town's celebrities, and so the woman in the office pulled out a file with his *Time* obituary and highlighted the route to his grave on a map. After that, I made my pilgrimage to the house on Smalley Avenue, and then crossed the Mississippi to see Bruce's childhood home from a different perspective.

The information concerning Marie's successful effort to transfer Bruce's papers to the Smithsonian Archives comes from a document titled simply "Abstract," which is part of the HTC. The *Natural History* article Marie wrote with Henry Frankel appeared in the October 1986 issue. Frankel's review of Robert Muir Wood's *The Dark Side of the Earth* appeared in the October 14, 1986, issue of *Eos*. Frankel's letters with Marie (one of which includes Marie's description of Bill Menard's visits to her house) are scattered throughout the HTC.

CHAPTER 30

My interviews with the Tharpophiles were conducted between 2007 and 2011, on the phone and in person. While most of the stories that appear in the beginning of this chapter were repeated to me over and over, the stories of Marie stealing ferns from a state park with Big John and getting frisked in D.C. came from Robert Brunke.

The letters to and from Marie that I quote in this chapter are part of the vast amount of correspondence on file in the HTC.

CHAPTER 31

My information about the transfer of Bruce and Marie's papers from her home in South Nyack to the Library of Congress comes from interviews with Gary North and the "Register for the Heezen-Tharp Collection" he wrote in 2005, which now resides in the GMD at the Library of Congress. While the register is comprehensive when it comes to the data Marie gave the Library of Congress, the personal materials I reference in this book are not included. Those materials rest in cardboard boxes, uncatalogued and unorganized, which made the process of studying those thousands of documents and photos very much like an archaeological dig: there was no way of setting out in the morning looking for one particular piece, I simply had to dig in and hope I'd uncover something remarkable.

Gary North's filmed interview with Marie was recorded on November 27, 1997, and is part of the HTC; the details about the awards and recognition the Library of Congress bestowed upon her came from my interviews with Gary North.

The letter Marie wrote to Worzel asking for assistance was written on May 22, 1997. David Lawrence's article "Mountains Under the Sea: Marie Tharp's Maps of the Ocean Floor" was published in the November/December 1999 issue of the now-defunct magazine *Mercator's World*. His book proposal is undated but available on his website, upheaval .davidmlawrence.com.

The congratulatory letters written to Marie upon her receipt of the Woods Hole Women Pioneers in Oceanography Award reside in a binder that's part of the HTC. Marie's statement about viewing The Harrassment more "objectively" is from a June 14, 1984, letter she wrote to Henry Frankel; it's part of the HTC.

Nearly every Tharpophile I spoke with mentioned the couple who may or may not have taken advantage of Marie's finances. The story of Marie's last few weeks and subsequent death comes from an interview with Fiona Schiano-Yacopino that took place in January 2010. Marie's *New York Times* obituary was written by Margalit Fox and published on August 26, 2006.

CHAPTER 32

The John Fowles article I refer to appeared in the July 1968 issue of *Harper's Magazine*. I visited Marie's house in January 2008.

CHAPTER 33

My understanding of the way modern-day scientists use satellite altimetry to map the ocean floor was drawn from Walter H. F. Smith and David T. Sandwell's article "Global Seafloor Topography from Satellite Altimetry and Ship Depth Soundings," which appeared in the September 26, 1997, issue of *Science* magazine; further interpretation was provided by Walter Smith. For an easily accessible and less technical explanation of that work, see their article on NOAA's website titled "Exploring the Ocean Basins with Satellite Altimeter Data."

In a June 27, 1997, letter to Tom Togashi on file in the HTC, Marie refers to having gotten a copy of the Smith and Sandwell map. I saw the map hanging above her fireplace when I visited her house in January 2008. Gary North told me a story of how, one day, he took a transparency of the 1977 World Ocean Floor Panorama and laid it on top of the Smith and Sandwell map so Marie could see how well her extrapolations and interpolations matched up with the newer map.

Walter Smith spent many hours on the phone helping me understand the current state of ocean floor mapping. The stories about the last few years of Marie's life that appear at the end of this chapter come from my January 2010 interview with Fiona Schiano-Yacopino.

ACKNOWLEDGMENTS

I became a writer because of my teachers: Susan Lohafer, who helped transform my telling of Marie's story from a series of fragments into an actual thesis; Jen Lee, who saw my imagination better than I could see it myself; Harry Kloman, who drilled the principles of journalism into me; and Judy Smullen and Leonard Perrett, who let me get away with a lot more than they'd ever admit. This book was also possible because of Dr. G. Alec Stewart—my "Doc"—who gave me the confidence to be my own kind of a scholar. He passed away in 2010; I wish he could have seen my first big attempt.

Documents are the bones of this book. It would have been impossible to reconstruct Marie's process and the events of her life without consulting the collections of the following organizations—and without the countless people who helped me maneuver through those archives. Thank you to the Heezen-Tharp Collection in the Geography and Map Division at the Library of Congress; the Bruce C. Heezen Papers at the Smithsonian Institution Archives; the Society of Woman Geographers; the American Institute of Physics' Center for the History of Physics; Columbia University's Oral History Research Office; the Lamont-Doherty Earth Observatory; the Maurice Ewing Papers at the University of Texas at Austin's Dolph Briscoe Center for American History; the Henry William Menard

Papers at the Scripps Institution of Oceanography Archives; the General Bathymetric Chart of the Oceans (GEBCO); and the National Geographic Society.

So many people provided me with insights while I was working on this book—into Marie, Bruce, their work and its context, and various scientific topics. Whether sitting down for interviews or trying to teach me about things like data density, these people gave this book its texture and imparted their expertise: Debbie Bartolotta, Dee Breger, Bob Brunke, Kerri Connolly, Ronald Doel, Jim Dollar, Kenneth Hunkins, Kim Kastens, Allen Lowrie, Suzanne MacDonald, Michael Rawson, Lex Reibestein, William Ryan, Steve Sagala, and Albert "Skip" Theberge Jr.

Early in this project, Gary North became a touchstone for me—the person I'd call when I needed to confirm or clarify a story from Marie's life, a gatekeeper whose trust I feel proud to have earned. Very late in this project, Walter H. F. Smith became my sort of scientific consultant. I don't know how many hours he spent talking with me on the phone or replying to my e-mails, but I know it was a lot—and that his encouragement was the kind of confidence elixir I think most writers dream of. Fiona Schiano-Yacopino welcomed me into her office, tracked down copies of maps and slides, put me in touch with sources, and spent hours telling me stories about Marie. She now owns Marie Tharp Maps (www .marietharp.com), from which you can purchase copies of the World Ocean Floor Panorama.

I began writing this book as a graduate student at the University of Iowa, and my teachers and peers in the Nonfiction Writing Program there deserve many thanks for having read early excerpts, versions, and drafts—particularly Amelia Bird, Danielle Bojanski, Matthew Clark, Bernadette Esposito, Patricia Foster, David Hamilton, Gabe "Saturday Scholar" Houck, Nathan McKeen, June Melby, David Peate, Bonnie Sunstein, and Stephen West. Thank you also to my Oregon readers Anne Bentley and Amelia Boldaji.

I hope I've properly expressed my deep respect for my talented researcher E. M. Kokopeli—your on-the-ground work in Austin was invaluable and perfectly timed.

My incredible agent, Wendy Strothman, somehow saw through all of the stylistic hubris of the pages I initially sent her and believed—again somehow—that a twenty-six-year-old with no scientific background could do justice to the life story of an oceanographic cartographer. She and Lauren MacLeod helped make my first draft readable and got it into the hands of my dear editor Marjorie Braman. Marjorie, you call 'em like you see 'em and I am eternally grateful that you saw promise in my writing. You shaped this book and taught me—sometimes wrangling, sometimes using a subtle hand, always enthusiastic—how to be a better writer. I hope this book is everything you thought it would be.

Gillian Blake and Allison Adler will never cease to amaze me. They adopted this book and guided me through the final stretch of the editing and publication process with extreme patience and kindness. As a first-time author, I needed virtually everything explained to me and I can't imagine that that was easy. So thank you for everything—for the things I know about and the behind-the-scenes details about which I remain clueless.

I'm enormously grateful to the MacDowell Colony for giving me time and space and basket lunches and sheep to look at and Reymundo to laugh at and introducing me to new friends: Kim Beck and Marina Zurkow, two of the biggest rock stars I know.

I'll never be able to fully express my appreciation for the Sitka Center for Art and Ecology. The sun may have been scarce, but at Sitka I had only to hike up Cascade Head or pop my head into the office to have my spirits lifted. Jalene Case, Mindy Chaffin, Ariel Kazunas, Ernie Rose, Eric Vines, and Rebecca Welti: you got me through my first Oregon winter and a serious case of writer's block—and had always worked half the day before I even woke up (we'll always have our Sessions). And Randall Tipton: even if I'd never written a single word at Sitka, all that construction would have been worth meeting you.

So many people opened their homes to me while I worked on this book. During my shorter sojourns to the Library of Congress, Kathy Beland and Peter Kokopeli provided me with a home away from home; this project never would have been possible without their generosity and encouragement (and delicious dinners). Thank you also to their friend Michael Agosto, who graciously lent me his condo in D.C. so that I could be closer to the library during an extended research trip. Lori Latham gave me her friendship and the keys to her home, showering me with stability and kindness during some particularly rocky months. Shout-outs to Angie, Todd, Ken, Julie, and particularly Cliff, all of whom gave true meaning to the word "neighbor" after my apartment got broken into. My aunt Sue and uncle Tim deserve a big thanks, too, for welcoming me to the bustling metropolis that is Ajo and helping out (you know how); Sue, you let yourself be called Aunt Sue by complete strangers in several states and for that you have my thanks—and apologies.

The rest of my family didn't get to see me as often as they wanted, but they were always supportive and there when I needed them. Boogah, Jerry, Sandi, Michele, Jen, and the Cotters—a million thank-yous for all that you've done. Mom, I got my creativity from you, my love of maps from you, my stubbornness and my strength—I'm so proud to be your daughter and I love you more than the world.

While writing, I ended up moving from Iowa to Maine to Pennsylvania to Oregon and back to Pennsylvania again. My grandmother died; I had my gallbladder removed; broke and sprained several limbs; my laptop was stolen—and much much more!—and through it all my best friends kept me going. Sometimes we were together and sometimes we could only talk on the phone, but all of you always knew how to make me laugh. You nursed me back to health, you read drafts of the book, you cooked meals for me, you let me knit you insane sweaters and accessories, you calmed me, you listened to me, you kicked my ass when I needed it, and helped me remember where I was going when I forgot. Matt, Em, Eva, and Stephanie—you're the family I found and want to hold on to forever. Let's not have any plummeting into puddles of indeterminable depth, okay?

ABOUT THE AUTHOR

HALI FELT teaches writing at the University of Pittsburgh. She received her MFA from the University of Iowa and has completed residencies at the MacDowell Colony, the Sitka Center for Art and Ecology, and with Portland Writers in the Schools. In the past, she has reported for the *Columbia Journalism Review* and the *Pittsburgh Tribune-Review*. She currently lives in Pittsburgh.